W9-DDX-545

THE WORLD IN THE CURL

THE WORLD IN THE CURL

AN UNCONVENTIONAL HISTORY OF SURFING

Peter Westwick

Peter Neushul

CROWN PUBLISHERS

NEW YORK

Published in the United States by Crown Publishers,
an imprint of the Crown Publishing Group,
a division of Random House, Inc., New York.

www.crownpublishing.com

CROWN and the Crown colophon are registered trademarks
of Random House, Inc.

Library of Congress Cataloging-in-Publication Data
Westwick, Peter J.
The World in the Curl : an unconventional history of surfing /
Peter Westwick and Peter Neushul.
pages cm.
Includes bibliographical references and index.
1. Surfing—History. I. Title.
GV839.5.W47 2013
797.3'2—dc23
2012051071

ISBN 978-0-307-71948-5
eISBN 978-0-307-71950-8

PRINTED IN THE UNITED STATES OF AMERICA

Book design by Jaclyn Reyes
Jacket design by Mike Krol
Jacket photography by Gabe Rogel

10 9 8 7 6 5 4 3 2 1

First Edition

For Kiley, Jamie, Ryann, Dane, and Caden

CONTENTS

PREFACE

We are surfers. Each of us has surfed for over thirty years, from California to Mexico, Hawaii, Indonesia, Australia, South Africa, and Europe. We know the sheer adrenaline rush that comes from arcing across a moving wall of liquid energy, and the peacefulness that comes from sharing waves and sunrises with pelicans and dolphins. That sense of stoke has consumed surfers for centuries and still motivates people to grab a board—be it a plywood plank on a West African coast, or a computer-shaped foam-and-fiberglass formula from an Orange County showroom—and ride waves. Surfing is flat-out fun. And that's why our kids are now out bobbing in the lineup with us.

But we are also, by training and occupation, historians. Not many historians surf. We practice deepwater history: we try not just to describe what's floating on the surface, but to peer below the surface to understand the deeper currents, and how they carry along the things we see up on top. For surfing, it turns out there's compelling stuff down in the depths.

The idea for this project came to the two of us on a sunny day of small surf at Cojo Point, north of Santa Barbara, as we sat in the water between waves and wondered how to combine our lifestyle with our profession. The immediate answer was to offer a course in the history of surfing at the University of California at Santa Barbara, where we both were teaching. Classes in the history of surfing were previously nonexistent, at UCSB and most everywhere else. But surfing has deep roots in Santa Barbara, and *Surfer* magazine regularly names UCSB a top campus for surfing students. So, after persuading various committees and deans that this would in fact be a serious class, and not just a bunch of surf flicks and field trips, we listed History of Surfing as a new course in history and environmental studies.

It was no surprise that on the first day of class we were inundated by students trying to enroll; what did surprise us was that most of them did not surf. Nonsurfers clearly wanted to learn more about the cultural phenomenon of surfing. Since most people are not lucky enough to be college students living by the surf in Santa Barbara, we decided to bring the surf to them. The result is the book you're reading now.

INTRODUCTION

Surfing today is pursued by an estimated 20 million people worldwide, including the forty-fourth U.S. president, and it supports a $10 billion global industry. It has acquired an inescapable cultural presence. Surfers grace Times Square billboards and sell beer and cars on TV and the Internet. There are thriving surf communities from Iceland and Ireland to Israel and Indonesia, and frequent media coverage of events ranging from formal competition to big-wave adventures regularly brings surf culture even to the landlocked masses. How did an ancient Polynesian pastime become a global commercial and cultural phenomenon?

Finding the source of surfing's cool cachet requires reconciling two popular images of surfing. The public receives competing visions of surfing: a refuge for rebellious hedonists dropping out of mainstream society to chase waves, beer, and girls, and a healthy middle-class sport, one equally capable of entertaining tourists in Africa, Australia, or Waikiki, bridging tensions in Gaza, or pushing athletic boundaries in awesome big-wave exploits. This split personality, which pairs subversive social rebellion and the middle-class mainstream, dates to the earliest encounters between European explorers and Polynesian surfers and has characterized modern surfing for the last century. The more popular and mainstream surfing becomes—thanks both to its intrinsic appeal and to the use of that cachet to make a buck—the more surfers hearken to its individualistic, natural roots. This book is about surfing's constant struggle to save its soul.

Surfing's split personality is not unique. Many so-called extreme sports combine an edgy, outlaw vibe with middle-class commerce and competition—just look at the X Games commercial juggernaut. Surfing is the first lifestyle sport. X Game staples like skateboarding and snowboarding were inspired directly by surfing. Being a surfer involves a different level of commitment from being a golfer or basketball player. Surfing is more than an athletic pursuit that you do a couple days a week at a course or in a gym. Even when surfers are out of the water, they are watching the weather, tides, and wind, monitoring distant swell patterns, and mentally tuning in the ocean. Surfing defines your life, in the same way that work—being a farmer or a carpenter or a blacksmith—used to define people's lives. Forty years ago Alvin Toffler's *Future Shock* called surfers "a signpost pointing to the future" for their embrace of a leisure-time "lifestyle," and in this case Toffler was right.

From a broader view, however, surfing's outlaw, subversive image is just that—an image. Surfers have an interest in viewing surfing as unique. That's the source of their cool: we're doing something all you other people can't do. Most surf writing is done by and for surfers, who perpetuate this perspective. As surfers, we know the thrill of wave riding and its attendant rituals (local lineup hierarchies, Hawaii pilgrimages, surf-trip privations, boat adventures, beach parties, surfboard sacrifices, and so on). As history professors, however, we know that social forces shape even the seemingly most isolated activities. Surfing is no exception. This book shows how surfing has intersected such forces as colonialism, capitalism, race and gender roles, the military-industrial complex, and globalization.

This is a thinking person's guide to surfing. Surfers are not just a curiosity, or a cool subculture; rather, they are a way to see the history of the modern world. For example, surfing's ultimate appeal is in the simple act of riding waves, but much of its cultural image derives from its Polynesian origins. Hawaii is the romantic soul of surfing and the original source of surfing's cool. Much of this romantic image is a myth, as the history of Hawaii is wrapped up in colonialism, warfare, racism, and sexism. Modern surfing emerged in Hawaii around 1900, just when white elites were overthrowing the native Hawaiian monarchy, developing a new tourism economy, and welcoming a major American military presence. This heady cultural context set the initial course of modern surfing. Similarly, cultural forces later helped surfing gain traction in Cold War California, post-cultural-cringe Australia, and apartheid-era South Africa.

Since this book is an intelligent guide to surfing, we do not aim for a detailed narrative describing every development in surf history. We do not include every possible milestone: the first surfer to ride this or that wave or land an aerial, or who won the Pipe Masters contest in 1987. We also do not want to lament a paradise lost, a once pure pursuit corrupted by commerce. Rather, this book shows how surfing, at every point in its history, reflected—and shaped—the world around it. We tell the story of surfing, from its ancient Hawaiian origins to today's global culture and industry, but at particular points we dive deeper into crucial themes, including technology, the environment, race and sex, localism and travel, big-wave riding, and the surf industry.

As a window on the modern world, surfing displays all the unintended consequences and ironies common to history. Among these we highlight the role of technology and the environment. Surfing is usually seen as a natural pursuit that doesn't require a lot of fancy equipment; just a board and surf trunks, and you're out there alone in the ocean. This literal immersion in nature is a large part of surfing's romantic appeal. This image, too, is false. New technologies have driven the phenomenal growth of surfing over the last century, and surfing is now a high-tech pursuit. Modern surfboards are a complex chemical cocktail of isocyanate-based polyurethane foams, fiberglass, and polyester resins, all initially mass-produced by the chemical industry for defense and aerospace applications. Wetsuits are another product of military research and development, by way of polymer chemistry. Surfers find good waves thanks to electronic buoys, satellites, supercomputer-based swell models, and the Internet. Even some waves themselves are man-made, as surfers seek to build the perfect wave through artificial reefs and wave pools.

Gazing through an environmental lens further highlights surfing's artificiality. As coastal development spreads, there are few truly natural waves left in the world. Harbors, piers, jetties, and seawalls change sand flow along the coast. Dams and concrete channels capture silt upstream on creeks and rivers and starve beaches of sand. Polluted runoff from industry, agriculture, and homes fouls the surf. Private property rights limit access to many surf spots. Climate change is killing coral reefs and inundating coastlines. For example, California's celebrated beach culture emerged only after a competing vision for California beaches, one based on oil drilling, was thwarted. In many ways the Army Corps of Engineers and international construction conglomerates like Dillingham in Hawaii have done more to shape modern surfing than most individual surfers—but you won't find them in histories of surfing.

Looking at surfing from the perspective of technology and the environment highlights the fact that, in many ways, surfing is an artificial pursuit, contrary to its romantic, natural image. The surf zone sits at the interface between an increasingly technological land-based civilization and the oceanic wilderness. Surfers are thus a perfect bellwether of human interaction with the environment. They stand—as did Rachel Carson—at the edge of the sea, bordering the world's last truly wild frontier. As stewards of this mysterious beauty, surfers are poised to either inform and preserve, or watch as humankind continues to overrun this last frontier. Surfers can only pursue their passion because of the presence of civilization—which provides not only the tools to ride waves, but also the leisure time to do so. But that very civilization threatens the waves themselves. Surfing is ultimately a story of the inherent contradictions between civilization and the wilderness, between modern society and the natural world.

NOTES TO THE READER

We give wave heights in mainland, not Hawaiian, units. That is, we refer to the actual height of the wave face. What a Hawaiian would call a twenty-foot wave actually rises forty feet or more from trough to crest. Most surfers outside Hawaii call that a forty-footer, and so do we.

We won't get into the long argument over why these competing measurements exist.

Also, our spelling of Hawaiian terms usually omits diacritical marks such as the 'okina, the apostrophe signifying a glottal stop—for example, in the native spelling *Hawai'i*. Use of these symbols varied over time and many of our sources omit them, so we do so as well.

1 THE CRADLE OF SURFING

The scene unfolded every year for centuries. In late spring, when big south swells began jacking on Waikiki's reefs, priests at the *heiau* on Diamond Head flew their kites to signal the surf was up. The best surfers paddled their longest boards to the outer reefs at Kalehuawehe. Those who first rode the waves earned the title of "Kalehuawehe" for the season, and were also called *mahi mahi* because of their powerful and streamlined physiques. On the biggest swells, surfers caught waves breaking all the way from Kalehuawehe through Makaiwa, Puuloa, and Mamala—from Diamond Head clear across to Honolulu Harbor, a phenomenal ride of several miles that is impossible today. Men who "rode the entire distance were looked upon with awe and veneration—as though they were supermen."

The history of modern surfing starts with Hawaiians. This is not to say that they were the only surfers. Polynesians surfed; in Peru, fishing villagers rode waves on reed boats called *caballitos*; in West Africa, young kids surfed on wooden planks. One can debate, as some do, which one of these places was first, but there is no disputing that modern surfing, the sport we know today, came out of Hawaii. How that happened is the crucial question. And answering that question requires us to look beyond

Hawaii itself. Hawaii's extreme geographic isolation makes it a crucial crossroads in the North Pacific, and after European contact the islands were a vital node in the network of global trade, a point of political friction on the boundary of several major empires, and a crucible for social and cultural mixing. These intersections almost led to the demise of surfing, but then they also sparked its modern renaissance.

SETTLING AND SURFING HAWAII

External influences started with the first Hawaiians, who arrived from other Polynesian islands—probably the Marquesas—around the fifth century AD, followed by a later wave of migrants from Tahiti around the twelfth century. Hawaii afterward developed in isolation for several centuries. These Polynesian sailors were among the most adept ocean people the world has known, capable of undertaking an unprecedented voyage across thousands of miles of open ocean, navigating by the stars in open double-hulled canoes propelled by woven sails. They likely brought surfing with them to Hawaii, and after arriving they applied their deep ocean knowledge in a social world with surfing at its center.

Hawaiians wove surfing into their entire culture, with religious festivals, political power, and gender relationships expressed through surfing. Many chiefs were expert surfers; surfing demonstrated the strength and skill that qualified one for leadership, and royalty enjoyed the most leisure time to perfect their ability. Chiefs had special servants who stood on the beach while they surfed and chanted of their skill and glory. One famous chant ran, "Give me the waves that I may ride upon them/Lest I be ashamed/When I reach the shore." The carving of surfboards from koa or wiliwili trees entailed special rituals and prayers to ensure success, and some surf spots included a beachfront *heiau* where surfers could pray for good waves. During flat spells, frustrated surfers might also enlist a priest, or *kahuna*, to lash the water with morning-glory vines and chant, "Arise! Arise, ye great surfs from Kahiki/The powerful curling waves/Arise with *pohuehue*/ Well up, long-raging surf."

Women were as keen on surfing as men. The surf spot Mamala west of Waikiki was named after an expert woman surfer and chief. One legend told of Kelea, another masterful woman surfer from Maui, whose brother was Maui's king: "she enjoyed surfing so much that at night she dwelt upon the morrow's surfing and awakened to the murmuring of the sea to take up her board." Abducted by Oahu warriors and sought by Oahu's chief, Lolale, she spurned Lolale, a landlubber, and married her kidnapper, Kalamakua, who shared her love for surfing. Women dominated many lineups, and woe to the man who dared paddle out to the queen's favorite spot. *Kalehuawehe* meant "loosened lehua," after the lehua flower used in leis. It was named after a handsome young man who surfed Waikiki at the same time as the queen and at the queen's request gave her his lehua lei. The queen then tricked him by taking off behind him on a wave; when he reached the beach, her servants prepared to kill him before another chief identified him as a relative and spared his life.

Surfing, though, was not just the sport of royalty. Everyone surfed in ancient Hawaii. Surfing's associations with sex added to its attraction. Surfing was a form of courtship, a way to demonstrate one's physical prowess and grace, with near-naked men and women mingling together in the warm water; custom encouraged a man and woman who shared a wave to follow it with an amorous encounter on the beach. Surfing was particularly important since the *kapu* system—the set of religious strictures, like taboos, that governed daily life—forbade men and women from working or eating together. If you wanted to meet a member of the opposite sex, surfing was one of your few options. Surfing's sexual undercurrent appeared as double entendres in chants, like the one about a chief riding his favorite surfboard, weaving up and down across the wave before finally reaching the crest. Another popular saying—"When the surf-rider is unskilled, the board is broken"—implied a dissatisfied lover.

Surfing also provided a competitive outlet, often between rival chiefs, spiced with Hawaiians' love of gambling. Hawaiians would wager livestock, canoes, fishing nets, or their own personal freedom on surf contests. One contest between Maui and Oahu champions involved a wager of four thousand pigs and sixteen war canoes. Some had even higher stakes. A famous story concerns Umi, a high chief and avid surfer, who ruled Maui and the Big Island of Hawaii in the late fifteenth and early sixteenth centuries. One day in Hilo he surfed against the local champion Paiea, with large bets staked on the outcome. On one wave Paiea ran into Umi; Umi then surfed up to Paiea, kicked him in the chest, and surfed in to victory. Umi later had Paiea roasted in an underground oven for his offense.

Contests, wagers, glorifying chants: these social aspects of surfing show that Hawaiians didn't ride waves just for fun. They also now surfed to impress the opposite sex, gain social and political status, and win prizes. Surfing was as much a social function as individual pleasure—and not for the last time.

Several factors helped Hawaiians become a surfing society, including geography, ocean knowledge, physical fitness, and nutrition. Hawaii was a natural paradise for surfing. Situated in the middle of the Pacific Plate, the Hawaiian Islands are one of the world's most exposed archipelagoes. The product of a "hot spot" in the earth's mantle, Hawaii, Maui, Lanai, Molokai, Oahu, and Kauai are a veritable catcher's mitt for waves. They have warm water and bountiful reefs not far from shore and enjoy good waves year round: summer swells from the South Pacific, winter swells out of the North Pacific. Almost all of the Hawaiian islands had good surf spots. On Oahu, Kalehuawehe was especially favored by royalty—Waikiki, the shore below the volcanic crater now known as Diamond Head, was long the seat of Oahu kings—but a select few also dared the winter surf at Pau Malu, now known as Sunset, on Oahu's North Shore.

With surf spots like Pau Malu, Hawaii presented a stiff challenge even for a water people. Big swells generated by polar storms travel unimpeded through open ocean to reach Hawaii; there they collide with sharp, shallow coral reefs, tower skyward, and plunge forward, creating some of the biggest and most spectacular waves in the world. Ocean knowledge in this environment was critical. Hawaiians had profound knowledge of the sea; only people with this knowledge could have made the open-ocean crossing needed to settle the islands. Hawaiians were oceanographers before the word existed, expert sailors and navigators who could read wind, waves, reefs, and tides. Anthropologists have concluded that Pacific island cultures had a sophisticated understanding of the marine environment in some ways surpassing that of modern scientists. Hawaii's extreme geographic isolation, in other words, made for better waves, because there was no land anywhere near to block ocean swells, and better surfers, because the people who could reach the islands had to be the most adept in the ocean.

Swimming was similarly critical to survival on islands surrounded by booming surf, where a wave could instantly claim the life of a swimmer or sailor. Hawaiians often learned to swim as infants. Before they could walk, they crawled. Ancient Hawaiians developed an overhand crawl stroke for swimming, an efficient stroke, still the fastest way to swim, that is the same motion used to paddle a surfboard. Native American swimmers with a similar stroke stunned Europeans in the eighteenth century when their crawl stroke far outpaced Old World side and breast strokes. The crawl served Hawaiians both as a means of survival and as a fundamental part of their sports competitions.

Hawaiian sports explain how this seafaring people evolved into some of the world's most accomplished watermen. During a visit to Hawaii in the 1930s, Franklin Delano Roosevelt witnessed a pageant that included a demonstration of Hawaiian sports. An impressed FDR urged the organizers to preserve Hawaiian pastimes. Charles Kenn, a twenty-seven-year-old student from Oahu, took the words to heart and undertook the task of resurrecting ancient Hawaiian games. It became his life's work. Kenn, whose grandmother was Hawaiian, mastered the Hawaiian language and interviewed scores of elderly Hawaiians. Because of Kenn, we know much more about ancient Hawaiian sports, including several aquatic games relevant for surfing.

The evolution of Hawaiians as a water people came from games that honed their ability to dive and swim. In *lele kawa* ("small splash") and *lele pahu* ("big splash"), contestants leapt off a cliff into the water with the goal of creating the smallest or biggest splash; participants held a guava leaf in their mouth to keep water from going up their nose. In *aho loa,* "long breath," competitors stayed underwater for as long as possible; the winner was the last to surface. Then there was *ulumi iloko oke kai,* or sea wrestling. Two players started in the ocean, where, at the referee's signal, they attempted to hold their opponent underwater and then quickly exit the water. Dunks were worth a point each, and the first person to leave the water while ahead in points won. A combatant behind in points could drag his opponent back into the water before he reached shore, prolonging the contest. *Ulumi ikoko oke kai* often took place in deep water where the participants needed swimming speed as well as breath-holding skill; they often dove underwater to avoid their opponent, since a dunk counted only when a person's head was forced under against his will.

All these aquatic sports developed the skills and fitness needed to ride big waves. Ancient Hawaiians got held underwater and swam in from distant reefs for fun, even when they weren't surfing. After getting dunked by a strong waterman in *ulumi ikoko oke kai* or holding your breath underwater for minutes in an *aho loa* contest, getting rolled by walls of whitewater while surfing was nothing to fear.

Hawaiians' remarkable fitness was enabled by their diet, which was tied to their leisure time by a highly developed food system. Surfers have always known that work gets in the way of surf. You can't surf if you're out finding food or shelter, or otherwise making a living. Surfing requires leisure time. Every society where surfing flourished has enjoyed enough resources to give people leisure time to surf. Hawaii became the cradle of surfing because food and shelter were easily had.

Shelter was the easy part in Hawaii's benign climate. For food, Hawaiians started with the surrounding ocean's natural bounty, since they were expert fishermen, whether spearing, trapping, netting, angling, or trolling. They did not stop there. Hawaiians very early developed a sophisticated system of aquaculture, or fish farming, that was unparalleled in Polynesia. They built walls of coral and sand to create ponds, with single ponds covering dozens of acres. The walls incorporated complex sluice channels or *makaha* that allowed young fish to escape while keeping mature fish for harvest. Hawaiians also understood that fish eat algae; they learned to encourage algae growth by lowering the water level, letting more sunlight reach the algae, and controlling salinity. Many Hawaiian villages, including Honolulu and Waikiki, featured a number of these ponds. Usually owned by kings or chiefs, the ponds themselves were probably built by forced labor of commoners. Once in place, the ponds provided a steady supply of food. There were hundreds of ponds, and each acre of pond yielded perhaps three hundred pounds of fish a year. The annual fish haul has been estimated at a thousand *tons*, a tremendous source of protein.

Hawaiians also developed extensive systems of terraces and irrigated fields for taro, and cultivated yams and sweet potatoes. Their agricultural surplus also sustained pig farming. The first Europeans to visit Hawaii commented on the endless supply of food, which gave Hawaiians ample time to surf. Surfing was a central part of the annual Makahiki Festival, around harvesttime in the Hawaiian winter, which celebrated the god Lono. The festival lasted three months, and work and warfare were forbidden during this period. In other words, Hawaiians basically took a quarter of the year off work. Not a bad vacation package. Good food meant Hawaiians were an exceptionally healthy and athletic water people who could surf all day, every day, for three months every year. That's a good way to master surfing.

Surfing has always been more than a sport. In ancient Hawaii it was a way of life, a philosophy. The word for surf, *nalu*, also meant to investigate, to search after truth and the origin of things. *Kanalu* was the highest order of priesthood in ancient Hawaii, introduced by early Polynesian settlers. Their ancient migrations proved to Hawaiians that life came from the surf, and would return to the surf. In recognition of this, *nalu* could also refer to the fluid that covered newborn babies. Hawaiians were literally born surfers.

DISPOSSESSION IN THE AGE OF EMPIRE: SANDALWOOD, SUGAR, SEX, SIN, AND SURFING

In January 1778 Hawaii's centuries of blessed isolation came to an end when two tall-masted sailing ships appeared over the horizon from the south. Before the ships made land at the island of Kauai, residents paddled out in canoes and greeted the light-skinned strangers timidly but warmly. If Hawaiians had known what would come of the encounter, they might have been less friendly.

The ships were the HMS *Resolution* and *Discovery*, British vessels commanded by Captain James Cook. In the previous decade Cook had systematically explored the South Pacific, initially looking for the Great Southern Continent posited by geographers. Cook found no continent, but in the process he mapped much of that vast oceanic expanse, including its many island chains. He had then turned his attention north, looking for a sea passage between the Pacific and Atlantic. The famed explorer was on his way into the North Pacific when he bumped into Hawaii.

Surfing's social prominence impressed Cook and his crew throughout the islands. The ship's artist, documenting the sweeping scene at Kealakekua Bay, where Cook harbored on the Big Island of Hawaii, included front and center a small figure on a surfboard. Surfing was a constant theme in the accounts of Cook's Hawaiian sojourn. Several of his crew wondered at the "almost amphibious" Hawaiians: "both Men and Women are so perfectly masters of themselves in the Water, that it appears their natural element"; "we never saw people so active in the water." Big waves struck fear in Western sailors, who tried to avoid them; Hawaiians viewed the same waves as a playground and sought them out for fun. David Samwell, surgeon's mate, declared, "These people find one of their Chief amusements in that which to us presented nothing but Horror & Destruction, and we saw with astonishment young boys & Girls about 9 or ten years of age playing amid such tempestuous Waves that the hardiest of our seamen would have trembled to face."

Cook himself, of course, did not return with testimony. His friendly relations with Hawaiians broke down over cultural misunderstandings. Hawaiians bedeviled his ships with petty thievery, absconding with anything not nailed down and even things that were—some intrepid natives dove under the ship to strip iron nails. Cook's crew escalated threats of violence to get their stuff back. Hawaiians were likely mystified by Cook's anger as they did not share his notions of private property and considered anything not *kapu* as communal. Since they shared their food and water with Cook's men, they expected him to share his goods with them. After some Hawaiians made off with a small boat, the ensuing standoff turned violent, and Cook was overwhelmed and clubbed to death on the beach.

In 1837 a Hawaiian scholar, David Malo, wrote, "If a big wave comes in, large and unfamiliar fishes will come from the dark ocean, and when they see the small fishes of the shallows they will eat them up. . . . The white man's ships have arrived with clever men from the big countries, they know our people are few in number and our country is small, they will devour us." The history of Hawaii after Captain Cook was a story of big fish devouring small ones.

What attracted the big fish to Hawaii? A series of booming markets in the nineteenth century lured white colonists trying to make a fast buck. The first was sandalwood. Hawaii after Cook was initially a way station for Pacific trade, especially the fur trade with Canton. By 1800 fur traders wiped out otter populations in the Pacific Northwest and began looking for new sources of income. They noticed that the Chinese valued sandalwood for building, incense, and medicine—and that Hawaii had abundant sandalwood forests. The sandalwood market took off at the same time that King Kamehameha was unifying Hawaii. Kamehameha, a tall, strong, fearless fighter—and skilled surfer—had been on Cook's ships and traded a feather cloak for iron daggers. The exchange signaled the young chief's priorities, and over the next two decades he set about conquering the major Hawaiian islands. By 1810 he had centralized control over land, including sandalwood forests, and since he lived on Oahu—first at Waikiki, then in Honolulu—traders began calling there to negotiate deals. This also led to the development of Honolulu, which had one of the few natural harbors in the Hawaiian islands—and harbors were crucial precisely because Hawaiian surf made safe anchorage scarce.

Kamehameha's control of the forests included a *kapu* on over-harvesting or cutting young trees. After his death in 1819 sandalwood agents began wholesale pillaging of the forests. By 1830 most of Hawaii's sandalwood forests had disappeared, and with them the sandalwood trade. By that time, however, sandalwood had started Hawaii's transition to a cash economy. Much of the income went to chiefs, who had developed a taste for fine Western clothing and furniture, ships, and guns. These chiefs shifted workers from fields and fish ponds to sandalwood harvests, and common people began to lose leisure time—including time for surfing. The sandalwood trade also began undermining Hawaiian social and religious customs, including the *kapu* system.

At least the sandalwood trade returned some money to Hawaiians, especially to chiefs like Kamehameha. The next major economic boom, whaling, returned less to Hawaiians and more to white colonists. Whaling filled the economic void just as sandalwood declined. In the first half of the nineteenth century whale oil provided the light and lubrication for the industrial revolution, and American whalers dominated the trade. Around 1820 whalers started using Hawaii as a base, especially after the discovery of major sperm whale grounds off Japan, when Japanese ports were still closed to foreign ships. Honolulu became the major port for the American whaling fleet in the Pacific. Hundreds of whaling ships called in Honolulu and Lahaina every year, each buying provisions, sails, timber, and entertainment—that is, booze and sex, which became a prime secondary business in Honolulu. Sailors, after months on a stinking, vermin-infested hellhole of a whaleship, arrived in Hawaiian paradise ready for fun, and prostitution boomed in Honolulu. Honolulu became a bustling port, filled with ships, piers, dockyards, and storehouses (and whorehouses); by 1830, forty thousand tons of American shipping passed through it. Whaling accelerated Hawaii's transition to a market economy and labor system. And more Hawaiians—and surfers—found themselves working long hours in shipyards or warehouses, with even less time off for fun.

Whaling peaked around 1850 and then declined. The discovery of oil in Pennsylvania replaced whale oil as fuel for lamps; the Civil War diverted the New England whaling fleet; and above all, the whales themselves had been hunted to the brink of extinction. The Civil War also interrupted the source of sugar in the American South, so sugar replaced whaling as the new economic engine. Sugar also benefited hugely from a major shift in property rights. Around 1850 the royalty gave up its monopoly on land, in a land division known as the Great Mahele. The change allowed commoners to buy land, but it soon expanded to allow foreigners to buy land as well. That meant another displacement of native Hawaiians, this time from their own land. By 1900 whites owned four acres for every acre owned by a native.

The Great Mahele provided vast landholdings for white colonists, which they turned into pineapple and sugar plantations. Then, in 1876, a treaty with the United States opened the American market to duty-free Hawaiian sugar. At the time sugar sold for 6.5 cents per pound, and the U.S. duty was 3 cents per pound; by getting rid of the duty, sugar growers basically doubled their profits. Sugar imports to the United States jumped tenfold from 1876 to 1890, and sugar growers made fortunes. Native Hawaiians did not share in the economic windfall. The land was in the hands of white elites, and the labor went to immigrants. Many natives quite reasonably refused to work in the cane fields under backbreaking conditions of indentured servitude, so plantation owners began importing Chinese and then Japanese workers. These Asian immigrants brought rice culture to Hawaii and supplemented Waikiki's fish ponds with rice paddies. Rice remains a major staple in the Hawaiian diet: Hawaii is the only place in the United States where you can go into a McDonald's and buy a bowl of rice to go with your Big Mac.

Sugar completed the economic dispossession of native Hawaiians. The introduction of a cash economy, starting with sandalwood and whaling and maturing with the sugar trade, stifled surfing. Instead of enjoying the bounty of their fish farms and taro fields, commoners were increasingly conscripted by chiefs for sandalwood harvests or relegated to work in whaling warehouses and shipyards. The market economy increasingly bifurcated Hawaiian society. Chiefs made more money and could afford luxury goods, but commoners had less—in particular less leisure time. And each new industry—sandalwood, whaling, sugar—increasingly concentrated economic benefits among white elites, not native Hawaiians. The increasing division between a few elites and many poor laborers meant economic hardship for most Hawaiians. As Malo predicted, the big fishes from the ocean deeps indeed devoured the little ones on the Hawaiian reefs.

THE MISSIONARY INFLUENCE

The economic dislocation brought by a cash economy has often been overshadowed by the dispossession of the Hawaiian religion. Standard accounts of Hawaiian surfing in the nineteenth century declare that white missionaries put an end to it. The story is not so simple.

The first Christian mission arrived in Hawaii from the United States in 1820. The British had dispatched missionaries to several South Pacific islands starting in 1796, and their success helped inspire the

American mission to Hawaii. The American missionaries enjoyed a stroke of amazing good fortune in arriving just after the death of Kamehameha. Before he died in 1819, the king had questioned the traditional *kapu* system of religious prohibitions. Commoners had seen that foreigners were flouting *kapus* and evidently not suffering retribution from the gods, and word got out that other South Pacific islands had abandoned *kapu* with no apparent consequences. Kamehameha also apparently disliked *kapu*'s regulation of meetings between the sexes and proposed abandoning it, which was indeed done after he died. The missionaries thus arrived to find the existing religious system in disarray. As one American described it, "After some hesitation on the part of the rulers of the islands, the missionaries, so opportunely arrived, were allowed to remain and commence their work."

Hiram Bingham and Asa Thurston led the first mission. Bingham, a stern New England Calvinist, played a stronger role, in part because he remained in Honolulu while Thurston went to Kailua on Oahu's east coast. Bingham was appalled on arrival by native nudity and sexual license. "The appearance of destitution, degradation, and barbarism, among the chattering, and almost naked savages, whose heads and feet, and much of their sunburnt swarthy skins, were bare, was appalling. Some of our number, with gushing tears, turned away from the spectacle. Others, with firmer nerve, continued their gaze, but were ready to exclaim, 'Can these be human beings?' "

Not all white colonists welcomed the missionaries. Whalers and U.S. naval sailors, who didn't mind having naked girls swimming out to their ships, grumbled about Bingham's virtuous campaign, which targeted them as much as it sought to convert native Hawaiians. (In 1827, irate sailors on an English whaler, denied prostitutes by a pious preacher, fired cannonballs at the missionary house; the previous year a Hawaiian female chief intervened to save Bingham from an angry mob of American sailors.) But Bingham's Christian dogma quickly filled the vacuum left by the abolition of *kapu*. The mission scored a coup in converting Kamehameha's independent and savvy widow, Ka'ahumanu, who was ruling as regent after the king's death. With the weight of royal sanction, Bingham was soon preaching to three thousand natives every Sunday.

What did this mean for surfing? Some observers perceived a decline in surfing at the time. A newspaper editor in the 1840s noted, "Formerly, old and young engaged in this sport, but now it is a rare sight." Later visitors similarly commented on surfing's decline. In 1892 anthropologist Nathaniel B. Emerson observed: "There are those living . . . who remember the time when almost the entire population of a village would at certain hours resort to the sea-side to indulge in, or to witness, this magnificent accomplishment. . . . Today it is hard to find a surfboard outside our museums and private collections."

Since the decline occurred after the missionaries arrived, some writers made the connection and blamed the missionaries. A visitor in 1838 declared that surfing and other games had been suppressed, "being in opposition to the strict tenets of Calvinism." Bingham and other missionaries initially supported such a view, boasting in 1829 that "the slate, the pen, and the needle, have, in many instances, been substituted for the surf-board, the bottle, and the *hula*."

The missionaries themselves, however, denied that they caused surfing's decline. Bingham complained about "unfriendly views" of missionary influence: "It was easy for vain men to accuse us of interfering, unreasonably, with the amusements of the chiefs and people." Bingham testified that missionaries had nothing against surfing itself. Rather, surfing was just collateral damage of the campaign against nudity, sex, and gambling—all those naked men and women frolicking in the water together and betting on surf contests. Specifically, "the adoption of our costume greatly diminishes their practice of swimming and sporting in the surf, for it is less convenient to wear it in the water than the native girdle, and less decorous and safe to lay it entirely off on every occasion they find for a plunge or a swim or a surf-board race. Less time, moreover, is found for amusement by those who earn or make cloth-garments for themselves like the civilized nations." Islanders also now devoted their time to "elementary instruction in reading, writing, morals, religion, arithmetic, geography, sacred song, and sacred history." (Surfboards were indeed turned into writing tables in some schools.) Bingham conceded that "the heathen sports of the nation nearly disappeared." But he declared, "The decline or discontinuance of the use of the surf-board, as civilization advances, may be accounted for by the increase of modesty, industry or religion, without supposing, as some have affected to believe, that missionaries caused oppressive enactments against it."

By the time Bingham wrote his self-serving account in 1847, the Protestant missions in Hawaii were in retreat. Queen Ka'ahumanu died in 1832, and with her the royalty's evangelical zeal and the alignment between religious and political leaders. Even at the peak of missionary activity, only half the native population attended church. The natives' faith was narrow, and shallow too: fewer than 1 percent of natives had been granted Communion. The dogmatic, self-righteous Bingham wore out his welcome by 1840 and fled back to New England. Few were sorry to see him go. By the 1860s, as one historian put it, "the retreat of the missionaries had turned into a rout." By 1870 only a quarter of Hawaiians were Protestant.

As the Protestant missions fizzled, the missionaries and their descendants turned their attention to business. They proved far more successful at making money than they were at making Christians. Missionary families acquired vast tracts of land in the Great Mahele or acquired property through marriage into landholding Hawaiian royal families. They turned this land into sugar and pineapple plantations and watched their fortunes grow. In the meantime, however, they wrote many accounts of Hawaii in this period that highlighted the newfound piety and discipline of the former heathens and shaded later perceptions of missionary influence. Dissolution of the *kapu* system (which the missionaries did not cause) certainly hurt surfing by ending the surf-centered Makahiki Festival. But the missionaries proscribed surfing itself only on the Sabbath. Queen Ka'ahumanu was scolded for surfing on Sunday—but that apparently did not stop her. One missionary complained that the queen, despite his warnings about violating the Sabbath, chose to go surfing anyway, with a "great multitude" of fellow natives. Even the threat of eternal hellfire did not deter Hawaiians from the waves.

Surfing survives the missionaries, as pictured in this illustration by Wallis Mackay in Charles Warren Stoddard's Summer Cruising in the South Seas. *(London: Chatto and Windus, 1873)*

Surfing, in short, survived the missionaries. Woodcuts and renderings depicted people surfing throughout the nineteenth century, and eyewitness accounts confirmed that Hawaiians continued to surf. A missionary wife in 1834 complained that surfing was "too much practiced at the present day," a view echoed by American explorer Charles Wilkes in 1840: "the time to see a Hawaiian happy, is while he is gambolling and frolicking in the surf." In the 1850s a visitor to Kealakekua Bay, site of Cook's demise, watched two dozen men, women, and children surfing in the bay, and added, "The healthful diversion is still the favourite of the few remaining national exercises of the natives. . . . Many of the natives spend whole days in enjoying themselves in this manner in the water." Mark Twain, on a visit in the late 1860s, saw "a large company of naked natives, of both sexes and all ages, amusing themselves with the national pastime of surf-bathing." (Twain added that he "tried surf-bathing once, subsequently, but made a failure of it. I got the board placed right, and at the right moment, too;

but missed the connection myself.—The board struck the shore in three quarters of a second, without any cargo, and I struck the bottom about the same time, with a couple of barrels of water in me.")

If surfing was the "national pastime," it clearly hadn't died out, nor had surfers' devotion. Around the same time as Twain, the Hawaiian writer Kepelino Keauokalani observed that "expert surfers going upland to farm, if part way up . . . look back and see rollers combing the beach, will leave work . . . hurrying away home they will pick up the board and go. All thought of work is left. The wife may go hungry, the children, the whole family, but the head of the house does not care. He is all for sport, that is his food. All day there is nothing but surfing." Decades later, an 1896 article in *Hawaiian Annual* noted that "necessary work for the maintenance of the family, such as farming, fishing, mat and tapa making, and such other household duties required of them needing attention . . . was often neglected for the prosecution of the sport."

European colonizers were no less entranced by surfing. The early explorers not only found Polynesian islands a far cry from the inhospitable North Atlantic (Magellan named it the Pacific Ocean for a reason), they also sent their reports to a continent wracked by revolution and war, especially the French Revolution and the Napoleonic Wars. Tahiti for the French and Hawaii for the British: accounts of tropical idylls, and especially surfing, provided a geographical, moral, and spiritual counterpoint to Europe's violent convulsions. While Europeans were perfecting the guillotine and bayoneting each other on the battlefield, tropical surfers were out riding waves. The surfer transcended politics, industry, and war, ignoring everything except "the most supreme pleasure" of wave riding. The contrast was not lost on Europeans. Historians have even suggested that such visions of surfing inspired "the pursuit of happiness" that underlay the French and American revolutions: surfers turned happiness from an abstract idea into a specific lifestyle, represented by a particular person and place—the surfer on a tropical wave. Surfing was not a heathen sport to eradicate; it was a transcendent, redemptive act to emulate. The revolutions, in other words, aimed to spread the stoke.

Religious authorities themselves took up this theme. British missionary William Ellis visited the Hawaiian mission in the early 1820s and marveled at the native surfers. "To see fifty or a hundred persons riding on an immense billow, half immersed in spray and foam, for a distance of several hundred yards together, is one of the most novel and interesting sports a foreigner can witness in the islands." Ellis took issue with surfing on the Sabbath but said nothing about surfers' nudity or gambling and otherwise conveyed no sense of disapprobation. On the contrary, he seemed to admire surfing. Similar approval came thirty years later from the Reverend Henry T. Cheever, a Protestant minister whose books on whaling inspired Melville's *Moby-Dick*. Cheever commented on surfing during a visit to Lahaina: "The sport is so attractive and full of wild excitement to Hawaiians, and withal so healthful, that I cannot but hope it will be many years before civilization shall look it out of countenance, or make it disreputable to indulge in this manly, though it be dangerous, exercise." In short, religious authorities observed that not only were natives still surfing, but that nonnatives were missing out—and that missionaries had not, and should not, make surfing disreputable.

Such views resonated with a new Western embrace of the ocean. Biblical accounts and other early theologies first instilled fear of the sea. Like forests or other wilderness, the ocean was a place to be avoided; you didn't venture into the abyss because you stood a good chance of dying. Around 1750 Europeans started to change their views, in what the great French historian Jules Michelet called "the invention of the sea." The sea first offered a medical cure for ailments such as melancholy and spleen. Seaside resorts sprang up in Europe and America offering sea bathing as therapy, the oceanic equivalent of spas or mineral springs; customers paid to get dunked in the surf as a bracing tonic. The emerging industrialized urban society fed this development with concerns about the physical fitness of urban classes. A mid-century movement called "muscular Christianity" gave exercise a spiritual and moral dimension and viewed swimming in particular as beneficial; the YMCA's dedication to swimming came out of this movement, with particular importance for surfing. Michelet himself saw the sea as a way to restore the enervated society of industrial Europe: "Have pity upon yourselves, all ye poor men of the West. . . . Nations! Attention! Earth supplies you with the means of laboring and living; THE SEA offers you the still better means of living WELL."

Sea bathing became a way to heal the spirit as well as the body. The Romantic poets and philosophers celebrated the ocean as a place for heroic action and self-realization; instead of fearing it, now you plunged in as a way to experience the sublime power of nature. Romantics from Goethe to Pushkin to Poe were avid swimmers; Byron swam the Hellespont at age twenty-two, and Swinburne likewise celebrated swimming and sea bathing. Shelley never learned to swim but should have: he loved the sea so much he died in it, drowning in the Ligurian Sea with a volume of Sophocles in hand. Byron's *Childe Harold's Pilgrimage* captured the thrill of the surf:

And I have loved thee, Ocean! And my joy
Of youthful sports was on thy breast to be
Borne, like thy bubbles, onward: from a boy
I wanton'd with thy breakers—they to me
Were a delight; and if the freshening sea
Made them a terror, 'twas a pleasing fear;
For I was as it were a child of thee,
And trusted to thy billows far and near,
And laid my hand upon thy mane—as I do here.

The erotic undercurrent was later expressed by the French writer Paul Valéry, another avid ocean swimmer, who called swimming "*fornication avec l'onde.*"

In the missionaries and the Romantics we see for the first time, but not the last, two opposing views of surfing: one as a decadent, heathen lifestyle; the other as natural, healthy outdoor sport. Much of subsequent surf history involves the tension between these two views: immoral versus moral, subversive versus mainstream. The idea that surfing was viewed as immoral, and that missionaries for that reason wiped out surfing, is overstated. The missionaries themselves had only limited influence for perhaps twenty years, and they dismissed accusations that they had suppressed surfing itself. Some of them, in fact, embraced the widespread view that surfing was healthy and even spiritual.

So, why the persistent belief that the missionaries suppressed surfing? Because this is where surfing first acquired its countercultural cachet. If the missionaries were against it, surfing must be cool. The missionary story is surfing's origin myth. Surfing was as mainstream as you can get in Hawaiian society, and, as we shall see, it became similarly mainstream in the twentieth-century world. But modern surfers who enjoyed surfing's subversive, countercultural image seized on the idea of missionary influence. It all started here, surfing's modern image of rebellious cool. But it's a myth.

DISEASE AND DEMOGRAPHIC COLLAPSE

Debating the missionary influence provided a convenient way at the time to ignore the real reason surfers seemed increasingly scarce. Caucasian colonizers did not kill off surfing through their missionary activity. Probably more damaging was the introduction of a cash economy through the sandalwood and whaling trades, which cut leisure time for many Hawaiian workers. Most important of all, white colonizers killed off surfing by killing the surfers. Surfing died out in the nineteenth century because of a catastrophic demographic collapse that left almost no Hawaiians alive to ride waves.

Before Cook, the isolation of Hawaii had insulated its people from infectious disease. Any germs that accompanied the original Polynesian settlers either infected their hosts and died with them or encouraged immunity in the survivors. The Hawaiian people encountered no new sources of infection over the ensuing centuries. Hawaii's remoteness, combined with its abundant food sources and benign climate, made Hawaiians extremely healthy, which enabled their pursuit of physical activities like surfing. There was no winter cold, no venomous snakes, and no beasts of prey on land; the only hazards were sharks, and other men.

This blessed refuge from disease, however, rendered Hawaiians uniquely susceptible when exposed after contact, since they lacked antibodies. Captain Cook and the Western sailors who followed him brought a veritable Pandora's box of afflictions: cholera, typhus, smallpox, leprosy, dysentery, influenza, rabies, polio, and venereal disease. The last was perhaps the most serious demographically, as it led to infant mortality and female sterility as well as debilitating illness. Venereal disease arrived with Cook's ships; on the trip to Hawaii, half of Cook's crew was unable to work due to its ravages. Cook and his officers tried to prevent infected crew members from mingling with native Hawaiian women, to no avail. Cook lamented that "the very thing happened that I had above all others wished to prevent." His sailors, seeing healthy young maidens after months at sea, avidly pursued them; the women, viewing Cook as the god Lono, thought his crew might also convey the god's *mana* to them and accepted liaisons with the sailors.

The result was a devastating onslaught of disease. (This was another reason to import Asian labor for plantations—because too few Hawaiians were around to do the work.) The communal nature of Hawaiian society boosted disease vectors, for instance in the sharing of eating utensils; so did the increasing urbanization of Hawaiian society, as natives followed whaling money to the boomtown ports of Lahaina and Honolulu, making Hawaii one of the more urbanized populations in the world by mid-century. Particular epidemics of cholera in 1803, whooping cough and measles in the 1830s, and smallpox in 1853 decimated the native population. The plagues brought by Westerners included alcohol and tobacco. The ancient Hawaiians had not discovered alcohol fermentation, leaving them blissfully free of alcoholism. Not so after Western contact. Since a number of Hawaiian leaders acquired the addiction, alcoholism accelerated the erosion of political independence.

The breakdown of basic sanitation hastened the spread of disease. In the early nineteenth century foreigners, many of them transient sailors, swelled Honolulu's population and proceeded to befoul it with their trash and sewage. These newcomers flouted the native *kapu* precepts on hygiene and sanitation, and the Hawaiians themselves then abandoned *kapu*. As a result, Honolulu soon resembled any other squalid seaport. Much of the trash and sewage went directly or indirectly into Honolulu Harbor and the surrounding ocean, where it stewed at tropical temperatures. Sailors the world over called Honolulu Harbor the "Cesspool of the Pacific." The introduction of grazing animals, particularly cattle, added greatly to the fecal burden, and cow pies flowed even easier from hillsides denuded of vegetation by grazing and woodcutting. Pollution likely stifled surfing more than the missionaries—one cannot blame Hawaiians if they shunned water turned murky from runoff and sewage, which promised further assaults on their immune systems.

By the mid-nineteenth century Western observers were well aware that Hawaiians were dying at an alarming rate. Early population estimates started from the one provided by Cook's voyage, of about 400,000. An estimated 142,000 native Hawaiians remained in 1823, down to 84,000 in the 1850 census and 67,000 in 1860. By the 1890s only 40,000 survived. More recently demographers have argued for a population pre-Cook of at least 800,000, and perhaps closer to 1 million. From 800,000 to 40,000: that would make the Hawaiian demographic collapse more extreme than the one suffered by medieval Europe during the Black Death.

As Hawaiians died by the hundreds of thousands, Westerners—not yet subscribing to germ theories of disease—attributed their susceptibility to some innate weakness, probably moral. That is, their decadent lifestyle made them prone to infection. Missionary Rufus Anderson flatly declared that "all the causes of the depopulation on the Hawaiian Islands, excepting several of the foreign epidemics introduced by the shipping, *were in full operation before the arrival of the missionaries.* The epidemics spent themselves chiefly on the most decayed portion of the people, and so had the singular effect, on the whole, considerably to raise the national tone of morals. They were like the amputation of diseased members of the body." Such attitudes discouraged public health measures to stem the tide of death.

It is hard to overstate the demographic collapse of the Hawaiian people in the short space of a century. The sweeping epidemics devastated Hawaiian culture—not just by killing Hawaiians, but by undermining their community and customs. A crisis of the spirit followed in the wake of disease. Lassitude, doubt, and drift replaced energy and enthusiasm.

How could Hawaiians summon the will to surf when everyone around them was dying?

ANNEXATION

The history of Hawaii after Cook was a series of dispossessions. Christian religious beliefs replaced the *kapu* system; sandalwood, whaling, and sugar trade displaced the native economy; the Great Mahele transferred native lands to white colonists; imported Asian workers flooded the labor market; and new diseases decimated the native population. In the 1890s came another dispossession, the loss of political independence—a final insult and injury in a century full of them.

Hawaiian political power had been eroding for decades, reflecting struggles for strategic influence in the Pacific among the United States, Britain, France, Japan, and Russia. In the 1840s Britain briefly took control of Hawaii, provoking a response by the U.S.; when the U.S. tried to annex the islands a decade later, the British and French fleets prevented it. Although the Hawaiian monarchs cannily played off the great powers against each other, American interests gradually dominated. In 1875 King Kalakaua, recently arrived on the throne, negotiated the Reciprocity Treaty with the U.S., which allowed Hawaiian sugar into the U.S. market duty free. The U.S. in exchange got exclusive access to Pearl Harbor. In the 1880s white elites led by Sanford Dole and Lorrin A. Thurston agitated for "reform," which meant more white control. Thurston, publisher of the *Honolulu Advertiser*, was the grandson of missionary Asa Thurston; Dole, a son of missionaries, was a local notary whose cousin was building the Dole pineapple empire. In 1887 Dole and Thurston led a rebellion against King Kalakaua. Backed by a small militia, they forced Kalakaua to sign a new constitution—hence known as the "Bayonet Constitution"—restricting his power and expanding their own. The U.S. Navy at the time also acquired a formal lease to Pearl Harbor.

In 1891 Kalakaua died and his sister Liliuokalani assumed the throne. A gifted musician who wrote "Aloha Oe," an eventual anthem for Hawaiians, Queen Liliuokalani was no pushover. In early 1893 she introduced a new constitution, written in secret, that undid the Bayonet Constitution and restored the power of the monarchy and native

Hawaiians. Infuriated white elites persuaded the U.S. Marines to come ashore and storm the palace in December 1893. Thurston and Dole led a "Committee of Safety" that took over the government, and Dole became president of a new Hawaiian republic on the symbolic date of July 4, 1894. After a royalist uprising in January 1895, the government arrested Liliuokalani, imprisoned her in the palace, and sentenced her to five years of hard labor (though she was soon paroled).

The new government appealed to Washington to annex Hawaii as a territory. Mainland opponents of annexation feared the effect of imperialism on American values; others, reflecting nineteenth-century racial attitudes, claimed that the Hawaiian people (and immigrant Asian laborers) might be unsuitable for democratic government. In the end, Hawaii's military significance tipped the balance. In 1890 military strategist Alfred Thayer Mahan had published *The Influence of Sea Power upon History*, an influential treatise that urged the U.S. Navy to project power in the Pacific, against Asia and especially Japan. The Navy became a strong proponent of annexation; the assistant secretary of the Navy, a Mahan disciple named Theodore Roosevelt, declared, "If I had my way, I would annex those islands tomorrow."

The clincher came in a tropical harbor a world away, in Cuba, when an explosion ripped the warship *Maine* in February 1898. The U.S. Navy was soon steaming off to Guam and the Philippines in the Spanish-American War, and Hawaii provided a crucial refueling station for coal-powered ships. Annexation passed Congress within months. Hawaii was now a U.S. territory, with a territorial government run by white Americans. In August 1898, the Hawaiian flag came down, and the Stars and Stripes flew over Hawaii. After losing their religion, their land, their livelihoods, and their lives, the Hawaiian people had lost their independence.

By the end of the nineteenth century, the *heiau* on Diamond Head was gone. No priests flew their kites to announce when the south swells arrived. Even if the kites had flown, there were few surfers around to see the signal. The Kalehuawehe, the surfing supermen who rode monster south swells all the way from Diamond Head to Honolulu, had disappeared. The waves themselves remained, however, at least for the time being. And the same historical forces that had almost extinguished the Hawaiian people provided a fresh breeze for a surfing revival. Within a few years, a couple of latter-day Kalehuawehe emerged to rekindle surfing's spark from the ashes of Hawaiian history.

2 THE DUKE, DILLINGHAM, AND THE WAIKIKI DREAM

On a hot summer day in 1917, during a once-in-a-lifetime south swell, Duke Kahanamoku paddled into a thirty-foot wave breaking far off Oahu's south shore. Duke negotiated the mountainous whitewater across a series of surfing's most famous reefs, from outside Castles through Queens to Canoes, an astounding ride that centuries earlier would have earned him the title of Kalehuawehe. Duke's legendary wave punctuated a surfing renaissance that had unfolded in the previous two decades, a revival enabled by the transformation of the Hawaiian economy after annexation and the engineering of Waikiki Beach itself. Duke surfed past several large hotels that did not exist two decades earlier and along a beach that his surfing forefathers would not have recognized. Environmental engineering fundamentally changed Waikiki and left a legacy for ensuing generations of surfers. But the romantic appeal of Waikiki, the cradle of modern surfing, remained. A surfer today, paddling out in the warm water at day's end, looking back at the purple glow of the sunset playing over Diamond Head, and hearing ukulele music wafting out from the beachfront clubs, can easily forget this history amid the simple joy of riding waves.

THE HAWAIIAN REVIVAL

Hawaii's loss of political independence in the 1890s, driven by American military interests in the age of imperialism, was the final insult in a century full of them. But it was this last dispossession that set the stage for a surfing revival. The resurrection from one perspective looks like another appropriation, by and for the white outsiders whom Hawaiians called "haoles." The tourist industry in particular used surfing to lure haoles to Hawaii so that other haoles could make money off them. Surfing hadn't completely died out, but most Hawaiians who surfed had died, and no one took their place in the empty lineup. Now, in the first years of the new century, surfing found a new group of people with leisure time. At the same time, the surfing revival did provide a way for Hawaiians to reclaim some of their culture after a century of dispossessions, and resume their place in the lineup alongside the newcomers.

Annexation played a central role in the emergence of modern surfing, but so did key individuals. The first was George Freeth. Born in 1883 in Honolulu, Freeth was the son of an Irish captain and a half-Hawaiian mother; blue-eyed and fair-skinned, but one-quarter Hawaiian himself, he was fascinated with his Hawaiian roots. As a child he saw an old painting showing his Hawaiian ancestors surfing and resolved to pursue the sport. He got the chance as a teenager, when an uncle, according to the story, encouraged his interest and gave him an old Hawaiian longboard, or *olo*. Freeth cut the sixteen-foot board down so he could carry it and taught himself to surf. He was soon the leading surfer at Waikiki, one of the few still around to ride standing and also one of the first, after the turn of the century, to angle across the wave instead of riding straight in.

At this point an unlikely character named Alexander Hume Ford entered the picture. No native waterman, Ford came from a wealthy South Carolina plantation family and took up writing for New York magazines and papers. Small and highly energetic, Ford had a sharp goatee that gave him a Pan-like appearance, and he conveyed his latest enthusiasm in torrents of one-sided conversation. A trip through Russia and China led Ford in early 1907 to Hawaii, where he tried surfing and found a new passion. He shaped himself a wood plank board and began spending several hours a day in the water; within months he was riding the outside breaks alongside Freeth and other Hawaiians. The diminutive newcomer fixated on Freeth. Ford effused, "There's something spiritual about Freeth that makes him stand out from the rest, like a bright light. He's a paragon of modern youth, yet he resists the mainland imports, and holds to the old pantheism. Water is his God, and it's all around and inside of him. When he rides the waves he's almost—dare I say it?—a Christ-like figure. No—I've gone too far: he's *pre*-Christian, of course."

The final character in this three-person act arrived onstage that spring. In May 1907 Jack London sailed into Hawaii on the *Snark* and with his wife, Charmian, checked into a small Waikiki hotel. At age thirty-one London was already famous for *The Call of the Wild*, and Ford knew his reputation as a manly adventurer. One evening Ford buttonholed London in the dining room of the Royal Hawaiian. Charmian recalled that Ford "talked a steady stream all through. . . . At present he is interested in reviving the old Hawaiian sport of surf-boarding on the breakers, and promised to see us at Waikiki later on, and show us how to use a board. When he left, we were able to draw the first long breath in two hours."

True to his word, Ford showed up a few days later with a board and took the Londons surfing. Charmian tried the gentler "wahine" (or women's) surf close to shore and caught one wave all the way to the beach, "slipping up to the beach precisely to the feet of some stranger hotel guests, who were not half so surprised as myself." Ford took Jack out to what London called "the big, bearded man surf that roars far out beyond the diving-stage." London didn't manage to stand up on a wave, but he caught a bunch on his stomach and watched Freeth in action. Caught up in the stoke, he stayed out for four hours, blissfully ignorant of what the midday tropical sun would do to fair skin. He spent the next week in bed with a blistering sunburn and couldn't get back in the water before the *Snark* sailed. But he was hooked on surfing.

London quickly wrote up his experience in a 1907 article for *Woman's Home Companion*, where he touted surfing as "a royal sport for the natural kings of the earth" and lionized Freeth as "a young god bronzed with sunburn." The article reached a still wider audience when it appeared as a chapter in *Cruise of the Snark* in 1911. Ford meanwhile did his part to spread the stoke with a 1909 article in *Collier's*, at the time probably the leading national magazine, with a circulation approaching 1 million.

London and Ford represented, and propagated, a resurgence of interest in surfing in the first decade of the century. Charmian London's account from 1907 mentioned a "fleet of young kanaka surf-boarders" bobbing around Freeth in the lineup. Why did they take up surfing? Easy: it was fun. It was fun for the ancient Hawaiians, and it was still fun in 1900. But what led to the revival at this particular time and place? One individual, George Freeth, was key. Freeth inspired Ford and London, who in turn promoted the surf lifestyle in their writing. Soon after London's visit, Honolulu's leading newspaper declared of Freeth that "no one has done more to revive surf riding. Through his exertions, what had seemed bound to become a lost art, has once more sprung into vogue."

One Hawaiian teenager did not revive surfing single-handed. There were broader social forces at work. What were Ford and London doing in Hawaii? They were tourists. Where did they meet? The Royal Hawaiian Hotel. Political annexation by the United States may have spurred young Hawaiians to reclaim their cultural independence, the same way young Freeth, intrigued by his cultural heritage, took up surfing as a link to his own past. At the same time, the interest of people like Ford and London came from another direction, that of Americans taking advantage of their new possession. That path led through Hawaii's emerging tourist industry.

TOURISM

The word "tourist," like tourism itself, did not exist much before 1800. Tourism required leisure time, which for most of humanity did not exist before industrialization. As the working and middle classes acquired free time in the industrial world of the nineteenth century, a tourism industry sprang up to cater to them, with travel agents, destination resorts, and transportation. Tourism took the travail out of travel, so to speak, and the tourist became a widget in the new leisure industry.

Hawaii at first did not make a great tourist destination. Alone in the vast North Pacific, it is one of the most isolated spots on the planet, two thousand miles from any other land. During the first several decades of the nineteenth century most visitors there were business travelers in the whaling, fur, or sandalwood trade, for whom Hawaii was not a destination but a way station. Hawaiian tourism picked up steam later in the nineteenth century, literally. Steamships replaced sailing vessels and cut the travel time from three or four weeks to under a week from the American West Coast. Regular steamship service to the islands began in the 1870s, subsidized by the Hawaiian monarchy, which also provided public funds to dredge Honolulu Harbor so that it could accommodate deep-draft steamships. The government also leveled the old fort downtown and used the rubble as a harbor breakwater, one of the first human efforts to transform Oahu's waterfront. The government pitched in further by providing bonds that paid for the construction and furnishing of a new first-class hotel in downtown Honolulu—the Hawaiian (later known as the Royal Hawaiian)—in 1872, as well as the land on which it was built.

Several factors encouraged tourism: expansion of the United States itself to the Pacific Coast, providing potential tourists and the ports to launch them; Gilded Age fortunes, which allowed the moneyed class to travel; and public interest in exotic natives encouraged by the emerging science of anthropology, carried along by the wave of Western imperial expansion. Tourism was one subject where the monarchy and white elites saw eye to eye, and white businessmen began their own enthusiastic marketing, with tourist-oriented periodicals such as *Hawaiian Annual* (published starting 1875) and *Paradise of the Pacific* (1888) to promote Hawaii's image. A few years later, in 1892, Lorrin Thurston started the Hawaii Bureau of Information, a short-lived tourism agency. On a trip to the United States to lobby for annexation, Thurston arranged a Hawaiian exhibit for the 1893 Chicago World's Fair. The Hawaiian display, featuring a volcano diorama and hula dancers, was a major attraction for the 25 million visitors on the fair's midway.

These efforts generated a steady stream of two thousand visitors a year to Hawaii in the last quarter of the nineteenth century. That was enough to sustain the Royal Hawaiian, which remained the only major hotel. But tourism was not yet an economic juggernaut. That only started after annexation, which aroused American interest in Hawaii and Hawaiian interest in American tourism dollars. Economic turmoil had nourished the annexation movement. In the sugar trade, the McKinley Tariff of 1890 nullified the Reciprocity Treaty by giving 2 cents per pound to mainland sugar growers. The Hawaiian sugar market plunged, compounded by the economic depression of 1893. The dire economic trends encouraged a search for new industries, and tourism filled the bill. In 1901 the Honolulu Merchants Association began touting the commercial potential of tourism, and in 1903 the local chamber of commerce created the Hawaiian Promotion Committee (later renamed the Hawaii Tourist Bureau), funded by the Hawaiian government as well as local business. Alexander Hume Ford was at the center of these efforts, helping to create the tourist bureau and editing *Pan Pacific Magazine* as a lure for tourists. Ford's celebration of surfing and buttonholing of Jack London were part and parcel of his promotion of Hawaiian tourism.

Annexation also spurred the construction of the first major hotel at Waikiki. In March 1901 the posh Moana Hotel opened for business right on the beach. The state-of-the-art Beaux-Arts hotel had seventy-five luxurious guest rooms with telephones, private baths, a billiard room, a parlor, a library, the first electric-powered elevator in the islands, and a hundred-yard wooden pier. Tourists could disembark from the Matson steamship lines at Honolulu and make their way to the Moana on newly paved Kalakaua Avenue. This developing tourism infrastructure—marketing, transportation, accommodations—soon paid dividends. The number of tourists doubled in the first four years after annexation, from two thousand in 1898 to four thousand in 1902, and continued growing.

What did all these tourists have to do with surfing? A photo of the Moana Hotel from 1907 features tourists strolling on the beach, apparently reluctant to enter the water. Tourism promoters had to make the ocean part of the Waikiki experience, and that meant surfing. The leisure industry itself had given the word "tourist" a pejorative connotation, with images of soft, pampered Westerners cut off from real experience. Vacationers instead sought to emulate the hardy "traveler," a sort of anti-tourist, who pursued originality off the beaten track. Surfing provided just this sort of authentic experience of an exotic culture—even if it was in fact packaged and sold by the Hawaiian tourism industry.

A 1905 article titled "Give the Tourists More Variety," in the pro-tourism journal *Paradise of the Pacific,* declared that "climate and scenery are well enough for the visitor at first," but true travelers craved "an insight into the wild life of the Polynesians." "Native color . . . is what the pleasure seeker likes to have imbued in his entertainment." And what better introduction to wild Hawaiian life than the sport of surfing? Surfing also presented a benign image to counter the popular misperception (spread by Twain, among others) that Hawaiians were violent and warlike, even persisting in cannibalism. Surfing images instead portrayed Hawaiians as peaceful and fun-loving. A Hawaii Tourist Bureau ad in *National Geographic* included a photo of a young white woman surfing, with this copy: "The water is a place to *play* . . . where bronze-skinned Hawaiians will teach you how to balance on speeding surfboards."

It was thus no accident that the Moana was right next to Canoes, Waikiki's most popular surf break. Canoes then and now is one of the best places in the world to catch your first wave, with long, gentle rides. The Moana quickly began advertising surfing as a new sport for tourists. One such tourist was the British scientist Francis W. Aston, who would go on to win the Nobel Prize in Chemistry in 1922 for his work on atomic isotopes. Aston visited Honolulu in 1909 and tried surfing. He there-after "considered it in many ways the finest sport in the world"—this from an active cyclist, skier, golfer, tennis player, and mountain climber.

Surfing also worked for tourism promoters thanks to its visually striking, dynamic images. Matson and other tourism promoters soon seized on surfing images for their posters and ads. One of the earliest tourist posters, from 1897, centered on a surfer angling across a good wave, framed by banana and palm trees against the backdrop of Diamond Head. This would become a Hawaiian staple, as tourism posters and articles abounded in photos of surfers streaking across waves with Diamond Head looming in the background. Hawaii's tourism marketing push benefited here from new printing technology; halftone reproductions allowed cheap, prolific reproduction of surf photos in

Two surfers at Waikiki. This photo appeared on the cover of Sunset *magazine in August 1916 and on the poster for the Mid-Pacific Carnival in 1917. (R.W. Perkins photo, Bishop Museum)*

magazine articles, advertisements, travel agency posters, and postcards, all of which propagated the surfing lifestyle through mainland society. By 1911 there were a hundred surfers out on an average day at Waikiki, where two decades earlier there had been maybe a handful.

ENGINEERING WAIKIKI

The proliferating surfers at Waikiki were witness to a changing landscape, brought on by coastal engineering of vast ambition. This decades-long project aimed at nothing less than the wholesale creation of a tropical paradise out of swampland and scrub brush. The tourism industry would not have boomed without it.

Waikiki in the nineteenth century was no tourist Mecca. The Royal Hawaiian was in Honolulu, and later developers likewise located their hotels downtown. In 1899 Benjamin Dillingham built a large resort at

Haleiwa, at the end of his rail line on Oahu's north shore. The 1880s and '90s finally saw small hotels built at Waikiki, along with a few bathhouses offering changing rooms, but the hotels soon went out of business. The Moana in 1901 was the first major hotel to make a go of it there.

Waikiki had natural advantages: a sandy beach lined with coconut groves, sheltered by reefs that kept the waves breaking far from shore, and set against the dramatic backdrop of Diamond Head. It was just a few miles from Honolulu, close enough for tourists to travel between them by horse in an hour or two, but distant enough to escape the pollution and sewage that befouled the Honolulu shoreline. Away from the strip of beach, however, Waikiki was mostly wetlands. Its name meant, literally, "spouting fresh water." Sitting on an extended coastal plain below steep valleys and mountains, it had three large streams that funneled the prolific local rainfall into hundreds of acres of swamps, rice farms, and fish ponds and drained muddy water into the surf.

Wetlands meant little buildable land, so tourists stayed in Honolulu and traveled to Waikiki by horse carriage. Transportation infrastructure was the first in a series of engineering initiatives. Building roads near beaches is a tricky business since waves and tides can wash them out. The first road to Waikiki, built in the 1860s, required a seawall for protection, which changed sand flow along the beach and drainage from the streams into the wetlands, which in turn affected sanitation. The drainage and sanitation issue introduced the first conflict between wetland farmers and beachfront homeowners and developers. The developers won the upper hand, and in the 1880s engineers widened the road and then added rails for horse-drawn Hawaiian Transways streetcars.

A road alone was not enough. To transform Waikiki into the most famous stretch of sand in the world, tourists needed a place to stay, beyond the smattering of bathhouses and hotels. And that meant land for hotels. The key event in the engineering of Waikiki was the creation of the Ala Wai (fresh water) canal, a plan by engineers to divert the three streams into a large canal running the length of Waikiki and to drain the vast swamps, rice paddies, and duck ponds. In the years following annexation, Lucius Pinkham, then president of the Territorial Board of Health, promoted the idea of a drainage canal to eliminate the "unsanitary" wetlands—and also to provide buildable land, in a vision of Waikiki that explicitly replaced poor farmers with wealthy developers. The discovery of a single case of yellow fever in 1911 spread fears about mosquitoes and added momentum to Pinkham's plan. Pinkham's appointment as governor of Hawaii in 1913 sealed the deal for what became known as the Waikiki Reclamation Project.

Walter Dillingham's Hawaiian Dredging Company won the job of draining the wetlands and creating the Ala Wai. This was no accident. Dillingham was the son of Benjamin Dillingham, founder of the Oahu Railway and Land Company and a major power broker in the economic development of Oahu. Benjamin Dillingham, a twenty-year-old Cape Cod native, came to Hawaii as first mate on the sailing packet *Whistler* and was left behind during a port call after breaking his leg falling off a horse. He made the most of his Hawaiian layover, marrying the daughter of a missionary and setting up shop in Honolulu with the son of another missionary, Alfred Castle. Thus well connected to local elites, he set about building a business empire embracing railroads, real estate, shipping, sugar, and pineapples. Not coincidentally, Lucius Pinkham spent the decade before his appointment to the board of health working for the elder Dillingham.

At the turn of the century Walter Dillingham was just starting a career that would literally reshape Hawaii. His Hawaiian Dredging Company incorporated in 1902 with Hawaii's first dredge and a contract to deepen Honolulu Harbor for the military. Why dredging? This was just another link in the remarkable vertical integration of business that made the Dillingham fortune: land bought cheap and planted with sugar and pineapples, railroads to transport the crop to the harbor, construction and control of harbors themselves, and even quarries that supplied rock for the harbor breakwaters. Starting a dredging business to build the harbors was just one more way to avoid paying someone else to do work.

Dredges, the ultimate earth mover of the coastal engineer, are used to pump silt out of channels, bays, and rivers, and to create beaches for shore protection and recreation. Few technologies have had a larger impact on surfing, and Dillingham controlled the dredging business in Hawaii. He was also, following in his father's footsteps, a land speculator. Anticipating a windfall, he bought up Waikiki wetlands for a song; by 1915, he owned 145 acres designated for reclamation. His dredges transformed the rice paddies into prime beachside real estate that he sold to developers at an immense profit. He also made money off the dredged material, to which he retained the rights in the Ala Wai contract. When the government issued permits for new buildings along Waikiki, it required contractors to build above sea level. So Dillingham sold developers the Ala Wai dirt, which they used to elevate their beachside building plots.

Work on the Ala Wai began in 1921 and was completed in 1923. The Ala Wai funneled the flow of the three streams into the canal and out into the ocean rather than into the now defunct wetlands or through Waikiki Beach. The sacrifice of the wetlands to create buildable land was pivotal to Waikiki's development as a tourist center. Dillingham's transformation of Oahu did not stop there; later construction projects included Ala Moana Park, Ala Moana Shopping Center, the dredging of Pearl Harbor as a naval base, the H3 highway, the building of Honolulu Airport on "reclaimed" land, and the Hilton Hawaiian Village. In Hawaii today, tourists are touched by Dillingham from the moment they land at the airport, grab their rental car, check into their hotel, and paddle out to the reefs along Waikiki.

The modern paradise of Waikiki Beach was a triumph of coastal engineering, at least from the viewpoint of the tourist industry. From an ecological standpoint, eliminating Waikiki's three streams and the wetlands had a profound impact on the beach and the surf. Waikiki had previously boasted a continuous beach stretching the length of the village, measuring over a hundred feet wide in places. Starting in the 1880s a wooden bridge was installed so that visitors could walk across the stream outfall between Kuhio Beach and Kapiolani Park, and then a seawall at the same spot began the literal erosion of Waikiki Beach. The sandy beach in front of the seawall disappeared almost immediately, the first local example of erosion caused by a man-made structure. More seawalls appeared in the 1890s with construction of the first buildings, and the domino effect began. By 1920, the entire length of Waikiki Beach was lined with thirty-seven seawalls. Hotel owners installed the walls close to the water to expand their real estate and protect their structures. Much to their chagrin, wave action quickly removed the sand. To make matters

Seawalls on Waikiki Beach in 1937. Note the lack of sand in front of the wall. The Moana Hotel is in the background. (Erwin N. Thompson, Pacific Ocean Engineers: History of the U.S. Army Corps of Engineers in the Pacific, *Honolulu District, U.S. Army Corps of Engineers, 1981)*

worse, the walls also prevented the flow of sand to the beach in front of the hotel next door; such littoral flows up and down shorelines are vital to maintaining natural beaches. Soon every plot of land on Waikiki had a seawall for self-defense, with little regard for the long-term effects on neighboring beaches.

Take away the beach and you lost the reason tourists came to Waikiki. Rather than remove the seawalls, the territorial government turned to more engineering to solve the problem. Coastal engineers installed a series of groins to hold the sand in place and solve the case of the disappearing beaches. The idea was that groins, projecting into the ocean from the beach at a perpendicular angle, would trap sand that flows along the shore. The Waikiki groins failed. By the mid-1920s the only beach left at Waikiki was between the Moana and Royal Hawaiian hotels, where there was no seawall. By 1928, the loss of Waikiki's beach threatened to stop the tourist industry in its tracks, and the territorial government conducted the first of several beach erosion studies, leading to eleven more experimental groins. One of these, a 368-foot groin at the Royal Hawaiian, captured a sizable amount of sand on the Diamond Head side. Three others created small beaches. Over the next fifty years forty-two groins were installed along Waikiki. Of these only five managed to hold sand on the beach. The successful groins shared one common feature: they were all very long. On the plus side they held sand; on the negative, sand that accumulated at the deepwater tip of the groin was lost to the shore forever.

Disappearing sand was only part of the problem. Rainfall in the valleys above Waikiki had emptied into the streams and wetlands below. This freshwater created channels through the coral reefs that determined the shape of the waves. Once the streams were channeled into the Ala Wai these reef gaps began filling with sand and coral growth, profoundly changing the surf lineup and rendering impossible some of the classic Waikiki rides from outside reefs to the beach; Duke's epic wave might have been impossible a few decades later. The reefs themselves, meanwhile, were targeted as a source of fill. In 1908 hotel owners began removing coral from near-shore bathing areas so that tourists could enjoy a swim without cutting themselves on the reef; they also blasted channels through the reefs for water skiing. Soon afterward the U.S. Army built Fort DeRussy on seventy-two acres of Waikiki wetland, using coral fill dredged from the reef flat and transported to shore in a channel blasted through the reef. On occasion the reef was dynamited, ground up, and spread in front of the seawalls as "beach."

The tourist paradise of Waikiki Beach, centered on the image of the surf lifestyle, was an elaborate fiction, engineered and maintained on behalf of the tourist economy. As Waikiki Beach continued to disappear, the government resorted to importing sand for replenishment. Beginning in the 1930s hundreds of thousands of cubic yards of sand were transported to Waikiki's beaches and spread in front of the seawalls. Some of this sand, subsequently scoured from the beach by wave action, settled on Waikiki's reefs, further changing wave patterns. The sand came from other parts of Oahu, from Molokai, and even from California. Most visitors to Waikiki, strolling along perhaps the most famous beach in the world, had no idea they were in fact walking on little bits of California.

DUKE

Although George Freeth was crucial for the revival of surfing in Hawaii, another figure is better known as the "father" of modern surfing: Duke Kahanamoku. Duke became the public image of the surfer—literally, a poster boy for Waikiki tourism—and, more broadly, of a new figure called the "waterman." Duke, however, certainly appreciated Freeth's contributions; a close friend, he continued to keep Freeth's legacy alive for decades after his death.

Kahanamoku, known universally as Duke, was born in 1890 in Honolulu. "Duke" was not a nickname; his father's name was also Duke, after the Duke of Edinburgh, who visited Hawaii in 1869. His family did have royal Hawaiian lineage, though his father was a delivery clerk. Duke was a first child, followed by five brothers, all of whom became accomplished surfers and watermen. Duke learned to swim as a toddler and was soon spending every day in the ocean at Waikiki near the family home at Kalia. He dropped out of high school, since his family needed the money he earned by diving and fishing. He had started surfing years earlier with other local kids, and Freeth, already a leader of the surfing revival, served as inspiration—and, soon, mentor and friend—to the youngster. In 1910, Duke made himself a ten-foot board, a few feet longer than the standard alaia board in the six- to eight-foot range. The longer board made it easier to catch and ride waves and allowed Duke to begin testing Waikiki outer reefs.

Duke first gained notice through swimming. At six foot one and 190 pounds, he was an impressive physical specimen, with size thirteen feet that powered the celebrated "Kahanamoku kick" in the water. At age twenty, in 1911, Duke shattered the American hundred-yard freestyle record by more than four seconds—and he did it not in a sheltered pool but in polluted Honolulu Harbor. Mainland swimming officials refused to certify the record, claiming either the timing or distance was wrong; no way could this unknown young Hawaiian be that fast. Duke traveled to New York and proved it, qualifying for the U.S. Olympic team. At the Stockholm Olympics in 1912 Duke won gold in the one-

Duke Kahanamoku paddling his board in Los Angeles circa 1920. (Source: Los Angeles Times *Photographic Archive, Department of Special Collections, Charles E. Young Research Library, UCLA)*

hundred-meter freestyle, after breaking the world record by three seconds in a preliminary heat. He had already charmed fellow competitors and spectators alike with his humility, sportsmanship, and good nature, strumming his ukulele poolside between heats. When he missed his semifinal heat, Australian champion Cecil Healy gallantly refused to swim unless Duke was allowed to swim in a special heat. Duke then beat Healy in the hundred-meter final, and also took silver in the four-by-two-hundred relay.

Olympic gold brought instant fame, and on his return to the United States Duke traveled the country giving swimming exhibitions. Duke gave surfing demonstrations as well whenever his tour landed in beach towns—Florida, Atlantic City, Newport Beach—and these displays, covered by local papers, helped sow the seed of surfing on the mainland. Duke's graceful, easygoing style and photogenic smile, in addition to his physical prowess, made him a natural ambassador for surfing. In late 1914 Duke embarked on a swimming tour in Australia, at the invitation of Australia's swimming association. Here too he gave a surfing demonstration, at Freshwater Beach north of Sydney, on a board he shaped out of local sugar pine. The Freshwater surf lifesavers offered to tow Duke through the shorebreak, but he declined and quickly outdistanced their surfboat on his way to the lineup. Several hundred spectators lined the beach as he caught wave after wave for over two hours. He capped the session with a headstand ride, then invited a fourteen-year-old local swimmer, Isabel Letham, to join him for Australia's first tandem surf. The crowd went wild. On his way out of the water he handed his eight-foot board to Claude West, a ten-year-old youngster who went on to become Australia's first champion surfer. Duke's gift grew into an Australian passion for the next century and beyond.

Duke undertook these swimming tours not just as a way to spread surfing stoke. He needed them to pay his bills. Surfers, like all human beings, need food, clothing, and shelter, which presents them with the fundamental question: how do you make a living and still surf? A few have gone the basic-subsistence route, diving for fish and poaching pineapples in Hawaii. Most have chosen to make a living, which means persuading some part of society to support them. For Freeth, this meant lifeguarding; for other Hawaiians, as we shall see, it meant giving surf lessons to tourists. Later surfers built and sold surfboards or surf trunks. The still later development of professional contests provided one more way, but far from the only one, of making a living off surfing.

How did Duke do it? He didn't, really. The ninth-grade dropout's unassuming personality, innocent trust in others, and aversion to self-promotion made him a poor businessman. As another Waikiki beachboy, George "Airedale" McPherson, put it, "if he would have had to earn a living, he would have starved. Out of the water, he was out of his element." In 1912, after his first Olympic triumph, Duke found work as a meter reader in Honolulu. Other odd jobs followed, including working chains for a surveying team and sweeping the floors and mowing lawns as the city hall janitor. In the 1920s, after winning two more Olympic gold medals in Antwerp, Belgium, Duke appeared in several movies filmed in Hollywood, or what he called "Haolewood," often cast as a faithful, exotic manservant to light-skinned leading men—including a later role alongside that other Duke, a young John Wayne.

In 1932, after a final run at Olympic qualifying, Duke returned to manage two gas stations for Union Oil. His friends joked with bitter irony that the most famous surfer in the world, a multiple Olympic gold medalist, was pumping gas and cleaning windshields. But Duke's fate was not unique. Many former athletes, especially those from underprivileged minorities or without built-in social support, fell on hard times after their glory days. Another celebrated Olympic champion of that era, Jesse Owens, similarly found himself working as a gas station attendant and going bankrupt.

Duke's connection with Hawaiian elites eventually eased his circumstances. After annexation, the sugar and pineapple barons learned to buy off the Hawaiian population with political patronage, dispensing jobs and favors in return for public support of their business empire. By the late 1920s all of the Honolulu police department and most of the fire department were filled by native Hawaiians. Duke had crewed on Harold Dillingham's yacht, and in 1934 the Dillinghams helped engineer Duke's election as Honolulu sheriff, a position he would hold for the next twenty-six years. Soon afterward Pacific System Homes, which mass-produced redwood surfboards in California, began paying Duke to endorse their boards, making him perhaps the first sponsored professional surfer. Even with the sheriff job, though, Duke struggled financially. In 1961 Duke declared to the *Honolulu Star-Bulletin* that he was "barely getting along." Around that time he teamed up with Kimo McVay, a commercial impresario, to promote his name. McVay provided the business and marketing expertise Duke lacked himself, and soon negotiated deals for restaurant franchises and Hawaiian shirts bearing Duke's name. One of the early headliners at the Duke Kahanamoku lounge in Waikiki was a young singer named Don Ho.

If Freeth was the first "professional surfer," Duke was the second. Though not paid to surf as was Freeth, Duke did essentially make a career, if not much of an income, off his accomplishments in the water. But the careers of Freeth and Duke proved that surfers, however talented they might be in the water, would need to find ways to make money from their surfing. Freeth and Duke were just the first in a long line of professional surfers who found themselves adrift, with little education or business experience, in the real world.

And their images relied on more than surfing. They instead helped invent the more general persona of the "waterman." The waterman did not just surf; he engaged the ocean in as many ways as possible, whether through outrigger paddling, paddleboard racing, diving, spearfishing, or the surfboard water polo that was dreamed up by the Kahanamoku brothers and a popular pursuit at Waikiki around the 1920s. Freeth fit this mold, and Duke himself called Freeth "the most consummate waterman I have ever known." Duke's waterman skills saved lives. In June 1925 Duke and two of his surfing friends, camping on Newport Beach to take advantage of a good south swell, rescued twelve fishermen whose boat had capsized off the harbor. Duke and his companions paddled out through the booming surf on their boards to ferry the victims to shore, earning them heroic front-page headlines in the *Los Angeles Times*. Newport's police chief called Duke's efforts "the most superhuman rescue act and the finest display of surfboard riding that has ever been seen in the world." Surfboards thereafter became standard rescue gear at lifeguard stations.

Above all, both Freeth and Duke built their waterman image, and their professional careers, on their fundamental swimming ability. Freeth was captain of Waikiki's Healani swim team; he probably would have competed in the Olympics as a diver, but officials declared that his lifeguarding pay revoked his amateur status. Duke continued his competitive swimming career after Stockholm; after the canceled 1916 Olympics, he won gold again in the 100 at the 1920 Olympics (and the world war probably robbed him of three straight golds). In 1924 he took silver in the 100 at age thirty-four, behind his young protégé Johnny Weissmuller, better known as Tarzan from his acting careeer. Sam Kahanamoku, Duke's brother, finished third. Duke good-naturedly joked that "it took Tarzan to beat me." Weissmuller, equally gracious, said of Duke, "I learned it all from him." In 1932 Duke missed qualifying for the Olympics in swimming and water polo at age forty-two, though his world record in the 50 freestyle still stood. That ended a remarkable span of two decades as one of the best swimmers in the world, in addition to the top surfer. Duke was Michael Phelps and Kelly Slater rolled into one.

EVERYBODY INTO THE POOL

It was no accident that Freeth and Duke, spearheads of the modern surfing revival, were competitive swimmers. Along with political annexation, tourism, and the engineering of Waikiki, swimming was the other fundamental social development driving the surfing revival. Swimming was crucial to the surfing renaissance in two respects. First, Freeth, Duke, and many other surfers in their cohort shared a swimming background. Second, and more important, the efforts of Freeth and Duke, and of surfing popularizers like Ford and London, would have had no effect if the general public itself could not swim. You can't surf if you can't swim. Hawaiian tourism promoters and California real-estate developers could not have gotten people off the beach and onto surfboards without the emergence of widespread swim lessons and swimming pools. The booming popularity of swimming in the late nineteenth century drove the surfing revival.

A century earlier, the only Americans who swam were mostly young working-class boys playing in lakes and rivers. Since such boys were usually naked, many cities passed laws against swimming. Increasing concern with urban health and sanitation, however, led several cities to build large pools as baths for the working classes later in the nineteenth century. Meanwhile, the rise of middle-class leisure time amid industrialization led to interest in swimming as exercise. The 1890s saw a general mania for physical fitness among middle-class clerks and managers whose desk jobs raised fears of a weakening American male. As a result, the public pools, initially built for lower-class sanitation, were reconceived as fitness facilities for the middle classes. Pools were now for swimming, not bathing. Dozens of cities built big public swimming pools around the turn of the century, and thousands of spectators could converge for swim meets at the Long Beach Plunge or the Fleishhacker Pool in San Francisco. In 1913, Duke and his Hui Nalu teammates competed before six thousand people at the Pacific Coast Swimming Championships, held at Sutro Baths in San Francisco, the world's largest swimming pool, built in 1896; the Baths could hold ten thousand swimmers, and included a faux tropical beach and palm trees. Another example was the Redondo Plunge, which opened in 1909 as the largest saltwater swimming complex in the world, and where Freeth led swimming lessons for countless newcomers. The Redondo pool was heated and open year-round, and could accommodate two thousand swimmers at one time. Private pools, at athletic clubs and especially at YMCAs, were also proliferating; the YMCA movement taught thousands of boys how to swim as a way to build physical strength and moral character. By early in the twentieth century, tens of millions of Americans were swimmers. This was the pool, so to speak, that surfing drew from.

In 1963 Duke was joined by fellow Olympian Johnny Weissmuller as cohost of the West Coast Surfing Championships at Huntington Beach. When the silver-haired Hawaiian stepped onstage to present the winners' trophies, the crowd of thirty thousand greeted him with a full-throated standing ovation before the announcers could make any introduction. Although Duke himself gave up surfing, he kept swimming in the ocean into his seventies. Toward the end of his life, during a hospital stay, Duke spent several days looking out over Waikiki from his ninth-floor balcony. From this vantage point he could check Waikiki's many breaks. In his lifetime Waikiki Beach had been destroyed and rebuilt by man. Waikiki's waves were dotted with boats, outriggers, swimmers—and hundreds of surfers out frolicking where once just a handful of elite watermen rode their heavy plank boards. Below Duke could see Waikiki's newest surfing spot—Ala Moana Bowls—wedged between a vast new resort complex called the Hilton Hawaiian Village and the new yacht harbor, created by dredging through the reef. To his left, the curve of Waikiki Beach was forested with high-rise hotels. Two blocks from his hospital, the Hilton Hawaiian Dome covered the plot of land where Duke grew up. The shore there was obscured by the Hilton Hawaiian Village adjoining man-made Duke Kahanamoku Beach, featuring a larger-than-life statue of the man himself. His old neighborhood, the wetlands, Waikiki Beach, and the waves themselves—all had been transformed. And yet the sound and smell of the surf still reached his high window.

3 THE DARK SIDE OF PARADISE: RACE AND SEX IN HAWAII

Americans with wealth and leisure time in the Roaring Twenties flocked to Waikiki, especially the rich and famous. In 1922 silent-movie actress Mary Miles Minter took her first dip in the water at Waikiki after a pleasant ride in a canoe piloted by Duke Kahanamoku. Minter wore "the most sensational purple imported French model bathing robe of the finest silk with the very latest 'Hula' model bathing cap." Waikiki bathers thronged the starlet. Miss Minter gushed, "Honolulu is just full of surprises and thrills and this was one of them. Your water is wonderful and I don't believe I'll miss a day after this." As Duke helped her to alight from her canoe, she asked, "Do you suppose I can learn to master the surf boards? I should just love it." The Hollywood actress typified the popular fascination with surfing and the Waikiki lifestyle that boosted surfing's continued revival. She was also, however, a white woman consorting with a dark-skinned male surfer. As surfing grew ever more popular, murmurings about race and sex darkened the sport's horizon.

HAOLES VS. NATIVES? OUTRIGGER AND HUI NALU

At one point in his swimming career Duke traveled to a swim meet at Lake Arrowhead in California and stopped at a restaurant. Viola

Hartmann, a champion swimmer and Duke's tandem-surfing partner, recalled the scene. "The waitress said, 'We don't serve Negroes. You need to go out,' gesturing towards the door. Duke started to ever so slightly get up gracefully, but we all spoke in unison, 'He's not a Negro. He's a Hawaiian and that is not the same.' The waitress was very puzzled and served us, and him."

Duke's racial limbo symbolized the central but ambiguous place of race in the surfing revival. In turn-of-the-century Hawaii, right after the final usurpation of native Hawaiian sovereignty by white foreigners, it would have been surprising if ethnic tensions had not affected surfing, especially those between dark-skinned native Hawaiians and haoles. Jack London glowingly described a native Hawaiian surfer at Waikiki as a "black Mercury," "a natural king," but after watching Ford catch a wave he exclaimed, "What a sport it is for white men too!" His wife, Charmian, meanwhile observed that Freeth was "only one quarter Hawaiian." Ford himself made the point clear: "To-day Judges of the Supreme Court in Hawaii, with their wives and daughters, ex-Governors and their families, and the greater portion of the prominent businessmen are surfboard enthusiasts. . . . At the recent surfing carnivals in honor of the recent visits of the American battleship and cruiser fleets, practically every prize offered for those most expert in Hawaiian water sports [was] won by white boys and girls, who have only recently mastered the art that was for so long believed to be possible of acquirement only by the native-born, dark-skinned Hawaiian."

Ford's view suggested that white Americans, having already claimed political, economic, and religious power in Hawaii, had also appropriated Hawaii's cultural legacy of surfing. But how then to explain the popularity of Duke, and the relative neglect of Freeth? One might say that Freeth was neglected precisely because he was more Caucasian than Hawaiian, and that Duke became known as the father of modern surfing because he was a full-fledged "native." Tourist promoters tried to play it both ways, presenting surfing as an exotic slice of native Hawaiian culture but also countering the belief, voiced by Mark Twain, that "none but natives ever master the art of surf-bathing thoroughly." In this case Ford overcorrected, saying that *whites* were the masters of the sport.

Ford was the first in a long line of writers to frame surfing's racial issue in terms of haoles versus natives. This racial tension is sometimes, but wrongly, viewed through the competition between two clubs, the Outrigger and Hui Nalu, representing, respectively, haoles and natives. In 1908 the ubiquitous Ford founded the Outrigger Canoe Club with the explicit goal of encouraging Hawaiian water sports, including surfing, in particular for youth. The development of private houses and hotels along Waikiki was making the beach hard to reach; the Outrigger aimed to make the beach accessible, as Ford put it, to the "small boy of limited means." He set dues at five dollars a year for young boys to make it "possible for every kid with guts to live at least half the day fighting the surf." He negotiated a cheap twenty-year lease on land next to the Moana Hotel and installed a couple grass shacks; within a couple years the Outrigger built a new, permanent clubhouse with storage lockers for boards.

By 1915 the Outrigger had 1,200 members and a long waiting list. These members had one distinctive characteristic: almost all of them were Caucasian. Despite Ford's stated goal, the Outrigger became a club for white elites, including such power brokers as Sanford Dole, who had helped overthrow the queen and became territorial governor after annexation, and Lorrin A. Thurston, likewise a descendant of missionaries, agitator against the monarchy, and publisher of the *Honolulu Advertiser* (and a major tourism booster). The Outrigger also limited membership to males until 1926. In response to the Outrigger Club, the story goes, several Hawaiian surfers, including Duke, Knute Cottrell, and Ken Winter, formed a competing club, called Hui Nalu. Dues were set at one dollar per year, with membership by election only. They had no clubhouse and just met under a hau tree in front of the Moana Hotel. An immediate rivalry developed between Outrigger and Hui Nalu, at times less than friendly; stories circulated of tensions between these two clubs, enhanced by ethnic divisions.

Portayals of a racial rivalry between haoles and natives oversimplify the picture. Outrigger and Hui Nalu had many things in common, stemming from the fact that both were as much about swimming and paddling as surfing. They had a common origin in the Waikiki Swimming Club, several of whose members then moved to these later clubs. Surf writers have focused on the name of Hui

Nalu, which in Hawaiian means "club of the waves," and assumed that members' sole activity was surfing. The reality is that Duke had to belong to an official club in order to have his swimming records recognized; the club name just reflected the other main interest of these swimmers. Duke and his supporters formed Hui Nalu as a new swim club to support the Hawaiian phenom's campaign to show the world just how fast he could swim. Hui Nalu and Outrigger were among several local swim teams, and Duke, Freeth, and other local surfers circulated among them. For a time Hui Nalu brought teams to the mainland to compete against elite swimmers from the Los Angeles Athletic Club and San Francisco's Olympic Club. This background underscores the importance of swimming to the emergence of modern surfing.

Hui Nalu was not a purely Hawaiian alternative to the haole-dominated Outrigger Canoe Club. Hui Nalu's doors were open to all, and two of the three founders were haole. Freeth, for example, was a charter member, though ethnically only one-quarter Hawaiian, and the club later included Tom Blake, a surfer and swimmer from Wisconsin, and Hal Prieste, a surfer and Olympic diver from Long Beach. Other prominent early members included Prince Jonah Kuhio Kalanianaole, Harold K. Castle, and William Rawlins. Castle's father had built the C&C sugar empire (with plantations served by Dillingham's railroads) and agitated for the annexation movement; Rawlins, a Yale law graduate and federal judge in Honolulu, saw Duke swimming at Diamond Head and encouraged his competitive career, later becoming Duke's first coach and accompanying the Hui Nalu club on trips to the mainland. Photos of Hui Nalu show mixed membership; one famous photo portrays an assembly of world-class swimmers, including Duke, his brother Sam Kahanamoku, Ludy Langer, Pua Kealoha, and Harold Kruger. Interestingly, there are two women in the photo, including world champion swimmer Ethelda Bleibtrey front and center. With Bleibtrey and Duke, Hui Nalu counted among its members the fastest male and female swimmers in the world.

Accounts of haoles versus natives begged a basic question: who was a "native" Hawaiian? Was it just someone born there? Or was it determined by ethnicity, and if so, what degree of Hawaiian ancestry qualified? The creole character of Hawaii complicated ethnic distinctions. As disease decimated Hawaiians in the nineteenth century,

Hui Nalu club circa 1921, with some of the fastest swimmers in the world, including Pua Kealoha, Ludy Langer, Ethelda Bleibtrey, Harold "Stubby" Kruger, Haig "Hal" Prieste, and Duke (fourth from right in the front row). Kealoha, Langer, Bleibtrey, Prieste, and Duke all won medals at the 1920 Antwerp Olympics. (Source: Bishop Museum)

white landowners seeking workers looked abroad—especially for sugar plantations, where brutal labor conditions deterred surviving Hawaiians; plantation owners in the American South and Caribbean had turned to slave labor because they couldn't find anyone to do it for money. Beginning in the 1850s, plantations began importing Chinese men for labor; after a couple decades, white landowners, alarmed at the growing Chinese population, started importing Japanese labor. Ensuing restrictions on Japanese immigration led to waves of Portuguese, Spanish, Germans, Puerto Ricans, Russians, Koreans, and Filipinos. (And each of these national communities could include several ethnic groups: Punti and Hakka from China, Tagalog, Visayan, and Ilocano from the Philippines.) Many of these immigrants were dark-skinned, and over time they mingled with each other and with natives through intermarriage. This ethnic mélange blurred any simple distinction between haoles and natives.

Nor did surfing belong solely to either white elites or downtrodden natives. Surf writers are often eager to romanticize the sport as a subversive counterculture. So, for instance, they depict the Hui Nalu as a bunch of underdog native surfers gathered under the old hau tree. Ford was right, in a way: white elites had already appropriated surfing, for the tourist industry and for their own recreation. It didn't get more elite in Hawaii than a Dole, Castle, or Thurston. Surfers, however, were not always on the outside looking in. Hui Nalu was not an underdog surf club, but rather one of the most accomplished swim teams in the United States, with elite members and support. Duke later joined the Outrigger and was connected to such power brokers as Judge Rawlins, the Dillinghams, and Doris Duke, the tobacco heiress and surfer, who dated one of Duke's brothers and later helped Duke purchase a home after his marriage to Nadine Alexander in 1940. Duke also swam for the elite Los Angeles Athletic Club, where local power brokers such as Henry Huntington and Abbot Kinney, among many others, were influential members. The LAAC hired George Freeth in 1913 to create a swim team, and Freeth attracted a world-class roster that included, besides Duke, Hui Nalu's Ludy Langer and Viola Hartmann, Duke's tandem surf partner. Duke and Freeth may not have hobnobbed with Thurston or Huntington, and both subsequently suffered more than their share of financial hardship. But Hui Nalu, the Outrigger, and the L.A. Athletic Club were not exactly on society's fringes. Surfing was already plugging into mainstream currents.

THE ORIGINAL BEACH BOYS

Long before the Beach Boys there were the beachboys. Unlike the harmonizing California kids from the sixties (only one of whom actually surfed), the original beachboys from Waikiki knew surfing, and did as much in their time to popularize surfing as the Beach Boys did later. The tourist economy provided one of the first ways for Hawaiians to make a living from surfing, and a generation of locals took advantage of the opportunity with relish, in the process defining the subversive spirit of surfing.

The increase in tourist traffic in the 1910s, with surfing as a central attraction, sparked demand for surf lessons and outrigger rides. The Moana Hotel hired several local surfers from the Hui Nalu to meet the demand, and the beachboy business was born. The next two decades appear as the golden age of the beachboys, enhanced by the opening in 1927 of the Royal Hawaiian Hotel, a posh pink-stuccoed palace right on the beach and adjacent to Canoes, Waikiki's most forgiving break. Hollywood stars from Mary Minter to Bing Crosby, Shirley Temple, Mickey Rooney, and Cary Grant became regulars at Waikiki, where the beachboys reminded them how to relax, laugh—and surf. The beachboys, meanwhile, made out quite nicely. A typical one-hour surf lesson earned them three dollars, compared to the twenty-three cents an hour earned by restaurant workers. That did not include the even more lucrative tips: the hundred-dollar handshake from high rollers and the cash-stuffed envelopes delivered on boat day, when the ocean liners took tourists home. Savvy beachboys knew they had leverage; Chick Daniels, beach captain at the Royal Hawaiian, relegated poor tippers to chairs in "Siberia," a distant stretch of beach.

The beachboys introduced thousands of travelers to surfing and defined the image of the surfer for the general public. This involved more than just riding waves; it was the entire waterman lifestyle, from surfing to spearfishing to outriggers. The beachboys also cultivated a reputation as talented musicians and perennial pranksters. Their steady stream of practical jokes, impromptu parades, and sunset ukulele and slack-key concerts ensured no dull moments on Waikiki. The beachboy image of pure hedonism, the single-minded pursuit of fun, included a casual attitude toward authority, which tourism promoters played up in photos of Duke and his brothers pulled over by a cop on their bicycle built for four, or another beachboy blithely flouting a "No Surfing" sign as he paddled out for a few waves. These publicity images reinforced the anti-authority, nonconformist image of the surfer. James Michener, in *Return to Paradise*, limned the beachboy lifestyle: "Without these remarkable people the island would be nothing. With them it is a carnival. . . . They are the perpetual adolescents of the ocean, the playboys of the Pacific."

"Playboys," of course, had another image, one propagated by a later Michener novel, *Hawaii*, where the dark, graceful, well-muscled beachboys gave "surf lessons" to vacationing women—and the surf lesson included a bit more than just surfing. Although surfing in ancient Hawaii was very popular with women, the modern surf revival, as part of the mainstream tourist industry in a newly annexed American territory, integrated surfing into the constraints of American gender roles. The trade-offs of the surfing revival, in other words, extended from native Hawaiian men to women as well. Thus Jack London's wife Charmian stuck to the "wahine" surf close to the beach when she tried surfing. Society still regarded women more as sex objects than surfers, at least according to popular images from the time. Many tourist posters featured women posing with boards, but never actually surfing unless accompanied by a man. In particular, tourism promoted the subtext of a casual sexual climate as part of Hawaii's appeal, and it extended beyond hula girls to the beachboys. Beachboys reversed the popular image of Hawaii and other tropical locales, which featured the dark-skinned maiden of unrestricted morals and sexual appetites. Here instead it was the athletic, tanned beachboy seducing white female tourists. A widely printed photo on the AP newswire in 1930 featured a young white woman cradled in the arms of a muscular Hawaiian as they zoom shoreward on a wave, with the caption, "Wouldn't you like to be rescued this way?" A *Vogue* magazine cover in 1938 similarly featured a young woman tourist surfing on her hands and knees with a Hawaiian crouched behind her steering the board. One young female visitor recalled a Waikiki surfing lesson from that time: "Can you imagine what it was like for me, going to a Catholic school on the mainland, to have a man take me surfing? To sit on top of me, on the back of my legs? The thrill I had. Skin to skin. In the water."

Not everyone was taken with the happy-go-lucky image of the beachboys. In particular, their reputed sexual license with haole women, whether perception or reality, sparked controversy. A 1932 mainland magazine insinuated: "There has been agitation against the tandem use of surf boards because of the long-distance rides which are sometimes observed. The white woman hires a handsome and muscular brown instructor. She lies prone in her scant bathing suit on the front of the board. The native lies behind, often stripped to the waist, in close proximity, and paddles out a quarter of a mile to the proper breakers. Sometimes they continue on to the outer reef, which is so far from shore that they are entirely lost from view." And (wink, wink) everyone knew what went on at that outer reef.

Surf lessons: A woman rides a wave with a Waikiki beachboy. (Source: Associated Press photo, May 30, 1930.)

On top of these racial and sexual tensions, Honolulu added a third dimension: the military. Hawaii was rapidly turning into a U.S. military garrison. The United States had won the use of Pearl Harbor in 1888, in exchange for duty-free sugar trade to Hawaii. The Spanish-American War expanded the U.S. military presence, and in 1902 Walter Dillingham's new company began dredging the coral reef across the harbor mouth to a depth of thirty feet to accommodate U.S. battleships. Native Hawaiians protested, since Pearl Harbor was the sacred home of the shark gods, who protected surfers and swimmers against shark attack. To no avail: the rise of Japan as an international power, signified by its victory in the Russo-Japanese War, led the U.S. Navy to dredge deeper channels and build dry docks and a naval yard starting in 1908.

Pearl Harbor eventually became one of the largest coastal construction projects in U.S. history, not far behind the Panama Canal in scale and expense. Dillingham's company would play a central role in transforming Pearl into the U.S. Navy's Pacific Ocean hub. But the military presence extended far beyond Pearl. The United States built a system of gun emplacements and forts to protect Pearl and the Honolulu waterfront. This included pillboxes on Diamond Head itself, that icon of Waikiki tourism, which the U.S. government bought and fortified in 1904, along with Fort DeRussy on Waikiki, with fourteen-inch guns for the defense of Pearl Harbor. (The guns were test-fired after the attack on Pearl Harbor, shattering windows in beachfront hotels; they were not fired again and were soon removed.) The U.S. Army also built Schofield Barracks on Oahu's central plain, which became the nation's largest Army base. By the late 1920s the United States had close to twenty thousand servicemen in Hawaii, the greatest concentration of U.S. military forces anywhere on the planet.

The U.S. military injected much money into the Hawaiian economy, and many servicemen married local women, but a line still existed between the military and civilians. In particular, many military officers hailed from the American South, and they brought Southern racial prejudices with them, referring to Hawaiians as "niggers." So here were all these white Southerners with strong beliefs about dark-skinned people, dropped into the middle of a strange place teeming with dark-skinned people. And some of these dark-skinned men, the surfing beachboys, were quite freely associating with white women.

These issues—sex, race, the military—came to a sharp focus in the Massie affair, a notorious murder trial that was the O. J. Simpson trial of its day. The episode centered on Thomas Massie, a young Navy officer raised as a Southern gentleman in Kentucky, and his wife Thalia, from a prominent Washington, D.C., family related to the Roosevelts. Thomas and Thalia were known for their rocky relationship. One evening in 1931, Thalia stormed out of a drunken party in Waikiki. She was found dazed near the beach later that night and claimed to have been raped. The local police detained five local Hawaiians, whom Thalia positively identified at the police station. The five went on trial, but the jury deadlocked and they went free.

At that point an enraged Thomas Massie, his mother-in-law, Grace Fortescue, and two sailors took the law into their own hands, kidnapping one of the accused, Joseph Kahahawai, and killing him in

Duke Kahanamoku took Clarence Darrow on an outrigger tour of the Waikiki reefs while Darrow was in Hawaii for the Massie case. Darrow is in the middle wrapped in a towel; Duke is the steersman at the back. (Associated Press photo, April 22, 1932)

a botched attempt to extract a confession. Now they were in the dock, on trial for murder. Famed attorney Clarence Darrow took on their defense in his last case (and for his highest fee). Darrow, celebrated for his support for minorities, the poor, and the oppressed, defended the lynching of Kahahawai as a justified "honor killing." At the time it was seen as Darrow's most famous case, more notorious even than the Scopes "monkey trial." The Massie affair became a global cause célèbre, with breathless media coverage. The *New York Times* ran almost daily articles, the *Chicago Tribune* called it "one of the great criminal cases of modern times," and Hearst papers in dozens of cities rallied around the defendants in daily headlines.

Darrow's defense worked. The court found Thomas Massie and Grace Fortescue guilty of manslaughter, not murder. Governor Lawrence Judd commuted their ten-year sentence to one hour, which they served in his office. The defendants immediately decamped for San Francisco, where they received a hero's welcome from the local admiral, a fellow Southerner. Hawaiians might say that the spirits got their revenge: the Massies soon divorced, his naval career stalled, and he was discharged from the Navy after being diagnosed as a manic depressive; he lived out his life a bitter man. Thalia made several suicide attempts and finally succeeded in 1963. Grace Fortescue was the only to come out unscathed—she inherited a fortune and lived out her days waterskiing in front of her Palm Beach mansion.

The Massie affair underscored and exacerbated racial tensions in Hawaii. The U.S. Department of the Interior commissioned a study entitled "Hawaii and Its Race Problem," which benignly concluded that, despite "much talk in the continental press of race antagonisms in Hawaii," race conflicts in the islands "are practically nonexistent." The mainland press indeed took a different view. Radio reporters warned that any white woman on the streets of Honolulu risked rape from gangs of dark-skinned natives. (In fact, there had been exactly zero reported cases of sexual assault on white women by Asian or Hawaiian men in the previous hundred years.) Another commentator cautioned darkly of "a paradise gone mad," and added, "living in Honolulu resembles living in a powder magazine. Something's going to explode soon."

Hollywood actress Dorothy Mackaill blamed the Massie affair directly on the sexually charged environment on the beach at Waikiki, with Hawaiian beachboys rubbing coconut oil on scantily clad female tourists: "What can we expect of these people when they see Kanakas openly receiving the attentions of American white women?" The good times on Waikiki were already dampened thanks to the Great Depression, and the Massie affair further stressed the beachfront tourist industry.

The Massie case served as a reminder of tensions beneath the fun-loving image of Hawaii, between male and female, military and civilian, and above all brown and white. Behind the beachboys cheerfully strumming ukuleles on the beach, the "Paradise of the Pacific" remained an American colony, dominated by the U.S. military and a cabal of wealthy whites. Ethnic minorities—in fact, the vast majority of the population—struggled constantly against poverty and racism.

Native Hawaiians and Asian immigrants labored on pineapple and sugar plantations for pennies an hour, in conditions that federal investigators compared to slavery; most of those who escaped the plantation system came to Honolulu, where real-estate redlining relegated them to slums and shantytowns. Tourist posters and glossy magazines papered over these inconvenient details, but the people of Hawaii did not. Their remarkable capacity for aloha had its limits. The Massie affair in the short run seemed a victory for the white elites; in the long run, however, it exposed how elite and foreign interests in Hawaii ran roughshod over justice, and it helped galvanize the beginning of political opposition by Hawaiians and Asian ethnic groups. Younger generations in particular were proving less deferent to haoles, with behavior that white Southerners would call "uppity."

This explains why natives dispensed the occasional beating to haole surfers. Gene "Tarzan" Smith, for example, was a California lifeguard who moved to Waikiki in the 1930s. Tall and exceptionally fit, he relished big waves and excelled as a paddler. He was the first to paddle solo from Oahu to Kauai, a thirty-hour, seventy-mile marathon that no one duplicated for sixty years. But when Smith, no shrinking violet, decided to enter the beachboy business and set up as an independent operator on Waikiki, the natives did not appreciate a haole entering their turf. On the way home from the local tavern one night Smith was jumped and severely beaten, suffering a fractured skull and broken ribs. The punch-outs extended to Tom Blake, an otherwise honored member of Hui Nalu, whose wholehearted embrace of surfing and Hawaiian culture could not overcome the basic transgression of hailing from Wisconsin. Blake would not be the last haole to get a beating from the locals.

4 INVENTING SURFURBIA: SURFING TO CALIFORNIA

When Hawaiian coastal engineers discovered in the 1920s that Waikiki's beaches were disappearing because of the engineering of Waikiki itself, they resorted to replenishing the beach with imported sand. Thereafter some of Waikiki's sand came from Manhattan Beach in California. That was only fair. Waikiki had already sent surfing to California, which helped turn coastal towns like Manhattan Beach into their own slices of paradise, in which surfing figured prominently. Hawaii gave California the beach lifestyle, and California gave back the beach itself.

MAKING THE BEACH SAFE FOR SURFING

Surfing had come to California in the nineteenth century. Richard Henry Dana, in *Two Years Before the Mast*, described Hawaiian "Kanakas" crewing on ships off the California coast and expertly surfing longboats through waves at Santa Barbara. As Dana put it, the Hawaiians were "complete water-dogs, and therefore very good in boating. It is for this reason that there are so many of them on the coast of California, they being very good hands in the surf." Later in the century three Hawaiian princes attending military school in San Mateo visited Santa Cruz in the summer of 1885, made some boards from local redwood, and went surfing.

These earlier episodes left no roots. The permanent California surf community stems from our friend George Freeth, to whom both Hawaiian and Californian surfing owe much. Soon after Jack London's surf lesson, in July 1907, Freeth left for California, in a trip apparently arranged by Alexander Ford's Hawaiian Promotion Committee. In other words, Freeth—and surfing—came to California in a marketing venture for Hawaiian tourism. Not such a good idea in retrospect: Ford no doubt thought to attract people to Hawaii to surf, but in exporting surfing he enabled Californians to stay home and surf—and to build their own tourist attractions around the surfing image.

Upon arrival Freeth went for a surf at Venice Beach (it was summertime, so the water temperature was tolerable). A local paper gave Freeth a prominent headline: "Surf Riders Have Drawn Attention." His exploit caught the eye of one Henry E. Huntington, the namesake of Huntington Beach, the Huntington Library, and other Southern California institutions. Huntington made his money off railroads—he was an original California railroad baron—but also, this being California, from real estate. He bought undeveloped, inaccessible land cheap, then ran rail lines through it to drive up land prices. The "Red Cars" of Huntington's Pacific Electric rail system defined early-twentieth-century L.A. These are the Red Cars memorialized in that well-known surf movie *Who Framed Roger Rabbit*, which features the classic line: "Who needs a car in L.A.? We've got the best public transportation system in the world!"

There was, in fact, a connection with surfing here. Huntington had run a line of his Red Cars out to Redondo Beach, where he just happened to own almost all the land. In 1905 he began building a three-story beach pavilion there, as a way to entice L.A. residents—and potential real-estate buyers—to Redondo. At the time many L.A. residents found their recreation shooting jackrabbits from streetcars in the San Fernando Valley, and Huntington sought to turn their attention toward the beach. Newspaper ads promised free rides on Red Cars to Redondo and touted the healthy beach lifestyle (in blissful ignorance of atmospheric chemistry): "Buy where the air is the pure ozone from off the health-restoring waters of the Pacific."

In 1904 a developer named Abbot Kinney, with a fortune from the cigarette business, proposed to build a town modeled on the real Venice, with canals, bridges, gondolas, the works. But Kinney added a California twist, building a pier with amusement rides and an enclosed saltwater swimming pool on the beach. Kinney's Venice vision was thus a direct competitor to Huntington's development at Redondo Beach. Huntington had been to Hawaii and knew how surfing attracted tourists. So after seeing the reports of Freeth surfing in Venice, Huntington hired Freeth to surf on *his* beach, in Redondo. In the summer of 1908 Freeth gave two surfing demonstrations each day in front of the Hotel Redondo. The performances attracted large crowds and much publicity, with Freeth touted as the "Hawaiian Wonder" and the "Man Who Walks on Water." Maybe Ford was not far off when he called Freeth "Christ-like."

Freeth's surfing exhibitions marked the first permanent roots put down by surfing in the mainland United States. They also marked the birth of professional surfing, as Freeth became the first person—though far from the last—who was paid to surf. In this case, surfing promoted the value of Redondo real estate and attracted riders to the Redondo Red Car line. It is not clear how long Freeth stayed on the Huntington payroll as a pro surfer, but he soon shifted to another job that would employ countless surfers in the twentieth century. Once again, it started with Freeth providing his skills for free for Abbot Kinney at Venice Beach, this time leading a new volunteer lifeguard service.

The need for beach lifeguards was driven by the very crowds that Freeth helped attract to the beach. Developers like Huntington and Kinney were basically inventing California beach culture in these beach towns later dubbed "Surfurbia"—that is, the nearly unbroken stretch of white-sand beaches, and beach communities, stretching from Malibu to Newport Beach. As with Waikiki tourism marketers, these developers wanted to get people off the boardwalks and piers, onto the beach itself, and into the ocean. Jack London saw the possibilities: "Take surf-boarding, for instance. A California real estate agent, with that one asset could make the burnt barren desert of the Sahara into an oasis for kings." And California real-estate agents had more to work with than the Sahara.

Creating beach culture, however, required making people feel safe. Local papers regularly publicized beach drownings, and parents in particular shied away from coastal real estate for fear of losing their children. Early beach tourists had gone to great lengths to avoid the ocean's dangers. English beach resorts around the turn of the century featured "bathing machines" for both safety and modesty; a bather sat inside the tublike contraption, which was pulled by horse or winch into the ocean for a brief dip. Venice Beach itself had an elaborate rope system stretching out over the shallow water, so that a bather at all times had a lifeline dangling within reach. The preferred approach, however, relied on lifesavers launching rescue boats through the surf; but this was designed to save ships in distress, not swimmers close to shore. Freeth revolutionized beach safety by introducing the concept of a lifeguard swimming out with a rescue buoy, connected to the shore by a cable, to beachgoers in distress. Unlike the old lifesavers, Freeth's new lifeguard was also proactive, using ocean knowledge to keep swimmers from hazardous surf, riptides, and undertows.

Freeth's techniques were soon tested and vindicated in a celebrated act of heroism. In December 1908 Freeth rescued eleven Japanese fishermen whose boats swamped offshore during a winter storm. Three times he dove in and swam out through the huge surf and frigid water to the foundering boats. On one of the boats he took an oar and, standing in the back, surfed the skiff in through the waves, depositing the grateful fishermen on the beach. By swimming through the lines of surf Freeth reached his victims, whereas a lifesaving crew could never have made it out in a rescue boat. The *Los Angeles Times* described his derring-do the next day, and added that Freeth had saved fifty other lives in the waters along Venice in the preceding two years. Freeth and his volunteer Venice Lifesaving Corps were instant celebrities and marched in the 1909 Rose Parade. Huntington's people again took note. The next summer they brought Freeth back to Redondo as a paid lifeguard at the new Redondo saltwater plunge.

While lifeguarding Freeth also gave swimming lessons and trained competitive swimmers; physical training was of the utmost importance to Freeth, and he encouraged his guards to stay in condition by ocean swimming, surfing, distance running on sand, and playing water polo. An ocean lifeguard, Freeth declared, had to be "at one with the water." Freeth's swimming and lifeguarding instruction created a cohort of young Californians with the ocean knowledge and physical fitness they needed to take up surfing. In 1912, Freeth and his Redondo swimmers founded the mainland's first surf club.

Freeth was thus crucial not only for promoting surfing as part of the beach lifestyle, which drove the development of beach towns like Redondo and Venice, but also for his revolutionary contributions to lifeguarding and swim lessons, which remain underappreciated. Freeth helped make beaches safe for the general public, further enabling California beach culture and, with it, the development of California's coast. In short, Freeth taught Californians that you could play in the ocean. California beach culture, however, had one more obstacle to surmount, as we shall see: a competing economic vision for California's coast based on oil, not the beach.

Freeth did not live to see the triumph of "surfurbia." After a stint as swim coach at the powerful L.A. Athletic Club, he struggled financially through a series of lifeguarding and sales jobs. In 1918 the community of Ocean Beach in San Diego hired Freeth as a lifeguard to restore public confidence in beach safety, after rip currents from large surf drowned thirteen swimmers on a single spring day. No one died the remainder of that summer under Freeth's watch, even though thousands of people flocked to the beaches to see his surfing demonstrations. For Freeth, though, the move south was fateful. San Diego then and now was a major military center, and many servicemen returning from World War I shipped through there. Many of the beachgoers Freeth watched over were off-duty servicemen. They brought with them the Spanish influenza virus, which was just exploding into the worst epidemic in the history of the United States. Freeth caught the virus. His exemplary physical fitness at first held the disease at bay, but he succumbed after months of struggle in early 1919, at the age of thirty-five. This central figure in the origins of modern surfing died alone and destitute in a San Diego convalescent home.

THE MEETING OF SKY AND OCEAN

While he was helping to midwife surfurbia, Freeth was riding the usual redwood plank. A subsequent boost to surfing's popularity stemmed from its intersection with a new California industry. Most surf history views surfboard design as an evolution from longboards to shortboards. In fact, in the modern revival most surfers were first riding shortboards: Jack London and Alexander Hume Ford were riding on boards about six feet long and two feet wide, which were very challenging to stand on; they needed a good wave to get up planing on the surface and even then were tippy. One of Duke Kahanamoku's main contributions was to introduce longer boards, ten feet long or more, and others soon followed his lead. The longer boards allowed surfers to angle across the wave face instead of riding straight to shore with the whitewater. More important, the big boards let beginners give surfing a try, either solo or in tandem with one of the Waikiki beachboys.

These bigger boards helped drive the surfing revival in the first decades of the twentieth century, but they had a crucial drawback: weight. Solid redwood boards were manageable at lengths of six or eight feet, but as board lengths passed ten and then twelve feet in the late 1910s, boards could weigh well over a hundred pounds. Just wrangling one of these monsters across a beach was no easy feat, and trying to hold on to one while paddling through walls of whitewater required tremendous strength. A world-class athlete like Duke or Freeth could handle these massive boards, but for a beginning surfer the prospect was downright dangerous.

In the mid-1920s surfers began experimenting with balsa, a very light wood that was readily available through its use in airplanes and relatively strong for its low density. Balsa was also very buoyant, unlike the much heavier redwood planks, which rode lower in the water and hindered paddling and wave riding. That low density and natural porosity, however, meant balsa acted like a sponge, soaking up water and eventually sinking your surfboard. Another solution emerged from Tom

Blake, who along with Duke Kahanamoku is celebrated as one of the early pioneers of surfing. Blake's path to surfing, like Duke's, ran through swimming, and his reputation rested on his abilities as an all-around waterman—and also on his innovations in surfboard design.

Blake was born in 1902 in that surfing hotbed of Milwaukee, Wisconsin. His mother died young and relatives raised him, and he developed a quiet, standoffish personality. At age eighteen, as a high school dropout, he met Duke in Detroit on one of Duke's swimming tours and came away impressed; he moved to Los Angeles, took up competitive swimming and paddling, and got good fast, especially in distance swimming. He also took a job lifeguarding at Santa Monica and tried surfing. Soon after, in 1924, he visited Hawaii, where the Kahanamoku brothers introduced him around and took him surfing at Waikiki. The Hawaiian beachboy lifestyle had him hooked, and he immersed himself in the sport and culture. The presence of this blond-haired youngster from Milwaukee in the supposedly locals-only Hui Nalu suggests that ethnic categories were perhaps fluid; but native Hawaiians also resented Blake, and attacked him, for showing them up at their own sport.

At the time no surf contests existed, and surfers found their main competitive outlet in paddle races. Hawaiians took great pride in their paddling ability, and the greatest surfers of that era were fixtures in the frequent races that took place along Waikiki Beach and in the Ala Wai channel. Blake was an avid competitive paddler, and his victories in these races were the source of resentment—but also drove him to a major step in surfboard design. For paddling, length provided an advantage, but so did flotation, and heavy redwood boards rode too low in the water. Blake thus looked for ways to reduce weight. In 1928 he was preparing for the Pacific Coast Surfriding Championship, a paddle race hosted by the Corona del Mar Surfboard Club; such meets were extremely popular at the time, attracting thousands of spectators. Blake shaped a new sixteen-foot board but added a twist. He drilled out hundreds of holes in the plank and sealed them with a thin layer of wood, and found it indeed cut down the weight. Blake took the board to the meet and won it going away.

This episode is usually viewed by surf historians as the triumphant introduction of the hollow board, but the story is more interesting. One of Blake's closest competitors at the Corona meet was Gerard Vultee, who had nipped at Blake's heels in previous paddling meets and was also an accomplished distance swimmer. Vultee was a member of the Corona surf club and the Los Angeles Athletic Club, where he met and competed against Duke Kahanamoku at LAAC swim meets. Vultee also surfed with Duke, and was one of Duke's surfing companions during the heroic rescue of a dozen fishermen off Newport Beach in June 1925.

So Vultee was an accomplished surfer, paddler, and swimmer. His day job, however, was as an aircraft designer at Lockheed. In the early 1920s, Vultee studied aeronautical engineering at the California Institute of Technology (better known as Caltech), where he made extensive use of Caltech's new wind tunnels and built a full-scale sailplane. After two years at Caltech he went to work with fabled designer Jack Northrop, first at Douglas and then Lockheed. Vultee and Northrop designed the Lockheed Vega, a radical new airplane that would be flown by Amelia Earhart and Wiley Post. Vultee and Northrop engineered the Vega to be fast but rugged, and the design stressed strength along with light weight. It used all wood construction; unlike, say, the fabric-covered design of Lindbergh's *Spirit of St. Louis*, the Vega was constructed using sheets of plywood over wooden ribs. Its particular innovation was its single wing, a long, thin, rounded shape, of plywood over wood struts, strong enough not to need external bracing. The Vega took flight in 1927 and was soon shattering speed records.

The next summer was the Corona meet, where Blake got to hang around with Vultee. No record exists of what Blake and Vultee talked about that day on the beach in Newport. But we know that Blake was seeking to build a lighter wooden surfboard, and Vultee had just finished designing a lightweight wooden wing—and Vultee knew the advantage of lighter surfboards. Within months Blake built a surfboard with, yes, internal ribs topped by a plywood sheath. This was the celebrated Blake hollow board; this design involved building a hollow board from the ground up, not drilling out a solid plank. Standard accounts, including Blake's own memories, portray him as a heroic lone inventor; the evidence suggests instead that crucial input came from California's burgeoning aircraft industry.

The subsequent history of the hollow board provides more evidence for the aviation connection. Blake filed for a patent on the hollow board, or what he called his "Water Sled," which was granted in 1932—apparently the first patent for surf technology. He then licensed the design for mass production and granted the initial certificate to the Thomas Rogers Company in Venice Beach. Why did Blake choose them? Probably because the firm was already expert at building interior strut frameworks with a wooden exterior skin: they were in the business of making airplane wings.

Blake's hollow board could be half the weight of a similarly sized solid plank, making it much easier for the average person to handle. Next to a hundred-pound redwood plank, a fifty-pound hollow board seemed positively svelte. It also rode higher in the water and paddled easier. Beginners especially liked the hollow board, since its paddling speed made it easy to catch waves. More important, beginners had easy access to the hollow boards because they were mass-produced. It was far easier to buy a Blake-licensed hollow board than to get your hands on a hunk of redwood and shape it yourself. Solid boards were not mass-produced until later in the decade. For those who couldn't buy a hollow board, Blake published do-it-yourself articles in *Popular Science* and *Popular Mechanics*. An article in *Modern Mechanix* made the aviation connection explicit: "The surfboards are constructed like airplane wings, being of hollow construction."

There is much talk today in the surf community about the threat of mass production. Most surfers forget that mass production isn't new. In addition to hollow boards mass-produced under Blake's license, a company called Pacific System Homes began mass-producing solid boards in the 1930s. Pacific System, a major builder of ready-cut frames for homes, saw in the surf market an outlet for their woodworking experience and tools—planers, routers, saws, lamination—idled by the slow housing market in the Depression. In a spectacular marketing misstep they first sold the boards under the Swastika label, chosen because of its traditional association with good health and good luck. Around 1938, as the Nazis gave swastikas more sinister associations, Pacific System switched to Waikiki for the brand name. The boards were widely available in sporting goods and department stores, and to increase visibility Pacific System paid Duke and other top surfers to endorse the boards, marking the first instance of surfing sponsorship.

Blake's "cigar boxes" were cheap, widely available, and easy to ride. They encouraged many newcomers to take up surfing in the 1930s, especially in California. The hollow board, in short, helped drive the growth of California surfing. It thus helps answer the question: why did California become one of the world's centers for surfing? Why did this Polynesian pastime become so popular there? The answer, in part, is the aircraft and aerospace industry, which injected new technologies that made surfing more accessible.

The popularity of surfing meant more people in the lineup, and a disillusioned Blake, fed up with crowds, eventually drifted away from surfing. Vultee became chief engineer of Lockheed when Jack Northrop left to start his own company, and Vultee struck out on his own in 1932, starting what turned into Vultee Aircraft; the company merged with Consolidated Aircraft in 1943 to form Convair, which became one of the largest aerospace firms in Southern California. Vultee did not live to see it. He died, along with his wife Sylvia, in an airplane crash in January 1938. Their plane went down in a snowstorm near Sedona, Arizona, with Vultee in the pilot's seat.

ENGINEERING THE CALIFORNIA COAST

The Blake board helped California surf culture flourish in the 1930s. The seed planted by Freeth and Duke was bearing fruit, watered by several broader developments. One was demographics: California's population doubled from 1920 to 1940, reaching almost 7 million people, a vast pool of potential surfers to draw on. And many of these people landed in beach towns. Huntington's plans were succeeding in L.A., and developers up and down the coast, from San Diego to Santa Cruz, were similarly marketing the beach allure to sell real estate. The Great Depression temporarily stifled surfing's growth, but even in the Depression, as historian Kevin Starr has argued, California saw "the emergence of a pleasure-seeking, leisure-oriented society that contained within itself the formula for post-war America."

Beach towns symbolized California's recreational culture, and surfing was central. In the 1930s surf communities coalesced in towns up and down the coast, evident in the surf clubs that sprang up from Palos Verdes and Corona del Mar to Santa Cruz. San Onofre, a beach near San Clemente, became the epicenter of this scene, with an old palm shack left over from a movie set becoming a hangout. Although many of these towns were relatively affluent—Newport Beach, Palos Verdes, Malibu—surfers embraced a down-at-the-heels, minimalist approach, sleeping on the beach or in their cars and living off the ocean. In particular they self-consciously mimicked the Hawaiian surf lifestyle: lounging on the beach between surf sessions, playing ukuleles, fishing and diving, playing pranks and starting food fights, partying and chasing girls. These "coast haoles," as they called themselves, brought the subversive spirit of Waikiki's beachboys to Southern California.

There's another reason why coast towns started to flourish later in the 1930s. It is also the reason why many coast haoles were further south, down the coast toward Newport and San Clemente. California was not yet committed to the surf lifestyle. The spread of surfing through California hinged on competing claims to the coast, and later centers of the surf world, such as Huntington Beach (which now calls itself "Surf City"), Santa Barbara, and Malibu, were drawn by alternative futures. Like Hawaiians on the artificial beaches of Waikiki, Californians surfed at the intersection of broad political, economic, and environmental interests. Private property owners, oil companies, railroads, the shipping industry, and pleasure boaters advanced different visions for the coast, involving fenced-off beaches, oil rigs, railroad right-of-ways, and harbors instead of wide-open beaches and waves. The future of California, and of surfing, rode on the resolution of these issues.

Malibu, for example, was off the surfing map early in the century. The reason was beach access and private property rights. When Tom Blake first surfed it with a friend in 1927, he had to break the law, trespassing on private property. It was not the last time a California surfer would trespass for surf—but legal wheels were already turning that would open up Malibu, and many other surf spots, to surfers.

Malibu Point sits at the mouth of a long wooded canyon, amid miles of beautiful coastline, rugged mountains, and sheltered coves. The south-facing point curves out to sea at the mouth of Malibu Creek, producing well-shaped waves that break anywhere from two to twelve feet, with rides up to a quarter mile. The beach got its name from the local Chumash tribe, who called it Humaliwo, "where the surf sounds loudly." The Chumash were a water people, who frequently voyaged to the Channel Islands offshore and fished local kelp beds; their plank *tomol* canoes were the largest vessels piloted by any North American tribe, sturdy craft that could handle ten-foot seas in the Santa Barbara Channel. There is no evidence the Chumash surfed, though it is hard to believe they didn't ride an occasional wave into the beach in their canoes.

By 1900 the land around Malibu Point had passed through Spanish land grants and wound up in the possession of Frederick Hastings Rindge, a wealthy heir from Cambridge, Massachusetts, who served as vice president of Union Oil and a director of Southern California Edison, and founded Pacific Life Insurance. Rindge fell in love with Rancho Malibu, and after his early death in 1905, his widow, May Rindge, took over the seventeen-thousand-acre ranch. For several decades the redoubtable May Rindge kept anyone from crossing her beloved Rancho Malibu. In her passionate fight she confronted powerful political and economic interests, but Rindge had her own considerable fortune to deploy. Her opponents included the Southern Pacific Railroad, the "Octopus," the largest employer and biggest corporation in California, whose political and financial clout ruled the American West and crushed most local opposition. Rindge stopped the Southern Pacific in its tracks, literally, by building her own standard-gauge railway along the Malibu coast, spanning occasional canyons with extensive trestles. Rindge built Malibu Pier in 1905 to transport hides and other products from Rancho Malibu; the pier served as her railroad's southern terminus. Rindge knew that federal law prohibited parallel railways, and the Southern Pacific was forced to turn its tracks inland. By stopping the railroad, Rindge left a stamp on Malibu that lasts to this day. Malibu is one of the few segments of Southern California coast where one cannot see a train whistling past surf breaks. Expelling the railroad kept new towns and commercial development from Malibu's shoreline; the tide of industrial and real-estate development instead flowed into the San Fernando Valley.

The Queen of Malibu's battle with Los Angeles County was less successful. The Rindge family zealously guarded access to their property against mounting public pressure for beach access starting early in the

1900s. After decades of litigation and early court verdicts in favor of Rindge's right to restrict access, L.A. County won the right to condemn a right-of-way for a coastal road, opened in 1921. A few years later the State of California followed suit, literally, in its bid to build a bigger highway; the case went to the U.S. Supreme Court, which ruled against Rindge and granted the state its own easement. When state construction crews showed up at the ranch gates, Rindge met them with forty armed guards on horseback. The standoff lasted a few days, but in the end the law prevailed. What was known as Roosevelt Highway—today, the Pacific Coast Highway—connected the entire Malibu coast in 1929, and enabled surfers to drive right up to Malibu Point, park their cars, and hit the waves.

May Rindge's mounting legal bills in these beach-access lawsuits compelled the breakup of Rancho Malibu. In the 1920s she began subdividing and selling lots, starting with beachfront lots leased to the Malibu Motion Picture Colony starting in 1927, just around the top of Malibu Point. Academy Award winner Ronald Colman, a friend of Duke Kahanamoku, purchased one of the first beach cottages at Malibu Colony and had Duke come visit and teach him to surf—the start of Hollywood's inroads into Malibu's waves. By the following year leases exceeded $2 million and houses were selling for $500 a square foot—no small sum at the time. May Rindge declared that Malibu's ranching days were over; the land's future lay in wealthy estates, their value built around the beach. This exclusive real estate ensured future legal battles over public beach access along the Malibu coast, but Malibu Point itself, thanks to the highway's route along the beach there, was now open to surfers.

The Rindge legacy did not end there. The Malibu wave that Tom Blake rode for the first time in 1927 was not entirely natural. Inside Malibu Point is a large lagoon, fed by Malibu Creek; in the rainy season the creek's flow opens the lagoon to the ocean, dispersing sand across the point. A year before Blake surfed the point, Rindge built a hundred-foot dam on Malibu Creek, creating a six-hundred-acre-foot reservoir to supply water for Rancho Malibu and the family's Malibu Tile Works. The Rindge Dam stopped the flow of sediment down Malibu Creek and changed the shape of Malibu Point. The dam silted in by the 1950s and now holds up to 1.6 million cubic yards of sediment, much of which would have ended up on Malibu Point. One can only imagine how this intercepted sediment changed Malibu's waves.

The development of coastal real estate included the construction of harbors and piers from San Diego to Santa Barbara, for recreational boaters, fishing, and shipping. These projects disrupted sand flows up- and downcoast—the rivers of sand that scientists call littoral flows—and fundamentally changed the coast. Littoral flow rates range up to a million cubic yards of sand a year in California—the equivalent of a dump truck full of sand moving down the beach every five minutes. Harbors and jetties in effect stop each dump truck and dump its sand in one spot, accumulating millions of cubic yards of sand there and starving downcoast beaches of coverage. In some cases new surf spots were the unintended by-product, but harbors also claimed prominent spots. One of the main surf breaks in this period was a sandbar at the Santa Ana River outlet in Newport called Big Corona. Created by jetties built early in the century to protect the anchorage, Big Corona was destroyed in 1932 when longer, larger jetties cut off the littoral flow and starved it of sand. Similar harbor construction killed Long Beach, one of the main surfing centers in the 1930s and site of the first National Surfing Championship in 1938. Within a few years Long Beach had become a surfing desert: the Army Corps began building a breakwater, fifty feet high and several miles long, to protect the Navy's Pacific Fleet during World War II, and eventually to protect the bustling port of Long Beach. The breakwater did its job: no more waves reached the beach.

The elimination of Long Beach surfing was, perhaps, just as well for surfers. Long Beach was where the Los Angeles River met the ocean. Before the harbor went in, surfers there were unwittingly soaking in a septic stew of runoff from the rapidly growing metropolis. Up into the 1920s the official L.A. city dump spilled into the river; even afterward, much of the city treated the river as its de facto disposal system. Oil and grease from downtown railroad yards; oil field runoff; iron, boron, chromium, and other toxic chemicals discharged from the burgeoning auto, rubber, steel, and aircraft industries; urine and manure from feedlots and slaughterhouses; and untreated human sewage, especially during heavy rains—all of it flowed into the surf at Long Beach.

Consider just a single source, the L.A. Union stockyard, the largest stockyard in the western United States, which handled over a million cattle and hogs each year in the late 1930s, and which sat right on the riverbank. Between 1930 and 1940, the amount of sewage carried by the river doubled, and a state hydraulic engineer called the river "foul and septic." Only in the 1940s, after a number of beach closures in Long Beach because of sewage, did the city and county attack the river pollution problem.

These halting efforts to deal with Southern California's escalating sewage problem help explain why surfing didn't catch on faster. Or, to turn it around, the growing appeal of the surf lifestyle helped convince local governments to finally confront coastal pollution. The Los Angeles River was far from the only polluted tributary. The population doubling that drove surfing's growth also doubled the sewage burden on the California coast. All that shit had to go somewhere. Usually that meant the Pacific. As with most American cities, the development of urban water-supply systems, including flush toilets, shifted sewage from cesspools and privies to waterways and, ultimately, the ocean. Until 1925, the city of Los Angeles discharged all its sewage directly into Santa Monica Bay. Beachgoers increasingly complained about swimming in raw sewage, amid dark jokes about a new oceanic species known as the Pasadena Brown Trout. In 1925 the city installed simple screens on the sewage flow, which trapped the trout but still allowed vast quantities of sewage and bacteria into the ocean, creating an ecological dead zone and requiring constant beach closures along the coast. Finally, in 1950 L.A. built a sewage treatment plant, but even that, as we shall see, failed to keep up with L.A.'s booming postwar population.

While L.A. was turning Santa Monica Bay into a cesspool, to the north and south the emerging economy of beach tourism and real estate competed with the equally thriving oil industry. Oil for a time had the upper hand. Southern California sat on extensive underground oil deposits, over 5 billion barrels' worth, and in the early twentieth century drilling in the onshore beach and tidal zone produced major gushers. A beachside oil boom ensued, and by the 1920s Southern California produced one-fifth of the nation's oil. Oil wells sprouted like weeds on beaches from Santa Barbara to Huntington Beach, befouling ocean and air with their plumes and fumes. Old photos reveal a surreal landscape of beachgoers and surfers frolicking amid this forest of oil derricks. Vast refineries often accompanied the oil fields. Standard Oil, for example, built a major refinery on the beach in El Segundo (the town so named because it was the second refinery in California). The company liked the beach location because it provided access to tankers, and the sand dunes limited fire hazards and could soak up oil spills.

So before they were "surfurbia," L.A. beach towns were "black gold suburbs," as residents flocked to oil industry jobs along the coast. The future of Southern California beach culture looked more likely to involve oil-well roustabouts and wildcatters than sunbaked surfers. A lengthy political and legal battle raged through the 1920s and 1930s over the best use of public beaches: industry or recreation. The oil industry mobilized its formidable lobbyists, who did not fail to point out the oil royalties flowing into government coffers. Beachgoers—and real-estate developers—organized a Save Our Beaches movement, and the otherwise business-friendly *Los Angeles Times* wished that swimmers could "cavort

Oil wells, belonging to Standard Oil, line Huntington Beach, circa late 1930s, after state and local officials barred drilling on the beach itself. (Source: Orange County Archive)

and gambol in the breakers and come out glistening with drops of pure salt water instead of having their bodies smeared with oil."

In the 1930s California decided the future of its beaches lay in recreation, not oil. Only then could beach culture, and surfing, finally flourish, as they did late in the decade. Although recreation and residential realty won this battle, oil's influence was far from over. The decision drove oil drilling offshore, to deepwater oil derricks, where it would continue to impact surfing. Meanwhile, oil had a knock-on effect in the construction of jetties and seawalls to protect oil fields and refineries, which further changed coastal sand flows and ruined surf breaks. Then, after the state restricted oil drilling, many oil firms simply walked away from a veritable junkyard of piers, wells, and drilling detritus on the beach—and in the surf. Some of these spawned surf spots, such as the aptly named Oil Piers south of Santa Barbara, where sandbars collected alongside piers. Others were downright hazardous, such as the many submerged pilings and remains of piers lurking in the surf and sand around Goleta's Ellwood Beach (Haskell's to the locals), waiting to impale the unwary surfer.

Most surfers only thought about these legacies of California's Oil Age when they literally ran into them. Surfing soon found its own uses for oil and became dependent on petrochemicals, although most surfers conveniently ignored where oil came from.

Fast-forward a couple decades, to when the teenage daughter of a Hollywood screenwriter began visiting Malibu in the mid-1950s. Kathy Kohner, better known as "Gidget," could go surf Malibu because it was no longer fenced-off private property; it was easily accessible on the gleaming coast highway; it wasn't covered in oil wells or other industrial development; and it was safe. Gidget came to personify surfing's postwar image of wholesome middle-class fun—but only because the beach had already been transformed into the central attraction of surfurbia.

5 WAR AND SURFING

On a big day exiting the surf at an unfamiliar break can be harrowing even for an experienced surfer. At Waimea Bay on Oahu's North Shore you have the option of coming in through the shorebreak or by the rivermouth. The current takes you toward shore and you need to make a decision. Choose wrong and you are in for either an underwater thrashing or an exhausting swim, or both. Ditch the surfboard and picture yourself and thirty-four friends sitting in a wooden Higgins boat weighing seven tons. Your destination: a beach lined with artillery and enemy soldiers trying to kill you. Half of your buddies can't swim, all of you are carrying sixty-five pounds of gear, and everyone is seasick. Inside, the beach is a sheet of fire and you can see Marines crawling across a dry reef just outside the lagoon. Your sergeant shouts at the Navy boatswain to gun it for the beach. As the boat next to you runs aground and is blown apart by incoming shells, you desperately hope the people in charge of this operation know what the hell they're doing. Do they know where the reef is, what the tide is? How big is the surf on the inside?

The gruesome debacle at Tarawa, the first American amphibious assault against determined resistance in the Pacific theater of World War

II, showed military commanders that they had much to learn about amphibious operations. Tarawa planners misjudged the tide, and the landing craft ran aground on the reef, leaving the Marines stranded under withering Japanese gunfire. Understanding the surf was now crucial. As amphibious assaults followed in Africa, Sicily, Italy, France, and hundreds of Pacific islands, the U.S. Navy turned to the nation's leading oceanographers for help. The result would transform surfing.

Surf forecasting was just one of several fundamental contributions by the military to surfing in this period. Aviation and naval research produced new materials and hydrodynamic theory that led to a revolution in surfboard composition and design. Naval research for Underwater Demolition Teams (UDTs)—today's Navy SEALs—developed the wetsuit, a crucial invention that opened up two-thirds of the planet to surfers. Surfing, that escapist pleasure, would seem to have little to do with warfare. But from surf forecasting to surfboard production to wetsuits, almost every surfer who paddles out today is using military technology.

SURF FORECASTING

Surfers are perpetually in search of waves. Even the most consistent breaks in the world are not rideable every day, so the question "Is there surf?" becomes fundamental to every dedicated surfer. The decisive answer to this question came from the military, starting in World War II.

The abject failure of the Dardanelles campaign in World War I, symbolized by the debacle of Gallipoli, left military logisticians with a jaundiced view of amphibious warfare. World War II strategists found no other option. Hundreds of thousands of men needed to move from ships offshore to hostile shorelines. Doing so in a ten-foot swell might cost lives and battles. That gave the question "Is there surf?" a whole different connotation; unlike today's surf forecasters, military oceanographers were in search of the smallest waves possible.

The answer came from physical oceanographers at the Scripps Institution of Oceanography. Walter Munk had enrolled as a graduate student at Scripps after receiving a physics degree from Caltech in 1939. An Austria native, Munk joined the U.S. Army's Mountain Brigade after the Austrian *Anschluss* to fight the Nazi takeover of his native country. After U-boats cut off supplies to Great Britain, Munk's mentor, Harald Sverdrup, director of Scripps and the most distinguished physical oceanographer in the United States, recalled him to join research on antisubmarine warfare for the Navy.

The Norwegian Sverdrup and the Austrian Munk wrestled with security clearances throughout the war. Some of the Scripps faculty pointed out that Sverdrup had relatives in Norway whom the Nazis might use for blackmail. That led to an FBI loyalty investigation at Scripps, and both scientists lost their clearance for the classified Navy antisubmarine research. They ended up working instead for the Army Air Corps on wave forecasting. By denying their clearances, the United States may have inadvertently won the war.

During the summer of 1941 Munk witnessed a large-scale Marine Corps amphibious exercise at New River, North Carolina. As Higgins landing boats (LCVPs) struggled ashore through the surf, Munk recognized that a successful assault could not take place in big surf that could capsize the craft. One LCVP broaching during an assault would not only drown the soldiers on board but also might block the path to the beach for all the boats behind it. The shallow-draft, plywood LCVPs were so vulnerable that large waves soon put an end to the New River exercise.

Munk concluded that successful amphibious operations could take place only in surf under five feet. He alerted Army officials to the problem and also sought the support of Sverdrup, a senior scientist, to promote the concept of predicting safe landing conditions. Sverdrup came to Munk's assistance and spearheaded the wave-forecasting project at Scripps. At the time the Navy was not in the wave-forecasting business; the only existing quantitative attempts at predicting surf had come from breakwater designers. Amphibious warfare created the new science of surf forecasting.

Shortly after his transfer to the Army Air Corps, Munk learned of Allied preparations for an amphibious winter landing on the northwest coast of Africa. This coastline is subject to heavy northwesterly swells from the Atlantic, with waves exceeding six feet on two out of three days during winter. To determine optimal conditions for a landing, Sverdrup and Munk needed meteorological data to forecast the generation of waves.

An LCVP in the surf zone near New River, North Carolina, in summer 1941. This exercise took place as a tropical storm brushed the Outer Banks, and it persuaded the military that waves this large would doom an amphibious assault. Walter Munk witnessed the exercise and immediately recognized the importance of surf forecasting. (Source: Scripps Institution of Oceanography Archives, UC San Diego Library)

Their fundamental insight was to connect wave data at a particular beach to weather data thousands of miles across the ocean. They then connected this weather and swell model to how waves broke on a particular beach, which required knowledge of bottom contours and topography. This novel combination of weather, waves, and topography—of meteorology, oceanography, and geology—underpinned their forecasting method.

Basically, Sverdrup and Munk needed to predict the surf the same way surfers look at today's buoy readings when they check if it is worth paddling out. Munk and Sverdrup developed a step-by-step process for predicting waves on the basis of meteorological data. To do this they first had to acquire wave data. This meant answering the simple question "What is a wave?" Where does a wave begin and end? How to define the height? Should you take the height of the tallest waves or sets of waves, or an average? And if an average, over what period of time? Sverdrup and Munk took observations from oceans, lakes, and wave tanks and came up with perhaps the first scientific definition of an ocean wave.

Their definition rested on the concept of "significant waves," a statistical reference to the average height and period of the highest third of waves in a given sea condition, terms that are universal today. Sverdrup and Munk came up with the three components of wave prediction: wind speed, fetch (the distance the wind travels), and duration. They then developed formulas to calculate wave heights at the end of a given storm. They soon found that the Army Air Corps, which handled meteorology, had little interest in storms thousands of miles away, since such weather did not affect flying conditions in the immediate theater. But such distant ocean storms were precisely the source of waves, so the scientists turned to meteorological data from Pan American Airways, whose Clipper aircraft flew to Europe via Bermuda and the Azores.

The importance of surf forecasting became clear in Operation Torch, the invasion of North Africa. For perhaps the first time, the occupants of the White House and 10 Downing Street wanted to check the surf. In September 1942, looking to the invasion two months hence, Roosevelt wrote to Churchill that "bad surf on the Atlantic beaches is a calculated risk." His fears were well grounded. Six-foot surf during the landings at Casablanca broached, stranded, or sank nearly two-thirds of the 378 landing craft and support craft.

Sverdrup and Munk refined their theory through 1943, and meanwhile had begun spreading the surf-forecasting gospel in a course at Scripps for Army and Navy meteorologists. These officers also attended crash courses in meteorology at UCLA in a program headed by famed Norwegian meteorologist Jacob Bjerknes. After completing their work at UCLA the students moved to the University of Chicago, where they studied under Carl Gustaf Rossby. A select few then went to Scripps for instruction in wave forecasting. Over two hundred officers passed through the Scripps wave course from 1943 until the end of the war, and its graduates predicted landing conditions at beachheads throughout the Atlantic and Pacific theaters.

John Crowell and Charles Bates, who were among those in the first Scripps graduating class, ended up making the toughest wave call in the history of surfing. Crowell had an undergraduate degree in geology from UCLA; Bates had one in geophysics from DePaul. These newly minted oceanographers were assigned the task of wave forecasting for D-Day in France. They headed for England to join the "Swell Forecast Section" in charge of the D-Day forecast, headquartered in Churchill's bunker, a converted Tube tunnel beneath the British Admiralty. The pair arrived to find the British already had a largely empirical wave-forecasting method devised by Commander C. T. Suthons of the British Naval Meteorological Service. The Americans came armed with the more theoretical Sverdrup-Munk approach, and a debate ensued over which approach should guide the D-Day forecast.

Crowell and Bates set up a network of observation stations manned by British Coast Guard officers. Crowell recalled that veteran British officers manning the weather stations were surprised when he instructed them to take detailed wave height and period data, and he soon learned the need for tact in dealing with skeptical Brits. Crowell also acquired data himself. On a visit to Casablanca, he used the bow of the Vichy battleship *Jean Bart*, aground in the harbor, as a wave measurement device. He rowed out to the *Jean Bart*, hauled himself up the bow in a bosun's chair, and painted wave-height markers up the side. He then relaxed at his hotel while taking wave data through binoculars.

Crowell and Bates soon marshaled an impressive body of data to compare the Sverdrup-Munk and Suthons forecasting methods. The Sverdrup-Munk theory proved more accurate than Suthons's and was adopted for use in all theaters for the rest of the war. Crowell and Bates connected North Atlantic weather data on wind speed, fetch, and duration to wave heights at particular beaches: for instance, if the wind blew in a particular direction at thirty knots over a five-hundred-square-mile storm fetch for twelve hours, you could calculate the wave height on a particular beach a number of days later. For each landing area Crowell made a nomogram, a graph that allowed one to calculate surf heights given a particular combination of weather variables.

In addition to weather and swell data, the Scripps forecasters drew upon contour data collected by UDTs and aerial photographs. In

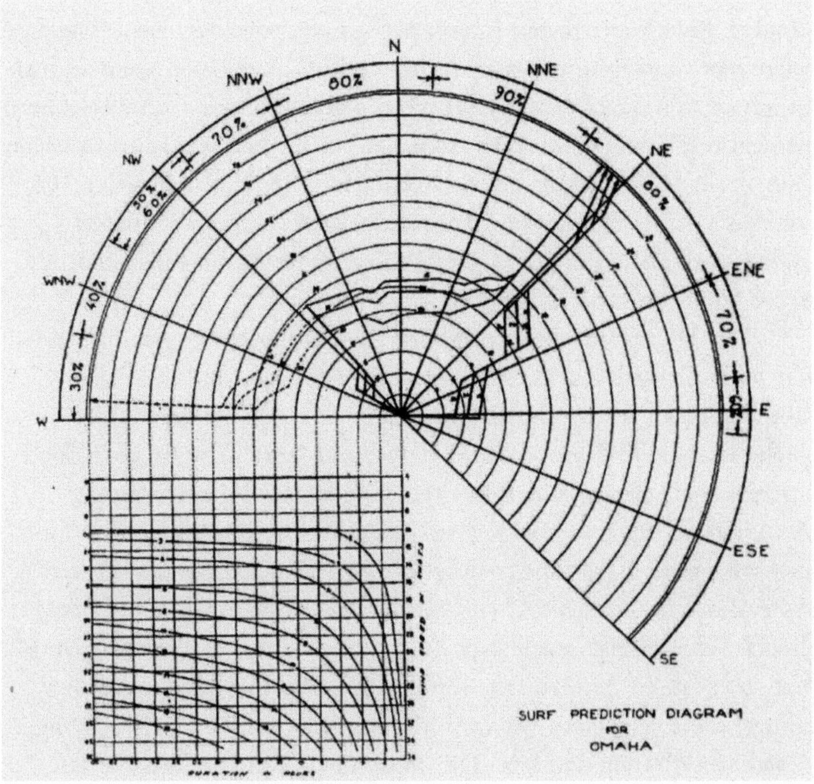

Allied surf forecast for Omaha Beach thirty days before D-Day. The upper diagram shows wave size and direction; the lower diagram shows the wind speed and duration that generated the swell. The data produced by the swell forecast group was correct 88 percent of the time for the period June 6–30. (Source: Charles Bates, "Utilization of Wave Forecasting in the Invasions of Normandy, Burma, and Japan," Annals New York Academy of Sciences 51, *(May 1949), p. 556)*

preparations for D-Day, both forecasters spent time with an amphibious operations unit. Crowell gained an appreciation for the capabilities of landing craft and the importance of understanding bottom contour when evaluating potential landing sites. At Omaha Beach, for example, tidal runnels, some of them nine feet deep, posed a potential hazard as well as affecting wave heights as the tide changed.

With its data in hand, the Swell Forecast Section could make the wave call for Normandy. Bigger waves predicted for the landing sites on

Monday, June 5, persuaded Eisenhower to postpone the assault one day, before more surf returned later in the week. Ike's decision went against the advice of some of his generals, who wanted to wait two weeks until the next tidal cycle. For a man from Kansas, Ike had good surf intuition. Two weeks later a storm suddenly changed track, causing twelve-foot waves at Omaha Beach that damaged or destroyed seven hundred landing craft and demolished one of the concrete harbors installed by Allied engineers for offloading supplies.

The D-Day surf forecasters may have changed the course of the war. Both Crowell and Bates received Bronze Stars, and the Swell Forecast Section set up similar wave data networks for anticipated amphibious landings in Burma, Malaya, and Japan. The Pacific offered different challenges to surf forecasters. Graduates of the Sverdrup-Munk forecasting course at Scripps formed a flying aerology team for surf forecasting. Beginning in August 1944 the scientists made aerial observations of weather and surf conditions, beach topography, and obstacles at potential beachheads on Japanese-occupied islands. During trial observations on Oahu the aerologists found they could accurately identify six- to eight-foot waves within one-foot accuracy while flying as high as two thousand feet. The group made accurate forecasts for the assault on Peleliu using the Sverdrup-Munk theory and assisted in invasion plans for the Philippines, Iwo Jima, and Okinawa. Two days into the assault on Iwo Jima, three aerologists were aboard the USS *Bismarck Sea* when it was hit by two kamikaze planes and sunk; all three were rescued.

Wave research continued after the war. The Office of Naval Research funded a program on waves and amphibious craft at Berkeley as well as Scripps. Berkeley had turned a campus swimming pool into a wave tank during the war, and scientists there pursued probabilistic theories of wave behavior and prediction; Hans Albert Einstein, the famous physicist's son, joined the program after the war through his work on sand transport. In one of the more death-defying stunts in the history of surfing, in fall 1945 Willard Bascom rode fifteen-foot waves in a DUKW amphibious vehicle off the Northern California coast. Meanwhile, by 1949 Scripps had produced over eighty of its bound "Wave Reports." Most of these were for the military, but Scripps soon expanded its horizons, literally. In 1967 Walter Munk helped produce a documentary film, *Waves Across the Pacific*, describing a Scripps experiment that followed a wave from an Antarctic storm all the way across the Pacific Ocean to Alaska. The experiment showed that open-ocean waves suffer little decay, and the film became a staple in high school classrooms.

Mid-century American oceanographic science and technology revolutionized surf forecasting by providing a new theory of surf and swell, including the basic idea of how to measure a wave. Walter Munk never surfed, but his research led to a revolution in the understanding of waves that touches millions of surfers every day. Some of those surfers ride waves every day at Scripps Pier, right below his laboratory window. On a big south swell, hundreds of surfers park their cars next to Scripps's Munk Laboratory without recognizing his legacy.

FROGMEN

How did Crowell and his colleagues obtain data on surf-zone bottom contours from hostile beaches? Very carefully. Before Allied landing craft made their way to the beaches of Normandy, British and American frogmen explored the intricate German defenses, the bottom contour and tides, and the composition of the beaches.

British frogmen used kayaks to probe the coast. Frogmen from the U.S. Office of Strategic Services (OSS), predecessor to the CIA, tested electric-powered rubber surfboards during World War II as they probed enemy coastlines. In the Pacific the Navy tested a motorized "warboard" designed for reconnaissance off the coast of Japan in preparation for Operation Olympic, the planned assault on the Japanese home islands. Warboards were hollow Tom Blake–style boards, about fourteen feet long and sixty pounds. The boards were camouflaged and had a built-in depth sounder and two-way radio. The Japanese surrender in August 1945 canceled Olympic and, with it, the military debut of the motorized surfboard.

The initial reconnaissance of the Normandy coast proved crucial, since the Germans had prepared a fiendish array of obstacles. On Omaha Beach the Germans installed twelve thousand "hedgehogs" created by welding three or four railroad rails together, like lethal asterisks. At low tide on the outer edge of the beach they implanted huge logs topped with mines that would explode if a craft sailed over at high tide. In the center of the beach were lines of steel antitank traps called "Belgian Gates" and thousands of barbed-wire entanglements; the beach itself was littered with six thousand land mines.

At Omaha Beach, Navy Combat Demolition Units (NCDUs) went in at low tide and set charges to clear eight full gaps and two partial gaps in the German defenses just as the first wave of boats headed for shore. This experience revealed an equipment shortfall that would eventually have a great impact on surfing. The NCDUs went into the frigid waist-deep water fully dressed and exposed to withering gunfire from the shore; of the 175 NCDUs on Omaha, 31 were killed and 60 wounded. British frogmen were better equipped, with rubber dry suits produced by Dunlop to help them withstand the frigid water. Italian frogmen were best equipped of all, with double-layer Belloni and Pirelli rubber dry suits. Led by the notorious "Black Prince," J. Valerio Borghese, Italy's Decima MAS set the standard for naval commandos in World War II. Among other daring raids, the intrepid Italians rode two-man torpedoes into the harbor at Alexandria and sank two British battleships; Churchill, impressed, wrote his generals, "Please report what is being done to emulate the exploits of the Italians in Alexandria Harbour."

In the Pacific theater, Admiral Richmond Kelly Turner, the father of modern naval amphibious warfare, knew that understanding conditions at a landing site was vital to the success of an assault. After the nightmares of Tarawa and Makin, Turner founded the UDTs. A primary mission for UDTs was to "walk" the Pacific reef flats of an amphibious assault underwater long before thousands of Marines and GIs clambered into their landing craft. Turner's new UDTs started training at Waimanalo on Oahu but quickly moved to a new base on Maui at Maalaea Bay.

The skills of Hawaiian watermen played a key role. John Kelly, a Navy man and pioneering surfer, had the task of readying UDT Team 14, the first to be trained on Maui. A skilled swimmer, Kelly introduced his raw recruits to rigorous training and ocean knowledge—for instance, teaching them not to fear sharks and moray eels—and numerous candidates dropped out from exhaustion. In an era before scuba gear the frogmen had to hold their breath for long periods, so Kelly brought in a pearl diver to give lessons and held contests. Whether he knew it or not, Kelly was duplicating the games of ancient Hawaiians. The frogmen kept gear to a minimum: bathing suit, fins, mask, a hunting knife, and a plastic writing slate and pencil to communicate, and for some missions a charge for detonating mines. Some sported necklaces made from bullets flattened by impact with the water surface, which they would catch underwater while evading enemy fire. UDT 14 participated in the assaults on Iwo Jima and Okinawa, two of the bloodiest battles in Marine Corps history, and lost just one officer and no enlisted men. Together they were awarded eleven Silver Stars and eighty-one Bronze Stars. Kelly received the Navy Marine Corps Medal, the same medal awarded to a young John F. Kennedy for saving crew members from his stricken PT boat.

At the end of World War II the Navy knew that frogmen held the key to successful amphibious warfare. In turn, reliable equipment was crucial to the UDTs. The Navy called on scientists to develop new equipment specifically for underwater swimming. One result was a technology that touches every cold-water surfer: the wetsuit.

Viewers of *Baywatch* from colder climes may think California beaches are a balmy paradise. Any such viewer who hopped on a plane to California and then jumped in the Pacific would soon be disabused of that fantasy. Most California coastal waters are below seventy degrees even in summer and are down in the fifties in winter. Since winter is the best time for surf in California, early surfers there—and in Australia and other surf communities—froze their tails off much of the year, and were often limited to ten-minute go-outs followed by a long defrosting before a fire on the beach. Paddling through constant walls of whitewater or swimming after a lost board was a bone-chilling experience.

The basic concept behind underwater suits around World War II was that as long as you stayed dry you stayed warm. In World War II frogmen had used solid rubber suits with a woolen undergarment, similar to the getup used by hard-hat salvage divers. Dry suits, however, tended to wrinkle and pinch wherever there were air pockets inside the suit. This dreaded "suit squeeze" was particularly uncomfortable when centered around the midsection on a male, something like having a wet towel wrapped around one's crotch and twisted with a stick—or, more simply, like putting one's testicles in a vise. Not a sensation you want while disarming large explosive mines.

Navy UDTs tested dry suits after the war but were looking for a better way. At the Navy's request, the National Academy of Sciences formed the Panel on Underwater Swimmers. The panel included the legendary frogman Douglas "Red Dog" Fane, who headed the UDT team at Coronado and whose experience provided the basis for the television series *Sea Hunt*; it was chaired by oceanographer Roger Revelle, best known today for his work on global warming. Revelle was very enthusiastic about the potential for effective underwater suits and wrote that "this underwater swimming business is in the same state the airplane was when man first stated probing the atmosphere."

The solution came from Hugh Bradner, a physicist who helped build the atom bomb. Bradner described himself as a "compulsive dabbler." His father, Donald, was an accomplished engineer and chemist who challenged his two sons to exercise their creative instincts at every turn. During World War I, Don Bradner worked for the Chemical Warfare Service in Maryland, where he invented a clever technique for dispersing smoke screens from airplanes. He taught his younger son to swim by tossing him into the nearby Gunpowder River, and Hugh grew up swimming. He attended Miami University of Ohio, majoring in physics and math while competing on the swim team. After graduation in 1937 he entered the doctoral program in physics at Caltech, perhaps the best science and engineering school in the country.

At Caltech, Bradner swam, coached water polo, and went abalone diving in the Southern California kelp beds. He and a fellow student developed their own closed-circuit rebreathing device and tested it in the Caltech pool. Diving in Baja gave him a healthy appreciation for the thermocline, the layer below the surface where the temperature drops sharply. Bradner finished his PhD in 1941 and joined the steady stream of scientists engaged in war work. During World War II, roughly half of Caltech's graduates went to work on military projects. Bradner first followed his older brother to the Naval Ordnance Lab, where he designed magnetic anti-shipping mines. He then got himself

Hugh Bradner at the Caltech pool, where he coached water polo and swimming and also tested a scuba prototype. (Source: Caltech yearbook for year 1939)

reassigned to a new laboratory at Los Alamos, the heart of the biggest scientific endeavor in world history—the Manhattan Project. Bradner was a highly qualified "gofer" for lab director J. Robert Oppenheimer, who had gathered an elite team of scientists on the remote mesa in New Mexico to build nuclear weapons. (The lab was so secret that when Bradner married Marjorie Hall, a secretary there, none of their parents were allowed to attend.) His first job was with Seth Neddermeyer in the explosives group, seeking a way to trigger the nuclear chain reaction. Neddermeyer's idea was to use conventional explosives to compress plutonium—in other words, to use an implosion to create an explosion. Many scoffed at Neddermeyer's "reverse" perspective—as one physicist observed, "explosions blow out, not in"—but the idea prevailed, and the bomb that obliterated Nagasaki was triggered by implosion.

After the war Bradner took a job at UC Berkeley, where he played water polo, went abalone diving on weekends, and got a good dose of freezing Northern California water. His physics job also entailed diving: in 1951 he traveled to Eniwetok Atoll in the South Pacific to work on nuclear bomb tests and made a number of dives. Bradner's diving fueled his concern with developing a suit. Larry Marshall, an electrical engineer at Berkeley, told Bradner about the Panel on Underwater Swimmers. Larry was a surfer and a very strong swimmer. He knew of Bradner's diving interests and urged him to join the panel. At the panel's request, Bradner attended a design session at Scripps where he proposed working on improved suits. Afterward Revelle arranged a summer study at Point Loma, where Bradner studied underwater heat transfer, and he soon began testing different materials for a better suit.

Bradner's background as a waterman helped this bomb-building physicist conceive a radically new suit. Bradner knew well how cold the ocean could be. He was also no stranger to taking unexpected approaches. Bradner had a sudden insight: dry suits limited mobility, so why bother keeping the swimmer dry? This was a fundamentally new perspective: you did not have to stay dry to be warm. Not everyone agreed, but Bradner persisted, recalling the doubts about Seth Neddermeyer's idea of implosion. Fortunately, Larry Marshall and the panel were receptive to Bradner's seemingly upside-down perspective.

Choice of material was the most important factor in the transition from dry to wet suits. Bradner's heat-transfer data showed that in order to keep a swimmer warm a wetsuit had to minimize water flow. He started by coating wool with a string-reinforced rubber, before turning to neoprene rubber produced by the Rubatex Corporation. The flexible rubber molded to body shape and kept water flow down. In fact, Bradner had two criteria for his suit, and warmth was only one of them. The other was ability to absorb shock underwater. The Navy and the panel were much concerned about the effects of underwater explosions on UDTs, and a wetsuit might improve chances of survival. Neoprene also satisfied this criterion. That is, the neoprene wetsuit was invented not just to keep divers warm; it was also designed to protect underwater commandos from explosive shock. A 1952 Navy memo reported that Bradner's choice of "unicellular foam rubber, neoprene . . . offers blast protection and warmth."

In April 1952, Bradner tested a prototype one-eighth-inch neoprene suit, snug but not watertight, in a swimming pool. He later tried the suit at Lake Tahoe while wearing a pair of booties also fashioned from neoprene, with encouraging results. The military bought material for prototype suits, and Bradner and his colleagues at nearby Livermore Laboratory, the nuclear-weapons lab that was sibling to Los Alamos, struggled to glue and stitch suits durable enough for UDTs. In order to meet the early demand from UDTs and research divers, Bradner's friend and fellow physicist Dave Garbellano formed the Engineering Development Company (EDCO). EDCO's founders made the first wetsuits in their garages and sent them to the UDTs in Coronado. Their design was called the "EDCO Beaver" because of the beaver tail attached to the jacket, a feature still found on many dive suits.

The key component to the wetsuit was neoprene, a synthetic rubber and another product derived from war. Synthetic rubber was first developed in Germany during World War I when the British blockade cut off the country's natural rubber supply. Over 90 percent of the world's natural rubber came from Malaysia, where rubber trees transported from Brazil pumped out latex like cows with roots. The United States faced a crisis in World War II when the Japanese captured Malaysia and duped the British into surrendering Singapore. Suddenly there was no rubber to feed the U.S. war machine. In fact, gasoline rationing during World War II was primarily designed not to save fuel but rather to preserve the rubber tires on the millions of U.S. automobiles.

American science and industry responded to the wartime crisis by developing a synthetic rubber industry, with neoprene among its products. Neoprene had first been produced in the United States by chemists at DuPont in 1930. Wallace Carothers, one of the fathers of polymer chemistry, led a team of chemists who isolated a new liquid compound, chloroprene, that produced a solid synthetic rubber very similar to natural rubber. Neoprene was more durable than natural rubber, and it became the first commercially viable synthetic rubber. Neoprene was highly resistant to heat and chemicals, making it an ideal material for fuel hoses and as insulating material for machinery and plumbing, although it was too expensive for use in tires. Best of all for the case of wetsuits, neoprene was easily glued using a solvent. Four years later, Carothers's lab at DuPont produced one of the most revolutionary polymers of the twentieth century—nylon. Nylon, best known for its use in women's stockings, had numerous applications, one of which was in wetsuits. The combination of neoprene and nylon makes up all modern wetsuits.

The first wetsuits were composed solely of neoprene. Like much rubber, it was often sticky. Getting into one of these suits required a liberal dusting of cornstarch or baby powder, and even then necessitated contortions that frequently tore the suit. Gluing nylon to the smooth neoprene improved durability and made the suits much easier to put on. (Nylon also gave manufacturers the ability to add color to the always black neoprene; during the neon 1980s wetsuit manufacturers pushed this button a bit too hard with retina-burning color combinations.)

Hugh Bradner never patented the wetsuit and never made a dime off it. At the time he had no idea the garment would have such a revolutionary impact on diving and surfing. He encouraged the Navy to file a patent but they declined; they had no need to patent it since they paid for the research and had the rights to it. As a result, Bradner's followers were not hindered by patent restrictions. The two most significant early manufacturers were O'Neill and Dive 'n Surf, which became Body Glove. Neither company patented the wetsuit, although both refined the garment for use by surfers. Both companies would also lay claim to "inventing" the surf wetsuit. The reality is that when surfers duck dive a freezing wave in the middle of winter, they can thank a bomb-building physicist whose combination of waterman's experience and inventor's instinct produced a suit that keeps you warm even when you are wet. Today's suits benefit from thinner, more flexible neoprene with special zippers, flaps, tape, hoods, and stitching. The concept, however, is identical to the wetsuit Hugh Bradner made for the Panel on Underwater Swimmers.

Over the past half century, wetsuits became a vital piece of equipment for surfers worldwide and a multimillion-dollar market. The wetsuit opened up countless surf spots outside the tropics. Body Glove founder Bill Meistrell declared that "nothing has put more people in the water, in more places, than the wetsuit," and another surf writer called the wetsuit "one of the most significant innovations—if not *the* Number One innovation in modern surfing history."

The key component of the wetsuit was not the use of neoprene. Rather, it was Bradner's idea that you don't have to stay dry to be warm—neoprene was just the means to the end. This insight was a crucial but unrecognized point for surfing. The experience of surfing is not the same if you stay dry. With the wetsuit, you're still constantly immersed in a thin layer of water, in direct contact with the ocean. Not so in a dry suit, which keeps the ocean out. The wetsuit helped surfing retain its primordial appeal of a direct immersion in nature. On the other hand, if oceanic pollution continues to increase, surfers might want to keep the water at a distance and return to dry suits.

FOAM AND FIBERGLASS

One of Bradner's fellow students at Caltech in the early 1940s, Robert Simmons, made an equally significant contribution to surfing that also utilized military technology. This was no coincidence. California was home to much of the U.S. defense industry, especially aircraft, which provided 2 million wartime jobs and countless new technologies. Also no coincidence, the state was home to several research universities that were world class in science and technology, Caltech foremost among them. The graduates of these schools helped the United States win World War II—and came up with crucial innovations for surfing. Bradner is just one example. Bob Simmons is another. The presence of people like Munk, Bradner, and Simmons helps explain why California became a center of global surf culture.

Simmons's central contributions, like Bradner's, came from new materials emerging from the alliance between the military and the chemical industry. Military aviation in particular demanded materials that combined high strength with light weight, and chemists at Bayer, DuPont, Dow, Owens Illinois, and Corning Glass developed polyurethane and polystyrene foams, fiberglass, and polyester resins. Foams and fiberglass, for example, provided lightweight insulation, and polyurethane coatings provided corrosion-resistant airplane finishes. Although some materials, such as polyurethane and fiberglass, predated the war, military needs drove their mass production for use on an industrial scale.

Simmons was born in 1919 and grew up in L.A. and Pasadena.

A long bout with cancer as a youth almost cost him his leg; then, while he was riding a bike to strengthen his bad leg, a collision with a car shattered his left elbow, leaving his arm crippled. In the hospital a fellow patient told him about surfing as a way to regain his arm strength. Simmons took up surfing in the late 1930s and built his first board from a Tom Blake hollow kit.

In fall 1939 Simmons entered Caltech to study mechanical engineering. Contrary to existing accounts, Simmons did not drop out in 1941, after just a couple years. He stayed full-time at Caltech for three years, through spring 1942, and then returned off and on through the war. In fall 1946 he had permission to receive his bachelor's degree upon completion of that term, but he dropped out for good only a few units shy of his degree. Caltech was one of the world's centers for engineering, and one of the reasons that Southern California became an aerospace hotbed. Few people think of Caltech as a surfing incubator, but several seminal figures in surf history—Munk, Bradner, and Simmons, not to mention Vultee—came out of there.

The mechanical engineering major at Caltech started with two years of math, including plane and analytical geometry and differential and integral calculus, and two years of physics. It also included a survey of hydraulics, combining both theory and experimental lab work on physical properties of water; hydrostatics; the flow of water over various surfaces and through pipes, nozzles, and channels; impulse and reaction turbines; and centrifugal pumps. Traditionally, Caltech hydrodynamics students used their newfound skills to work for Robert Knapp, Simmons's hydraulics professor, who founded the Caltech Pump Lab in the basement of the mechanical engineering building. Knapp turned Caltech into one of the best places to be if you wanted to study hydrodynamics.

The Pump Lab originally studied how to bring Colorado River water to Los Angeles, but during the war Knapp and his colleagues turned to research on cavitation of high-speed submarine propellers, and then an even larger program on torpedo design under the wartime Office of Scientific Research and Development, or OSRD. The OSRD sought to develop torpedoes that could be dropped from higher altitudes yet still find their targets. American torpedo bombers were decimated by antiaircraft fire at the Battle of Midway, because existing designs required pilots to fly so low that they were sitting ducks. OSRD funding allowed Knapp to transform the Pump Lab into a full-fledged Hydrodynamics Lab—what the *Los Angeles Times* called "the world's outstanding hydrodynamics laboratory," including a fully instrumented high-speed water tunnel. The torpedo research involved theoretical calculations for streamlined bodies moving through fluids, including drag and lift coefficients and boundary layer effects, and an extensive experimental program using the water tunnel, ten- and twenty-five-foot test tanks on campus, and an elaborate facility at nearby Morris Dam for full-scale testing of air-dropped torpedoes.

It is not clear whether Simmons worked directly for the torpedo project, but with Caltech's almost total commitment to the war effort, it would have been hard for him to avoid it. His hydraulics class, taught by Knapp, likely used the Pump Lab, and his older brother, Edward "Dewey" Simmons, worked in the Pump Lab before the war. Simmons may also have intersected Caltech's wartime research through his employer. His uneven attendance at school stemmed from the fact that he was working for Douglas Aircraft. Defense work schedules suited Simmons: he worked the night shift, leaving days open for school—or surfing empty wartime waves. Caltech sent its torpedo project reports to Douglas, whose TBD-1 was the only U.S. torpedo bomber for the first years of the war.

Simmons first ran across the new materials either at Douglas or through his brother Dewey, who encountered polystyrene foam—Styrofoam—as an insulation material in his wartime work on aircraft radar and, by one account, showed it to Bob. Whatever the conduit, Bob Simmons was soon using fiberglass and resin, first to reinforce the noses of wood boards, then to seal and strengthen the whole board, and finally in combination with Styrofoam to make a remarkably lightweight yet strong surfboard. Simmons's hybrid boards had a core of Styrofoam, balsa rails, and a plywood veneer sealed with fiberglass and resin.

Simmons's contribution was not only in new materials; he also revolutionized board design. Here Simmons relied on a combination of

Bob Simmons, age 25, explains a model airplane to his three-year-old nephew Rick Hilts at the Simmons family home in Pasadena. At the time of this photo, 1944, Simmons was finishing a year of coursework in machine design and hydraulics at Caltech and working for Douglas Aircraft. Fifteen feet out of this frame is the garage shop where Simmons made his surfboards. (Source: Richard Hilts.)

military R&D and his Caltech science and engineering training, which had immersed him in advanced hydrodynamics. Simmons's subsequent source for the hydrodynamics of planing hulls was wartime research conducted by the Navy on Patrol Torpedo (PT) boats. PT boats had planing hulls designed to reach speeds up to forty knots; they were often called "mosquito boats" because they appeared to skim along the water. The United States marshaled a fleet of PT boats during World War II, the most famous of which was the ill-fated PT109 captained by Lieutenant John F. Kennedy.

To improve PT boat design the Navy funded hydrodynamic research on high-speed planing hulls that tested the limits of hull design. The experiments took place at Pearl Harbor and were led by Lindsay Lord, a naval architect from Maine. Lord began building speedboats during Prohibition when rumrunners outran the Coast Guard. During World War II, Lord used his expertise to help design faster PT boats.

Afterward, he published his wartime research in a book entitled *Naval Architecture of Planing Hulls* (1946), which became Bob Simmons's bible for surfboard design. Lord's book worked through detailed hydrodynamics theory, tested against experiments using various surfaces towed at high speeds behind boats. Lord's test surfaces closely resembled surfboards: flat, thin wooden shapes, with varying templates (or outlines), rails (rounded edges), and foils (thickness profiles), all aimed at minimizing drag and maximizing lift and planing.

Lord's calculations, impenetrable to anyone without a math or engineering background, caught Simmons's eye. He worked through them in detail and applied them to surfboards. The result departed dramatically from the existing boxy surfboards with curved bottoms and narrow tails. The Simmons boards featured a flat or even concave planing surface on the bottom behind a scarfed nose; a wide, flat tail; downturned rails; and twin fins to direct water flow off the tail. He also began experimenting with shorter boards, down to six feet in length, four to six feet shorter than standard boards. Simmons thereafter insisted that his designs were not surfboards but rather "hydrodynamic planing hulls."

Simmons sprang his radical new designs on the postwar surfing community at Windansea and Malibu, and they soon proliferated through lineups from San Diego to Ventura, with the top surfers at each break trying to wangle boards from the new leading surfboard shaper. As Bev Morgan, one such surfer, put it, "Simmons was the one. . . . It was a quantum leap from the old Pacific Homes blanks and Tom Blake paddleboards." Peter Cole, another legendary surfer from the time, flatly declared that "Simmons has done more for modern surfing than any other surfer."

Simmons never profited from his designs, devoting himself to riding challenging waves on ever-changing board designs. He traveled the California coast, sleeping in his car and eating canned food. His eccentricity did not approach that of his brother Dewey, who wandered the Caltech campus dressed in medieval garb, down to the slippers and tights, until his death in 2008. The brothers argued constantly and finally stopped talking to each other altogether. Bob tired of the crowds at Malibu and migrated south, surfing big swells at Tijuana Sloughs while a legion of imitators filled the demand for the new shapes and materials. Simmons died in 1954 while surfing Windansea in San Diego. The surf was big but nothing he hadn't handled before. Simmons got hit in the head by his board and collapsed on his way to the beach. Today, the dangerous, shallow break on Windansea's north end is called Simmons Reef.

6 THE SURF BOOM

On movie screens across America in 1959, a perky blond teenager nicknamed Gidget jumped on her couch in an impromptu demonstration of surfing for her parents. Balancing on the cushions, Gidget gushed, "Surfing is out of this world! You just can't imagine the thrill of shooting the curl—it positively surpasses every living emotion I've ever had!" Her beaming dad, the epitome of the middle-class fatherly font of wisdom, replied, "Well, I don't mind learning my daughter enjoys the pleasures of an outdoor sport." In a later scene on the beach, however, Gidget meets the Kahuna and hears of his vague plans to visit Peru, or perhaps Hawaii. Gidget, incredulous, gasps, "You can't mean . . ." Kahuna nonchalantly confirms her fears: "I'm a surf bum. You know, ride the waves, eat, sleep. Not a care in the world." Gidget: "Well, it might be awfully naive of me, but when do you work?" Kahuna: "Oh yeah, well, I tried that once. But there were too many hours and rules and regulations." *Gidget* thus captured the familiar, competing visions of surfing—as healthy outdoor sport or the domain of dropout delinquents—and forced surfers to struggle with their own self-image as rebels versus the commercial possibilities in postwar America.

CALIFORNIA DREAMING

The standard story is that *Gidget* created a huge surf boom at the end of the 1950s that ran well into the '60s: *Gidget* ended surfing's age of innocence and sparked commercialism, consumerism, and the invasion of previously empty beaches by hordes of clueless kooks. The standard story is wrong. There was indeed a boom in surfing, but *Gidget* was as much an effect as a cause of it. For one thing, there was the source for the movie, the original Gidget herself, a fifteen-year-old named Kathy Kohner, whose diminutive stature—five feet tall and ninety-five pounds soaking wet—earned her the nickname "girl-midget," or Gidget. What was this teenage girl doing at Malibu in the first place that summer of 1956? She was there because her parents, like countless others along the California coast, thought the beach was a good, healthy place for her and her cousins to spend time. Once at Malibu, Kathy found a cast of characters who had been hanging around the point for years. In short, the surf boom was well under way even before Gidget strolled up to the point at Malibu. That's why, when it came time to make the *Gidget* movie, they had to film it nine miles up the coast at Leo Carrillo. Malibu itself was already too crowded.

Surfing boomed in postwar California for several reasons. It started with a strong base from the 1920s and '30s, the "coast haoles" who spread up and down the new coast highway. The first prerequisite for the surf boom is the one we saw aiding the initial revival of modern surfing: the general spread of swimming ability. Again, you can't surf if you can't swim, and in the 1930s the federal and local governments further boosted swimming capability among the general American public. Amid the Great Depression, the federal Civil Works Administration and then the Works Progress Administration built nearly 750 municipal pools and remodeled several hundred more. To supplement swim lessons offered by the YMCA and local athletic clubs, California beach towns such as El Segundo and Santa Barbara taught swimming as part of physical education classes, so that students learned swimming alongside math and reading. Meanwhile, celebrity swimmers such as Duke and Johnny Weissmuller, along with more comfortable and functional swimwear, further enticed Americans into the pool. By 1934 *Fortune* magazine was calling swimming "the New Great American Sport." Gidget herself declared, through her father's fictionalization, "I'm just crazy about swimming. I really am. I must have been thrown into some Southern California swimming pool when I was six months old, and I've been in the water ever since."

The popularity of swimming allowed Californians to flock to the surf long before Gidget. Photos of some spots even before the war show packs of surfers pursuing waves. Malibu by the late 1940s had dozens of surfers in the lineup, and six guys on every wave during a good swell. These were not exactly the pristine empty waves recalled by nostalgic old-timers, though they might have seemed so after the postwar boom. War had interrupted the fun but also increased surfing's appeal. Veterans rejoining civilian life could find it dull and meaningless, and seek an alternative to the mundane work world. Some of them just went surfing. This was Kahuna's path, in *Gidget*; he became a beach bum on returning from the Korean War.

More important, the Cold War drove the continued growth of Southern California. California became the "aerospace capital of the world," as billions of dollars in defense contracts, plus billions more from the civilian National Aeronautics and Space Administration (NASA) and the space race, supported hundreds of thousands of well-paid white-collar engineering jobs. All of this made California the capital of middle-class leisure culture. Teenagers in aerospace surfurbia weren't getting up early to milk cows or mine coal. They were enjoying the bounty of affluent society in Southern California, and a benign climate that allowed outdoor recreation year round. They not only had money to buy surfboards and trunks; they had cars, gas money, the new freeway system to get them to the beach, and above all the free time to enjoy it all.

The Cold War also boosted surfing outside of California. In 1966 *Sports Illustrated* ran a cover story on "surfing's East Coast boom." Most of that centered on Florida, where the spaceport at Cape Canaveral, launch pad for Mercury, Gemini, and Apollo missions, drove development of the whole "Space Coast." White-collar engineers flooded into Cocoa Beach, Satellite Beach, and other coastal towns, and their kids hit the surf. As in California, aerospace enabled the middle-class lifestyle that supported surfing.

The defense economy drove California's demographics, which in turn boosted the surf boom. California's population doubled from 1940 to 1960, making it the most populous state in the nation. As California's economic, political, and social influence grew apace, much of American culture now came from the Golden State, instead of emerging on the Eastern Seaboard and flowing west; Wallace Stegner famously declared that California was like the rest of America, only more so. Population growth doubled the number of potential surfers—or more than doubled, since many of the new Californians were young, thanks to the baby-boom generation created by returning World War II vets. By 1960 there were close to 16 million people in California, 2 million of them in their teens and twenties, and many of them living close to the coast. In 1963 the *L.A. Times* estimated a 100,000-strong "army" of surfers in Southern California. That meant, in theory, a few hundred surfers for every mile of coast. In practice, however, even more surfers collected at popular breaks, such as Malibu, where hundreds of surfers invaded the lineup on good days.

All these baby boomers riding the wave of Cold War California aerospace constituted the demand for the surfing boom. Aerospace also provided the supply. Simmons, as we know, introduced polystyrene foam, fiberglass, and polyester resins from wartime defense projects to surfboard design. Shapers quickly embraced fiberglass and resin to seal and strengthen balsa boards. In the mid-1950s they abandoned wood altogether for another complex chemical from the defense industry, polyurethane foam. Polyurethane could be traced back to nineteenth-century German isocyanate chemistry but got a boost in the 1930s when Bayer Chemical in Germany, the discoverer of aspirin and sulfa drugs, developed new urethane foams that combined strength and elasticity. When the Allies entered Germany in 1946, military intelligence reports described German progress in urethane foams; the U.S. Air Force expressed interest, and DuPont, Monsanto, Goodyear, and Lockheed jumped into urethane research using Bayer licenses.

Polyurethane foams had hundreds of commercial applications in the postwar era (for instance, as insulation for refrigerators), but the U.S. military sustained the polyurethane market as the largest consumer. Urethane foams were used to fill voids in aircraft, and Lockheed chemists soon patented a rigid polyurethane known as Lockfoam. General

Dynamics also worked with National Oil Products Chemical Co. (Nopco) in New Jersey to develop Lockfoam for nuclear submarines, in the process solving several problems in foam production. Nuclear subs like the *Skipjack* contained twenty thousand pounds of Lockfoam—seemingly a lot of foam, but using it instead of the conventional fillers cut a sub's overall weight by over eight tons. Nopco built plants in New Jersey and Los Angeles with a combined annual capacity of 2 million pounds of urethane and vinyl foams. In the early 1960s, the company began focusing on isocyanates, the raw material that went into urethane, producing 20 million pounds a year.

Meanwhile, Owens Corning was busy refining fiberglass to a point where the flexible strands were one-fifteenth the thickness of human hair with a greater tensile strength than steel. The aerospace industry supported much fiberglass production, using it, for instance, as ablatives in rocket nozzles and reentry vehicles. Surfers began using some of these more advanced weaves in the 1960s: twist weaves instead of flat weaves, and so on. Fiberglass may have had an unconscious attraction for surfers: it was basically spun glass, or sand; surfers in a way were still lying on the beach, even when out in the water.

Polyurethane foam entered the world of surfing in 1956. Dave Sweet purchased his first surfboard from Bob Simmons and, following Simmons, experimented with Styrofoam before focusing on balsa. In 1954, after a friend showed Sweet a block of polyurethane foam, he began blowing his own foam to make polyurethane surfboard blanks (a blank is the raw block of foam that shapers turn into a surfboard). Sweet obtained his chemicals from Nopco and his first steel-and-fiberglass mold from Techniform, an L.A.-area aerospace machine shop. Sweet at one point shared his mold with his younger brother and Cliff Robertson—yes, the actor who played Kahuna in *Gidget*, and who surfed in real life—to make molded pop-outs for Robertson/Sweet Surfboards. Others followed Sweet into the foam-blank business, like him relying on cheap raw materials from the huge chemical conglomerates, which in turn were sustained by Cold War military demand.

Foam blanks by the hundreds and thousands allowed surfboard shapers to scale up operations to meet demand in the surf boom. A power planer cut through polyurethane foam like butter. Instead of laboriously chipping balsa blanks by hand, a shaper could turn a foam blank into a surfboard in an hour or two. Starting in the late 1950s, major surfboard makers scaled up production lines, and a handful of large labels, named after individual surfer/shapers—Velzy, Hobie, Weber, Noll—exerted a virtual monopoly, shipping cheap, mass-produced boards across the West and East Coasts and to Hawaii. Hobie made one hundred boards a week by the late 1950s, and by the mid-1960s Dewey Weber was making three hundred a week. Greg Noll knocked out two hundred a week, thanks to seventy employees in a twenty-thousand-square-foot factory featuring high-tech ventilators, temperature controls, and separate facilities for making foam, shaping boards, laminating, and sanding.

Manufacturers also tried the pop-out approach, using molded foam blanks that eliminated the process of planing the foam by hand. For a time in the early 1960s pop-outs outproduced hand-shaped boards. Problems with foam strength and consistency undermined pop-outs, but the main problem was price: pop-outs weren't cheaper than shaped boards, since shapers like Hobie or Noll could hire eighteen-year-old kids for close to nothing to crank out boards all day in exchange for the cachet of working for a big-name shaper.

Fiberglass and resin aided one other design innovation that opened up the California coast to surfers. The flat planks used before the war tended to sideslip down the face of the wave, what surfers called "sliding ass," which usually meant losing your board and a long swim to the beach. Hawaiian surfers tried carving keels at the tail of their planks to provide purchase in the wave face, calling the result "hot curl" boards, since they allowed angling high across the wave face close to the breaking curl. Tom Blake, meanwhile, tried a fin, like a solid rudder. Blake was an avid sailor and understood the importance of keels for sailboats; he attached a discarded boat skeg to a board and found it worked great. The idea did not catch on at the time, however, in part because it was hard to attach fins to boards. After trying screws and bolts, surfers glued on fins, but few glues could withstand salt water. With the fiberglass-resin combination, however, surfers could glass on the fin instead of gluing it.

In postwar Southern California, technology, demographics, economics, environment, and culture combined to create the surf boom.

Cheap boards provided an easy entry point for the thousands of teenagers enticed by the surf scene. They weighed much less, were easier to ride, and were available in sporting goods stores and even department stores.

The new surfboard designs transformed the act of surfing. Surfers no longer stood stiffly erect and rode waves straight to the beach or at gentle angles running from the breaking curl. Now they were arcing up and down the wave face, maneuvering to stay as close to the curl as possible, crouching and quick-stepping from nose to tail of their boards. A new "hotdogging" style emerged, with a vast repertoire of bottom turns and cutbacks, tail stalls, soul arches, drop-knees, cross-steps, head dips, wave scratches, and above all the hang ten, where the surfer perched on the nose like a hood ornament, with ten toes draped over the tip. Hotdogging was the surfers' way of expressing individuality and style in the 1950s age of *The Organization Man* and *The Man in the Gray Flannel Suit*.

The most prominent surfers developed distinctive styles: Phil Edwards, known for his quiet, classy grace; Lance Carson, a dark-haired partyer and nose-rider extraordinaire, who could ride the length of the beach casually hanging ten; sporty and easygoing Mike Doyle; diminutive Dewey Weber, known as "the Little Man on Wheels" for his quick cross-stepping across his board; the equally diminutive Johnny Fain, blond-haired and flamboyant, playing to the crowd with handstands on waves; and Fain's nemesis, the tall and dark Miki Dora, shoving Fain and anyone else off waves and flipping off the crowd, and yet, to Fain's chagrin, winning it over.

The new style affected surfing's geography. Before the war, surfers favored slower mushy rides, at places like San Onofre. The new postwar materials caused surfers to seek out long, peeling waves to showcase trimming and turning. They found them at point breaks: Rincon, a pristine point break just south of Santa Barbara, and in particular First Point Malibu, that prominent bend in the coast that focused swells into long, fast lines. One surf journalist, in a fit of hyperbole, declared that "Malibu is the exact spot on earth where ancient surfing became modern surfing." Waikiki already occupied that spot, but Malibu was indeed seen at the time as the epicenter of California surf culture.

The new lightweight boards also encouraged women to take up

the sport in much greater numbers. Joe Quigg, one of the first shapers to follow Simmons with the new materials, introduced a forty-pound "girl board" that was shorter, lighter, and more maneuverable than the solid wood planks or Blake's hollow boards—eventually so light that a five-foot-tall, ninety-five-pound girl the size of Gidget could handle one of them. Gidget might not have been as keen on surfing if she'd had to struggle with a sixty-pound thirties-era board, let alone a hundred-pound plank from 1910. Her twenty-pound board, a marvel of modern chemistry, was pure fun.

The surf boom also advanced surfing's commercialization, as surfers joined the consumer class. In addition to driving demand for mass-produced surfboards, it gave many surfers a job path in the surfboard production industry and opened up commercial opportunities in the emerging surfwear industry. Surfers first bought suits from mainstream swimsuit makers tapping the new surf market. Jantzen, for example, had entered the swimwear business in 1910 and had a national "Learn to Swim" campaign to get more people swimming—and buying swimsuits. Among those endorsing Jantzen suits was Olympic champion Duke Kahanamoku. In the early 1960s Jantzen began marketing to surfers and sponsoring top surfers, an early step in the professionalization of surfing. Among those Jantzen paid to surf were big-wave legend Pat Curren; Ricky Grigg, who earned $2,000 a year from Jantzen for his surfing ability; and Corky Carroll, later famous for his beach-bum persona in Miller Lite beer ads. Jantzen also added John Severson to its payroll. The publisher of then-new *Surfer* magazine, Severson sustained his business by establishing the symbiosis of advertisers and surf media. Surfers also created their own surfwear companies. The most successful was Hang Ten, which built an ad campaign around a team of sponsored surfers, including Phil Edwards, Dewey Weber, Mike Doyle, Greg Noll, and Hobie Alter.

Madison Avenue meanwhile began using surfers to advertise consumer products with no connection at all to riding waves. Linda Benson promoted Triumph cars, Joey Cabell hawked Keds shoes, and Hamm's beer used photos of Rusty Miller dropping in at Sunset. Surfers selling commercial staples like cars and beer highlighted public interest in surfing.

STRAIGHT OUTTA HAWTHORNE . . . AND HOLLYWOOD: SURF MUSIC AND FILMS

While the aerospace industry helped Southern California become the epicenter of surf culture, another Southern California industry spread that culture across the nation, and the world. What else was Southern California known for? The entertainment industry, of course. A couple dozen miles from Malibu, Hollywood and the music business helped American pop culture glom on to the California surf scene.

First, of course, was *Gidget*, which started as a book written by Frederick Kohner. An Austro-Hungarian Jew with a PhD from Vienna, Kohner had fled the Nazis and by the 1950s was a Hollywood screenwriter living in Brentwood. His daughter Kathy started surfing at Malibu in 1956 and hanging around the Malibu crew. She confided about her new friends to her father, who knocked out a short novel about the Malibu surf scene. The book came out in the summer of 1957 and quickly sold a half million copies. Surfers were unimpressed. *Life* magazine hit Malibu to ask them about surfing's new publishing phenomenon. One of them replied, "If I had a couple bucks to buy a book, I wouldn't. I'd buy some beer." But many nonsurfers who did plunk down money for the book came away inspired by Kohner's descriptions of the rush of riding waves.

The movie version soon followed in 1959 (Kohner was, after all, a screenwriter) and became a national hit. The film starred Sandra Dee in the title role, James Darren as her love interest Moondoggie, and Cliff Robertson, who surfed in real life, as the mysterious, seductive Kahuna. Malibu regulars Miki Dora, Mike Doyle, and Johnny Fain were stunt doubles, with Mickey Muñoz, wearing a blond wig and bikini, doubling for Sandra Dee. The film spawned several sequels: *Gidget Goes Hawaiian*, *Gidget Goes to Rome*, and so on. As the Rome setting suggested, surfing was secondary in many of these, as it had become for Gidget herself: Kathy Kohner left for college at Oregon State and gave up surfing.

Hollywood, however, was just getting started. Soon came the "Beach Party" movies with Frankie Avalon and former Mouseketeer Annette Funicello crooning and cuddling in the surf, starting with *Beach Party* in 1963 and evolving, or devolving, through *Beach Blanket Bingo*, *How to Stuff a Wild Bikini*, and *Muscle Beach Party*, the last one with the immortal tagline "When 10,000 biceps go around 5,000 bikinis, you *know* what's going to happen!" Despite the innuendo, these movies presented a safe, acceptable alternative to the darker, antisocial examples of the beatniks and other social outcasts: this was Frankie Avalon, not James Dean. Even the *Beach Party* producers, American-International Pictures (or AIP), saw the light; the company had first made its name in the 1950s on low-budget films featuring sexually aggressive teenagers rebelling against dysfunctional adult authority. By the 1960s, however, the company abandoned this formula for mainstream respectability—and bigger box office. So where the original *Beach Party* script featured sex and drugs, the director quickly scrubbed it to present the "clean teen" image.

The *Beach Party* movies featured Frankie Avalon and Annette Funicello—East Coast Italians who did not exactly look like blond California kids. And they were not exactly teenagers either: Frankie was twenty-six, and married with kids, at the time of *Beach Blanket Bingo*. This was not the first or last time studio heads ignored ethnic realities to appeal to urban audiences. On the other hand, the brown-haired *Gidget* was played by blond Sandra Dee. Improbable casting came to a head in the inevitable Gidget TV series, aired in 1965 and starring Sally Field as the perky, rambunctious teenager. Field provided the requisite squeaky-clean image; she would go on to fame as the Flying Nun. The wholesome image, however, was already passé, along with the Gidget phenomenon, and the series mercifully expired after one year of bad ratings.

The music business joined Hollywood on the surfing bandwagon. In the early 1960s a new music category called surf music emerged, soon becoming the second most popular in the United States, second only to Motown. Surf music mostly came out of Southern California, but the first contribution came from a nonsurfing band from Seattle, the Ventures, whose "Walk Don't Run" reached number two on the charts in 1960. Then in 1961 Dick Dale recorded "Let's Go Trippin'," which surfers regarded as the first surf song; Dale was himself a surfer from Southern California and was already popular in the surf community for his blistering live shows in Newport. The next year he released "Misirlou," whose searing guitar solo cemented his reputation as "king of the surf guitar." Other groups and hits followed: the Surfaris' "Wipe Out" of 1962, and later the theme to *Hawaii Five-O* from the Ventures.

These groups shared a characteristic sound: electric guitar–based instrumentals with heavy reverb effects. Purists regarded this as true surf music, but another group at the same time became identified with surfing. The Beach Boys came out of the aerospace hotbed of Hawthorne. They matched layers of harmonizing vocals with lyrics celebrating the California surf lifestyle. A string of hits—"Surfin'," "Surfin' USA," "Surfer Girl," "Catch a Wave"—reinforced the image of waves, sun, girls, and cars. The Beach Boys era reached well into the 1960s, but they hearkened back more to the conformist fifties than to the sixties. In candy-striped shirts that suggested a barbershop quartet, they conveyed a sentimental and safe image, even as their sound was overtaken by more turbulent times and the British Invasion. Some hard-core surfers at the time thought the Beach Boys were phonies, and their music tame and lame; Dennis Wilson was the only Beach Boy who actually surfed. But the popular image of surf music continued to center on the Beach Boys, not Dick Dale; that is, on wholesome harmony, not yowling feedback.

All these movies, TV shows, and music added up to an extended American fixation with surfing, centered on the Malibu image of surf, sun, sand, and girls. This was hedonism of a certain type: not subversive, just wholesome kids having fun. Hollywood brought surfing to the heartland and further fueled a pop-culture boom. Inlanders flocked to the beach, especially to Malibu, to try the sport. Inland in this case usually meant not Kansas, but instead the new inland suburbs springing up around Southern California—especially, for the case of Malibu, just over the hill in the San Fernando Valley, where industrial and real-estate development flowed thanks to May Rindge's victory over the railroad. Valley kids grew up in middle-class suburban homes with the requisite backyard pool, where they mastered swimming before heading over the hill to the 'Bu. California's beaches in a sense became an extension of the suburban backyard.

The pop-culture surfing fixation also signaled a shift in surfing's epicenter, from Hawaii to Southern California. Where surfing's popular image in the 1910s and '20s had focused on Waikiki, surf culture in the fifties and sixties became identified with Southern California.

BLUE HAWAII

Although Hollywood's infatuation with surfing focused on California, it extended to the original beachboys in Waikiki. In 1961 Elvis picked up a surfboard for *Blue Hawaii* and went on to make two more surf-themed movies in Hawaii. In the movie Elvis played a returning soldier happily reunited with his surfboard. The military motif was apt. The U.S. military dominated Hawaiian life more than ever during World War II and the Cold War.

America's path to World War II ran through Hawaii, literally and logistically. Over a million troops passed through the islands on their way to the Pacific theater; in 1944 soldiers accounted for half of Hawaii's total population of 860,000, and federal outlays in the islands approached a billion dollars. The swift onset of the Cold War kept Hawaii mobilized; after a few short years the Korean War began, followed after another too-brief interlude by Vietnam. For over three decades Hawaii was, essentially, a war zone, and Oahu a military garrison. Joan Didion sensed the military presence in a visit in 1966: "If there is a single aura which pervades Honolulu, one mood which lends the lights a feverish luster and the pink catamarans a heartbreaking absurdity and which engages the imagination as mere paradise never could, that mood is, inescapably, one of war. . . . War is in the very fabric of Hawaii's life, ineradicably fixed in both its emotions and its economy, dominating not only its memory but its vision of the future."

Surfers did not escape the military's extensive reach. Surfing was not part of the Cold War, unlike the many sports that provided a proxy realm for international competition (the Olympics), espionage and territorial claims (mountaineering), or diplomacy (Ping-Pong). For starters, many Communist countries forbade surfing, apparently for fear surfers would hop on their boards and paddle across the Baltic or the Caribbean to freedom. But, as we shall see, surfing maintained its link to the U.S. military during the Cold War, through several technologies that profoundly reshaped the sport. More generally, the Cold War influenced surfing by bringing hundreds of thousands of people to Hawaii and providing them with the economic leisure to hang out and catch a few waves. Many did, and were hooked.

American military interests bound the islands more tightly to the United States and helped Hawaii win statehood in 1959. That, in turn, enticed more Americans to come visit the newest American state. The military presence rubbed shoulders with a redoubled tourist industry. A postwar wave of popular interest in Hawaii followed the backwash of the earlier wave, as returning veterans from the Pacific theater told tales of tropical isles, and Tiki rooms, Trader Vic's, and Don Ho were soon bubbling through middle-class culture in the United States and Europe. Elvis crooning "Blue Hawaii" was the zenith, or nadir, of the postwar tropical trend.

Soldiers, statehood, and commercial air travel brought mass tourism. In 1950, for the first time, tourists arriving by plane outnumbered those coming by ship. The jet age for tourism started in 1958, when Boeing 707s and then Douglas DC-8s cut the flight time in half again. Instead of a weeklong sea voyage, tourists sank their toes on the beach after a few hours in the air. The number of tourists jumped by an order of magnitude, from 50,000 visitors in 1952 to 500,000 in 1965. (Many of them arrived at Honolulu Airport, newly expanded with material dredged from neighboring wetlands; a later runway was built entirely offshore on fill dumped over an existing reef.) By the 1970s, with millions of visitors arriving each year, tourism overtook the U.S. military as the main economic driver in Hawaii.

Mass tourism turned Waikiki into a Las Vegas for surfing. High-rise hotels proliferated along the beach; Sheraton bought out several Matson hotels, followed by Hilton, Hyatt, and other vertically integrated, multinational corporations in the global tourism industry. The Dillingham conglomerate did much of this construction, but a new name emerged in the 1950s to engineer Hawaii for the demands of tourism. In the early 1950s Henry J. Kaiser visited Hawaii and was startled to find that his hotel could not honor his reservation; all the rooms were full. Kaiser overcame this initial affront and fell in love with Hawaii. He moved into a house on Kahala Beach and determined to ensure that future visitors would have rooms when they arrived in tropical paradise. He had missed out on tourism bonanzas in Florida and Palm Springs and was not going to let the Hawaiian opportunity pass him by.

Kaiser's Hawaiian enterprise was the final chapter in a career that reshaped the world. He accumulated vast wealth as the greatest builder of the twentieth century. In the 1930s, Kaiser built Hoover Dam on the Colorado and the Grand Coulee and Bonneville Dams on the Columbia. In World War II Kaiser mass-produced Liberty cargo ships at a breakneck pace, building more than 2,700 ships over four years, at one point knocking out an entire ship in four days. Kaiser developed a network of steel mills and concrete plants to supply his building interests and hospitals to serve his workforce. After the war Kaiser mass-produced cars, but upon moving to Hawaii, Kaiser handed these enterprises to his son, Edgar, and focused on his new goal of transforming the islands.

Surfers at the western end of Waikiki in the early 1950s could look toward shore and see the old Niumalu Hotel, dating to 1928, and not much else. Within a decade Kaiser engineered a new beach and more than doubled the number of hotel rooms available on Waikiki. "Kaiserland" created a cluster of hotels amid a destination resort where a visitor's every need was met. The $20 million project kicked off when Kaiser ended a furor over land-use rights by purchasing the Niumalu and adjoining land that included Duke Kahanamoku's childhood neighborhood. Kaiser now held the largest open plot on Waikiki with the exception of acreage controlled by the adjacent Fort De Russy. Kaiser's construction led to expansion of the yacht harbor and of Waikiki Beach itself. His Hawaiian Village included a new beach and man-made lagoon with a small-scale replica of the Hawaiian Islands and palm trees. When it came time to name the beach, Duke's name came up. After all, Kalia was where Hawaii's greatest surfer grew up. Critics said that "Kahanamoku" was too hard to pronounce and that nobody on the mainland knew the name. City fathers conducted a stateside survey and learned that Duke's name was synonymous with Hawaii and Waikiki. The new stretch of Waikiki was duly dubbed "Duke Kahanamoku Beach."

Kaiser's gigantic hotel had a profound impact on Waikiki, creating land where none existed before and lengthening the beach. *Parade*

Waikiki Beach from the air in 1961. Henry Kaiser's new Hawaiian Village, with artificial lagoon adjoining Duke Kahanamoku Beach, is just above the harbor at center. Note the several jetties, and the Ala Wai canal running the length of Waikiki behind the beachfront. This photo predates the construction of Magic Island on the other side of the harbor and the further carpeting of Waikiki with high-rise hotels. (Source: Laurence Hata photo, Bishop Museum.)

magazine called Kaiser "the Pasha of the Pacific." A local Honolulu politician looked instead to Hawaiian history and compared Kaiser to Kamehameha the Great: "we now have that great warrior of finance,

Henry J. Kaiser, who in turn would like to capture the Islands, his starting point being Oahu, destination Hawaii." To sustain the ambition of a latter-day Kamehameha required a special relationship with the Hawaiian people and their political representatives. For anyone else this might have proved fatal. Hawaiian business was still dominated by a few wealthy families who did not look kindly on a newcomer calling for thousands of new hotel rooms. Kaiser, however, was no stranger to political opposition and the potential intransigence of labor. He garnered the necessary support from local politicians and then addressed the construction challenge. Money was no object. If a contractor or union representative questioned a contract, Kaiser immediately spent what was needed to keep the project moving forward. Kaiser was convinced that color television was a must for his hotel, and when he learned that Hawaii had no color broadcast capability, he built his own station; when the existing broadcaster complained, he bought out the company. Kaiser did not keep a low profile. His official color was pink. Every item of equipment was painted pink, and the boss himself often wore red-pink slacks and pink sport shirts. Hawaii's new Kamehameha was not hiding from anyone, least of all Hawaii's elite.

Walter Dillingham's Hawaiian Dredging Company was among the many benefactors of Kaiser's development plan, driving piles for the Hawaiian Village, creating more beach for Kaiser's tourists to lounge on, and dredging out ten acres of coral in front of the hotel for water-skiing. Kaiser's building ambitions and demand for raw material exceeded the capability of local contractors, particularly when he decided to build a new Kaiser community, known as Hawaii Kai, along the bay just past Diamond Head. Tired of dealing with shortages, Kaiser proposed building his own Permanente Concrete plant to supply the project. In doing so, Kaiser ran afoul of Walter Dillingham and his son Benjamin, who owned the existing Hawaiian Cement Company and had a lock on Hawaiian development.

The threat was enough to drag Walter Dillingham out of retirement. At a community meeting in Waianae, the eighty-four-year-old patriarch who had ruled Waikiki for half a century squared off with Kaiser. Kaiser accused Dillingham of "underhanded attempts" to kill his project. Dillingham called Kaiser "a visitor here [and] I don't think it is a very nice thing for a visitor to Hawaii, no matter how many millions he's spent here, to attack a son of mine, and of Hawaii." The locals sided with Kaiser, whose plant created jobs. Kaiser did not forget Dillingham's challenge. He created an alternative to Dillingham's Hawaiian Dredging empire, shipping his own dredge and an army of earthmoving equipment to Oahu to build Hawaii Kai.

What did all this mean for surfing? This postwar surge in Waikiki tourism introduced countless thousands of tourists to surfing, many of whom returned to the mainland to spread the surf boom. But the tourist hordes helped drive hard-core surfers away from Waikiki, up Oahu's west coast to Makaha and eventually, as we shall see, to the North Shore. The tourist invasion also ended the romantic beachboy era on Waikiki. The prewar beachboys worked on an individual basis, building personal relationships with visitors over surf sessions, ukulele choruses, and late-night beers, and seeing the same faces year to year. Such personal relationships did not endure the influx of hundreds of thousands of visitors. In the 1950s the beachboys became more of a business than a lifestyle, and as licensed and regulated surfboard concessions proliferated up and down Waikiki, a little spark of aloha left the beach.

The influx of millions of tourists also turned the cradle of surfing into a toilet bowl. By 1940 the local Chamber of Commerce had sponsored a sanitary survey of the waters between the Diamond Head and Kewalo sewer outfalls, which spewed raw sewage into the ocean on both ends of Waikiki. Territorial health officials concluded that sewage levels were unacceptable for recreational beaches and urged the construction of sewage treatment plants. In the postwar population boom, though, sewage treatment continued piecemeal, with much new housing relying on septic tanks and cesspools that leached into groundwater. Only in the 1970s, after the Clean Water Act of 1972, did Honolulu build a large treatment plant on Sand Island, just off Honolulu Harbor, with its outfall two miles offshore—though that did not end Waikiki's sewage problems.

The Kaiser juggernaut sputtered to a halt after "Hurry-Up Henry" passed away in 1967. At his funeral he was eulogized as "a modern *ali'i*," a member of Hawaiian nobility. By that time this preeminent industrialist had built Waikiki into a factory for the mass production of tourism and recreation. Kaiser's legacy endures. At the western end of Waikiki there is a surf spot called Kaisers. The wave faces Kaiser's sprawling Hilton Hawaiian Village, fronted by man-made Duke Kahanamoku Beach. This was the vista the Duke himself gazed on in his waning days from his vantage point in the old Kaiser Hospital, built in the 1950s by the Kamehameha of construction. In the 1980s the hospital was demolished, and the rubble dumped in the ocean off Ewa Beach to create an artificial reef.

THE ENDLESS SUMMER

Back in California, real surfers were mocking the Beach Boys and Gidget, but they could not gainsay one final expression of the surf boom. A film by a dyed-in-the-wool surfer crossed over to mainstream success and provided a catchphrase for surfing's appeal: "the endless summer."

In 1964 filmmaker Bruce Brown was twenty-six years old and had a string of surf films under his belt. Brown, Greg Noll, and other surfing filmmakers at the time had a low-budget business model: set up a camera on the beach during surf sessions, string the resulting clips together with a soundtrack, and take the film up and down the coast, screening it in high school auditoriums and gyms. Brown undertook a new film with the simple premise of following two top surfers to lineups around the world. He filmed it for $50,000, most of that for travel, not technology; he kept his camera gear simple, since he had to carry it everywhere. He screened the 16-millimeter film to surf audiences in 1964 and met enthusiastic reactions. Thinking the film might have broader appeal, he took it to Wichita, Kansas, for a test screening in the dead of winter. The crowd went nuts, and Brown knew he was onto something. He went back to California, blew up the film to 35 millimeters, and released it in 1966 to general theaters.

The Endless Summer was a breakout hit, earning $30 million—not a bad return on Brown's investment. Critics raved. The highbrow *New Yorker* lauded "a brilliant documentary . . . [that] perfectly expresses the surfing spirit. . . . Great movie. Out of sight." *Time* magazine called it "an ode to sun, sand, skin and surf" and declared Brown "a Bergman of the boards." *Newsweek* named it one of the top ten films of 1966. The movie poster, designed by a twenty-two-year-old graphic artist named John Van Hamersveld, became a cultural icon and now hangs in New York's Museum of Modern Art. (Van Hamersveld went on to design many classic album covers, including the Beatles' *Magical Mystery Tour* and the Rolling Stones' *Exile on Main Street*.)

Why was *The Endless Summer* so successful? It had a simple plot, following surfers Robert August and Mike Hynson around the world as they chased summer, and good waves, from the Northern to the Southern Hemisphere. It included their cornball antics and encounters with local people but with no dialogue, just Bruce Brown's comic, deadpan voiceover. The film captured surfing's carefree appeal, the urge to drop everything and just follow the surf. If it had a dramatic arc, it was the search for the perfect wave, which culminated at Cape St. Francis in South Africa. Brown framed the scene as a dramatic discovery, with Hynson and August trekking across desert sand dunes like surfing Lawrences of Arabia before cresting the final dune and spotting flawless head-high waves spinning down the Cape. What moviegoers did not know was that the whole segment was a setup. Brown and the surfers had checked into a local hotel and seen the Cape up the beach from the hotel; they had cruised up the beach and surfed it for about forty minutes before it went flat. The next morning Brown got them to journey across the dunes to simulate the dramatic "discovery." Surf travelers soon learned, to their chagrin, that the Cape was extremely fickle and rarely surfable.

Although the film's appeal lay partly in the old surf-bum image of just following the sun and surf, it also rested partly on its conservatism. It appealed to places like Kansas precisely because of a comforting, harmless message. Although it appeared in 1966, the film showed little trace of the emerging sixties sex-and-drugs counterculture; here were August and Hynson, clean-cut and earnest, walking through LAX in suits and ties. The only traces of sex appeared when Hynson tried and comically failed to pick up girls on the beach. Surfing here was still just wholesome outdoor fun.

Like the Beach Boys, *The Endless Summer*, a product of 1964, owed more to the long decade of the fifties than to what we think of as the sixties. This revived the old tension in surfing between counterculture and mainstream. Was surfing a bunch of bums shirking work, drinking beer, and chasing girls in between waves or a wholesome outdoor sport? Was it a holdover from the conformist fifties or a harbinger of the deca-dent sixties? In Gidget's terms: was frat-boy Moondoggie or beach bum Kahuna the real surfer?

Surfing's old associations with sex, rebellion, and general laziness, going back to the Christian missionaries in Hawaii, persisted. Surfers saw themselves as deliberately challenging the drab conformity of 1950s middle-class culture. Greg Noll, whose public image combined big-wave heroics with beer-soaked debauchery, reveled in the "RF," the rat-fuck: the practical joke played on friends, preferably scatalogical, and better yet the prank that flipped stodgy middle-class society the bird—like Lance Carson riding through a Winchell's Donuts parking lot hanging ten on a car's hood, stark naked save for a single donut amidships. Noll recalled the general vibe: "Something went to hell in the early '50s. It's like someone threw a light switch. . . . All of a sudden a bunch of guys came along and they go, 'screw the money, I'm having all the fun I can possibly have.' . . . For the first time ever, they had a group of guys who didn't give a rat's ass, dropping out of the basketball team and the football team and just giving the whole thing the finger, going, 'I don't give a shit about that, I just want to go surfing.' "

Surfing was not unique in this respect. At the same time, in the late 1950s, rock climbers at Camp 4 in Yosemite were dropping out of the rat race and dodging park rangers to indulge their outdoor passion, in this case climbing the big walls of El Capitan. Yvon Chouinard has said, "We took special pride in the fact that climbing rocks and icefalls had no economic value in society. We were rebels from the consumer culture. Politicians and businessmen were 'greaseballs,' and corporations were the source of all evil. The natural world was our home." There were also, of course, the Beats, who were equally keen on rejecting middle-class expectations and career tracks. The same impulse that drove Jack Kerouac on the road in search of kicks drove surfers to the beach in search of waves. It was no coincidence that the books *Gidget* and *On the Road* appeared the same year, or that surfer Miki Dora was eulogized decades later as a "Kerouac in shorts."

The Cold War encouraged a live-for-today philosophy. By the mid-1950s both the United States and the Soviet Union had developed multimegaton hydrogen bombs, and were rapidly building up nuclear stockpiles and perfecting the means to deliver nuclear warheads across the world on a moment's notice. The Fishbowl nuclear tests in 1962, whose nuclear flash lit up Waikiki, provided a literal and figurative atomic-age backdrop to postwar surfing. For American youth, brought up on duck-and-cover drills and bomb shelters and living with the constant threat of nuclear Armageddon, why plan for the future and build a career when it all might go up in a mushroom cloud tomorrow? Why not hit the beach and catch a few waves?

Though surfers mocked the culture of conformity and consumerism, like the Beats they couldn't completely escape it. Greg Noll, while busy giving society the finger, was also busy setting up his surfboard factory. Mass production meant disciplined management, as the casual surfers who ran these companies had to crack down on teenage employees who blew off work to go surfing. One of his employees summarized his management philosophy: "No matter if the surf was up, you had to work. Heavy demand from the East Coast meant that you had to meet your shipment deadlines. Making surfboards had become big business." Noll was the corporate manager putting the screws to the workforce, to the point of creating a surf-world version of the management poster exhorting productivity. This one featured Noll dressed in sombrero and serape, brandishing a machete, with the bold caption "Watcheth, for ye know not when the master cometh." Noll, in short, was The Man.

Surfers could not escape middle-class culture. The only reason the Beats could chase their kicks, or surfers the endless summer, was because society was affluent enough to support them. Like the ancient Hawaiians, middle-class Americans in the 1950s enjoyed material abundance that made leisure a common privilege. The United States emerged from World War II as the dominant industrial power, taking up the economic slack from the nations laid waste by the war. The poor souls scrapping for food in postwar Europe (or Africa, or Asia) couldn't lounge on the beach strumming ukes, no matter how nonconformist they might be. They were too busy trying to earn their next meal. Alvin Toffler, in the runaway 1970 bestseller *Future Shock*, made this point: "Affluence makes it possible, for the first time in history, for large numbers of people to make their withdrawal a full-time proposition." Toffler used surfers as a prime example of how "a leisure-time commitment can also serve as the basis for an entire lifestyle." They were the first "fun specialists," organizing their lives around play instead of work. Toffler concluded, "The surfing subcult is a signpost pointing to the future."

In *Gidget*, clean-cut Moondoggie got the girl (and Kahuna got a job). It was, after all, still the 1950s. In 1963 one writer described surfers as "young nonconformists, but of a more healthy and unpretentious cast than the beatniks." The next year the United States Surfing Association advised members to "conduct yourself as a gentleman on the beach; act like a surfer." Such advice may have been needed because surfing's image was changing. A few years earlier the *Los Angeles Times* had posed the question "Are surfers good, clean American youth having fun at South Bay beaches? Or are they gangs of rowdies defying parental and school authority?" By 1964 writers were describing "200,000 half-naked surf buffs [in] varying types of immorality, from cutting school to throwing sexy twist parties. They tend to be rebellious. They are suspicious of outsiders. They have no desire to conform." Descriptions of surfers with "no ambition and a penchant for getting in trouble" accelerated as the sixties set in. *Time* magazine noted that "riding a board through the surf is a little like going on hashish."

In the summer of 1965 Tom Wolfe strolled onto the beach at Windansea in search of the surfer. He famously conveyed his experience in *The Pump House Gang*, with insolent teenaged surfers lounging on the beach and mocking square tourists. Wolfe captured the sense of youthful rebellion, the age segregation that cast anyone over twenty-five as a hopeless fuddy-duddy. But he also noted that most of these young surfers were from upper-middle-class homes whose affluence enabled their surfing lifestyle. Wolfe recounted an encounter between a wealthy rancher and a barefooted, towheaded Bruce Brown tooling around a big ranch on his motorcycle. " 'Hey! You!' 'Yeah' says Bruce Brown. 'Don't you know this is private property?' 'Yeah,' says Bruce Brown. 'Well, then, why don't you get your ass off it?' 'Because it's mine, it's my private property,' says Bruce Brown." The millionaire Brown, made rich by *The Endless Summer*, was now the propertied class. The encounter summarized surfing's combination of rebellion and affluence.

The Windansea crew had the last word. They had immediately pegged Wolfe, in his wingtips, bespoke suit, and natty tie, as a kook himself. That's why he ended up hanging around some kids a block down the beach at the pump house; the real surfers were under Windansea's traditional palm shack fronting the reef. After his piece appeared, the locals graffitied the pump house: "Tom Wolfe is a dork."

MIKI DORA

One Malibu surfer symbolized surfing's split personality. Miki Dora acquired legendary status for his rebellious image, and he is still revered today as a mysto figure in the surf world. Dora was one of the most talented surfers of this era, a hotdogger with inimitable style who earned the nickname "Da Cat" for his feline grace on a wave. But he was perhaps better known for his image as a rebellious, creative genius who refused to conform, giving the establishment the finger, literally as well as figuratively. Dora in this sense was a quintessential product of Southern California, where people felt free to invent a persona. Dora's Hollywood background and friendships affected not only his act on land, but also his surfing. Riding waves was a performance, a show; Malibu was the stage, and he was the star.

Dora's main role was as anti-establishment rebel. He never in his life had a real job. Dora stories have filled books; a notorious prankster, he sent turds in the mail to magazine editors and released jars of moths at surf movies to ruin the show. He always mysteriously materialized whenever the surf was good at Malibu; a fellow surfer tailed him once and found Dora sneaking down a dirt driveway above the point to check the waves. Only if it was good would he pull loudly into the Malibu parking lot, proclaiming how tuned in to the ocean he was. He made a public display of tossing his trophies in trash cans and for one famous photo posed provocatively on a crucifix of surfboards. In his most celebrated stunt, at a Malibu contest in 1967, he supposedly dropped his trunks and mooned the judges. (The more prosaic version is that his old, threadbare trunks just split down a seam.) Dora was among the first to complain about crowds, railing against all the newcomers flocking to Malibu and competing for waves. When other surfers dropped into waves he was riding, he shoved them off or kicked his board at their heads. These exploits earned him another nickname, "the Black Knight." He also developed a career as a petty thief, targeting friends as well as strangers. Charged with credit-card and check fraud in the United States, he jumped bail and fled abroad; his disappearance only fueled his legend, as rumors of Dora sightings in exotic places percolated through the surf community. He finally returned in 1981 and served about a year in assorted American prisons, then again moved abroad in exile.

In his Malibu heyday, Dora very deliberately capitalized on surfing's commercialization. He appeared as a stunt double in the "Beach Party" films and in the original *Gidget*, where he doubled for the clean-cut Moondoggie. He also rolled out a signature line of "Da Cat" surfboards from the Noll factory in a savvy, provocative ad campaign. In short, while railing against commerce and crowds, Da Cat was cashing in with mass-produced boards for the Malibu hordes. And Dora's rants against the crowds—what he called "the football-punchy Valley swingers"—ignored the fact that he himself was not originally a Malibu local; like the newcomers, he too started surfing as an inlander, making the drive to the coast from Hollywood. Dora, that is, was part of the postwar inlander beach rush that had turned Malibu into a phenomenon before Gidget ever set eyes on a surfboard. All of these surfers enjoyed the results of the Rindge saga decades earlier, benefiting from her stand against the railroad, which saved Malibu from industrial development, but also her defeat over beach access and the construction of the coast highway, which Dora, Gidget, and the others drove daily to reach the beach. Dora the rebel surfer, rejecting society, was nevertheless trapped in the environmental gyre.

By the time Dora fled abroad in the 1970s Malibu had lost its luster. The crowds drove away several other mainstays, and developments of the 1960s—drugs and new surfboard designs—shifted the spotlight to other breaks. Finally, the ocean itself rose up to punctuate Malibu's golden age, as the monster El Niño–driven storms in the winter of '69 shifted sand patterns on the point for years. By the time Malibu Barbie arrived in toy stores in 1971, Malibu's beach party had long since ended, and the hangover was setting in.

7 CHARLIE DON'T SURF: SURFING AND COUNTERCULTURE

The iconic chronicle of 1960s surf culture, *The Endless Summer*, came out in 1966, but it projected a 1950s image, with a clean-cut Mike Hynson and Robert August strolling through the airport in suits and ties as they left on their "surfari." Hynson's suitcase, however, included a big bag of pot. He did not think he could survive the boredom and frustration of extended surf travel without some psychochemical escape.

Hynson's stash foreshadowed a change in surfing's image, from safe conservative sport to subversive lifestyle—in Gidget's terms, from Moondoggie to Kahuna. This shift, around 1964, coincided with the general onset of "the sixties" (which did not exactly overlap the 1960s). Surfing intersected two of the most potent symbols of the sixties: drugs and Vietnam. But it was not just a case of sixties culture affecting the surf community. Rather, surfers helped define the sixties culture itself. That culture in turn helped drive changes in surfing, including another shift in surfboard design and associated changes in performance and surf geography.

DRUGS

Part of the sixties counterculture was, of course, drugs, which entered the surf community as they did many other parts of American society. If anything, drugs especially permeated surfing, with its youth-oriented, nonconformist culture based on leisure and free time, especially between swells. It is hard to overstate the pervasiveness of drugs in the surf community of the late sixties and early seventies; it started with pot, then hash, embraced psychedelics such as mushrooms and LSD, and finally included heroin and cocaine, and by the 1970s a surfer who did not do drugs became the exception.

Some of the most accomplished North Shore surfers in the late 1960s enhanced their surf sessions with chemical stimulation. Jeff Hakman and Jock Sutherland, for example, rode Honolua Bay dosed on LSD, and Hakman's career soon entered a tailspin as he sank into heroin addiction. Hakman was probably the best surfer in the world in the early to mid-1970s, along with Australia's Michael Peterson, who was similarly spiraling into heroin addiction. Try to think of another sport where the two best athletes could be smack addicts, getting loaded before championship contests. (Heroin is not, by almost any measure, a performance-enhancing drug.) Sutherland meanwhile gained notoriety for an amazing trifecta, surfing forty-foot Waimea Bay . . . at night . . . on acid. Friends found his board washed up on the beach later that night and presumed him drowned, but found him hours later strolling casually up Kam Highway.

Sutherland was one of the lucky ones. Drugs claimed many surfing casualties, including Bunker Spreckels, Clark Gable's stepson, who had prodigious natural surfing ability and an equally prodigious inheritance as heir to a sugar fortune, which he spent lavishly on globetrotting, drugs, and women before flaming out at the age of twenty-seven. Spreckels lost his life to drugs; Ron Stoner, an important chronicler as a *Surfer* staff photographer, lost his mind; 1970 world champion Rolf Aurness, like Hakman and Peterson, lost his career.

Just as important are the far more numerous, less famous surfers who succumbed to drugs. Here the grim toll grew to include entire communities, from Huntington Beach to Oahu's Westside to Australia's Gold Coast. Rabbit Bartholomew's description of Coolangatta may stand for all: "The town was insane. I called it the invasion of the bodysnatchers, because one day you'd see someone and they'd be fine and then the next time you saw them, they'd have beady little eyes, the pinners, and they would kill you for $200. . . . The dealers moved in and they were selling the stuff on the beach, virtually calling guys out of the surf." Bartholomew added, "The second half of the year was the worst, when the northerly winds kicked in and the surf might stay flat for weeks and weeks on end. That's when the smack would really flow, and that was easily the most dangerous time of the year." Some cynical surfers saw this as not a bad thing: it was one way to cut down on crowds. But many individuals and families lost their futures—or their lives—to drugs, and addiction would continue to plague the surf community for decades.

One must consider, however, not only the impact of drugs on surfing. Of equal importance was surfing's impact on drugs. Surfers were not just passive victims; they played a central role in the creation of the sixties drug culture. Allan Weisbecker, for example, took a break from surfing the North Shore to visit the source of his Moroccan hash. As he discovered there, "You could buy 40 bucks' worth and sell it for $1000 stateside. You didn't have to have an MBA to figure out you could make some serious money doing that." Opting for a more accessible source, Weisbecker and a surfer friend soon had a sailboat running bales of pot from Colombia, with one run of twenty thousand pounds netting them each a million dollars. Weisbecker said, "Back then, the whole smuggling thing was just a bunch of long hairs, mostly surfers, throwing bales to their buddies and it was sort of fun. . . . Jimmy Buffett was singing about us so we thought we were pretty cool. A 20-something guy flying around in Lear jets with surfboards in the back? C'mon, it was cool." He was far from alone. Even the top North Shore surfers got in on the act. At one point Jeff Hakman, "Mr. Sunset," sustained his habit by transporting hollow surfboards filled with hashish across the Tijuana border, then upped the ante with a failed drug run from Lebanon using the same hollow-surfboard approach.

A group of Laguna Beach surfers raised this technique to the peak of sophistication in an enterprise that mushroomed, so to speak, into a global drug-smuggling ring worth $200 million, responsible for half the LSD and hash in the United States. The group was known as the Brotherhood of Eternal Love. Its founders had made a couple of keen observations: surf travel was beginning to flourish, much of it to places with good drugs; and surfboards themselves provided a handy stash spot. Surfers thus had a natural excuse to visit drug sources and a way to get drugs back. They started on a small scale, smuggling dope from Mexico on their way back from Baja surf trips. Formally incorporated as a tax-exempt organization in Laguna in 1966, the Brotherhood developed a system of secret bank accounts, false identities, chemical labs cranking out millions of "Orange Sunshine" LSD doses, and smuggling routes from South America, Hawaii, and Central and Southeast Asia.

The Brotherhood's network brought in hash and pot measured not by the ounce or the pound, but by the ton. Surfing's image helped the organization escape the attention of law enforcement. The feds refused to believe that a bunch of hippie surfers were capable of running such a complicated operation. The U.S. government belatedly recognized it as "one of the largest and most complex drug systems in the history of this country's narcotic law enforcement efforts" and added that the drug ring had made Laguna "the psychedelic drug capital of the world."

The Brotherhood had started with idealistic motives, exemplified by founder John Griggs, who believed that meditation and psychedelic drugs would lead to a society-wide spiritual awakening. Griggs fell in with Timothy Leary, who came out to see what these Laguna surfers were doing. Surfing entranced the guru. Leary later gave popular talks titled "The Evolutionary Surfer," which proposed that surfers "are truly advanced people . . . you could almost say that surfers are mutants, throw-aheads of the human race." Surfers, Leary enthused, rode nature's energy bands, expressing their individuality through pure contact with nature. He concluded, "Surfing is the spiritual aesthetic style of the liberated self."

Hanging around the Brotherhood eventually got Leary busted by the local police. Griggs meanwhile died, disillusioned, in 1969 of a major psilocybin overdose. By that time the movement had embraced the more earthly rewards of the drug society, with mountaintop retreats, sprawling ranches, and fast cars. Despite the mystical beliefs of Leary's crowd, one young Laguna surfer recalled that "the bond, the thing

David Nuuhiwa, Brotherhood founder John Gale, and an unidentified youth in Laguna Canyon, 1971, the year Nuuhiwa won his second U.S. surfing championship. (Source: Jeff Divine.)

that tied us up together was surfing and dope and balling." John Gale represented the hedonistic side of the Brotherhood, and the side geared to drug smuggling. A surfer and founder of Laguna's Rainbow Arts Surfboards, he was a free spirit (once gleefully selling dog turds to narcs on a hash buy) but an astute businessman. Gale provided the original brainstorm of using surf travel as an excuse to visit drug sources and hollow surfboards as the smuggling tool. Gale shaped the hollow boards, scouted new smuggling routes on surf trips, and recruited young surfers as mules.

The Brotherhood gave away its smuggling secret in *Rainbow Bridge*, a 1971 film about a commune on Maui and their trek to a Jimi Hendrix concert on Mount Haleakala. The film focused on surfers as cosmic messengers, the advance guard of an enlightened extraterrestrial civilization. Several leading surfers lent their talents, including David Nuuhiwa, Barry Kanaiaupuni, Herbie Fletcher, and, yes, Mike Hynson, the clean-cut kid from *The Endless Summer*, who had now grown out his hair and taken up with the Brotherhood. Hynson was smuggling drugs in hollow boards while living on High Avenue, literally as well as psychochemically, in La Jolla. The film's surreal opening scene depicted a rifleman on horseback shooting a surfer, who turned into a Christlike figure ascending to the heavens. A later scene had surfers cracking open a hollow board and pulling out big bags of hash, which they then joyfully sampled; elsewhere another surfer discussed the ten hits of acid he took in one sitting. The Brotherhood, in fact, used the film as a front for drug smuggling, and it may have helped open the eyes of the feds. An interagency drug task force the following year recommended that "all surfboards coming in from Hawaii should be broken. The indications have been that they do contain hash—however, there are so many surfboards coming in to the United States that it is impossible to break them all." Instead, the report suggested focusing just on the fin and fin box.

The Brotherhood continued to dodge the feds but eventually ran up against less laid-back competitors. In 1982, while free on $250,000 bail from a $2.7 million cocaine bust, Gale lost control of his Mercedes convertible on a turn at high speed near Dana Point Harbor, allegedly evading Mexican cartel enforcers, and ran it through a chain-link fence. His pursuers snatched a briefcase from his car and fled. Gale gave no resistance; the fence had come through the windshield and decapitated him.

Many surfers besides the Brotherhood recognized the economic opportunities of drug smuggling. One was Mike Boyum, a charismatic young American surfer who, like John Griggs of the Brotherhood, viewed surfing and psychedelics as a path toward higher consciousness, as well as a good way to finance surf travel. Jeff Hakman, who had made his own hollow-board drug runs, hung out with Boyum in Bali in the mid-1970s. Hakman would later help found Quiksilver USA, but in 1979, when Hakman was strung out on heroin, Mike Miller bought out his founding shares in Quiksilver for $100,000, a 10 percent stake in the company. Miller was noted for his travels around the Pacific on his sixty-eight-foot catamaran, and he eventually held substantial real estate in Hawaii and Sun Valley, Idaho. In 1997 the feds arrested Miller and his brother on charges of marijuana smuggling, seizing more than $14 million in property and $20 million in cash from a drug network that dated to the early 1970s. Miller pled guilty.

VIETNAM

The other defining feature of the sixties also intersected surf culture. Many male surfers were distracted throughout this period by the military draft, especially all those baby boomers who fueled the California surf explosion and who were now in their late teens or early twenties, precisely the age of interest to draft boards. Many surfers found creative ways to dodge the draft, at least in California; Hawaii had long familiarity with a military presence and Hawaiian surfers accepted military service with less draft-dodging and protesting. A case in point: Jock Sutherland, who had survived his famous session night-surfing Waimea on acid, but was not the stereotypical drug-addled hippie. Well, yes, drug-addled, thanks in part to connections to the Brotherhood of Eternal Love. But it did not seem to slow him down. In the winter of '69 Sutherland set new performance standards on the North Shore, especially tube-riding, to the point where *Surfing* magazine said, "Hey Jock, why don't you lay off for a year and let the rest of the world catch up?" Sutherland complied, by walking into a local Army recruiting office and enlisting.

Sutherland ended up riding out the war in California. Some surfers in the service weren't so lucky and came back scarred by their experience of war—if they made it back at all. They also brought a surfing sensibility to the conflict itself. Out of 2.5 million U.S. military in Vietnam, 350,000 were Californians, or about one in seven. Since a fair fraction of these Californians were surfers, it is a safe bet that the average platoon included a surfer or two. California was also the departure and return point for most servicemen and servicewomen, many of whom trained at California bases—Marines at Camp Pendleton, the Army at Fort Ord, the Navy in San Diego. Surfing defined their character; as Ron Sizemore, the 1962 U.S. surfing champion who found himself in the Ninth Infantry Division, U.S. Army, recalled, "If you let people know that you surfed or word got out that you surfed, yeah, you were a California surfer." Oliver Stone agreed, including a surfer as one of the characters in *Platoon*, his Oscar-winning Vietnam War film.

Soldiers loading up a LARC amphibious truck for some tow-surfing at Cam Ranh Bay, 1967. (Source: Gregg Samp.)

Some of these surfers noticed that Vietnam had a long coastline facing the South China Sea, and U.S. servicemen were soon riding good waves in Cam Ranh Bay, Nha Trang, and Vung Tau. The U.S. military also set up a famous R&R center, called China Beach, farther up the coast near Da Nang. Surfers came out of the jungle on leave, saw the surf, and sent back to the States for surfboards. Before long they had a stash of boards, a shack on the beach, and a name: the South China Sea Surf Club. The club logo featured an M16 rifle crossed over a longboard, which some club members sported as a tattoo. And, with so many nonsurfing soldiers on the beach and in the waves, the U.S. military posted several lucky surfers to China Beach and to Vung Tau's Back Beach as lifeguards, where they served out their tour in safety and style—and showed in-country soldiers what surfing was all about. Soldier-surfers learned to tolerate the occasional VC rocket barrage peppering the lineup and to accept rides to the beach on tanks; one officer flew regularly to Da Nang for supplies with a surfboard strapped under his helicopter.

Surf-crazed helicopter commanders appeared prominently in perhaps the most celebrated Vietnam War movie, *Apocalypse Now*, which highlighted surfing's association with Vietnam. Recall the famous early scene featuring Colonel Kilgore of the Air Cavalry (played by Robert Duvall), who targets a coastal village in order to surf the waves off the point. Informed that the Viet Cong control the village—"That's Charlie's point, sir"—Kilgore declares, "Charlie don't surf!" Kilgore especially wants to see Lance Johnson, a former pro surfer from California, surf the place. (Johnson, true to type, spends the rest of the movie on a drug bender.) After Kilgore's helicopters swoop in, blaring Wagner's "Ride of the Valkyries," he has a couple of surfers test the waves amid harrowing VC mortar fire. Captain Willard to Kilgore: "Are you crazy goddamn it? Don't you think it's a little risky for some R&R?" Kilgore, stripping off his shirt: "If I say it's safe to surf this beach, Captain, then it's safe to surf this beach. I mean I'm not afraid to surf this place, I'll surf this whole fucking place!"

Why did filmmaker Francis Ford Coppola devote twenty minutes of his Vietnam epic to surfing? One might say that Kilgore in his cowboy hat combined the surfer with that other American archetype, producing what the *New York Times* has called "the California surfer as existential cowboy." In Vietnam the surfer supplanted the cowboy and other American stereotypes to make California a particular touchstone. According to *Apocalypse Now* screenwriter John Milius, "The Vietnam War was a California war. . . . It was a clash between California culture and Asian culture. . . . The surfer is a cliché for the Vietnam War in the same way that the kid from Brooklyn stuck in the B-29 tail gunner position was the World War II cliché." War correspondent Michael Herr called Vietnam "some unnatural East-West interface, a California corridor cut and bought and burned deep into Asia." Some American servicemen made a more literal identification of Vietnam as the mirror image of California: they noticed that Vietnam's outline looked like California's upside down, and superimposed an inverted Vietnam over California on U.S. maps. On such maps China Beach became a cartographical twin of San Onofre.

The influence of surf culture extended into the heart of the military-industrial complex. Daniel Ellsberg, a longtime strategist at the Rand think tank in Santa Monica, returned from a tour in Vietnam a pronounced critic of the war. The late 1960s found Ellsberg living in a Malibu beach house, smoking dope—and bodysurfing every day: "there was nothing in the world I liked better." His moral and strategic opposition to the war led him to release the Pentagon Papers, a top-secret report whose publication helped turn the tide against American involvement in Vietnam. Surfing may not have turned Ellsberg against the war. But after staying up all night photocopying the Pentagon Papers, the first thing Ellsberg did was to drive to Malibu and catch some waves.

THE "SHORTBOARD REVOLUTION"

Sixties culture also produced a major change in surfboard design, and with it surfing performance and style. The changes dated back to the 1950s, after Simmons introduced new materials and designs. Shapers began playing with different outlines, rails, and bottom contours, as well as fin shape and fin placement. This experimentation led, by the late 1960s, to the "shortboard revolution." Surfers still debate what the revolution was about, who was in it, and where it took place. But by the 1970s there was a new approach to surfboard design and production.

The revolution took inspiration from an unlikely source: kneeboarding, where surfers ride in a kneeling position instead of standing fully upright. The key figure was George Greenough, born in 1942 and raised on a Santa Barbara estate. Perpetually barefoot, with a haircut self-inflicted with a Swiss army knife, Greenough was an eccentric, creative inventor, tinkering in his backyard on boats, cameras, and surfboards. Greenough had started surfing as a teen in the 1950s but switched to kneeboarding and mat surfing because he liked being closer to the water. He soon discovered that kneeboarding got him into places on the wave longboards could not: carving in the pocket, close to the wave's breaking lip or even under it, what surfers called being in the tube. Greenough logged remarkable tube time in the cylinders of Rincon and at reefs and points to the north at Hollister Ranch. To convey this experience to the uninitiated he designed a shoulder-mounted camera rig and shot in-the-tube footage from his knees for his 1970 film *The Innermost Limits of Pure*

Fun. The band Pink Floyd was so captivated by the footage that they donated music for Greenough's next film and projected it as a backdrop for their concerts. Coca-Cola used Greenough's tube sequences in a 1975 television ad with a similar psychedelic soundtrack.

Greenough started shaping balsa boards in high school wood shop and later, in the mid-sixties, switched to a flexible board boasting a foam outline around a fiberglass center. He added another innovation: instead of the usual blocky, keel-shaped fin, he designed a highly curved fin supposedly inspired by the raked tail fin of a tuna. Greenough traveled to Australia in 1964 and dazzled locals with his high-speed, full-rail arcs and turns. Robert "Nat" Young, a rangy and talented young Aussie, switched to a Greenough fin and won the 1966 World Championships—and shortly afterward described Greenough as "the greatest surfer in the world today."

Bob McTavish, meanwhile, saw Greenough carving on his kneeboard and aimed to allow upright surfers to do the same things on a wave. McTavish, a stocky, brash surfer from Queensland, had visited Santa Barbara in 1966 and seen a short, seven-foot-eight-inch board Greenough had designed years earlier for turning in the pocket. The following year McTavish started shaping shorter boards and adding a new twist, a deep V-shaped keel toward the tail. Nat Young and Wayne Lynch, another talented teenage Australian, tested and popularized the new boards in Australia, showing that they allowed sharper changes in direction and new ways to ride waves.

Some of the finishing touches came from a shaper named Dick Brewer, whose role reveals another connection between surfboard design and the Southern California aerospace industry. Brewer's father had moved the family from Minnesota to Long Beach to take a job at North American Aviation as a machinist. The younger Brewer followed in his father's footsteps, working night shifts as a machinist while studying engineering at Long Beach State. He left college twenty units shy of an engineering degree to become a surfboard shaper, thus also retracing the career path of Bob Simmons. He moved to Hawaii and began shaping boards with narrow tails and noses that overcame the limitations of McTavish's designs in bigger waves.

Jeff Hakman highlighted Brewer's importance: "As far as I'm

concerned, RB was the guy who took a longboard and made it work as a shortboard—outline, fins, edges, lightness, etc. He was the man." Brewer is often left out of standard accounts of the shortboard revolution, perhaps because of his prickly personality. Hakman continued: "It took a long, long time to get a board from him in those days, though the Brazilians could get 'em 'cause they had coke. So I came into the shaping room and Brewer says, 'Here it is, what do you think?' And I looked at it and said, 'Nice, nice,' and then I said, 'The tail seems a little bit pulled in, don't you think?' 'A little pulled?' he asks. 'I can fix that.' And he got a saw and cut a foot off this perfect board, and the pintail just dropped on the floor. 'How's that?' he asked me. 'Is this better for you?' "

Brewer has also been neglected because Australians early and often defined the "shortboard revolution" as an Australian invention. John Witzig set the tone in a chest-thumping article in *Surfer* magazine in 1967, titled "We're Tops Now." Witzig pointed to Young's World Championship in 1966 and declared that Young's " 'power' school of surfing . . . has crushed the 'pansy' surfers of California and the east coast: the 'mediocre' competition surfers have paled into insignificance in the face of his aggression." Such claims did not endear the Aussies to the wider surf world.

Bob McTavish similarly recalled a visit to Hawaii a few years earlier: "We were a little surprised at the stiff and average surfing of many of the big-time North Shore names. In Australia we'd have written them off as total egg rolls. . . . Nice guys, but average surfers." McTavish conveyed some of this attitude directly to the locals, including Brewer. McTavish recalled hanging out in Brewer's shaping room "as he painstakingly crafted beautiful, obsolete guns. I tried to be respectful, but I think I gave him a brash mouthful or two." McTavish also took pot shots at Californians, declaring that with his nine-foot board it was "Goodbye Yater. Goodbye Dora," thus dissing two icons of California surfing. This marked the start of nationalist tension in the international surf community, which came to full fruition in the 1970s. Some Australians would pay a price for brash words in Hawaii.

From one perspective, the so-called shortboard revolution was no revolution at all. Revolutions, on closer historical examination, are rarely very sudden or sharp. McTavish's nine-footer was not all that short, and was still three feet longer than the alaia boards ridden at Waikiki sixty years earlier. One could see the new boards as just one more step in a long-term evolution from alaias to Duke's redwood planks to Blake's hollow boards to postwar foam-and-fiberglass. The new designs consisted of several elements besides shorter boards: the narrowed nose and tail, V-shaped bottoms, and the Greenough fin. These elements came from three different centers—California, Australia, and Hawaii—and merged in a rough consensus for the new shapes. By contrast, earlier innovations, such as Blake's and Simmons's, came from a particular place and source—in these cases, California aerospace. The shortboard revolution merged several widespread changes, in part because the surf community in the 1960s started to go global. The emergence of surf media helped create a shared community and culture, as did the advent of jet air travel in the late 1950s, which allowed Californians, Hawaiians, and Australians regular visits to each other's hotbeds.

One other thing these far-flung surf communities shared was a fondness for drugs, which played a large part in the shortboard revolution. Tales abound of shapers corking bong hits or dropping acid and then turning out radically new designs. Gerry Lopez described a late 1967 meeting of Brewer, Greenough, and the Australians in Hawaii: "A little chemical stimulation helped pique Brewer's interest until he and McTavish were so deeply engrossed in discussing surfboard design that the other Australians finally got in their car, started it up and began beeping the horn before they got Bob to leave. Meanwhile Brewer was all fired up, we followed him over to the shaping room where my blank was sitting on the rack, and he immediately took the saw and cut two feet off the tail." As Allan Weisbecker recalled, or rather didn't recall, "There are large parts of '69 I don't even remember. But I do remember buying blanks from a guy living in a tree house for a baggy of pot, then I'd give Brewer another little baggy to shape it, take it to this guy Wolfman to finish. The whole thing would cost me like 80 bucks. For a Brewer, man! The Holy Grail of boards." Weisbecker concluded, "It's not a coincidence that the acid movement and the revolution in surfing came at the same time. . . . We were so high we would have tried riding a barn door."

This drug use reflected the general atmosphere of upheaval and experimentation we now associate with the sixties. It is no accident the new surfboard designs emerged around 1968, the year youth culture in general declared a revolution. In this view, shortboards were surfers' way of taking part in the revolution. In a bit of generational hyperbole Drew Kampion, editor at *Surfer* in those years, called the shortboard revolution the "greatest conceptual shift in surfing history."

The upshot of all this activity was that within several years surfboards had indeed changed. Some surfers pushed the envelope too far; at the 1969 world championships Wayne Lynch rode a five-foot-eight, Nat Young a five-foot-ten, and both lost. By the end of 1971, boards were settling around the six-foot-six to seven-foot range, still a third shorter than the standard longboard of five years earlier, and shapers were starting to experiment with multiple fins in addition to new templates and bottom contours. The "shortboard revolution" involved more than just the shape of surfboards, however. It also affected production modes, performance, and surfing's geography.

First, surfboard manufacturing shifted from mass production to a craft mode of surfboard production. Instead of major manufacturers like Greg Noll and Dewey Weber churning out thousands of standard models from their factories, surfboard shapers turned to custom boards shaped in backyards and garages. This was in part because shortboards are more sensitive to an individual surfer's size and style. A six-foot board that can float a 140-pound surfer may sink under a 200-pound rider. These two surfers, though, could happily swap waves on the same ten-foot board without noticing too much difference. The shift to craft production also reflected the ethos of the sixties. Counterculture rebellion against large-scale production and technology produced a do-it-yourself movement represented by Stewart Brand and the *Whole Earth Catalog*, and by the emerging "small technology" or "appropriate technology" movement. In this age of backyard tinkerers making their own gear, Greenough was surfing's version of Yvon Chouinard forging his own rock-climbing hardware or Burt Rutan building airplanes in his garage. By the early 1970s, there were hundreds of shapers where previously a handful—Noll, Hobie, Weber, Velzy—had dominated. Surfboard shaping was a craft, not an industry—or, as *Surfer* magazine intoned in the spirit of the times, it was "an art form . . . a 'zen' brain game." But these zen sculptures continued to rely on the complex chemicals—polyether and polyester polyols and isocyanates—cranked out by vast chemical conglomerates and blown into foam by industrial-scale surfboard blank makers.

Shortboards changed the ways surfers rode waves. It let them surf like Greenough kneeboarded: no longer confined to the wave face, safely away from the breaking lip and the steepest part of the wave, they could now carve turns around the pocket of the wave and, above all, try to ride underneath the breaking lip itself. The tube ride replaced the hang ten as the ultimate goal of surfing. This shift in performance also changed the geography of surfing: instead of long, hotdogging point breaks, surfers began seeking out beachbreaks and reefs for the tube rides they offered.

On the North Shore of Oahu one wave in particular emerged as the center of attention for surfers: Pipeline, whose very name conveyed the new surf style. Pipeline in winter presents an awesome spectacle, with twenty-foot waves pitching out over a shallow reef a few dozen yards off the beach. Surfers had tackled Pipeline in the early 1960s but could barely survive it on longboards, let alone really ride its gaping barrels. In the late sixties, surfers armed with the new shortboards tamed Pipe, pulling so deep into the tube that they disappeared entirely behind the lip before shooting out amid a blast of spray as the wave collapsed. It did not hurt that Pipe broke so close to the beach and was front-lit in the morning, which made it an ideal spot for surf photographers from the new surf magazines.

The Pipeline crew, led by Hawaiians Gerry Lopez and Rory Russell, began setting new performance standards with their tube-riding, which embodied the sixties ethos in its emphasis on "going with the flow." A famous photo from that period shows Brewer, Lopez, and fellow Hawaiian Reno Abellira in blissful yoga poses next to their boards. Lopez, in particular, seemed to tap into an almost mystical connection with the waves, an uncanny sense of how waves would break. The Zen approach exemplified by Lopez stood in marked contrast to the aggressive assault of Nat Young and the Aussies, who called their style the "Animal" approach for its raw carnal power. Instead of flowing with the wave, the Aussie approach sought to dominate the wave, and "carving" or "ripping" the wave apart was the ultimate goal. Witzig, naturally, threw down Australia's gauntlet: "We're on top and will continue to dominate world surfing. California surfing is so tied and stifled by restrictions that are its own creation. . . . An end must come to this monotony. Vigor will replace lassitude; aggression will replace meek submission." In the 1970s a new crop of young Aussies brought their aggro approach to Pipeline and helped transform surfing yet again.

THE COUNTERCULTURE AND SURFING: WHAT IT ALL MEANT

The sixties changed surfing's public image. Surfing had earlier evolved from an exotic but harmless tropical pursuit to a mainstream middle-class sport; it now shifted again to something subversive and menacing. Surfers were no longer clean-cut kids enjoying a little wholesome outdoor recreation; they were dope-smoking rebels giving American society and middle-class culture the finger. Surfboard manufacturers were no longer large employers with high-tech, high-volume facilities and responsible management; they were backyard operators trading shaping jobs for bags of pot. For sixties youth, this image added to surfing's appeal, and tens of thousands of new surfers joined Southern California lineups. For all those young baby boomers looking to escape boring middle-class culture, what better way than to load a few surfboards in your VW van and head for the coast? In Gidget's terms, the surf bum Kahuna, not the clean-cut Moondoggie, became the real surfer. This subversive, rebellious image shaped popular perceptions of surfing for decades.

Images, however, do not always match reality. As we know, surfing's clean-cut 1950s image ignored its countercultural undercurrents, and so could the sixties rebellion obscure surfing's continued middle-class conformism. Surfing's contributions to sixties social transformations, that is, were selective. The sixties comprised several main elements—civil rights, feminism, New Left, Vietnam, and the counterculture—only a few of which engaged surfers. The sixties offered two paths, political activism or hedonist escapism. Surfers chose the latter. In general, surfers did not spend the sixties protesting racial and sexual discrimination, social and economic injustice, or bourgeois consumerism. They instead followed Leary's exhortation to "turn on, tune in, drop out."

Thus for Vietnam, individual surfers may have protested the

draft, but apparently often from the selfish motive of avoiding service, not from any deeper consideration of Vietnam's postcolonial history and the geopolitical strategy of containment. And while the image might be of the "California war," with the surfer as the stereotypical soldier, the reality was that Vietnam, the first war with a desegregated American military, was a brown-skinned person's war—and such people, at least in California, didn't surf. Indeed, the vast majority could not swim. Most draftees came from the urban poor, while many middle-class suburban whites rode out the war in college. African Americans bore a disproportionate share of combat: from 1961 to 1966 they accounted for less than 10 percent of the military but close to 20 percent of combat deaths. Surfers fought and died in Vietnam, but so did African Americans, in greater numbers.

The most potent domestic issue of the sixties, civil rights, seems to have escaped the surf community altogether. Surfing, as we shall see, remained an overwhelmingly white sport, involving few blacks or other ethnic minorities outside of Hawaii. In the hot August of 1965, a dozen miles inland from summer swells, black Angelenos sat astride a powder keg in Watts, a sweltering ghetto. With images of Alabama state troopers clubbing and teargassing civil rights marchers in Selma fresh in their minds, African Americans turned a drunk-driving arrest into a six-day race riot that left dozens of people dead, thousands injured, and a thousand buildings in ashes. Some surfers viewed the carnage not as a crisis in American race relations and inner-city poverty, but instead as an excuse for a party. A group of Windansea surfers, in Tom Wolfe's account, "attended the Watts Riots as if it were the Rose Bowl game in Pasadena. They came to watch 'the drunk niggers' and were reprimanded by the same for their rowdiness."

As for feminism, as we shall see, male surfers happily approved the sexual revolution while ignoring women's possible interest in surfing, and continued to view women more as sex objects than as potential fellow surfers. Even when it came to the environment, the political issue one would expect to engage them, surfers stood aloof. *Surfing* magazine lamented in 1970 that "the people who stand to lose the most because of pollution, the surfers, have done the least to protest." Surfer Craig Lockwood summed it up in a 1968 plea for action that fell upon deaf ears: "Surfers are among the most politically powerless groups in the U.S.A. today. We have no voice."

Although individual surfers may have taken part in the sixties political movements, they were not a conspicuous presence, and the surf community as a whole seems to have skipped politics. For all its countercultural trappings—the drug use and drug smuggling, the Maui communes, the surfing soldiers in Vietnam—surf culture remained more reactionary than revolutionary in many respects. Surfers weren't marching on Montgomery or Washington; they were too busy with "surfing and dope and balling."

8 SURFING TURNS PRO

The shortboard revolution of the late 1960s, although overhyped, fostered a new climate in the 1970s. Part of the shift came from a newcomer on the global surf scene: Australia. Surfing's center of gravity had started out in Hawaii, then tilted toward California. In the 1970s it swung Down Under. Aussies brought new attitudes to surfing, including an embrace of competition and a drive to turn surfing from a leisure activity into a professional sport. Although Australian influence on the growth of pro surfing has been overstated, the overstatement itself reflects characteristics of the Aussie contribution.

The growth of pro surfing moderated, but did not erase, surfing's countercultural image, but in one prominent way surfing very much reinforced the dominant culture: it remained an overwhelmingly white (and male) sport in most places outside Hawaii. This was most clearly the case in South Africa, which rode colonial sports enthusiasm to a prominent role in pro surfing while adhering to apartheid. But surfing in Australia and California also showed little ethnic diversity, which suggested that for all its countercultural cachet, surfing very much reflected mainstream attitudes when it came to race.

AUSTRALIA ÜBER ALLES

One reason the "shortboard revolution" was proclaimed so loudly is that the Australians who participated in it were staking a claim on the world surfing stage. Upstart Aussies, resentful of perceived slights by Hawaiians and Californians, felt they had to be brash just to make themselves heard. The emerging Australian surf community differed in several respects from those in Hawaii and California, and those differences would affect surfing everywhere in the 1970s.

Surfing in Australia dated back to Duke's visit in 1914, and the country's abundant beaches encouraged some locals to take up the sport, especially along the eastern seaboard, well exposed to South Pacific swells. Australian surfing sputtered along until sparked by a 1956 visit by several Californians, who brought with them the new lightweight boards dubbed "Malibus" by the Aussies. In those days, before surf magazines and films, design and performance ideas were carried by word of mouth or just by traveling surfers—so particular communities were more isolated, and surf culture was less universal and more local.

What was already thriving in Australia was lifeguarding. Duke's surfing demonstration in 1914 was organized by a lifesaving club, and the Surf Life Saving Association, or SLSA, was crucial to Australian surf culture. Each beach generally had its lifesaving club, which patrolled the beach and also competed in regular meets, or surf carnivals. The highlight of these meets was the march-past, a quasi-militaristic display where club members high-stepped in formation past their competitors, all in uniform with banners flying. The development of lifeguarding in this British dominion early in the century reflected the values of Victorian Britain. Lifesavers not only ensured public safety but also enforced current moral and legal standards of public decency, both for bathing costumes and for how close male and female bathers could get to each other. This context of moral rectitude and discipline stood in marked contrast to the hedonism of Hawaiian beachboys and California beach bums, and the lifesaver became a national icon, a symbol of the manly image of Australia. One of the main centers of Aussie beach culture was, in fact, Manly Beach, named by a British colonial administrator impressed by the vigor of the natives.

The growth of Australia's surf community led to some conflict, as surfing's countercultural associations clashed with militaristic lifeguard culture. Long-haired surfers in baggy trunks mocked the "clubbies" in their swim caps and Speedos (budgie smugglers, to surfers). Lifeguards trying to enforce surfing bans at some beaches almost sparked brawls. More important, though, were the overlaps between lifeguard culture and surfing. Lifesaving clubs provided an entry point for many school-age Aussie grommets, and one much appreciated by parents: they gave kids a supervised hangout on the beach and got them swimming, fit, and ocean savvy.

These attributes, and lifeguarding's frequent club contests, spilled over to surfing, as surfers formed counterpart clubs for their local beach and engaged in regular contests with nearby clubs. This junior circuit bred a generation of young Australian surfers keen on competition and contest tactics. California had surf clubs as well, but these were more a social venue for locals, a base for partying rather than interclub competitions. (Australians, though, could also party as hard as they competed.) Lifesaving culture also influenced Aussie surfing style, which, as we know, stressed aggression and power over flow and glide. The SLSA aimed to subdue and defeat the ocean; Aussies lionized lifesavers as "gladiators of the surf" and "Australians against the sea." Australian surfers reflected this goal of dominating the ocean, of bending it to their will; Hawaiians, by contrast, generally expressed respect for an unpredictable ocean and sought to go with its flow, taking what the wave gave them.

Two other factors underpinned the Aussie surf uprising. One was economic. By the 1960s Australia ranked among the top ten wealthiest nations in the world, per capita; in 1974 it passed the faltering United States. As in the postwar United States, economic prosperity bolstered the Australian middle class and leisure culture, and hence surfing. The other reason was cultural. Australians had long suffered an inferiority complex as a British colony, and one originally populated by felons at that. Australia's convict-colony origins offered the opposite image to that of Hawaii: not a Polynesian paradise enjoyed by leisurely natives in a state of moral grace, but a prison populated by the worst of England's criminal class. Aussie commentators spoke of the "cultural cringe," evident when Australians viewed an Aussie accent as inferior to a proper British accent. These writers lamented that for too many Australians, as the old joke went, "Australia" indeed rhymed with "failure."

This began to change in the 1970s, spurred in part by the growing youth culture (from the same postwar demographics that drove California surfing), and also by the ascendance of a new liberal government after a series of prime ministers who had stressed backward-looking, British-friendly values. These trends reinforced each other, and a general anti-British movement produced an outpouring of national pride by Australians. This busting down of conservative cultural values and the British colonial mentality, with the new belief in a distinct Australian national identity, reverberated in the Aussie surf community.

Economic and cultural trends converged on surfing. Economic modernization in Australia marked a shift from an agricultural to an industrial society, from rural to urban landscapes, and hence from a national identity centered on the bush to one framed around the beach—especially since most of Australia's population lived near the coast. So the "new nationalism" of the late sixties and early seventies seized on a new icon: instead of the fabled bushman of the nineteenth century, the prototype modern Australian was the surfer.

GOING PRO

Growing Aussie pride, filtered through the competitive lifeguard culture, contributed to the growth of a pro tour, which has since been celebrated as the birth of "pro surfing." Since such statements have often come from participants staking their historical claim, similar to those of the shortboard revolution, we should consider them skeptically. But the creation of a world circuit by Hawaiian promoters in the mid-1970s did lead to a career opportunity for contest surfers.

A group of young Australians (plus one South African), all around twenty years old, led a charge against the surfing establishment in the mid-1970s. It didn't hurt that the group included some outsized personalities, with charisma, flair, and media savvy. Most notable in this respect was Wayne "Rabbit" Bartholomew, whose media-friendly persona borrowed explicitly from Muhammad Ali and David Bowie.

Rabbit came out of the highly competitive Gold Coast surf clubs well schooled in aggressive contest tactics, including a well-deserved reputation as a drop-in artist. One of his longtime Gold Coast rivals was Peter Townend, known as PT, whose volubility more than made up for his diminutive stature. PT burnished his public presence with a penchant for riding pink surfboards. Ian "Kanga" Cairns, from Western Australia, presented a rougher front—loud, opinionated, physically and psychologically intimidating, and equally prone to dropping in on fellow surfers. Quieter but equally competitive, Mark Richards (MR) earned the nickname "the Wounded Gull" for his distinctive style, swooping through turns with his long arms outstretched.

Cairns and PT took the media-friendly approach to a new level in 1976 by forming the Bronzed Aussies. The idea was a cross between a surf team and a marketing gimmick, a way to attract sponsors and media attention. The Bronzed Aussies presented a wholesome, clean-cut image, traveling as a team and showing up at surf contests in matching velour sweatsuits adorned with the Bronzed Aussies label. The sweatsuits and the general goody-goody image won them much ridicule from fellow surfers, but the team did momentarily garner some media attention as the apex of Australian professionalism.

Though very much part of the new crew, Shaun Tomson stood apart as a South African. Tomson, articulate and stylishly coiffed, with an upper-class upbringing, had a more polished image. His good looks won him modeling work when surfing did not pay the bills. His Jewish background further set him apart in the surf world. Tomson was not really part of the matey Australian gang; among the menagerie of Kanga, Rabbit, and the Wounded Gull, Tomson was the only one without a nickname. (The Aussies tried to call him "Shaun the Prawn," but Tomson managed to shed the moniker.)

The reputations of Rabbit, Tomson, MR, PT, and Cairns did not just ride on media savvy. The group spent the winter of 1975–76 on the North Shore pushing the performance envelope, especially the tube-riding possibilities of shortboards. Tomson learned to turn in the tube to generate speed, making it in and out of waves that others could not, and Rabbit and PT applied their extensive experience in smaller Gold Coast barrels to the much larger specimens on the North Shore. The group also brought the characteristic Australian approach of aggressive, vertical surfing to the North Shore, tackling big waves at Sunset and Pipe the same way they attacked small waves back home.

That winter of '75 to '76 has acquired the color of legend, helped first of all by their subsequent accounts of it, but also by a film, Bill Delaney's *Free Ride*, which focused (literally) on Rabbit, Shaun, and MR. Delaney financed it in part from a bet on a two-on-two schoolyard basketball game and persuaded Jan-Michael Vincent to narrate it. *Free Ride* featured not only remarkable surfing performances at Off-the-Wall and Pipeline, but also groundbreaking camera work by Dan Merkel, who daringly swam a 16-millimeter camera into the lineup and inside gaping North Shore tubes. Merkel's up-close, slow-motion sequences of surfers passing by him in the tube were a credit to his swimming ability and lensmanship, and defined what became known as the "Free Ride generation," comprising the Aussies plus Tomson. They also inspired the makers of *Big Wednesday* to hire Merkel the following year for water cinematography. *Free Ride* also popularized the notion of pro surfing. Five years earlier, the landmark film *Five Summer Stories* had portrayed surfing as a lifestyle, not a competitive sport. But in the intervening five years the sport aspect had gained acceptance, and *Free Ride* pointedly referred to the *sport* of surfing.

The Free Ride generation loudly proclaimed its arrival. In a *Surfer* interview in May 1976, modestly titled "We're Number One," Ian Cairns compared his Aussie cohort with the Hawaiians: "Our surfing has improved outrageously; whereas theirs, as a group, has stagnated slightly." Rabbit stirred more outrage with a subsequent *Surfer* article titled "Bustin' Down the Door": "The fact is that when you are a young emerging rookie from Australia or Africa, you not only have to come through the backdoor to get invitations to the Pro meets, but you have to bust the door down before they hear ya knockin'." Rabbit heralded "the hard rock-ripping, full-tilt boogie band, which, in true 'Story of Pop' fashion, has for its first time climbed to the top of the hit parade, and now band members such as Shaun, Kanga and Mark Richards are top-billed features at many inside-out, upside-down jam sessions."

All of this—the boasting, the drop-ins, the matching track suits—rubbed some surfers the wrong way. Especially the Hawaiians. When the Australians arrived the following winter for the annual North Shore sojourn, Hawaiians greeted them with death threats and, in Rabbit's case, a beating. Rabbit and Cairns spent much of the winter in hiding, fearing for their lives. The immediate threat abated only after the Aikau family, well-respected locals, intervened, persuading the Hawaiians to back off and in the process teaching a chastened Rabbit and the Aussies something about the Hawaiian Islands' history of appropriation by outsiders. But the bad blood between Australians and Hawaiians lingered for years.

In the meantime an arena was emerging where Aussies could express their competitive urges. Later claims that this group midwifed the birth of pro surfing depend on the definition of "pro surfing." Surfers going back to Freeth and Duke earned a living at least in part from surfing, and sponsored pros proliferated in the late 1950s and 1960s. Contests had likewise been around for decades, with huge crowds converging on the Makaha International Championships in the 1950s and then on the periodic World Championships in the 1960s. The Duke contest in 1969 offered a cash prize of $1,000; the following year the Smirnoff offered a total pot of $6,000, half of it to first place; and Australian contests were dangling even bigger purses.

By 1975 the North Shore hosted three premier contests: the Pipe Masters, the Duke at Sunset, and the Smirnoff at Waimea. That year's Smirnoff top placings: MR, Cairns, and Rabbit. (MR at the time was eighteen years old.) But while Aussies were starting to reap the rewards of the emerging contest circuit, a couple Hawaiians were the organizers and promoters behind it. Fred Hemmings and Randy Rarick were accomplished surfers, Hemmings in the sixties, the younger Rarick in the early seventies. Both were *kama'aina haoles*: light-skinned people born in or longtime residents of Hawaii. Rarick had surfed in contests before dropping out for extensive surf travels around the world. Hemmings won the World Championships in 1968, beating Nat Young, among others. He then shifted into contest promotion, winning sponsors for a contest at Makaha in 1970 and the Pipe Masters starting in 1971, and persuading TV networks to cover surf contests. Hemmings was a bit of a black sheep in the surfing community, not as a counterculture rebel but as precisely the opposite; when he won the world title he showed up for the awards banquet in suit and tie and close-cropped hair—this in 1968. His conservative style did not hew to the surf community's expectations (he later won a seat in the Hawaii state legislature as a Republican), and his willingness to knock heads together to get things done won him the nickname "Dead-Ahead Fred."

In 1976 Hemmings and Rarick formed an outfit called International Professional Surfers (IPS), with the goal of unifying the pro contests into one system, with uniform judging standards, scoring, and ratings points for each contest; the world title would be based on end-of-the-year ratings, similar to tennis or Formula One. The IPS in effect was a sanctioning organization; it gave out no prize money itself but set the standards for contests in every country. Hemmings had the promoting experience and affiliation with the Hawaiian events, and Rarick knew the contest organizers in Australia, South Africa, and elsewhere thanks to his travels. Rarick called up these promoters, who happily agreed to include their contests in a world tour since it provided free publicity. Most surfers didn't even know that a tour was in the works, but Townend and Cairns had an inkling and made sure they showed up for all the contests to accumulate points. So when Hemmings and Rarick counted back to award points for earlier contests in 1976, the title went to Townend. A sense of jerry-rigging marked the nascent tour; for the ceremony bestowing the world title on Townend, held at the Outrigger Club, Hemmings realized he had no trophy to award. He nabbed one from the Outrigger's trophy case behind them and turned it around so the engraving didn't show; the assembled media took the obligatory photos of the champ with his trophy, and when the photo op ended the trophy went back in the case.

The advent of the pro tour did not suddenly mean surfers were rolling in dough. When they formed the pro tour, many surfers probably thought that they'd be raking in hundreds of thousands of dollars by 1980. In 1977 Shaun Tomson won the world title and counted total winnings for the year of about $20,000, most of it eaten up by travel expenses. Far from making a living, he was barely breaking even. And that was the guy on top of the heap, not the dozens of guys finishing lower and making even less. MR was perhaps the first to really make money, earning $25,000 in winnings in 1979 plus another $15,000 from surf-industry sponsors, enough to buy himself a Porsche. And for these young men in their early twenties there were other compensating factors: some of the young pros happily upheld surfing's sexualized image with the nubile young women who hung around surf contests.

The formation of the world tour had elements of the Hawaiians-versus-Australians standoff, with Hemmings and Rarick resenting Australian claims of having invented pro surfing. The surf media viewed the Australians (plus Tomson) as the driving force in part because their competitiveness and charismatic personalities attracted attention. But so did their performance in the water. Hawaiians may have preferred dues paid in the form of respect to locals, but the Aussie visitors paid a different price in punishing wipeouts at Pipeline, Off the Wall, and Sunset, earning grudging respect even from some North Shore locals. Aussie domination of the tour's first years reinforced their belief that they were laying the foundation: after PT won the inaugural title in '76, Tomson won in '77, Rabbit in '78, and then MR for four years running before Tom Carroll won two more for Australia. The first nine world titles went to Australia and South Africa, with none to Hawaii or California. This was not a coincidence, a fluke based on the appearance of especially ballsy and talented individuals in the same generation. Rather, it stemmed from the general competitive ethic, the surfer-as-athlete perspective, cultivated in the colonial sports hotbeds of Australia and South Africa, and specifically from Australian lifeguard culture and emerging Australian national identity.

But pro surfing involved more than the Free Ride generation. The IPS was created by and for the contest directors, not the surfers. There was a reason for that. As Rarick put it, "you couldn't get two surfers to agree on the time of day," and expecting the surfers themselves to organize the logistics and finances of a fourteen-event, yearlong tour spanning several continents was asking for trouble. Some surfers, however, argued that surfers should run the show. Although Hemmings and Rarick were accomplished surfers, with contest results to prove it, the Aussies viewed them as mere promoters. And not very successful ones at that, as expectations of rapid growth—that surfing would soon be as lucrative as, say, tennis, the usual point of comparison—soon led to disappointment.

The Bronzed Aussies in particular pushed for faster growth, and led a palace revolt that resulted in the new Association of Surfing Professionals led by Ian Cairns. Hemmings, relegated to running the Hawaiian contests, declared, "Ian Cairns is an asshole. I created him. He came to my contests for years, and now look what he's done." Cairns, who was in fact not so far in his dead-ahead philosophy from Hemmings, declared that "the days of hippies and the sixties and seventies are now over"—in short, "surfing goes corporate." With surfers—specifically, Cairns—on top, more money went directly to surfers instead of promoters. But surfers did not make the best administrators, and dysfunctional committees plagued the tour. Rarick recalled "ridiculous meetings." "There was just never a consensus, nothing ever got done. The first few years of the ASP were just nightmare marathons. We'd sit there for five days discussing the drop-in rule."

Australians dominated the ASP, starting at the top with Cairns, and one of their first acts was to shift the end of the tour from Hawaii to Australia. Under the IPS the tour had ended in the Hawaiian winter, which meant contests that tested the pros in big surf on the North Shore. The Hawaiian winter, however, coincided with Australian summer, which meant big crowds on Australian beaches for contests. Aussies went with the "bums on the beach" philosophy (bums meaning backsides, not deadbeats), and preferred the media spectacle offered by big crowds over that of big waves. The result: the world tour was decided in smaller Australian waves, far from the sport's ancestral home—a symbolic upending of surfing's values.

Ensuing surf tour politics cost some surfers their careers. In response to the ASP's shift, Hemmings created the Triple Crown, a sort of mini-tour consisting of the three main North Shore events, still held during Hawaii's winter—in conflict with the Australian season-ending leg. Cairns and the ASP, who wanted all the top pros at their events Down Under, declared that tour surfers could not surf in the Triple Crown. Hawaiian surfers said, in effect, screw that, and surfed in their home contests. The ASP fined them $1,000 each. A few Hawaiians paid up, but a few refused, including Dane Kealoha, then one of the top contenders for the world title. The ASP refused to lift the fine and Kealoha lost his place in the standings. An embittered Kealoha left the tour at the age of twenty-five, at the peak of his talent. His fellow Hawaiians viewed the episode as another chapter in the Hawaii-Australia rivalry—a sort of petty Australian payback for the beatings and stink-eye doled out by Hawaiians to uppity Aussies. Hawaiians felt damned either way: pro contests brought aggressive crowds, but when the pro tour shunned the North Shore, it snubbed Hawaii's historic place at the center of surfing.

Not everyone welcomed the new professional movement. Once again surfing's romantic, countercultural ideals confronted the money-driven modern world of consumer capitalism. One reason it took so long to get a tour started was resistance among surfers, in what became known as the "sport versus art" debate. So-called soul surfers contended that surfing was a medium of individual aesthetic expression, and that professionalization and commercialization perverted an essentially spiritual pursuit. Claiming to objectively judge a surfer's wave was akin to assigning a score to a piece of art. Hawaiian Kimo Hollinger saw "the system" at work at a Waimea Bay contest: "The kids started paddling out with numbers on their bodies. Numbers! It was incongruous to the point of being blasphemous. . . . The system is like an octopus with long legs and suckers that envelop you and suck you down. The free and easy surfer, with his ability to communicate so personally and intensely with his God, is conned into playing the plastic numbers game with the squares, losing his freedom, his identity, and his vitality, becoming a virtual prostitute."

Such views had killed earlier movements, in the late sixties, to combine the various contests into a world tour, and in the early seventies several top surfers dropped out of contests, including Rolf Aurness, the 1970 world champ. In 1970 prominent surf journalist Drew Kampion proclaimed the "Death of All Contests" in a *Surfer* article and instead advanced the idea of "Expression Sessions," which brought several leading surfers together in a demonstration with no judging. Groovy idealism did not overcome petty rivalries. At the inaugural Expression Session that year, Hawaiian surfers protesting their exclusion in favor of "chickenshit California surfers" sparked a brawl at the opening "good karma party."

WHATEVER HAPPENED TO CALIFORNIA?

Above all, the surfing-as-art view kept pro surfing out of that linchpin of the global surf community, California. *Free Ride* and the ASP signified the ascendance of the Australian view, against Hawaiian resistance. But where was California in this story? California had been central to surfing in the early sixties, but faded from the picture in the 1970s, when Australia and Hawaii dominated the frame. Not only did no Californians win a title in the tour's first nine years; none even came close. In 1975 *Surfing* magazine ran a cover story titled "Where Are the Hot Californians?" Another article asked, "Is California Terminally Ill?"

Drugs wreaked havoc in California, with the Brotherhood and others making them readily available. But drugs decimated surf towns in Australia and Hawaii as well. Aussies said instead that Californians had missed the new performance wave, and were still trying to hang ten when Australians were ripping waves with their power approach on shortboards. Californians, however, were as quick as anyone to embrace shortboards. California also suffered, as we shall see, from crowding. Thanks to the earlier surf boom, there were more surfers than waves by the 1970s, and young surfers just could not get enough rides to hone their talents.

One main issue was that California lacked the competitive climate of Australia. Californians had organized a few events, such as nose-riding contests based on time spent in a hang ten, but while these often featured high gamesmanship they were not as organized or cutthroat as the Aussie circuit. California surfers had looked to Hawaii for inspiration (recall the "coast haoles") and imbibed a noncompetitive ethic, and hence embraced the surfing-as-art movement. Californians displayed not only apathy but downright resistance to the sport movement. The night before a contest sponsored by Smirnoff at Santa Cruz in 1969, locals tipped the judging stand off the bluff at Steamer Lane. The Smirnoff moved the next year to Hawaii, and California did not host a world-tour event until 1981.

Another, broader factor drove the sense of malaise in California surfing. In 1977 *Time* magazine asked, "Whatever happened to California?" Southern California in the early 1970s entered a deep economic recession. The space race sputtered after Apollo, and détente with the Soviets accompanied a decline in defense spending. After two decades of boom times, the aerospace economy entered a tailspin, amplified by the ensuing economic shock of the oil crisis, and layoffs and cutbacks percolated resentment through Southern California's society. To economic woes one could add sewage and pesticides in the ocean, smog in the air, and a general hangover of anxiety after the boom years of the fifties and sixties. *Time* concluded, "California has clearly lost the magic it once had." As middle-class California struggled to keep its head above water, surfing floundered along with it.

After the emergence of the world tour and Australian dominance, some Californians decided if you can't beat them, join them. In 1980 the fledgling National Scholastic Surfing Association, an amateur surfing group, hired Townend and Cairns as coaches in an explicit attempt to import the Aussie competitive model. The former Bronzed Aussies soon set about incubating a new generation of Californians with a junior contest circuit. In the meantime, a renewed defense buildup starting in the late 1970s got a huge boost under Reagan in the 1980s, and the revival of the aerospace industry brought good times back to Southern California.

The general revival and the NSSA in particular restored California's place in world surfing. Although this is often portrayed as a success story, one may also see it as a loss. It reduced youth surfing to competition and raised successive generations of California kids on heat strategy and point-counting instead of enjoying and developing their surfing. The pro tour in general, which developed objective judging standards in pursuit of fairness, aided by the surf media, which propagated images of performance standards around the globe, replaced individual expression with a uniform style designed to please judges. The Free Ride generation were known for their distinctive individual styles, from MR's knock-kneed, wide-winged swoops to PT's soul arches and Tomson's wide-stanced weaving, but the pro tour that they helped midwife led to a homogenization of surfing style. By the mid-eighties *Surfer* magazine ran an article titled "Is Style Dead?" A few years later Hawaiian Reno Abellira's lament for the loss of "Hawaiian style" extended to idiosyncratic approaches from anywhere: "If aloha is really out and aggro is king, then riding waves with any special

Hawaiian flavor attached—or any flavor at all, for that matter—is history."

Pro surfing had one additional effect—on the attitude toward drugs. Here Hemmings and the Aussies saw eye to eye. The Australian surf lifesaving movement had presented a clean-cut athletic front against the drug-addled hippies of the sixties, and surfing's Free Ride crew similarly challenged surfing's drug associations in their arguments for surfing as an elite competitive sport. Mark Richards attacked the general view of surfers as "drug addict dole bludgers," and Shaun Tomson acknowledged Michael Peterson, perhaps the most talented Australian of the early 1970s but also a prodigious drug abuser, as "a great surfer" but added, "That guy held surfing back. He held sponsorship back from the sport." The new clean-cut image, however, belied the sources of money underpinning the pro tour.

THE WIDE WORLD OF SPORTS

Surfing was not the only sport to go pro in this period. Several other previously marginal sports, with similarly rebellious, outlaw images of beer-drinking bums and social misfits, also started formal contest or tournament circuits in this period, with sponsors and prize money. This broader trend reflected not the agitation of a few aggro Aussie surfers, but rather deep-seated changes in American sport, television, and advertising, which found their way through circuitous routes into surfing.

In the 1960s, for example, beach volleyball developed a loose collection of local tournaments with prizes on the order of a case of beer to the winners. In 1974, 250 spectators watched the first commercially sponsored tournament, with Winston cigarettes offering $1,500 in prize money; a couple years later, 30,000 gathered for a tourney sponsored by Olympia beer, with a $5,000 first prize. A couple years after that Jose Cuervo tequila sponsored a whole tournament circuit, joined a few years later by Miller Brewing Company. By 1983 a formal Association of Volleyball Professionals ran twelve tournaments with $137,000 in total prize money from Miller. Similarly, but earlier, bowling had ridden a wave of postwar popularity to the emergence of formal tournaments with prize money and, in 1958, the creation of the Pro Bowlers Tour, which was soon regularly covered by ABC Sports and sponsored by Miller beer. Drag racing likewise went from an informal network of races to a national circuit under a formal body, the NHRA, with commercial sponsors gradually increasing the prize money.

Winston, Olympia, Cuervo, Miller . . . one detects a trend. For all of these marginal sports the tobacco and alcohol industries were pivotal early sponsors. The trend reflected broader developments, in particular greater willingness by the federal government coming out of the 1960s to regulate social behavior. One key event was the passage of the Public Health Cigarette Smoking Act, which banned cigarette advertising on TV. The law took effect January 2, 1971 (not New Year's Day, mind you: tobacco firms lobbied to keep their ads on the college football bowl games). Tobacco executives reasoned that perhaps they could no longer advertise on TV—but what if they supported sporting events that just happened to have TV coverage? They would not be buying ad time, but their name and product would feature prominently on screen. So tobacco firms jumped into indirect advertising by sponsoring televised sporting events. Established sports like baseball and football certainly benefited from tobacco advertising, but instead of putting their name on the World Series or Super Bowl, tobacco firms found cheaper opportunities in previously marginal sports like auto racing, bowling, tennis—and surfing.

In 1975, an R. J. Reynolds marketing executive toured Hawaii. After first noting that R. J. Reynolds's Salem brand was lagging far behind its main competitor, Kool (whose name, he lamented, especially resonated in the islands), he came away enthused about the marketing opportunities: "The most popular sports activities are water related and . . . the most renowned, of course, is surfing. . . . Surfing is 'big business' in Hawaii." He added that a cigarette brand would fit perfectly on a surfboard deck. The trip including meetings with Fred Hemmings and Wally Iaea, head of the Hawaiian Surfing Association, and the marketing exec recommended that R. J. Reynolds sponsor amateur surf contests with up to $20,000. He noted that "the renowned sport of Hawaiian Surfing" might help them "reach our target audience, the young adults," though they would want "to avoid sponsoring events that are designed for children." That particular deal failed to materialize, but

Skoal chewing tobacco sponsored the Pipe Masters in the 1970s, and for three decades, from 1970 to 1999, the Gunston tobacco company sponsored the Gunston 500 in Durban, South Africa, one of the main stops on surfing's pro tour. The relationship ended only when South Africa passed a law banning all tobacco advertising, including sports sponsorships. Rarick recalls wondering about the Skoal deal, "Oh my God, can we really do this?" But tobacco companies loved surfing's youthful image and demographic, and Rarick and Hemmings overcame their qualms: "At that stage of the game it was: take anything we could get. And it was totally against our nature."

Meanwhile, the American Distilled Spirits Council was honoring a self-imposed ban on TV advertising in order to fend off stricter regulation of print and billboard ads. (This self-imposed ban eroded in the 1990s, as today's TV viewers know.) But like their tobacco colleagues, they realized that sponsoring sports events provided a neat way around that restriction and still got their brand on TV, perhaps even more consistently than in isolated commercials. Beer companies, though not restricted, soon followed suit. Hence the Winston, Cuervo, and Miller beer beach volleyball tournaments; Miller bowling events; Virginia Slims tennis tourneys; and race cars festooned with Budweiser and Miller logos.

It therefore should not have been surprising to see surfers Mark Foo and Brian Bulkley stroll onto the North Shore in the early 1980s with boards airbrushed nose to tail with Budweiser and Michelob logos, thanks to sponsorship from Anheuser-Busch. The beer boards were, literally, a sign of the times. Smirnoff supported the most prestigious surf contest from 1969 to 1977 and sponsored 1978 world champ Rabbit. Jose Cuervo stepped in after Smirnoff, and other early sponsors included Lancers and Lucky Lager, which provided the additional perk of a case of beer in each contestant's hotel room. Later, Budweiser in the United States and Foster's and 4X in Australia sponsored contests and junior circuits.

In the 1980s the surf industry itself grew large enough to sponsor contests, and today Quiksilver, Billabong, Reef, and other major surf firms underwrite the main contests. Although a few surfwear companies in the 1970s sponsored events, contest organizers at that time—like their colleagues in other marginal sports—often had to look to other industries

Mark Foo on his Michelob board, circa 1984. (Source: Bob Barbour)

for financial backing. It was their good fortune to find alcohol and tobacco firms seeking new marketing outlets and demographics. Surfing in particular needed money from outside sponsors; unlike other sports, it had no "gate"—it made no money off tickets for spectators, unless it fenced off the beach. Lacking this revenue stream, surf promoters looked to outside sponsors for funds—and found them in alcohol and tobacco companies.

One reason for the attraction of these marginal sports to sponsors was increasing television coverage. Pro surfing in Hawaii got wide exposure in this period thanks to ABC's *Wide World of Sports*. What was ABC doing on the North Shore? The network created *Wide World* in the early 1960s to get into sports telecasting; the program covered marginal sports because ABC could acquire TV rights for little or no money, unlike football, baseball, or basketball. (And it got off the ground in large part thanks to alcohol and tobacco advertisers.) So *Wide World* covered figure skating, rodeo, water-skiing, cliff diving, bowling, track and field—and surfing. Hemmings and Rarick were happy to provide the TV rights to their contests for a song in exchange for the visibility, which attracted sponsors.

These developments were as important to the emergence of pro surfing as the activism of contest-happy Australians, and they help explain why the pro tour emerged in the 1970s and not earlier. This is not to take away from the performance standards pushed by the Free Ride generation. Rather, it is to note that "bustin' down the door" would have meant little if there hadn't been sponsors standing on the other side with pots of money. If surfers noticed the irony of presenting themselves as healthy, drug-free athletes while alcohol and tobacco underwrote their sport, they overlooked it as a necessary expedient.

In short, surfing was not the only sport to go pro at the time. From bowling to bass fishing, from hot rods to beach volleyball, a host of marginal sports, many with an outlaw image, formed pro tours in this period. The trend reflected leisure culture, increasing federal regulations, television advertising contracts and constraints, and sponsors' marketing strategies, especially in the tobacco and alcohol industries. For many of these sports, professionalization led to complaints that "suits" had taken over the sport—that it had been corrupted by Madison Avenue types who had never surfed (or rebuilt an engine or spiked a volleyball). But for surfing, the suits did not run the sport. If they did it might have done better. With ASP's board dominated by young men in their twenties with no college education and no business experience, it is a wonder that surfing managed to attract any money at all.

Or, rather, public and commercial interest came not from the business savvy of the tour but rather from the intrinsic attraction of the sport itself, and from the persistence of its subversive attitude, even amid the trappings of commercialism. At the Pipe Masters contest in the epic winter of '75, ABC's crew was on the beach waiting to roll film. The surf was pumping, with thirty-foot faces exploding on the shallow reef scant yards offshore. The director asked for a shot of surfers waxing up their boards and charging into the surf. But when he called "Action!" the assembled surfers stayed on the sand, warily watching a set detonate on the reef while they waited for a lull. The director strode up to demand that they follow instructions. Hawaiian pro Rory Russell replied with a profanely graphic suggestion that was, alas, drowned out by the surf.

SURFING AND RACE

Although part of surfing's appeal lay in its countercultural image, in one crucial aspect surfing reinforced mainstream culture: race. It remained a sport practiced almost exclusively by whites (as well as by males). Almost every other American sport was integrated during the twentieth century, albeit with substantial resistance, and even country club sports like golf and tennis had seen some limited inroads before Arthur Ashe, Tiger Woods, and the Williams sisters brought color to the top of their sports. Surfing had Hawaiians, in all their ethnic complexity, but was otherwise conspicuous in its whiteness. Duke, as we know, managed to sidestep prejudice aimed at African Americans. Surfing's lack of color applied not only to the mainland United States but also to Australia, in particular to Aborigines, and above all to another new member of the surf community, South Africa.

How did South Africa join the surfing world? Most accounts focus on Shaun Tomson's sudden emergence in the 1970s, but he was just the first of many competitive surfers to emerge from South Africa. Surfing there dated to the 1920s, both from locals reading about it and from a visiting Australian who gave demonstrations in Durban. In the 1930s local lifesaving clubs began making hollow boards, but the surf community remained very small when Bruce Brown visited in 1963. *The Endless Summer* led to greater interest, especially after the discovery of Jeffrey's Bay, one of the world's premier point breaks. As important, South Africa resembled Australia in that it was a former colony, with a similar competitive, sports-oriented culture. The government included a National Sports Council to promote athletic ability, and hence national pride. The Council underwrote the trips of South African surfers, including Tomson, to Hawaii; in 1975 it sent a team of nine South Africans for the North Shore season.

South Africa, of course, had an uglier distinguishing characteristic. In 1948 the ruling white minority initiated the official policy of apartheid, a system of legal segregation and discrimination against blacks.

The apartheid laws covered all aspects of society, including surfing. In 1960 white politicians discovered that "land" as defined in apartheid laws did not include anything below the high-tide line, so they passed an amendment extending apartheid to include the beach and ocean out to three miles and dispatched lifeguards and police to enforce the segregation. The racial policy may have contributed to the South African government's support of surfing. Starting in the 1960s, international sports including track and field, soccer, and swimming began excluding South African athletes as a protest against apartheid. Surfing remained one of the few unsanctioned sports, and hence offered an international stage for South African athletes.

Like Duke in America, visiting Hawaiians were caught up in South African racial discrimination. Eddie Aikau visited for a contest in 1972 and found himself barred from "white" hotels and beaches. Local authorities had to issue a special permit for him to surf at the contest beach, and he ended up staying with Shaun Tomson's family. After the growth of the pro tour in the 1970s, the South African leg forced pro surfers, individually and collectively, to consider the politics of racism, as Hawaiians such as Dane Kealoha again faced discrimination there. In the 1980s international pressure increased on the South African regime, and surfers joined in. Four leading surfers—Australia's Tom Carroll and Cheyne Horan, California's Tom Curren, and South Africa's Martin Potter—boycotted contests there in 1985, despite the potential cost to their careers. The pro tour itself, however, continued to hold the South African events, and most pros elected to compete—three-fourths of the top sixteen in 1985, and over half in 1986. Other nations retaliated: Brazil refused a visa to Shaun Tomson, which kept him out of the Brazil contests; protests before a Barbados contest targeted top pros who had surfed the South Africa events. The ASP tour director declared that surfing did not involve politics, a refrain taken up by many surfers—including Tomson, who publicly criticized the apartheid regime but also argued passionately against political interference in sport. As a result, however, surfing distinguished itself as one of the only international sports willing to hold events in South Africa. The pro tour continued to hold contests in lineups that were off-limits to black South Africans.

Whites-only beach near Cape Town, South Africa, 1976. (Source: Getty Images)

Only after the downfall of apartheid in the early 1990s could blacks freely surf beaches in South Africa.

South Africa provided an extreme case of legal discrimination, but racial discrimination certainly existed elsewhere—including Australia, whose immigration policy for most of the twentieth century was known as "White Australia." These policies, and the history behind them, help explain why almost no Aborigines surfed. This was not because they didn't like it, but because of demographics and access. The British colonists settled along the coast and decimated indigenous coastal populations with disease and physical violence. Surviving coastal Aboriginals were then gradually herded into settlements in the outback and effectively cut off from the beach. And the lifesaving clubs, with their quasi-military, uniformed march-pasts, did not exactly encourage racial minorities to hang around the beach.

So while some Aboriginals surfed, they were the exception. In 1971 Bob Cooper Surfboards in Australia ran a magazine ad featuring Aboriginal surfers, a novelty that only highlighted Aborigines' absence from surf media—at least until very recently, when indigenous surfer Dale Richards began moving up the Australian pro ranks. Race in Australia, however, was not confined to Aborigines. It was rather a triangular relationship, with Aborigines as an internal presence to be subjugated and Asians an immigrant presence to be excluded. In 1901 the new Australian parliament passed the Immigration Restriction Act, more popularly known as the "White Australia" policy, which curtailed non-European immigration and targeted Pacific Islanders and Asians previously imported to work in the Queensland sugarcane fields.

The government dismantled the White Australia policy in the 1960s and '70s, extending basic rights to Aborigines and accepting Asian immigration. That represented a landmark improvement in race relations, but it did not end the legacy of racial discrimination. Despite happy talk about multiculturalism, increasing Aboriginal visibility and rising Asian immigration sparked a backlash. The rise of the One Nation party and its racist populism in the 1990s demonstrated the persistent potency of racial issues in Australia. And the image of Australian surfing remained overwhelmingly white and male.

Of course, one did not see a lot of African Americans surfing in the United States. Beaches were often not congenial places for minorities. In 1960s Florida, civil rights activists organized "wade-ins" to highlight the existence of segregated beaches, leading to scenes of billy-club-wielding police beating blacks on American beaches. The issue was not limited to the Jim Crow South. California surfers, as we know, were not noted for their contributions to the civil rights movement, and de facto segregation extended to the beach. By the 1920s, redlining real-estate covenants kept African Americans from buying property near the beach. In 1924 the city of Manhattan Beach claimed eminent domain over the homes of several African American families and evicted them from a beachfront neighborhood known as Bruce's Beach. At a "swim-in" at Bruce's Beach in 1927 police arrested the head of the local NAACP chapter and several others. Although Manhattan Beach officials capitulated, the city and county of L.A., fearing that blacks might manage to acquire beachfront property, meanwhile began buying beaches to ensure they would remain white. African Americans wound up barred from almost all local beaches, through either formal ordinance or informal intimidation, which meant black L.A. residents were paying taxes to buy beaches they couldn't visit.

After subsequent confrontations between black beachgoers and the police at several L.A.-area beaches, blacks began congregating at a polluted patch of sand near Bay Street in Santa Monica, which became known as the "Ink Well." In the early 1940s Nick Gabaldon taught himself to surf at the Ink Well and was soon a regular at Malibu. He died in June 1951 after colliding with the Malibu pier during a big south swell. Black surfers since then have been few and far between. In 1965, *Ebony* ran a feature on eighteen-year-old Frank Edwards of Hermosa Beach, who was one of two African American students in his graduating class at Redondo Union High School. Edwards was one of a "minute number of Negroes who have taken up the sport of surfing." A native of Alabama who grew up with relatives in California, Edwards started surfing at fourteen years of age, rode for the Jacobs Surf Team, and placed fourth at the international surfing championships in Santa Monica. Stanley Frison, another Alabama transplant, was a standout at Malibu later in the decade. In the 1990s, Cab Spates, a pro surfer from Virginia Beach, still appeared as a novelty, "one of the few black surfers to be found in American lineups."

In 1979 one surfing magazine ran an article titled "Why Blacks Don't Surf." The article found the answer in lack of beach access, lack of tradition, and a lack of role models. It did not consider racial attitudes within the surf community. A few years later, *Surfer* magazine juxtaposed dark-skinned Hawaiian surfer Buttons Kaluhiokalani with a photo of a gorilla. There was also that prominent feature of postwar California surf culture, the "Surf Nazis," which featured German army uniforms, Nazi salutes, and swastikas spray-painted on the Malibu wall, and later became a popular term to describe hard-core, dedicated surfers. The surfers involved would say this was just young kids getting a rise out of square grown-ups, a way to give society the finger with some souvenirs their dads brought home from the war. But while it might have seemed harmless fun to the surfers doing it, to those not in the group, including potential surfers, these images likely appeared in a different light. It is especially hard to excuse these antics when they were only a decade or two removed from Auschwitz.

And for some of the surfers involved, it was apparently not just harmless fun. Miki Dora was notorious for spray-painting swastikas on his board at Malibu. This may have been part of his rebellious image, but consider where Dora ended up living for many years: South Africa in the apartheid era. An earlier Dora story had him manning an *anti*-civil-rights desk at a 1965 UCLA protest. In later letters Dora ranted about Mexicans and "niggers" overrunning the United States and declared, "From now on I love American Nazis." With good waves and apartheid, South Africa may have appeared a congenial spot for exile. While there he apparently developed friendships with blacks as individuals, even as he adhered to a generalized racism. In a letter in 1986 from "deepest darkest Africa," he wrote about the blacks: "They're not like the blacks in the US who just kick your ass and take your wallet. These MF's are flesh-eaters. Give these guys the rights and you'll get white-man jerky for export." In the early 1990s, eyeing the imminent collapse of apartheid, Dora wrote: "Everything is going to hell in S.A. [South Africa]. . . . I'm trying to make a move to South America somewhere before the Blacks take everything." Nat Young has lent credence to such a view: "Dora's take is push the black man under. He's a supreme racist, always has been. When I was younger, I believed it was all just in mirth, that he was just jivin' it all; but no, he believes absolutely in white supremacy."

As a youth in mid-twentieth-century America, Dora was perhaps just a product of his environment. But that environment was not the American South, but rather the California surf community. Dora was a complicated, charismatic man, charming and intelligent, and an outstanding surfer. But the surf community's continued infatuation with him, and its tolerance for his obvious bigotry, only raises troubling questions about the surf community itself.

As in Australia, race in the United States was not just an issue of black and white. A major demographic trend, especially in California, was the growth of the Hispanic population. In 1970 California counted 2.4 million Hispanic residents, less than one-eighth of the state population; by 2007 that number had risen to 13 million, over one-third of the total. The surf community largely failed to reflect this development. At the turn of the twenty-first century pro surfer Bobby Martinez, out of Santa Barbara, was notable precisely because Hispanics had been so rare in surfing (unless one counted Gerry Lopez, Sunny Garcia, and other surfers generally considered Hawaiians despite their Hispanic heritage). The increasing presence of Brazilians in pro surfing would seem a contrary and welcome trend, but the surf community's response—such as mutterings about their flamboyant, cocky behavior on the North Shore—perhaps reinforced the prevailing impression.

The fact that surfing has not represented the ethnic makeup of the surrounding society does not necessarily make surfing, and surfers, racist. The sport, after all, first came from Polynesians, and Hawaiians have always played a central role in its history. Surfers have frequently defended their darker-skinned peers, from Duke Kahanamoku to Eddie Aikau, against the racism of wider society. This has encouraged most surf writers to dismiss charges of racism. But the fact remains that contemporary surfing, in the mainland United States and in many other countries, is ethnically unrepresentative. The main reason is socioeconomic. Surfboards and wetsuits are not cheap. Yes, you could conceivably pick up a board for $100 and surf in summertime, and surfing is not as expensive as, say, skiing. But it is not free. And beach communities are generally expensive places to live. A kid in Newport Beach or La Jolla lucky enough to have parents who could afford the million-dollar real estate could just walk down to the beach. A kid in East L.A. had to find a parent willing to spend an hour in the car, paying for gas and parking, to drive him or her to the beach. The general lack of mass transit in Southern California made beach access even more difficult; there are not a lot of buses or trains running between East L.A. and the coast.

The other basic problem: many minorities don't learn to swim. In 2008 USA Swimming commissioned a study which found that while 31 percent of white children could not swim, 56 percent of Hispanics and 58 percent of blacks could not. That is, minorities were almost twice as likely not to know how to swim. Minority children between ages five and fourteen were three times more likely to die of accidental drowning. The findings correlated strongly with the parents' experience—if parents don't know how, kids don't know—and also with the parents' income and education, independent of race. That is, class was as important as race, or even more so.

Why didn't blacks or the urban poor learn to swim? The many public pools built around the turn of century were originally integrated but then increasingly segregated starting around the 1920s. Greater public tolerance for gender integration at pools, allowing men and women to swim together, helped the growth of women's surfing by encouraging women to swim. But it had the unhappy effect of barring blacks from pools for fear that black men would then be swimming with white women. By mid-century blacks in large cities were confined to one or two Jim Crow pools or excluded altogether. In small towns with just one pool, blacks were out of luck. As whites retreated to private backyard pools, most towns then refused to spend money on maintenance or build new pools, and eventually closed the dilapidated pools. The upshot: by the 1970s few usable public pools remained for the urban poor, and the few that remained were often wading pools for little kids, not swimming pools.

Some college students today, we can sadly report from experience, still believe the canard that "blacks don't like the water." Besides being essentially racist, such attitudes can become self-perpetuating: if blacks don't like the water, we don't need to build inner-city swimming pools or offer minorities swim lessons. Such beliefs are easily contradicted by the fact that African Americans have become Olympic swimmers, or the evidence that West Africans tried surfing independently in the past and happily do so now if given the chance. But the result of racial assumptions is that many minorities don't learn how to swim. And you can't surf if you can't swim.

9 ENGINEERING THE COAST

Rachel Carson, the iconic environmental writer, drew her inspiration from the surf. She wrote raptly about the vastness of "Mother Ocean . . . where life itself began," and called the beach her "favorite place to reconnect with myself and with my surroundings." Her classic books about the ocean—*Under the Sea Wind* (1941), *The Sea Around Us* (1951), and *The Edge of The Sea* (1956)—molded the minds of millions. *The Sea Around Us* is among the most successful books ever written about the natural world, influencing even the young Gidget, who gushed about "that terrific book *The Sea Around Us*." Carson's writing about the ocean explored the connectedness of nature, a perspective that later became the rallying cry of the environmental movement. Several years later, while dying of breast cancer, Carson rocked the world with *Silent Spring*, a book that questioned the wisdom of man's quest for "better living through chemistry." Her target was DDT, a broad-spectrum insecticide that was killing far more than insects. *Silent Spring* described a sterile world without birds, fish, or children; its bleak vision led to investigation of insecticide use and a ban on DDT, and ignited the environmental movement of the 1960s.

Despite Carson's lifelong interest in the ocean, this bastion of life has been last on the list for the environmental movement she sparked. The largest human populations border the oceans, challenging the seemingly limitless capacity of what Carson called "our Mother Ocean." There are few significant ocean "parks" or "preserves." Even after centuries of studying fisheries, humankind is decimating ocean fishes and destroying the oceanic environment. We use the ocean as a dump and a latrine. (Think about that the next time you order raw oysters, a bottom-dwelling filter-feeder.)

For surfers the act of catching a wave is bonding with nature. Gliding through the primordial soup, riding the energy bands raised by distant winds, is a close encounter with Mother Nature. Surfers would seem to rank among the deepest of ecologists. The ocean is earth's last frontier, a dangerous, dark, and unexplored place of unfathomed mystery, and surfers ply the edge of this abyss, at the interface between civilization and wilderness. Too often, though, they focus on the wilderness and forget about the civilization part. Surfers spend most of their time in the water sitting on their boards, looking out to sea. They literally have their backs on the civilized world. That perspective has often rendered them indifferent to what is going on behind them. But civilization's increasing encroachments on the natural world—through pollution, development, and coastal engineering—eventually roused some surfers to action.

CONCRETE AND SAND

Most surfers—indeed most people—do not think about the extensive engineering that allows people, including surfers, to live on coastlines. Dams, concrete riverbeds, and seawalls protect houses from the environment but also profoundly reshape the coastline, whether it's in California, Hawaii, or Australia. For example, Los Angeles abuts the ten-thousand-foot San Gabriel Mountains, which regularly send down mudslides during heavy rains. To protect housing developments, the U.S. Army Corps of Engineers erected dozens of stadium-sized debris basins and flood-control reservoirs around the foothills. These measures have trapped 20 million tons of sediment that would otherwise have flowed through neighborhoods—and to the beach.

The environmental engineering of the L.A. basin did not stop there. Some of the rainfall in the San Gabriels flows through our friend the L.A. River. Falling seven thousand feet in forty miles from its headwaters to the ocean, the L.A. River flows quickly. The Mississippi, for comparison, falls six hundred feet in two thousand miles. During wet winters, the rampaging river regularly overran its banks, flooding homes and businesses, and the flatness of the L.A. basin allowed the river to change its course from year to year, finding new places to flood. The spread of development only increased the flood-control problem: more paved streets and parking lots meant more runoff. By 1940, half of L.A. County was in a floodplain, amounting to several hundred thousand acres. To make L.A. livable, the Army Corps built over one hundred mountain debris basins, five massive valley flood control dams, and 350 miles of concrete river channels. The channelized L.A. River became a 50 mile-long concrete storm drain, and that's during the rainy season; in the dry season, sewage treatment plants upstream provide half of the river's flow. That is, the "source" for the L.A. River for most of the year is not a babbling brook in the San Gabriels; it is the vast treatment tanks of the Van Nuys sewage plant.

Flood control in the Los Angeles basin had a substantial impact on surfing. Channelization of the Los Angeles River—and the similarly concrete-lined Santa Ana and San Gabriel Rivers, not to mention countless concrete stream beds throughout Southern California—saved towns from flooding but also changed the flow of sediment to the beach, where it formerly replenished sand scoured by winter swells into offshore canyons. Before these rivers were dammed and channelized, many of Southern California's beaches were known for their high-quality sand. Indeed, as we know, there was so much fine-grained white sand at Manhattan Beach that some of it was shipped to Hawaii to replenish Waikiki Beach. Faced with disappearing beaches, some towns have recently resorted to buying sand while searching for a long-term solution.

Since beach sand is what stands between the Pacific Ocean and some of the most expensive real estate on earth, shore protection became a major priority. The quest for shore protection, however, often embraced technological solutions—jetties, groins, seawalls—that interrupted natural sand flows and undermined, as it were, the goal of saving sand. As one book on America's shrinking beaches put it in 1983, Americans responded to coastal erosion "by throwing more and more technology at the sea." But beaches are not static; sand is constantly flowing up- and downcoast in littoral cells and from the beach into offshore canyons, always pushed by the perpetual surf; the same book observed that "trying to 'stabilize' the beach was like trying to stabilize the ocean itself."

Beach erosion is a nationwide problem. Scientists estimated in 1984 that 80 to 90 percent of America's once-sandy beaches were sinking beneath the waves, threatening property and livelihoods. But the problem is particularly acute in California, where 90 million people visit beaches at least once a year, generating billions of dollars in tourism. Each year, an estimated million cubic yards of sand disappears from beaches in Southern California. Yet California spends only 7 cents per capita annually on shore protection compared to $1.11 in New York and 71 cents in Florida.

The government agency responsible for protecting America's coastline is the U.S. Army Corps of Engineers. The Corps traces its origins to the construction of defenses at Bunker Hill during the Revolutionary War. Army Engineers continue as an integral part of the armed forces today but are also responsible for a wide range of "civil works." Chief among these is their responsibility for the "waters of the United States," an exceedingly broad mission that includes dams for water supply and flood control, navigation, wetlands, and shore protection. The Corps touches California surfers every time they check wave heights at the Coastal Data Information Program (CDIP), which features the Corps' castle logo on its web page. The Corps funds the Scripps database because the agency measures wave heights as part of its continual shore protection program. Basically, the Corps is in charge of ensuring that a big swell does not wipe out coastal communities along the entire West Coast from Washington to the Mexican border. Environmental groups invariably cast the Corps as a villain for building dams that drown ecosystems and for dredging rivers and wetlands to make waterways and harbors. As we will see, the Corps' impact on surfing is not so simple.

WAVES CREATED AND DESTROYED

Many surfers fail to recognize that civil engineering projects miles from any beach affect them. The most obvious are the projects that created some world-class waves but destroyed others, a process that continues today. A few brief examples will illustrate the engineering of the surf environment.

Sandspit

In the El Niño winter of 1983 a hall-of-fame swell hammered the California coast, pushing huge surf into breaks from Santa Cruz to San Diego. The swell of '83 reverberated through the surfing world for years to come. Tom Curren, a Santa Barbara high schooler, was already turning heads at Rincon during the early eighties. The '83 swell hit Rincon, but it also crashed into the Sandspit at the Santa Barbara Breakwater, home of one of the best tube rides in Southern California. Film of Curren deep in tube after tube launched the career of the future world champion. Sandspit is a perfect surfing arena: spectators and photographers can stand on the beach to the inside or along the railing at Stearns Wharf a hundred yards south of the break, or, more foolishly, on the breakwater itself. The dramatic backdrop of huge waves pounding into the breakwater, sending twenty-foot sheets of water skyward, makes for a visual spectacle. Since '83, whenever a swell hits Sandspit, pro surfers fly in from around the world to join crowds of locals sampling its spinning barrels.

Like many of the world's renowned breaks, Sandspit is entirely man-made. The wave is a product of the breakwater that protects the Santa Barbara Harbor. Santa Barbara's breakwater does not use arrowhead jetties typical of other man-made harbors in California. Local movers and shakers thought such jetties ugly and opted for a more aesthetically pleasing barrier that ran parallel to the coast. Early in the last century Santa Barbara needed a port, and the local yacht club commissioned a study that concluded the best site would be the natural wetland east of Stearns Wharf, where a large lagoon—site of today's Bird Refuge—offered the beginnings of a natural harbor. Many of California's man-made harbors are former wetlands dredged out to accommodate boats. The Army Corps of Engineers agreed with the yacht club study, knowing from experience that the city's proposed jetty would interfere with sand transport and denude the downcoast beaches. Aesthetics and money prevailed, however. Max Fleischmann, the yeast king, needed a harbor to dock his two-hundred-foot yacht *Haida*, argued for the breakwater approach, and agreed to pay for half of it. The city fathers accepted his $200,000 check and installed the parallel breakwater west of Stearns Wharf.

As predicted, sand built up behind the jetty, creating an entirely new beach and enough new real estate to build Santa Barbara's La Playa Football Stadium. Some sand also worked its way around the breakwater's tip, forming a sandspit that blocked the passage into Santa Barbara Harbor—and that also created a freakishly tubing wave on the perfectly angled winter swell. Also as anticipated, the beaches downcoast from the new harbor were the one area the sand did not reach. Soon the broad protective beach east of Stearns Wharf was gone and waves were lapping at the doorstep of the Bath House and farther south. At this point the city and county turned to the Corps of Engineers to dredge the harbor mouth, opening a boat passage and pumping the sand to downcoast beaches. The sand bypass program at Santa Barbara was one of the earliest efforts at shore protection along the California coast. The city purchased its own dredge with an $80,000 check from Fleischmann, but it eventually failed and the Corps resumed the bypass, constantly compensating for the harbor's interruption of sand transport. The continuous, costly dredging is one legacy of this episode. The other legacy is the Sandspit, one of the best waves in the world.

Newport Beach

Danny Kwock, Quiksilver's wunderkind who dreamed up the phenomenally successful girl's brand Roxy, cut his teeth surfing the "hottest hundred yards of Newport Beach" between the 54th and 56th Street jetties. Kwock's home was near the most spectacular Army Corps wave, the "Wedge," located at the northern edge of Newport Harbor. The Wedge rebounds off the harbor jetty, creating a freakish slab of water, a pyramidal peak a couple stories high that unloads just yards off the beach, in only a few feet of water. Particularly big swells are reminiscent of Hawaii's Pipeline, with huge tubes that regularly launch surfers skyward in spectacular wipeouts—or pile-drive them into the sand in literally backbreaking explosions of whitewater. Clips of Wedge mayhem often grace the evening news at the end of steamy summer days. The Wedge attracts mostly bodysurfers and boogie boarders, and Kwock made a name for himself as one of the few who dared to drop in standing up on a surfboard.

The Wedge and the Newport Jetties are artificial waves. The Newport surf scene would not exist without extensive coastal engineering. But then neither would Newport Beach itself. Newport's coastal engineering can be traced back over a century. In the late nineteenth century ships landed at the marshy lagoon there to trade with local ranchers, who soon built a wharf extending from the shallow bay of the peninsula to deeper water so that larger steamers could dock. In 1905 Huntington's Pacific Electric railroad connected the town to Los Angeles, and tourism and vacation real estate followed in its wake to create what became known as Newport Beach. Access to Newport from the sea was a continual problem as shifting sand surrounded the wharf with shallows. To maintain deep water, the city installed rock jetties to the east and west of the harbor mouth. During the early 1930s the Corps and the county dredged the Lower Bay, extended the jetties, and created the present-day contour of Newport Beach around the harbor—in the process erasing the surf spot known as Big Corona.

In World War II the harbor became a naval hub, and the military influx began to change Newport from a seasonal resort to a year-round community. The Santa Ana Freeway, completed in 1956, brought even more citizens to Newport, and housing development spread along the entire beachfront. On vacation weekends, meanwhile, up to half a million visitors from the sweltering inland of L.A. and Orange Counties descended on Newport's beaches.

The economic value of Newport's beachfront brought the issue of shore protection to the fore. By the mid-1960s waves were threatening to obliterate what was now some of the most expensive shorefront property in the nation. During 1966 Newport's beachfront shrank from 136 feet to 25 feet. The city trucked in sand, but the fill ended up in the Newport submarine canyon faster than they could replace it. To save Newport Beach the Corps' L.A. District proposed a half-mile breakwater paralleling the shore to intercept incoming waves, creating a still-water trap where sand would settle before being lost in the canyon. The Corps postulated that the 4 million cubic yards of sand needed to restore the beach would accumulate in the breakwater trap and then be dredged and pumped downcoast to resurrect the beach. The public disagreed and the Corps shelved the offshore breakwater.

Instead, the Corps proposed a seventeen-mile groin field extending along the entire western stretch of Newport Beach. After that beach experienced further severe erosion in the fall of 1966, the desperate local government agreed, and the first experimental sheet-metal groins appeared at 40th and 44th Streets. The groins trapped sand on the beach and, at the same time, generated incredible waves. After severe storms in 1969 eroded the sand in between the jetties, the Corps dredged 800,000 cubic yards of sand from the Santa Ana River to create an additional twenty acres of beach. In 1972, the Corps began sheathing the sheet-metal jetties with stone and adding two new stone groins. To anchor the jetties, the district used seventy thousand tons of granite boulders for bedding, followed by mid-groin rocks weighing up to six tons, topped by a layer of rocks weighing ten tons or more, designed to bear the brunt of ocean waves. The eight jetties extended several hundred feet into the ocean, with dredged sand filling the beach between them. They were considerably longer than the public expected and led to concern amongst surfers—until they found that the longer groins actually enhanced the waves, thanks to the sand that built up around them. In the 1980s, the new spots became a center of media attention; the 54th Street jetty became known as "Studio 54," as photographers from the nearby surf magazines descended on it to chronicle the flamboyant surf antics of Kwock and his posse. Saving Newport's beach—and creating new waves—cost $51 million, $34 million from the federal government and $17 million from local government. The Army Corps solved Newport's beach erosion puzzle and created epic surf in the bargain—but at vast effort and expense.

Killer Dana

Newport, not coincidentally, is now an epicenter for the global surf industry, as Kwock's career suggests. The former center of gravity was down the coast, around San Clemente and Dana Point; surfers farther north joked about the "Dana Point mafia." There, coastal engineering claimed waves instead of creating them. The mafia's hangout was the main point break, called "Killer Dana" for its big, peeling walls that broke up to twelve feet on a good south swell. The waves were so good that Richard Henry Dana—the spot's namesake—waxed poetic on the "pulsations of the great Pacific" at the point, in *Two Years Before the Mast*. Duke Kahanamoku brought surfing to Dana Point in the 1920s, and it had been an epicenter of California surf culture ever since. In the 1960s some local residents and politicians began agitating for a harbor to encourage sportfishing, sailing, and pleasure boating. The Army Corps responded with plans for an eight-thousand-foot breakwater enclosing a harbor with capacity for two thousand boats. The Corps dropped the first eleven-ton boulders into place in August 1966, to the cheers of harbor enthusiasts, and Killer Dana never broke again. Locals there still talk reverently about it, and the trauma of losing their local break. "Killer Dana" remains a sort of shorthand for surfers: a reminder that coastal engineering can claim waves as well as create them.

Maalaea

The Corps' influence extended to Hawaii. Maui was long difficult to reach via boat because it lacked shallow draft harbors. The Territory of Hawaii remedied this in 1952 when it built a breakwater at Maalaea on Maui's south central coast. The harbor acquired an additional breakwater in 1958, and a small community developed to service the boats and sport fishermen. One unforeseen benefit of the second breakwater was a new surf break that became known as the "fastest rideable wave in the world." Surfers call it "Freight Trains"; it peels right off the end of the breakwater and breaks only on a huge south swell. Freight Trains may go unseen for years at a time; on the rare occasion when it breaks, surfers fly in from other islands to surf it.

Maalaea's new harbor mouth soon proved vulnerable to storms. After complaints from local businesses, the State of Hawaii approached the Corps about blasting out a bigger harbor and building a new seawall. The first proposal in the early 1960s roused opposition from environmentalists, especially the Sierra Club, which pointed out potential damage to coral reefs and to humpback whales. In one of the earliest surfer-led efforts to preserve a wave, Save Our Surf of Hawaii weighed in for Freight Trains.

That did not end the saga of Maalaea. Battles over coastal development can last decades, especially when local interests favor a project. During the 1980s, the Corps produced new plans for an improved harbor at Maalaea. The Surfrider Foundation, formed in 1984, joined other environmental groups in protesting the expansion, not only for environmental reasons but also on the grounds that a new breakwater might destroy the artificial wave generated by the 1959 structure. Environmentalists, again led by the Sierra Club, held off the expansion, but Maalaea still faced periodic proposals for harbor expansion in ensuing decades. Finally, in 2012, after over forty years, the Corps and state Department of Land and Natural Resources announced that based on input from the community "we are choosing not to move forward on this project at this time." Lucienne de Naie, a board member of Maui chapters of the Sierra Club and the Surfrider Foundation, called the decision a "triumph of common sense."

This brief survey of man-made surf spots could be expanded exponentially, and globally—Florida's Sebastian Inlet, Hawaii's Ala Moana, Kirra on Australia's Gold Coast, Mundaka in Spain, the Bay of Plenty in South Africa. So could the list of waves destroyed, such as Stanley's, killed by a freeway off-ramp for California's coast highway. Even seemingly remote spots are altered by humans. Consider Petacalco in Mexico, a premier wave discovered in 1973 by traveling Californians, who spoke wonderingly of "the most outrageous, hollow, makeable, grinding tubes that I'd ever seen." Petacalco's pristine beach-break barrels provided some of the biggest waves ever surfed outside of Hawaii, thanks to a deepwater canyon offshore that focused incoming swells and the Rio Balsas river mouth, which provided well-shaped sandbars. Surfers only had a couple years to enjoy it. Construction of a massive hydroelectric dam upriver, built to supply a new steel mill, starved the beach of sediment. This was soon followed by construction of a harbor just north of the beach, which stopped downcoast sand flow. By August 1975 Petacalco sand, and its waves, disappeared.

Most surfers remain blissfully ignorant of the extensive engineering that allows vast populations to live at the oceanic interface—and that shapes surf spots along almost every populated coastline. As a result, most surfers fail to recognize that the surfing environment is increasingly artificial. In particular, the Army Corps of Engineers has done more to shape surfing than any of the celebrated heroes of surf culture. For surfers, the Corps has been a double-edged sword. Shore protection erased surf spots like Killer Dana but created amazing waves at the Wedge, Newport Jetties, Sandspit, and Maalaea.

Surfers often cast the Corps as an environmental villain, but the Corps is not a mindless, coastline-consuming juggernaut. It is a federal entity that responds to the American public. Corps engineers must negotiate a welter of public interests, including those of coastal property owners, the local fishing industry, pleasure boaters, rail transport, shipping, and tourism, as well as surfing. It is not the Corps that wants a new breakwater or harbor; it is some segment of the public, often supported by its political representatives, to whom the Corps responds. Some might argue that the Corps consists of engineers who want to build things, and that when you are a hammer, everything looks like a nail. But many Corps engineers are themselves surfers; in the engineering of Newport Beach, for example, 90 percent of the local district's engineers were active surfers who understood the impact of jetties on a major surf community. For the Maalaea breakwater, the agency responded when the public—here including whale-watching and snorkeling tour operators—asked it to perform a task. Especially in the environmental era, Corps personnel are required to work with local communities to balance competing public interests. Often, not every group is satisfied with the outcome, and sometimes that includes the surf community.

There is one more environmental aspect that surfers often conveniently ignore. In this case, if they knew more about it, they might stop surfing altogether.

SEWAGE

Humans and animals on this planet produce a Bandini mountain of Himalayan proportions each year: 232 million metric tons of excrement from humans and 5.5 billion metric tons from livestock, not counting all other wild and domestic animals. Most of this is carried by rivers and runoff into the surf zone, and most of it is untreated in the developing world. Even in developed countries, vast amounts of untreated sewage flow into the waves. All this offal is crawling with pathogens that can survive for weeks or months in salt water at a wide range of temperatures and salinities. This mind-boggling and stomach-turning fecal burden is only increasing as human and animal populations grow.

Surfing takes place at the interface between civilization and the ocean. Many of the most desirable surfing spots are located near large concentrations of people, for whom the ocean is their ultimate toilet bowl. The standard philosophy for sewage treatment held that "the solution to pollution is dilution." That is, send sewage to the ocean, and it will be diluted to harmless levels. *Seinfeld* fans will recall the episode where Jerry and George watched a fellow health club patron peeing in the shower and debated whether the shower drains and urinals led to the same place. They do indeed: for coastal cities it all ends up in the same pipe, headed, if the city is environmentally enlightened, to a sewage treatment plant and from there into the ocean. Basically, if you relieve yourself in New York or L.A. in the morning and surf a few days later there's a good chance you will reunite with a little piece of yourself, not to mention millions of your fellow citizens.

Take a surfer's tour of California's best waves. At many of them surfers are stewing in sewage. Santa Cruz disgorges its effluent offshore of Steamer Lane in a plume that reaches Monterey Bay. Just south at Pleasure Point was a nice peak known as Sewers, thanks to the nearby outfall. Surfers normally call tube rides the "green room," but at Sewers they called it the "brown room." A head-dip maneuver during tube rides at Sewers was decidedly unpopular. Santa Barbara pumps its sewage just off Campus Point and at Butterfly Beach in Montecito; in between, Mission Creek spews polluted urban runoff into the lineup at Sandspit. At Rincon, "Queen of the Coast," a polluted creek and leaking septic tanks flavor the waves with fecal coliform. Santa Clara Rivermouth, a great beachbreak in Ventura, was notorious for sickening surfers, not only from the agricultural and industrial waste injected by the river itself, but also from the sewage treatment plant just yards from the beach whose fragrant aroma greeted surfers in the parking lot.

Malibu has no sewage treatment system, so all local waste goes into septic tanks and from there into the water table and then the ocean. Effluent in Malibu Creek is not limited to that generated by the immediate community. For many years, the Los Virgenes Water District, miles inland from Malibu, sent its treated sewage into Malibu Creek. During the summer months, the district's Tapia sewage plant could produce up to 10 million gallons of treated sewage daily, making a summer south swell at Malibu a potentially pungent proposition.

Pollution only increases as we head south. In addition to the L.A. River, which carries such urban detritus as shopping carts, refrigerators, and entire automobiles to the sea, there is the sewage from L.A. itself. In 1950 L.A. built a secondary treatment facility known as the Hyperion plant, a sprawling complex occupying two hundred acres in Playa Del Rey, across the coast highway from what became Dockweiler State Beach. The Hyperion plant could not keep up with L.A.'s booming population, and within a few years the new plant was discharging primary effluent five miles offshore; another seven-mile ocean outfall discharged the waste solids known as sludge left behind by secondary treatment. By the 1980s the city was pumping 25 million pounds of sludge—essentially, concentrated crap—into Santa Monica Bay every month. In the ecological dead zone around these outfalls, the only living things were worms and a particularly hardy species of clam. The surf break off Hyperion was known colloquially as Shit Pipe.

Keep heading south. For decades the White Point sewer outfall in Palos Verdes carried, in addition to the usual offal, tons of DDT from a local chemical plant, effectively turning offshore reefs into a toxic waste dump. It has since been declared a Superfund site. At Newport, the Santa Ana River disgorges Orange County's urban effluent. At Doheny in Dana Point, sewage spills regularly force beach closures. In San Diego, on top of the city's own sewage problems, untreated sewage from Tijuana regularly plagued surf breaks near the border. The break known as Tijuana Sloughs, a popular big-wave spot in the 1940s at the mouth of the Tijuana River, became virtually unsurfable due to pollution.

And that's just California. Consider also surfers on Long Island and the Jersey shore. A brown stream of effluent known as the Hudson River Plume carries sewage from 20 million New York residents past Sandy Hook and Rockaway Beach. Jersey locals called the plastic tampon applicators littering their beaches "the New Jersey seashell." In summer 1988 Long Island and New Jersey surfers found colostomy bags, used bandages, and syringes floating in the lineup during one of the summer's best swells. The nauseating waste included balls of sewage two inches thick and blood vials tainted with hepatitis B and AIDS. The pollution prompted *Newsweek* and *Time* magazine to run cover stories on what *Time* called "Our Filthy Seas."

Australia? Sydney's major sewer outfalls for decades fouled its main surfing beaches, Bondi and Manly. (More outfalls defiled Cronulla and Maroubra, surfing centers south of Sydney.) Into the early 1990s, huge brown plumes regularly wafted to shore, especially with southeast breezes, and Sydney surfers learned to dodge turds in the lineup, known colloquially as "Bondi cigars." The pollution's impact on tourism eventually provoked measures to cut down the sewage, or at least pump it farther from the beach. As for Hawaii, we already know those pristine tropical waters off Waikiki were polluted. Until the 1970s, when Honolulu built the Sand Island treatment plant, tourists flying into Honolulu could spot the offshore sewage plume on their descent to the airport. Elsewhere in the islands, sewage often just went straight into the ocean. On Oahu's North Shore, most homes remained on septic tanks or cesspools. A 1998 study noted that 40 percent of the cesspools failed frequently, and even those that worked leached most of the sewage into groundwater and hence eventually to the surf. The sewage burden included the local population of 12,275 residents but also up to a half million tourists who visited the area each year, many of them for the beaches and surf. County planners identified sewage treatment as "the highest priority" for the North Shore, but as of 2012 the community still lacked a sewage treatment plant, and local surfers were reporting patches of raw sewage, including large turds, at Sunset Beach.

Treatment plants alone were not enough. In 2006, a forty-year-old Waikiki sewer pipe failed during heavy rain, sending 48 million gallons of raw sewage through the Ala Wai Canal into Waikiki surf breaks. A surfer who fell into the Ala Wai during the spill contracted a massive bacterial infection and died.

In recent years environmental organizations and government agencies have begun testing beach water quality for fecal coliform (the intestinal bacteria that inhabit human and animal excrement). The so-called BEACH Act of 2000 (Beaches Environmental Assessment and Coastal Health Act) provided EPA grants for water quality testing—but while these tests warned surfers when to stay out of the water, they did not identify the source of contamination or do anything about it. Coliform counts usually peak during rainstorms, when treatment facilities are overwhelmed by runoff and simply release sewage straight to the sea, leading to health warnings and beach closures. Surfers have learned to avoid the water after big rainstorms (a daring few get a hepatitis vaccine and take their chances). In fact, however, fecal coliform counts are always present. So-called clean days are just when fecal coliform counts remain below a certain standard number. The counts are never zero. Surfers of today are still swimming in shit.

Surfers are the canary in the coal mine, or rather the sewage line. They spend many hours soaking in the ocean zone closest to sewage outfalls. They are often the first affected by pollution—for instance, during heavy rainfalls, which regularly overwhelm sewage systems and send polluted plumes miles out to sea, sickening surfers with gastrointestinal and sinus infections and skin rashes. They have also been the primary beneficiaries of environmental activism that, over the twentieth century, tightened sewage treatment standards. Raw sewage is no longer pumped straight into the surf, at least in many developed countries; it is treated and pumped farther offshore. But environmental laws have loopholes. The Clean Water Act of 1972 regulated water pollution by requiring all sewage to receive at least secondary treatment. "Primary" treatment uses sedimentation to settle out solid waste; "advanced primary" uses chemicals to remove more solids; "secondary" removes bacterial and viral pathogens through microorganisms. Enforcement of the law was lax. In 1977 the EPA sued the city of L.A. for breaking the law but granted it until 1987 to comply. So L.A. got a ten-year reprieve while it continued to dump sewage sludge from its Hyperion plant. Thanks to pressure from other communities that were similarly unable or unwilling to comply, in 1977 Congress amended the Clean Water Act to allow local governments to grant waivers allowing less than secondary treatment. Many sewage districts took advantage of such waivers; the agency in Aliso used one to continue discharging 12 million gallons of sewage a day off Laguna Beach in the 1980s.

On the one hand, surfers might not be able to surf at all without the gradual development of sewage treatment over the last century. On the other hand, who can say how many potential surfers shunned the sport to avoid a close encounter with a Pasadena Brown Trout or Bondi cigar? As sewage burdens increase and sewer infrastructures age and disintegrate, surfers will continue to ask themselves whether a few good waves are worth risking their health.

COASTAL POLITICS, ENVIRONMENTAL ACTIVISM, AND SURF APATHY

Despite their direct experience of swimming in sewage surfers have not been in the vanguard of environmental activism, and indeed have been noticeably apathetic about their environment until very recently.

The modern environmental movement began with Rachel Carson and *Silent Spring*, but it was catalyzed by an event that directly affected surfers. After the defeat of onshore oil drilling in the 1930s and the subsequent flourishing of California surfing, the oil industry did not go away; it just moved offshore. In 1958 Standard Oil planted the first offshore derrick in the Santa Barbara Channel, Platform Hazel, in one hundred feet of water off the old oil fields of Summerland. More offshore derricks followed over the next decade, so that the channel was speckled at night with the lights of a dozen oil rigs. In January 1969 Union Oil's Platform A suffered a catastrophic blowout, spewing 3 million gallons of crude oil into the channel. It was the largest oil spill to that date in U.S. history. The thick crude coated thirty miles of Santa Barbara's coastline and killed thousands of birds as well as uncounted dolphins and sea lions. National media ran daily headlines and newscasts of dying wildlife and blackened beaches. The spill coincided with one of the best winters in memory for surfing; huge El Niño swells foiled attempts to contain the oil but also beckoned surfers. The news images included surfers emerging from the waves covered in oil.

The oil spill sparked the fledgling environmental movement and a host of local and national environmental laws, including the National

Environmental Protection Act, Clean Air Act, and California Coastal Act. The last had particular consequences for surfers. In 1971 several environmental groups formed the Coastal Alliance to push for a California Coastal Act preserving the coast from rampant development. The Coastal Alliance collected over 325,000 signatures and got Proposition 20 on the ballot. There ensued a pitched battle for California's coast, with the environmental alliance squaring off against oil, utility, and land-development companies. The industry group spent $1.7 million campaigning against Prop 20, more than four times the amount generated by the Coastal Alliance. The pro-development campaign paid for billboards that proclaimed "Save the Coast, vote NO on 20." The bare-knuckle politics lit a fire among environmentalists, and membership in the Coastal Alliance swelled from eight to over seven hundred organizations. Proposition 20 passed with 55 percent of the vote, and a few years later the state legislature, taking note of public interest, confirmed and extended its provisions in the California Coastal Act of 1976.

The act created a permanent coastal protection program overseen by the California Coastal Commission, a panel of twelve appointed by the governor. It established a coastal zone extending three miles seaward and generally about a thousand yards inland. The commission oversees development permits along the California coast and ensures that any construction conforms to the provisions of the Coastal Act. Since shore protection measures take place within the coastal zone, the Corps of Engineers must obtain permits from the commission for its projects. The California Coastal Commission was among the first agencies in the United States to regulate the use of dwindling coastal resources. Like most environmental agencies formed in the 1970s, it was a "look before you leap" agency, requiring public input, environmental impact reports, and permits before, say, a developer built a new marina in a coastal wetland.

Surfers were notably absent from the environmental response to the Santa Barbara spill. This was not because they recognized that almost all surf equipment came ultimately from petrochemicals: foam, resin, leash, wax, wetsuit, and surf trunks, not to mention gas to get to the beach. No, surfers did not admit that the oil industry enabled modern surfing at the same time it threatened it. Rather, surfers were just plain indifferent. A year before the spill, surfer Craig Lockwood, an editor for *Peterson's Surfing*, noted the lack of protest from surfers over the demise of Killer Dana and several other nearby breaks lost to coastal engineering. Lockwood described the surf community as "a passive minority so caught up in our own pursuits that we allowed the thing we love the most to be destroyed."

Thus when members of GOO (Get Oil Out) tried to rally surfers to join protests against the Santa Barbara spill, one frustrated organizer compared rallying surfers to "herding cats." Another was "disheartened with the attitude of many local surfers. It seemed that they weren't very concerned with the spill—and yet of all people, they had the most to lose. They were just plain apathetic!" The surf media tried to light a fire, urging surfers to "start flexing their political triceps" and starting regular columns on "Our Mother Ocean," but the main refrain of these articles was complaint about surfers' continued apathy. Of the seven hundred groups in California's Coastal Alliance for Proposition 20, only one represented surfers, the Western Surfing Association—and it soon expressly disavowed "surf-related politics and legislation" to focus on promoting surf contests. A *Surfer* writer concluded, "From city to city, from coast to coast, we are getting the proverbial shaft, an ever-growing obituary to our innocence and inaction."

The one spark of environmental protest appeared in Hawaii, where hot curl pioneer John Kelly cofounded surfing's first environmental group, Save Our Surf, in 1961. Born in San Francisco in 1919, Kelly moved with his artist parents to Hawaii as a young child. He learned to surf on a seven-foot redwood plank shaped by David Kahanamoku, Duke's brother, and became an accomplished waterman, training some of the Navy's first UDTs for combat in the Pacific theater. He also earned a degree in music from the Juilliard School and was an accomplished artist. Kelly's activism, which started with protests against nuclear weapons after World War II, cost him his job as a schoolteacher. He then turned to fighting coastal development in Hawaii. Kelly liked to say, "Big fish eat little fish until little fish get organized." After he watched harbor improvements at Ala Moana destroy a surf spot, he and big-wave pioneer George Downing founded Save Our Surf. Kelly owned a printing press and circulated leaflets against new development projects; he also wrote *Surf and Sea*, a 1965 treatise on surfing and the ocean environment. One of Save Our Surf's main targets was the Dillingham conglomerate, which had proposals to dredge coral reefs around the east and southeast shores of Oahu. Save Our Surf also foiled plans for offshore airport runways built on dredge fill, new high-rise hotels also on remains of former reefs, beach-widening projects at Waikiki, and the eviction of families from an ancestral fishing village to make room for a runway extension. Downing summed up Kelly's integrity: "You couldn't buy John. . . . People tried."

Finally, in 1984, California surfers found their own forum when three Malibu locals—aerospace engineer Glenn Hening, environmentalist Tom Pratte, and Lance Carson—formed the Surfrider Foundation to prevent bulldozers from channeling the Malibu lagoon. Surfrider won an early victory with a successful lawsuit against a new breakwater in Imperial Beach in San Diego. But it otherwise struggled for traction. By 1990 Surfrider's total membership amounted to fewer than four thousand, a pitiful percentage of the 2-million-plus surf community, and its budget could support only one full-time employee in addition to Tom Pratte. *Surfer* magazine declared such apathy "an absolute disgrace." Almost all Surfrider's funding came from small, grass-roots donations and in-kind legal work. In 1991 it received $200,000 in cash donations, perhaps $20,000 of that from surf companies. For an industry with sales of perhaps $2 billion, that amounted to another vanishingly small fraction, and Surfrider began publicly calling out the surf industry for its lack of support.

Part of Surfrider's problem was confusion over its mission. Its goal of preserving surf breaks at times landed it in awkward positions, since so many breaks were in fact man-made. For instance, Surfrider found itself arguing against the removal of two decrepit oil derricks south of Santa Barbara, since they caused sandbars and created a wave called Oil Piers. Surfrider pushed its mandate even further into "surf enhancement," or artificial reefs. The group wasted much energy—and environmental goodwill—after it proposed in 1989 to build an artificial reef, consisting of giant polymer sandbags, near Ventura, with backing from outdoor gear maker Patagonia. Although Surfrider eventually abandoned "Patagonia Reef," it continued, as we shall see, to embrace the idea of artificial reefs.

Surfrider's triumph in a major 1991 lawsuit against paper mills polluting surf breaks in Humboldt County, California, exposed another basic question over its mission. Represented by a young lawyer named Mark Massara, Surfrider joined other environmental groups in negotiating a multimillion-dollar settlement, including a half million dollars to Surfrider for its legal fees. The victory represented a major coup; the *New York Times*, the *Wall Street Journal*, and CNN covered the case, and the front page of the *Los Angeles Times* heralded Surfrider's arrival as a "major environmental player." But the victory also threatened to tear the group apart. The dispute was ostensibly about money—specifically, about the amount of the settlement that went to Massara, who first brought the case to Surfrider and then worked on it for two years. But the compensation debate stemmed from a deeper philosophical difference over the organization's direction. One faction, based in Southern California, thought Surfrider should focus on grass-roots programs like education and water testing, not legal action. Massara's side, mostly from Northern California, thought only aggressive lawsuits would stop polluters. Surfrider board member Rob Caughlan, a Massara ally, declared, "All the educational programs and brochures and T-shirts in the world were not going to stop those pulp mills from polluting the surf. It took direct and vigorous confrontation, nothing less." In a sharply divided vote, Surfrider's board chose the path of education, not lawsuits, and one-third of the board, including Massara and Caughlan, promptly resigned. Surfrider's image took a beating, for the controversy itself and because the foundation had run up $100,000 in debt and was in danger of folding. (That might explain the focus on education; lawsuits take resources.)

Surfrider eventually shamed the surf industry into matching environmental rhetoric with hard cash; meanwhile, human assaults on the surf environment were becoming ever harder to ignore. Surfrider flexed its political muscle in 2008, after developers campaigned for a toll road that would block access to Trestles, an exceedingly popular break that on many days attracted hundreds of surfers. Trestles and the adjoining breaks at San Onofre had been sacred to California surfers since the 1920s, and had provided surfers an early education in beach-access issues: first when the Marines at Camp Pendleton kept the waves off-limits through beach patrols, then again during the Nixon administration, when the nearby Western White House further limited access until the president struck a deal to create a state park there.

Surfrider rallied hundreds of members to speak in defense of Trestles and enlisted celebrities ranging from Kelly Slater to Eddie Vedder and Clint Eastwood. The California Coastal Commission held a series of boisterous public meetings. Commissioner Sara Wan called the toll road "something out of the 1950s" that "drives a stake through the heart of the Coastal Act." Wan and her colleagues rejected the road in an 8–2 vote. The developer appealed to the U.S. Commerce Department, which upheld the commission's decision. The well-publicized episode suggested that surfers might have finally found their political voice.

Sara Wan was involved in an earlier episode that highlighted an issue of much concern to surfers. It's very hard to surf if you can't reach the beach. By the end of the 1960s California's population approached 20 million, 80 percent of it living on the coast. A small fraction of this coastline is open to public access; almost all of it is privately owned or controlled by the military, making beach access a major issue.

California's beach access law is confusing and lends itself to conflict. Unlike laws in Oregon, Texas, and Hawaii, where beaches are public to the first line of vegetation, California law only guarantees public access seaward of the mean high tide line. As a practical matter, that means the public portion is on the damp sand. The California Coastal Commission, however, can improve public access through its ability to regulate construction in the coastal zone. If, for example, a homeowner wishes to expand a home in the coastal zone, the commission may grant a permit only if the owner provides public access to the beach.

All of that is why Sara Wan, a Malibu resident and biologist, spread her towel on the warm sand at Malibu's Broad Beach during the summer of 2003, ignoring the threats from a private guard on an ATV. Wan was not there to surf, but her presence that day was supremely important to surfers. Broad Beach is some of the most expensive, beautiful, and controversial land in the world, zealously guarded by extremely wealthy homeowners (or, rather, by their hired guards—shades of May Rindge). Billionaires don't like surfers trooping through their compounds on the way to the waves. Five sheriff's deputies arrived that day on ATVs to arrest Wan but left when she produced documents showing that the landowner did not own the beach she was sitting on and had, in fact, granted public access twenty-two years earlier. The general public won that round; but surfers will face more such battles over access as the coastline becomes ever more exclusive.

NATURE AND ARTIFICE

Fifty years after Rachel Carson rallied support for "our Mother Ocean," surfers continue to face a host of environmental issues: beach access; sewage, pollution, and oil spills; and environmental engineering, whether for inland flood control or coastal development involving harbors, piers, breakwaters, and seawalls. Despite these encroachments on the surf zone, most surfers have proved to be indifferent environmentalists, even when they've found themselves swimming in oil and excrement or watching their beach bulldozed. What little political activism surfers did muster faced the formidable forces of real-estate development, transportation, and other outsized political interests. Surf activism also led to difficult questions. Is environmental engineering justified to preserve a good wave? Should homeowners risk their homes, or their lives, just so surfers can keep a surf spot? How should the rights of a few surfers be balanced against those of the broader public? Although many surfers would consider themselves environmentalists, many found it easier to duck such questions and just go surfing. That was, in part, because admitting the wide range of human influence on the surf would undermine the image of surfing as a pure communion with nature, as a quasi-mystical "aquatic nature religion." Surfers paid the price, however, when they found rows of condos blocking the footpath to their local break, or when the water became so polluted that even perfect waves were unsurfable.

10 BEATING THE CROWDS, LITERALLY AND OTHERWISE

You can't believe your luck. You pull up to an unfamiliar beach and see the surf is firing. You paddle out, ecstatic, wondering how you managed to score with so few other surfers out. Heading for the outside peak, you immediately swing into a perfect set wave. As you paddle back out more set waves go unridden. Suddenly the day darkens. A couple younger guys in the water fix you with stink-eye and mutter warning curses. A graying forty-five-year-old paddles up and tells you flatly to show some respect. Evidently you're supposed to sit inside and not only let the locals catch every wave, but also watch classic waves peel off unridden. You back off, seething, an epic day ruined. Continuing to ride waves could end with a fistfight on the beach, rocks tossed at your head as you walk up the path, a broken windshield, or slashed tires. You have just experienced localism.

This scenario could play out at any number of "localized" surf breaks around the world. Surfing's increasing popularity has meant crowded lineups. The problem with surfing is that surfers like to ride each wave by themselves. There may be many surfers in the lineup, but each wave, in theory, will be ridden by only one of them. Usually there are four or five waves a minute, or, say, three hundred waves per hour, perhaps a third of them good-sized "set" waves. If there are fifty or a hundred surfers out, an individual surfer can go a long time in between waves. A complicated set of informal rules and hierarchies imposes order on most lineups, but surfers get impatient and greedy. That's when the trouble starts.

During the 1970s, with ever more surfers competing for a limited number of waves, locals defended certain spots in Hawaii, Australia, and California with violence and vandalism. As crowds and localism spread through surf communities, disillusioned surfers took to the road in search of empty waves. The result was a surge in surf travel and the spread of surfing beyond the confines of California, Hawaii, and Australia to far corners of the globe.

The trend transformed surfing in fundamental ways. Surf travel helped dilute localism: it was hard to go surf waves around the world and then feel too territorial about visitors at your home break. Surf tourism also propelled surfing into debates over the economic development of the postcolonial world. Many surf destinations were located in lands previously colonized by conquering Europeans that were now independent states. Surf tourism, depending on one's point of view, could appear as either an economic boon for these new nations or another form of imperialism, and it begged the question: was surfing good or bad for these societies? Meanwhile, surfing's hedonistic lifestyle brought it into the gun sights of radical Islamist terrorism.

HAWAII: HAOLES AND DA HUI

Localism has had a long history in surfing, one that predated recent crowds. The first examples of localism emerged very soon after modern surfing itself, in its birthplace of Waikiki, where haoles such as Tom Blake and Gene "Tarzan" Smith received beatings because they were white.

In the 1970s a new group emerged to enforce Hawaiian localism. A group of North Shore surfers created the Hui O He'e Nalu, or "club of wave riders," in 1977 to defend local breaks against the invasion of haole surfers. They became known more generally as Da Hui, and also as the "Black Shorts" after their standard surf trunks. Da Hui came out of the so-called Hawaiian Renaissance, a flowering of interest in native Hawaiian culture and politics in the 1960s and 1970s. Many American ethnic groups in this period, sparked by the civil rights movement, asserted their unique identity and cultural heritage. Scholars and the Hawaiian public likewise began reconsidering the history of Hawaii as another example of colonial conquest. This movement of reviving native Hawaiian traditions and forming cultural clubs came to surfing with Da Hui.

Although the Hawaiian Renaissance included many nonnatives, Da Hui presented itself as a native movement to recover ancient Hawaiian culture. The group took its logo from an ancient Hawaiian petroglyph depicting an early surfer. Outside observers have since celebrated Da Hui as an indigenous political protest against continued white imperialism. In this view, Da Hui embraced aggressive resistance to undo the nonviolent submission of the Hawaiian monarchy to white elites eighty years earlier. It is true that many Hawaiian surfers embraced the cultural reclamation project and the associated criticism of white political dominance, but the apparent basis for Da Hui was not political activism but garden-variety localism.

Consider the background of Da Hui cofounder and ringleader Eddie Rothman, who hailed from Philadelphia and only moved to the Islands as a teenager. Rothman, known universally as "Fast Eddie," became an accomplished North Shore surfer, charging heavy waves at Sunset and Pipeline. Rothman also, however, led Da Hui's embrace of intimidation outside of the surf, some of it allegedly in support of an extensive drug smuggling business. Da Hui became known as the "North Shore mafia," with rumors of beatings, or worse, dispensed to those who crossed them. Rothman was later charged with extortion and with holding "the North Shore in a state of feudalism for years." A few years later Rothman was again arrested and charged with first-degree burglary, kidnapping, and extortion, after he and two associates threatened to kill some North Shore residents in a dispute over a truck. Rothman was acquitted in both cases.

Stories of beat-downs administered to haole surfers fed the group's fearsome image in the surf community, fueled further by sensational media coverage that seized on images of violent surfers. For decades, visiting surfers on the North Shore feared a violent encounter with a black-shorts-clad local. But whatever the thuggish means employed, the

Hawaiians had a point. In addition to the Hawaiian Renaissance, the context of Da Hui included the inundation of the Hawaiian Islands by tourism. The number of annual visitors exploded after the advent of jet air travel and American statehood, rising from a few hundred thousand a year in the late 1950s to over 3 million tourists each year by the mid-1970s. With economic growth came population growth: in addition to tourists, Hawaii added about 150,000 new residents each decade, with the resident population almost doubling from 1950 to 1980, most of them on Oahu. All these people, tourists and residents, began spreading across Oahu, some of them reaching the North Shore.

The growth of Hawaii first of all meant there were many more Hawaiian surfers, who then found themselves competing with hordes of Australians, Californians, and other visitors. That was just on average days. Then they found themselves barred from certain beaches on the best winter days because of surf contests, because the other immediate context for Da Hui was the growth of the pro tour in the mid-1970s. The contests not only increased demand for waves, by attracting many more would-be pro surfers to the North Shore. They also decreased the supply, by taking over the best spots at the peak of winter for contests.

Local Hawaiians naturally protested the loss of their breaks. In 1970, an anonymous Hawaiian pondered the question "Why do I feel like stomping a haole?" in a short article titled "Haole Go Home!" for *Surfer* magazine. North Shore locals began refusing to leave lineups during contests. Contest organizers faced the spectacle of locals shamelessly stealing waves from visiting pros at crucial times during heats. The solution: contest directors hired the biggest offenders as "water patrol" to clear contest lineups. Having a few menacing locals in black shorts paddle out certainly cleared the lineup—but directors then had to contend with their "water patrol" helping themselves to waves during heats. Directors hit on the idea of requiring the patrol to use paddleboards instead of regular shortboards, with the justification that they might have to rescue somebody. In essence, the pro tour tried to co-opt Da Hui. Eventually the water patrol evolved into a legitimate and respected group of local lifeguards and watermen; meanwhile the local government worked out a permit system, with only a certain number of contest days allowed per spot and free days interspersed to let locals surf there. But still, every day from October to March there was a contest under way somewhere on the North Shore, monopolizing waves at one of the local spots and jamming the two-lane Kam Highway to the point where a simple trip to Foodland for a carton of milk was impossible.

Da Hui may have mellowed over the years as members grew old and had kids and grandkids, and the group softened its image by sponsoring community events like Easter egg hunts and beach cleanups. Da Hui also became one of the many contest organizers trying to block out Pipeline for their annual "Da Hui Backdoor Shootout." Da Hui's actual influence in surf lineups may have been more perception than reality. Anything that undermined tourism, Hawaii's major economic driver, did not sit well with the Hawaiian government. "We don't condone it at all," said Lester Chang, Oahu's director of parks and recreation. Local Hawaiians excluding people from surf spots "would be very disturbing to us."

CALIFORNIA: THE BAY BOYS AND SILVER STRAND

Compared to California locals, North Shore surfers could seem relatively generous. For example, the point break at Rincon south of Santa Barbara remains one of the few world-class waves never to host a pro contest. For decades the only contest held at Rincon has been one put on by locals, for locals, thanks to a widespread assumption that for any other contest the locals would refuse to share waves with visiting pros.

Although we have been referring to the state as a single entity, California is a collection of diverse communities (a clarification that applies to Australia as well). In addition to the SoCal/NorCal division, each of the prominent surf towns—Windansea, San Onofre, Huntington Beach, Malibu, Santa Barbara, Santa Cruz—has a distinct culture. For example, Newport Beach and San Clemente have long been surf-industry towns, image conscious and trendy, home to colorful boards and wetsuits; Ventura and Santa Barbara stayed out of the limelight and preserved a soulful image, favoring unadorned white boards and black wetsuits.

Surfers in some of these places grew particularly protective of their waves. One of the most exclusive towns, in several senses, was Palos Verdes, a wealthy coastal enclave south of Los Angeles. Palos Verdes is home to Lunada Bay, one of the few big-wave spots in Southern California. On a big winter swell there twenty-foot waves break across a rocky lineup, protected by cliffs lined with million-dollar homes. On big swells the cliffs often featured local surfers threatening outsiders with violence if they tried to surf the bay. In the 1990s one fed-up visitor came with a TV news crew, which caught the subsequent scuffle on film; the inevitable lawsuit named the aggressive local but also the local city government, which the suit alleged had turned a blind eye to the violence for decades. In the settlement the offending surfer paid $15,000 and received a restraining order, and the city agreed to police the area and ensure visitor access; but several years later Lunada locals were still assaulting visiting surfers.

Palos Verdes represented localism by an elite, exclusive community. A different example lay in the poorer areas between Ocean Park and Venice Beach, just south of the ritzier neighborhoods of Santa Monica and Malibu. The area known in the 1970s as Dogtown was an early skateboarding hotbed but also an aggressively localized surf scene centered on the Pacific Ocean Park Pier. The decrepit pier, a relic of the Huntington-era beach amusements, collected sandbars that made for good waves, but the jutting pilings also made for extremely hazardous surfing. The documentary film *Dogtown and Z-Boys* included locals reminiscing fondly about throwing rocks and bottles at outsider surfers.

Another violent scene emerged farther north, near Oxnard, whose population included a large number of immigrant farm workers. It had previously been off the surfing map, but in the 1970s the shortboard and leash opened up Oxnard's classic hollow beachbreaks like "Hollywood by the Sea." As visiting surfers began arriving to sample the waves, Oxnard locals defended their turf in now-familiar ways: slashing car tires, throwing rocks, physically pummeling visitors—and, according to local legend, surfing with razor blades stuck in the nose of their boards.

Idiocy crossed class lines. Palos Verdes and Oxnard seem to be polar opposites: one a wealthy white enclave, the other a lower-class ethnic community. So, what did these towns have in common? Not just crowded waves; many California surf spots had worse crowds without the same degree of physical violence. Consider instead the history of both towns. They were among the few beach towns in Southern California that did not depend economically on tourism. Palos Verdes thrived on property taxes from pricey residential real estate; Oxnard depended on agriculture and a nearby Navy base. It was not that tourists made for friendly lineups. Rather, the level of tourism affected law enforcement. Palos Verdes and Oxnard did not, until recently, actively pursue locals for threats and violence (and even now seem to be selectively active). Tourist towns, by contrast, could not and did not tolerate visitors being assaulted on the beach. Two separate convictions in the fall of 1981 for surf-related assaults marked, according to *Surfing* magazine, "the arrival of the Law into the lineup."

AUSTRALIA: "SURF RAGE" AND THE BRA BOYS

However violent the California locals, Australia may have been worse. The hypercompetitive spirit that made Australia a pro-surfing powerhouse also made it a hotbed for localism. Nat Young, perhaps Australia's most celebrated surfer, declared that "America is far less aggressive and hateful than Australia." Young spoke from experience. While surfing his home break in Angourie in 2000, Young got into an argument and received a pounding that left him with broken eye sockets and cheekbones. The dispute led Young to write a book titled *Surf Rage* criticizing violent localism.

Young was not entirely innocent. Back in 1966 Young was in San Diego for the world championships and got hassled by a Californian. As Young related the encounter to a reporter at the time, "I did what any other Australian would do—I hit him." Young did not mellow with age. The Angourie incident began when Young slapped a school-age boy who had accused Young of dropping in on another surfer. The beating came from the boy's father, who was also in the water and paddled over to defend his son.

As in California, Australian localism affected tony neighborhoods as well as poor ones, such as Narrabeen, a well-off northern Sydney suburb where one creative local liked to drive golf balls from the beach at unwanted surfers in the water. In addition to redefining "water hazard," Narrabeen locals also invented the "grommet pole," a light pole in the parking lot where they would tie up and torment impudent kids.

The most notorious localism in Australia was at Maroubra, a beachside suburb of south Sydney. Although it had a working-class history thanks to earlier public housing projects, in the 1980s Maroubra experienced rampant real-estate development, and many new residents embraced surfing as part of the suburban beach lifestyle. First they had to do something about the large sewage plant that spewed poo off the north end of the town beach; local surfers dubbed that wave the "Dunny Bowl."

When outside surfers began competing for the ever more crowded waves, Maroubra locals exerted control with violence. One group of young men in particular claimed priority, calling themselves the "Bra Boys," short for Maroubra Boys. The Bra Boys enhanced their tough-guy image with chair-throwing brawls in local pubs, one of which, the Coogee Bay Hotel, banned the Boys altogether. Their fearsome reputation soon extended across Australia, and Russell Crowe expressed an interest in a documentary film about the Boys. The resulting film, narrated by Crowe, included nauseating clips of beatings administered to visiting surfers. There was talk of a Hollywood film, but instead the Boys got a nod in the recent HBO comedy series *Angry Boys*, featuring the "Mucca Mad Boys," a surf gang from the fictional town of Narmucca Bay that was clearly modeled on the Bra Boys.

The Bra Boys did not stop at fistfights. Jai Abberton, a prominent member of the Bra Boys, was accused of shooting to death a local man and dumping his body in the surf. Jai's brother Koby, a professional surfer making $300,000 a year from his sponsors, was charged as an accessory to murder and faced the possibility of forty years in jail. Koby did not help his case when, a few days before facing the judge, he was arrested in a bar and charged with inciting a riot against police. A few years later he spent time in jail for slugging an off-duty police officer in Hawaii. Jai Abberton was eventually acquitted on grounds of self-defense; the murdered man was a well-known thug, a convicted rapist—and a fellow Bra Boy.

The Bra Boys recently began surfing a new spot, a dangerous ledge just off a jagged rock point. They named it "Ours." The name brilliantly summed up the base attitudes behind localism. It also carried an ultimate irony. "Ours" lay just around the headland from where Captain Cook first set foot in Australia in 1770, shooting one of the indigenous Gweagal tribesmen in the process of claiming the continent for Great

Britain. The Gweagal, the real locals, were shut out of the local waves, and just about everything else they valued, for the next two centuries. "Ours" was theirs.

IS LOCALISM OVERBLOWN?

Localism challenged surfing's romantic image as a solitary, peaceful, even spiritual pursuit. Surfers bumping into each other in crowded lineups introduced the usual human traits of pettiness, greed, and violence. Even relatively empty lineups, however, incubated violence. Traveling surfers could encounter some of the heaviest localism at isolated spots in Northern California and Oregon. Localism tapped instead into the outlaw, rebellious perception of surfing, and the mainstream media reveled in stories of supposedly laid-back surfers beating each other up on the beach. Hollywood movies such as *Point Break* and *Blue Crush* fed this image with scenes of surfside violence. Some surfers are happy to encourage the image, because it keeps people away from their beach. In fact, however, many surfers manage to visit these places and surf unscathed. Surfing's informal code regulates most lineups, and fights are rare (and often involve the more hotheaded surfers). Surfers themselves have resisted formal regulation. In 1999 San Diego's chief lifeguard proposed a new "Open Waves" law against violent localism, but after the surf community and surf media heaped scorn on the plan the state legislature abandoned it. Surfers, it seems, did not want cops in the lineup, or even on the beach.

Like many other aspects of surfing, even localism became commercialized. Both the Bra Boys and Da Hui launched surfwear lines, trading on their violent notoriety by turning it into a brand. The Bra Boys line is My Brother's Keeper (MBK), drawing on the gang's heavily tattooed slogan. Da Hui clothing includes an ultimate-fighting line, complete with faux blood spatters, alongside the surfwear in their advertising. This development might not be a bad thing. While the thuggish image helps underpin the brand, the commercial imperative may temper actual violence. How tough can the Bra Boys or Da Hui be when kids are buying their trunks at Costco?

SURF TRAVEL

One other development helped to dilute localism: the rise of surf travel. As one surf journalist noted, "Oxnard surfers are not travelers. The guys who fight a lot can't go anywhere else." North Shore regular Owl Chapman provided a pithy aphorism: "A local is just a dirtbag who can't get his shit together to travel."

Surfers had been hitting the road for decades, starting with George Freeth and the Duke. In the 1960s, after the advent of jet air travel, *The Endless Summer* popularized what the Beach Boys were calling the "surfing safari," better known as the "surfari." The shortboard revolution further encouraged the trend. It was hard to lug a ten-foot, thirty-pound longboard around the world. Although the Morey-Pope shop began experimenting with folding boards in the mid-1960s to get surfboards onto airplanes, the idea did not catch on. A seven-foot, ten-pound board, however, was another story.

In the 1970s surf travel took off, as surfers hit the road in search of the perfect, uncrowded wave. A pair of young Californians, Kevin Naughton and Craig Peterson, explored Central America and West Africa and sent back articles and photos documenting their finds in *Surfer* magazine, encouraging others to follow in their footsteps or blaze their own trail. So-called feral surfers like Naughton and Peterson pioneered early breaks by trekking through jungles and sleeping on the beach in pursuit of surf. (On one Africa trip, they wondered why natives kept shouting at them about something in the water named Bill Harzia, whom they assumed was a fellow surfer—not, as they later learned, the parasite bilharzia, also known as schistosomiasis.) But the ferals soon found themselves crowded out by more deluxe and high-tech forms of surf travel.

One area in particular was opening up: Indonesia, which was an easy hop for Australians, the equivalent of Baja for Californians. The early exploration of Indo focused on Bali because it had a developed tourist industry. In the late 1960s Qantas flight attendants on a layover in Denpasar passed the time surfing in nearby Kuta. Others followed their lead, and a surf scene blossomed in Kuta. At the same time, Bali was acquiring a countercultural reputation as a hedonistic hippie haven, with free-flowing pot, hash, heroin, and magic mushrooms, accompanied by sexual license. Bali's Kuta Beach became a favored stop on the international backpacker trail, and also for U.S. servicemen escaping Vietnam. Visiting surfers soon discovered the nearby break of Uluwatu, a long, winding left-breaking wave barreling over a coral reef, and images of its spinning emerald cylinders were soon mesmerizing surfers through magazines and films. Meanwhile, surf shops, bars, and hostels proliferated in Kuta, turning the beach town into a garish circus for drunken yobs.

Footloose surfers were already seeking the next undiscovered spot. In 1972 American surfer Bob Laverty was on his way to Bali and spotted surf from the plane. He checked a map and saw a setup similar to Uluwatu on the southeast corner of Java, near the fishing village of Grajagan. Laverty and his buddy Bill Boyum rode motorcycles up the deserted shoreline to get to the spot and found six-foot barrels peeling perfectly down a mile-long reef. They pigged out on surf for three days before heading back to Bali. They soon returned, and Boyum's brother Mike began carving a surf camp out of jungle near Grajagan, or what became known as G-Land. The camp opened in 1978, and G-Land became the hot new destination, with surfers lining up to pay a thousand bucks a week to share a hut. Actor Bill Murray was one visitor, learning to surf on a small inside section. By 1985 Mike Boyum was pulling in annual revenue of $250,000.

A few years later Boyum was gone. G-Land sat in the Plengkung forest in Alas Purwo National Park, home to several endangered plant and animal species. The Indonesian national park system, like that of the United States, sought to balance tourism with environmental preservation, but the government often sided with tourism (and money). Boyum apparently obtained permits to hack away the forest to build his surf camp, but with every change in government he had to renegotiate his deals. Finally, fed up with the bureaucratic hassles, he burned it down. Literally: he poured gasoline around the camp, struck a match, and walked away.

The G-Land camp was soon rebuilt by a local, Bobby Radiasa, and other camps sprang up nearby. The G-Land complex marked the emergence of a new industry, surf tourism, designed to help surfers reach new waves. In the process, surfers crossed the line of that old distinction between travelers and tourists. The new resorts abandoned the feral jungle camp typified by early G-Land for luxury accommodations; instead of roughing it in jungle huts, surfers enjoyed swimming pools, pool tables, and well-stocked bars to help pass the time between surf sessions. Once again, romantic counterculture gave way to commerce. By the 1980s and 1990s, all the baby boomers who had started surfing in the 1950s and 1960s were middle-aged and had no interest in roughing it, and they were willing and able to pay for amenities.

Meanwhile, the search for new spots had led farther afield in Indonesia. In 1975 Aussies Kevin Lovett and John Geisel were exploring the island of Nias, eighty miles off the coast of Sumatra. As with the discovery of G-Land, while perusing a map they saw a potential surf spot at one bay. They rented motorbikes and struggled up the dirt path to the bay, where they were greeted with the sight of perfect six- to eight-foot surf. They bolted to retrieve their boards and stayed for six weeks in a jungle shack, until their fifty dollars in savings ran out.

Nias stayed secret for a few years, but word began trickling out. In 1979 *Surfer* magazine ran an iconic photo of an empty wave breaking across a palm-framed bay, a surfer's tropical paradise. The article disguised the location as "Sian," but the following year Aussie filmmaker Dick Hoole published photos that identified the spot and literally put Nias on the map. Surfers started flocking to Nias, and local villagers built guesthouses to accommodate them and their money.

One result of these developments: crowds. Within ten years Nias had fifty people out on good days. By the mid-1990s Uluwatu had fifty guys out, G-Land had crowds of forty or more, and Nias over a hundred. These exotic destinations were as crowded as the most popular spots in California or Australia, with occasional fistfights on the beach over waves, and many surf travelers began to wonder just what they had gotten away from.

Meanwhile, few surf travelers bothered to wonder what they had left behind on these surf trips. All these surfers generated a substantial amount of sewage and trash in places with little means of treatment and disposal. Most of it just went into the jungle or the ocean. Along with environmental pollution, surf tourism brought coastal development. In 1996 Kevin Lovett returned to Nias to find coconut groves along the beach chopped down to build guesthouses; in the process Nias had lost twenty-five meters of beach along the point. Surf resort development thus threatened the original attraction, the wave itself. As for Bali, by 2011 well over 2 million tourists were visiting the island every year. Infrastructure did not keep pace with resort development; trash piled up on beaches, swimmers began suffering skin infections from pollution and sewage, and coral reefs died from polluted runoff.

Surf tourism did, however, provide benefits for local villagers—money, for one thing, for people often living on bare subsistence, and also health care, in disease-ridden tropical climates. Malaria in particular ravaged many of these areas; several early surfers at Nias died of it, including John Geisel, and surf tourism brought a mosquito eradication program to Nias. So, was surf tourism "good" or "bad"? That depended on your point of view, and there were no easy answers.

Another question: how did these surfers pay for all this? Some worked and saved and then hit the road during the good surf season (winter, or May to October in the Southern Hemisphere). Others financed surf travel by smuggling drugs. Surfers, as we know, had recognized that Southeast Asia had world-class drugs as well as waves, and that surf trips might provide a good cover for drug running. Some of the early Indo pioneers happily joined the global drug trade. Mike Boyum himself was an avid smuggler as well as consumer of drugs; he was in Bali in part because he was on the run from the law in the United States. After burning down the G-Land camp, Boyum and several surfer friends—including Peter McCabe, perhaps the premier surfer at G-Land in the 1970s—were busted smuggling in New Caledonia and spent years in prison. Another of the first visitors to G-Land, Rick Rasmussen, was known for surfing G-Land stoned almost to the point of unconsciousness. Rasmussen was later shot and killed in New York in a Boyum drug deal gone awry.

At one moment of freedom in this period Boyum was hanging out with Martin Daly, a New Zealand surfer with a marine salvage business. Daly had bought a big boat, the *Rader*, that sported bullet holes in its hull from its prior career in illicit business, essentially as a modern pirate ship. Boyum proposed using Daly's boat to pick up four tons of hash from Pakistan, for which Daly would make a half million dollars. Daly turned him down, and found another way to make a fortune: surf tourism.

Daly found his gold mine in the Mentawais, an island chain on the west coast of Sumatra, basically off the coast from Nias. The chain features several islands with lava shelfs topped with coral reefs and exposed to Indian Ocean swells. In 1989 Daly got a job hauling a wrecked timber barge off a reef on one of these islands. On his way to the job he noticed a series of world-class waves and took notes. The next year he came back for the surf, and the year after that he began chartering his boat, renamed the *Indies Trader*, for surf industry execs. News about the Mentawais began percolating through the surf community, and a magazine article in 1994 brought it to a boil by identifying the breaks. The publicity put Daly as well as the waves on the map, and he built up a fleet of boats to serve his thriving surf charter business. As other surfers noted his income and lifestyle—getting to surf perfect empty waves as part of the job—they started their own boat tours. By the mid-1990s, only a few years after Daly's first trip, surf charters were swarming the Mentawais, and customers were complaining that they weren't paying thousands of dollars to surf in a crowd. A form of localism emerged even here: boats that arrived first claimed priority over any surfers who arrived later. Daly freely admitted that he opened up the Mentawais to commercial exploitation: "I prostituted myself to keep surfing."

These so-called boat trips added a new twist to surf tourism. Instead of staying on land in a surf camp, surfers lived on a boat for a week or two. This avoided the environmental impact of land-based surf camps, with resorts carved out of rainforests and tropical beaches to house tourists, and native villages could retain their traditional culture and economy. The surfers, however, missed the whole point of travel, which is to experience other cultures. They hung out on the boat with a bunch of other Westerners, with well-stocked beer coolers and on-board chefs; their only goal was to surf, not to engage with other people and cultures. That made them worse than cruise ship tourists, who at least made the occasional day trip into a port of call; surfers on boat trips only ventured in as far as the waves. And since the average boat trip could run several thousand dollars for a week or two, they were only accessible to affluent surfers. The old distinction between travel and tourism—

the traveler accepts hardships in search of authentic experience, while the tourist is the pampered product of the leisure industry—applied now to surfing, where the surf tourism industry indeed took the travail out of travel. The feral surf traveler who hitchhiked and camped cross-country gave way to the jet-set surf tourist, flying in to score a few days of swell amid deluxe accommodations.

Boat trips also failed to benefit the villages. In 2002 the provincial West Sumatra parliament passed a law licensing a handful of tour operators in the new Mentawais Marine Tourism Association, with limits on the number of boats and surfers at any time. By 2008 the local government was collecting about 1.2 billion rupiahs from these fees—but that was only about $130,000 in U.S. dollars. At that point tour operators were building several beachside surf resorts that promised to further undermine the premodern Mentawai culture, already besieged by modernity. And the fragile ecosystem, already assaulted by dynamite fishing and onshore logging, now had to deal with surf-tourist pollution.

WHO OWNS THE WAVES? THE PRIVATIZATION OF SURFING

The Mentawais regulation dodged a basic legal issue: can someone own the surf? Most surf zones are under state control; under the "freedom of the seas" legal concept dating to the seventeenth century, nations control the sea out to three miles, the "cannon shot" rule, and beyond three miles the oceans are for anyone's use. In the twentieth century many nations, including the United States, sought to extend that boundary to exert control over fisheries and minerals. "International" waters now could begin anywhere from three to two hundred miles offshore, depending on whom you talked to. In the 1970s the UN began negotiating a new standard, the Convention on the Law of the Sea, which included the definition of a twelve-mile coastal zone as "territorial waters." By the 1990s, 155 countries had signed it; the United States signed, but the Senate did not ratify it.

The new convention meant that a government could grant long-term leases to particular interests, as they do for oil and mining rights. A surf resort in Fiji sparked a debate by winning such rights to the waves off the tiny island of Tavarua. The resort operators insisted that only guests of the resort could surf the breaks there, and they chased off nonpaying surfers on boats—including neighboring villagers—with physical force.

In the early 1980s a young American surfer named Dave Clark went to American Samoa to teach and surf. Clark had just graduated from the University of California, Santa Barbara; his senior thesis, on artificial reefs, mentioned the prospect of surf resorts and included the concept of "carrying capacity," or how many surfers a spot could sustain. He heard from a visiting sailor about a likely surf break off Tavarua, a small island of about thirty acres five miles off Fiji, deserted except for the occasional villager from neighboring islands picking coconuts. What Tavarua did have was two great left reefs, one with smaller waves peeling over shallow coral just off the island and a bigger open-ocean spot a mile offshore.

Clark found Tavarua, camped there to surf for two months, and returned the next year with his wife Jean and a friend, Scott Funk. The offshore reef in particular turned out to be a world-class wave that Clark called Cloudbreak. In addition to discovering the waves, Clark learned that in Fiji native landowners have fishing rights, called *qoliqoli* (ng-O-lee-ng-O-lee), for the surrounding ocean. Two nearby villages on Fiji held these rights for Tavarua, and Clark befriended the chief, Druku, from one of these villages, Nabila. Druku agreed to a sixty-year lease of Tavarua island. Clark did not get the rights from the other village, Momi, but decided not to worry about it. He and Funk built some huts and opened up Tavarua Surf Resort. A 1984 *Surfer* article by surf travelers Kevin Naughton and Craig Peterson popularized Cloudbreak, and surfers began flocking to Tavarua.

By 2005 the Tavarua resort was pulling in $5 million a year. By the terms of the lease, the resort committed 5 percent to local villages; the resort volunteered additional contributions up to about $1 million, or 20 percent of revenue, which helped provide housing, schools, electricity, and medical supplies. The resort also employed perhaps a hundred locals. Villagers seemed happy to have this economic windfall, but the money also introduced greed and conflict. The resort implemented Clark's notion of carrying capacity by allowing only fifty people on the island at a time. Some surfers avoided the resort's monopoly by boating in from mainland Fiji. But when Momi villagers began running surfers out to Tavarua in boats, Nabila villagers came out to enforce the resort's exclusive claim with physical intimidation and violence. Even Fijian surfers were threatened with beatings by the surf camp enforcers. In short, localism came to Fiji, intensified by economic interest.

The dustup did not exactly mesh with the image of tropical paradise. In 1996 the Fijian government issued the Tavarua resort an exclusive license, but it had to allow a limited number of outside surfers on Saturdays. The violence just continued the rest of the week, and finally in 2010 the Fijian government issued the Surfing Areas Decree, which revoked all exclusive licenses to surf spots. Surfers could now boat into any Fijian lineup and surf it for free. Tavarua soon had crowds of sixty surfers jockeying for waves, amid jokes about "Crowdbreak."

Fiji's tourism minister declared that Fijian natives would now "profit directly and indirectly by way of engaging in businesses themselves as opposed to relying on handouts from hotel operators." The mini-ster's rhetoric marked a postcolonial moment. Tavarua's resort owners had defended their exclusive rights by pointing to the benefits they brought to local villages. To the developing world, such rhetoric was familiar. The British spoke it in India, the French in Algeria, the Americans in the Philippines, and the Dutch in Indonesia. It was the language of colonialism, of foreign occupiers extracting wealth from local resources and justifying it by the uplift of natives. However, just as surfing intersected the Cold War, so did it cross that other main development of the later twentieth century, postcolonialism. Starting after World War II, most of the world emerged from colonial government to political independence, including such surfing hotspots as Indonesia, independent from the Dutch in 1949, and Fiji, a British colony until 1970. Such countries, finally enjoying political autonomy, resented the continued exploitation of their natural resources by Western industries, as economic imperialism persisted amid political independence. Waves in this view could seem like minerals, oil, or timber, a natural resource plundered by outsiders: the G-Land camp was started by the American Boyum; Australians Daly and Rick Cameron led the boat brigades in the Mentawais; and Americans took most of Tavarua's revenue.

Not all surf camps fit this pattern; in Nias a native landowner,

Ana Dalin, was the main developer of surfing guesthouses. The overdevelopment of Nias, however, did not suggest it as a model for other surf resorts. And surf tourism in some cases indeed returned benefits to natives. Perhaps without the foreigners, the natives would never have tried to make money off the resources. Foreign surfers put much of their own time, money, and sweat into building up their businesses, and surf resorts did regulate the impact of traveling surfers. But the fact remained that almost all the money from surf tourism went to American or Australian operators.

The Fijian government thus presented the surf decree as a blow against economic imperialism. The decree also bucked a general trend toward privatization in surfing. Tavarua was not the only resort asserting an exclusive claim to waves, as surf resorts from the Mentawais to the Maldives claimed exclusive access to surf spots. International environmental policies might support this trend. The United States and a number of other countries have proposed granting private rights to fisheries—something like the Fijian concept of *qoliqoli* on a global scale. Such "dedicated access privileges" aim to avoid the "tragedy of the commons," where, if a resource belongs to everyone, there is no incentive to conserve it. If fishermen are granted an ownership stake in a fishery, they won't overfish it.

This bid to "privatize the seas" could conceivably extend to surf breaks. Surfing, though, is different from grazing pastures or ocean fisheries. Whereas overfishing or overgrazing could wipe out a natural resource, "oversurfing" a spot won't wipe out the waves. The number of waves will essentially be the same no matter how humans behave (except, as we know, for environmental engineering). What privatization can do is control crowds. Some economists indeed argued that privatization provided a way to control localism and surf rage, by making costs commensurate with supply and demand. Privatization might also reduce surfing's environmental footprint, by limiting the empty beer cans and human sewage that hordes of traveling surfers leave behind. Some surfers, after the Tavarua decree, similarly backed more privatization of surf spots. Such proposals embracing the precedent of private ownership begged the question: what would keep a surfer's own local spot from being bought and fenced off?

HOLLISTER RANCH

Dave Clark wasn't around Tavarua to worry about the effect of the new surf decree. He had sold the resort and retired to a spot on the California coast that enjoyed its own version of a surf monopoly. In the United States, property rights end at the waterline, but that has not stopped the owners of the Hollister Ranch, where Clark now lives, from threatening surfers who try to ride the waves there.

Hollister Ranch occupies eight miles of empty coastline above Santa Barbara. It is one of the few undeveloped stretches of coast left in Southern California. It also boasts several good surf spots, which surfers discovered in the late 1950s, when the Hollister family still owned it and ran cattle on it. Visiting surfers did not endear themselves to the ranchers; in one story, Dewey Weber took a break from surfing to jump on a cow for some impromptu bareback rodeo. The Hollisters did, however, allow members of the Santa Barbara Sportsmen's Club to use the ranch for hunting and fishing. Some enterprising surfers made a deal: if the Hollisters included surfers under the exception for the Sportsmen's Club, they would limit the number of surfers and police the beach. Their dues paid for a guard at the gate, and the era of restricted surfing at Hollister began, initiated and enforced by surfers.

In the late sixties the Hollisters sold the property, known in the surf world simply as "the Ranch." The initial buyers planned a major recreational development, with thousands of campsites and cabins, RV parks, roads, and fishing piers, but after they went bankrupt new owners emerged with a plan to divide the Ranch into over one hundred parcels of a hundred acres each, which were put up for sale. The beachfront parcels were kept in common ownership. (The hundred-acre size satisfied California's Williamson Act, which provides property tax breaks for land kept in agriculture.) The sale also, however, scuttled the surfers' agreement with the Hollisters for access to the waves. The new ranch manager, Dick LaRue, announced to surfers that "the Ranch is closed."

There was a loophole, however, if a surfer could afford it. LaRue added, "I just have to tell the kids—the only way they can use The Ranch is to buy a parcel." The homeowners' association allowed partial interests of a one-twelfth share in a parcel, which gave you no right to build on the property but did give you a pass to the Ranch gate. For a number of surfers, this was all they wanted. Currently a one-twelfth share sells for over $300,000, compared to several million for a full parcel. (Monthly association dues for a one-twelfth share are a few hundred dollars a month.) Not all Ranch owners are wealthy, especially the ones who bought in early, and not all of them surf. But the one-twelfth owners tended to be surfers, whose overriding interest in their shares is surf access. They are owners, not residents. And most of the recent arrivals are well off. In short, for many members the Ranch has become a surfing country club.

The issue of surf access is not new, as we know from the Rindge estate at Malibu. Ranch owners sought to do what Dave Clark achieved and extend property rights to the surf zone. This is not legally the case at the Ranch, since California law guarantees public coastal access below the high-tide line, but in practical terms it is the case. Sure, you could walk in at low tide, but long stretches of rocky cliffs (and the miles of distance to cover) deterred walkers. More surfers tried to boat in, anchoring just outside the surf lineups, only to face Ranch owners threatening physical violence or vandalism to their boats. The Ranch owners spent a lot of money for exclusive access to these surf spots; their attitude was, if you haven't spent the money, don't try to surf here. Santa Barbara County and the State of California for years sought public access through biking and hiking trails but were thwarted by Ranch lawyers. Such intransigence spurred the state legislature to add specific language to the California Coastal Act in 1982 to ensure public beach access to Hollister Ranch. But little has been done to enforce the law.

Ranch owners have fiercely defended their property and the surf beyond it. The Hollister homeowners' association hires full-time security guards to enforce private access. Santa Barbara surfers showed great resourcefulness over the years in their efforts to evade the guards, launching commando-style raids, complete with camouflaged bikes and boards, to score surf. But Ranch owners demonstrated equal resolve to keep people off the Ranch, and to keep publicity away from it. In the late 1990s George Greenough, who was among the first to surf the Ranch and enjoyed legendary status in the area, named a few Ranch spots in photo captions for a surf magazine. Ranch owners wrote angry letters to the magazine denouncing him, despite the fact that all of the spots by this time were well known. Even Ranch owners who brought in more than one or two guests returned from a surf to find their car tires flattened by a fellow owner. Once again, the guys letting air out of car tires were not teenage derelicts but rather wealthy, middle-aged men.

Ranch owners view themselves, with some merit, as environmental stewards. By keeping the land in agriculture they saved a precious coastal ecosystem from development. There is a useful analogy to Irvine Ranch, which did sell out to developers and which is now a master-planned community carpeted with tract houses, McMansions, and shopping malls. The Hollister Ranch owners have spared eight miles of coast from the fate of Orange County. It could have been different: the Hollisters refused offers from oil companies who wanted to buy their land and drill on it, and also refused buyers who planned intensive development. Sticking to their principles no doubt cost the Hollister family money. For Ranch owners, preservation required restricted access; the end justified the means. As one Santa Barbara writer put it, "It could have been 20,000 people and a 24-hour mini-supermarket. Better a private paradise than no paradise at all."

But Ranch owners have not been consistent environmentalists. In the late 1990s the National Park Service proposed to create a new national seashore on the Gaviota Coast, which would protect forty-five miles of California coast from development. Hollister Ranch fell within the proposed stretch of coastline, some of which was already targeted for real-estate development. The catch: the new national park would include public access to Hollister Ranch. Faced with a clear choice between environmental preservation and private surf access, Ranch owners hired a lobbyist, to the tune of several hundred thousand dollars, to help shoot down the plan. Full-page ads in the *Santa Barbara News Press* showed a mythical Orange County traffic jam winding its way into the Ranch. Ranch owners gave lip service to coastal preservation, but when offered a chance at long-term preservation, they actively lobbied against it. Ranch owners have also not always been model environmental stewards. They bulldozed illegal ramps through the beachside bluffs so they could drive their SUVs onto the beach. This habit of driving on the beach and occasionally beach-launching boats chewed up the fragile coastal zone, which included a nesting ground for an endangered local bird species.

As a sort of surfing country club, the Ranch might symbolize the future of surfing. If national governments indeed grant property rights to the ocean, privatization could conceivably extend to surf breaks. Places like Tavarua and Hollister Ranch raise a basic question: Is surf free? Most surfers assume so, but history and present trends suggest a more restricted alternative, what has been called "cash localism"—that is, surf spots protected not by fists and flattened tires but by private property rights. Surfers viewed their sport as inherently populist, since the surf is free; and privatization of surf spots, not to mention wave pools, smacked of country-club elitism. On the other hand, ever-increasing crowds—and the aggression and pollution that came with them—could make private resorts appear a more attractive, sustainable option. Even Kevin Naughton, the original dirtbag surf explorer, came around to the Tavarua philosophy. "All things in life—even miracles—come at a price," Naughton declared. "I'm the last person to say the planet would be a better place with restricted access to all First Class surf spots, but neither do I want to see a world full of Malibus. . . . If that means restricting access to some spots on a pay-to-play basis, so be it."

The Ranch meanwhile has entered popular culture through another commercial channel: Abercrombie and Fitch now sells a line of Hollister Ranch clothing, which has turned the mystical allure of empty surf lineups into a marketing brand.

NEW SURF SEEDBEDS

Surf travelers—starting with Freeth's first visit to California, and Duke's to Australia—helped spread the sport around the world like some new infectious disease, but they were just one disease vector. Another was native people traveling to an already infected locale and returning, such as the Peruvians who made the pilgrimage to Hawaii and returned as surfers; yet another was locals who read about surfing and found a way to try it, whether on a lifeguard rescue board or just a piece of plywood.

In this way surfing infiltrated every continent—including Antarctica, thanks to recent explorations. Many countries now have well-established surf communities and cultures: Morocco and Liberia, Peru and Chile, Germany and France. Popular Moroccan spots have a hundred surfers in the water on average days. Japan has about a million surfers,

Brazil a million, Britain about a half million. In Bulgaria, dozens of local surfers chase windswell on the Black Sea; the Greek surf community has hundreds of members. Newcomers in these distant realms perhaps have a truer sense of stoke than jaded Californian surfers. Surfing still represents freedom to them, not the commercialized, competitive, technologized pursuit it has become. New technologies have driven the spread of surfing, especially improved wetsuits, which opened up frigid frontiers from Ireland and Iceland to New England and Nova Scotia. Canada and Alaska, for example, have tens of thousands of miles of coastline, and surfers are out there exploring it. On Vancouver Island in British Columbia, the town of Tofino has four surf shops and five surf schools; on good days lineups there have forty surfers.

New surf spots included seemingly surfless locales, such as the Mediterranean coasts of Italy and Israel, and the shores of the Great Lakes. Even European riverbanks attracted surfers. In England, the Severn Bore, created by flood tides funneled up the Severn River, allows surfers to ride a head-high wave several miles upstream, on what is probably the longest rideable wave in the world. Surfers similarly flock to the Eisbach and Flosslände Canals off the Isar River in Munich. These are standing waves, where the current flows over an obstruction; instead of traveling with the wave, the surfer rides the wave to stay in one spot. The Munich surf community now boasts several hundred surfers, and Quiksilver hosts surf contests there.

With surfers came surf culture and surf industry. Surf towns such as Biarritz in France and Newquay in Britain, with their surf shops, local shapers, and weekend contests, are almost indistinguishable from their counterparts in California or Australia. A surfer from anywhere on the planet can paddle out in one of these places and immediately recognize the lingo, performance styles, and surfwear—in part thanks to the globalization of American pop culture, which surfing helped define, and in part thanks to the surf industry. The industry's insatiable search for new markets helped propagate the sport. Like missionaries seeking souls to convert, surfwear firms sought customers to receive the surf gospel—and buy T-shirts. Surf companies identified promising markets, then went there to sponsor surf contests and advertise in local media. For example, by 2002 British surfers were spending hundreds of millions of dollars on surfing merchandise, and as a surf industry sprang up around Newquay, local universities began offering degrees in surf business.

These new surfing seedbeds could reflect the local culture, much as the Hawaiian, Californian, and Australian surf scenes differed in their particulars. Anecdotal evidence suggested that Japan and England were less localized than, say, the hypercompetitive Aussies. (This may be in part because Japan seems to have many women surfers, perhaps the highest proportion anywhere; to speculate further, this in turn may reflect a long history of extremely accomplished women swimmers and divers, including the tremendous waterwomen who dove for pearls, shellfish, and seaweed.) But even Japan had a few localized spots, such as Inamura Point, with rumors of intimidating enforcers in the water. Garden-variety surf localism appeared in such unlikely, isolated places as Mauritius, the Canary Islands, British Columbia, and Alaska. Some Bali locals mimicked Da Hui with their own version of the Black Shorts, complete with violent confrontations. Stories circulated about Eisbach surfers throwing rocks at visiting photographers, apparently out of fear that touring surfers would be soon be swarming to Munich. As traveling surfers carried surf culture to new hosts, localism often appeared as an ugly symptom of infection.

Surfing could also suffer from its association with Western culture. In this respect surfing intersected that other key historical development of the late twentieth century, the rise of fundamentalist Islam. This applied in particular as surfers proliferated in Indonesia, the largest Muslim nation in the world in terms of population. After 9/11 surfing drifted into the gunsights of radical Islam. In October 2002 a suicide bombing in the surf shop and nightclub district of Kuta Beach, on Bali, killed 202 people. Many of them were surfers.

11 SURF TECH

Fred Hemmings is among a select few surfers to grace the pages of *Life* magazine. In a 1970 feature Hemmings is seen riding a wave at "Waikiki Beach." The wave was in fact 350 miles from the nearest ocean, and the article was titled "Surfing in the Desert." Big Surf in suburban Tempe, Arizona, was the first American wave pool; every forty seconds, it generated a five-foot breaker that spilled into a four-hundred-foot lagoon lined with an artificial Waikiki, complete with Polynesian beach huts and palm trees. Clairol funded the project and hired Hemmings to put on scuba gear, swim through the gates, and help configure the wave. A Honolulu native and member of Duke Kahanamoku's surf team, Hemmings had won the Makaha International surf contest twice and the Surfing World Championships in 1968, and later helped found the world pro tour in the 1970s. With Hemmings's assistance, Waikiki was reborn in the desert. Hemmings christened the concrete Kalehuawehe with a nose ride across the face of a man-made wave, duly documented by *Life*'s photographer.

Surfing has become high tech. Hemmings's nose ride underscored that surf technology extended from board-riding equipment—surfboards, wetsuits, surfwear, and leashes—to the waves themselves. In the twentieth century surfing entered the modern world, but the culture around surfing, a premodern, Polynesian pastime, discouraged surfers from thinking too much about such high-tech associations—or their environmental implications.

Surfers, for example, have tried their hand at environmental engineering by building artificial reefs. Erstwhile environmental organizations, such as Surfrider and Patagonia, backed plans to dump concrete or giant plastic sandbags on the ocean floor in order to build new surf spots, and companies began eyeing a new market niche in artificial reef construction. Wave pools meanwhile allowed landlocked surfers to ride chlorinated waves but introduced their own environmental issues about water and energy use.

The presence of surfers in marine ecosystems also meant that they were in the food chain. The threat of shark attacks forced surfers once again to consider the trade-offs between environmentalism and surfing. Protecting seal and otter species, for instance, drove up shark populations and shark attacks. Shark nets to protect beaches drowned innocent dolphins and fish. When it came down to it, would surfers sacrifice good waves for the sake of the environment?

Most examples of human impact on the surf environment were local. But a profound new influence emerged on a global scale. Global warming threatened rising sea levels, killing of coral reefs, and bigger and more frequent storms, all of which promised fundamental changes in the surf landscape.

TOOLS OF THE TRADE

Surfboards themselves have gone from hard-carved wooden planks to a blend of industrial petrochemicals from Bayer, Nopco, DuPont, and other major chemical firms: polyether and polyester polyols and toluene diisocynate in foam, with freon or chlorofluorocarbon blowing agents; and styrene monomer resin, catalyzed by methyl ethyl keytone peroxide (MEKP). This toxic soup of volatile organic chemicals, once turned into a surfboard, is chemically inert (unless thrown in a fire, which surfers occasionally did as a ritual "sacrifice" to attract waves during flat spells, usually after a few beers). This inertness means that surfboards will last for centuries when buried in the local landfill.

Some surfers sought even higher-tech boards. Manufacturers continued experimenting with molded "pop-out" boards in the 1960s for mass production. In the early 1970s, amid the resurgence in backyard board designers, several top shapers—Dick Brewer, Phil Becker, Ben Aipa—provided standard molds for hollow boards from W.A.V.E. surfboards, founded by former aerospace engineer Karl Pope. The label's acronym smacked of high tech: Wave Apparatus and Vehicular Engineering, Inc. The W.A.V.E. boards used an aluminum composite skin from ski maker Hexcel, sealed with "aerospace grade" fiberglass and epoxy resin. Molded surfboards didn't catch on widely, yet. Other board makers, meanwhile, continued toying with the next step, motorized surfboards. Several models appeared in the 1960s, the most successful out of Australia; then in 1980 Surf-Jet came up with a nine-foot board with a two-stroke engine, controlled by a cord on the nose, and capable of thirty knots; the $1,695 price tag no doubt deterred many surfers. The U.S. Coast Guard christened a sixteen-foot motorized surfboard in 1983 to patrol San Diego beaches; decked out with official Coast Guard markings, the board could do ten knots. More recently, Surfango of New Jersey introduced the Powersurf FX as "the ultimate surfboard," with a four-stroke, 9.5-horsepower engine that could reach a speed of twenty-five miles per hour. And a company called WaveJet has made inroads with a battery-powered, water-jet-propelled surfboard capable of seven miles per hour. No more tedious paddling.

Wetsuits were equally reliant on high technology, specifically the petrochemical industry. Since Hugh Bradner did not patent the wetsuit, several firms sprang up to market his concept to surfers, most notably O'Neill in Santa Cruz and Body Glove in Redondo Beach. These companies capitalized on advances in neoprene chemistry from firms like Rubatex that made production of lighter, warmer, more flexible suits possible; some of these new neoprene formulas marked as large an advance, and an impact on surfing, as the coincident shift from longboards to shortboards in surfboard design. A particular leap came with Rubatex G-231, a nitrogen-injected neoprene originally developed in the late sixties to seal headlight gaskets for the automobile industry, but soon marketed by Rubatex to wetsuit companies.

Surf wetsuit firms continued to rely on the chemical industry for the raw material. The typical wetsuit started as a fifty-five-pound bag of neoprene chunks, about the size and shape of potato chips, from large chemical firms such as DuPont and Rubatex, with petroleum as a primary component but with fiercely guarded proprietary formulas. The neoprene chips then traveled to Asian firms where they were melted and merged with fillers, plasticizers, and other chemicals into a rubber dough, then pressed into inch-thick sheets and baked; then they were shaved into thinner sheets and laminated with nylon on one or both sides. One reason for shipping the neoprene to Asia for this hot, dirty, and dangerous process was to avoid American workplace safety regulations. The neoprene-and-nylon sheets then traveled back to California for cutting and sewing by wetsuit makers. The wetsuits on the rack in the local surf shop betrayed little hint of the industrial chemistry behind them.

Two other products of modern chemistry transformed surfing in the 1970s. The first was the leash. Surfers had long wearied of exhausting swims to the beach after every wipeout to retrieve their lost boards. In 1971 a Santa Cruz surfer named Pat O'Neill, the son of wetsuit scion Jack O'Neill, connected one end of some surgical tubing to his surfboard with a suction cup and the other end to his leg. He tested his invention in a surf contest in Malibu and was disqualified for an unfair advantage. The rubber leash didn't catch on for several reasons. One was cultural, the belief that swimming was part of surfing; that's why surfers mocked leashes as "kook cords." But the other main reason was technological. Rubber cords had a snap-back effect, especially in big surf, where an eight-foot leash could stretch to over twenty feet, then rebound with violent force. Pat's father Jack O'Neill lost his left eye when his board snapped back into his face; his eye-patched, bearded visage later became the well-known image of his wetsuit company.

The solution came from the chemical industry—specifically, from urethane, which provided a less lethally elastic but durable alternative. Urethane at the time was also revolutionizing skateboarding, a surf-derived pursuit; unlike the old clay or steel wheels that stuck on every piece of gravel, launching you into a close encounter with pavement, urethane wheels rolled smoothly over such small obstacles—and spawned the whole surf-skate crossover. Meanwhile, Bob Neely, a surfer, water polo player, and history teacher from San Clemente, perfected the union between board and body by attaching a urethane cord to a Velcro ankle strap and swivels. Neely transformed leashes from kook cords into efficient tools and founded Surf More in 1973 to market his advance. The company's name hinted at Neely's goal: to allow surfers to spend more time riding waves and less time swimming for lost boards.

The urethane leash revolutionized surfing. It opened up new spots to surf, especially along rocky shorelines or distant reefs, where losing your board ruined either the board or your health. It greatly increased crowds: for a specific lineup more people would be at the takeoff spot, since no one was swimming in after boards; and more people were surfing in general, since it was easier for beginners to learn without having to swim after every fall. The leash promoted new performance standards; with no penalty for falling, it was easier to go for that tube ride or aerial. Finally, the leash started the divergence between swimming and surfing, which had previously been fundamental to the sport. All this is why Surfing magazine, soon after the leash's invention, declared that "no innovation has had a greater impact on the sport, for better or for worse." But the changes wrought by the leash also made it a central question for surfers; Surfing said that "to leash or not to leash may have been the greatest moral issue in surfing in the 1970s."

The second major invention was the boogie board, a new tool for wave riding that brought the thrill of surfing to millions. Its inventor, Tom Morey, grew up riding waves in Southern California and earned a degree in math from USC in 1957. He went to work as an engineer for Douglas Aircraft, Bob Simmons's old employer, helping develop the process chemistry for new composite materials. This included a new honeycomb material Douglas manufactured for its aircraft, which Morey soon incorporated into surfboards. After a couple years he moved from Douglas to Avco, which was working on rocket nozzles for the Nike-Zeus missile. Among the ablative materials Avco engineers tested for the nozzles was a special crystalline fiberglass that allowed the resin to burn off, as well as more exotic tungsten-silver combinations. This experience led Morey to try different materials in surfboards, including special fiberglass weaves from aerospace; in general it encouraged his experimental mindset, introducing him to materials off the radar of most surfboard builders. After several years he left aerospace to start a surfboard business.

In 1971 Morey began thinking about how to get even more people surfing—and buying his boards. At the time many sporting goods stores and drugstores sold mass-market bodyboards: inflatable surf mats and plain, unglassed Styrofoam boards. In addition to breaking at the first opportunity, Styrofoam boards could do little besides ride waves straight in; surf mats offered durability, but only skilled riders could extract any performance out of them. Morey understood these shortcomings and looked for a way to combine durability with performance and democratize surfing. The result was the boogie board.

Morey's boogie board drew on his knowledge of new materials, in this case a polyethylene foam developed by Dow Chemical with a denser, stronger bead than polystyrene. Morey took an electric carving knife to a slab of this foam to carve out a small bodyboard template, and then used an iron to add an exterior skin like papier-mâché. The result was a board soft enough not to hurt if it hit you, but rigid enough to plane on water at speed and to hold a turn with its edge. The skin provided a slick, hydrodynamic surface and kept the water out of the foam. In short, the boards were fast, fun, and safe—and not too hard to make.

In 1973 Morey trademarked the "Boogie Board" name and made the boards available as a kit through mail order, advertised in *Surfer* magazine. Some assembly was required. For twenty-five dollars Morey sent a shaped core, two skins, a razor blade, sandpaper, and a xeroxed copy of his handwritten instruction manual. However downscale the production values, people figured it out and boogie boards began sprouting in California lineups. As the mail-order business grew Morey expanded into surf shop sales and then into other stores. By 1977 he was producing eighty thousand boogie boards a year, far beyond the capacity of even the highest-volume board makers of earlier eras. That level of production maxed out Morey's capabilities, and in 1978 Morey sold out to toy maker Kransco (which was later purchased by Wham-O, then later Mattel). The transaction apparently involved only the trademark, since Morey did not file a patent for the boogie board. He thus did not capitalize as much as he might have from the invention, especially considering that, by one estimate, 20 million boogies had sold by 2003.

The upshot: mass-produced boogie boards offered cheap, widely available entry into wave riding for hundreds of thousands in the late 1970s, and over the ensuing years have introduced millions to the sport of surfing. There was virtually no learning curve or wrong way to ride one; you just lay down on top, caught a wave, and away you went. The proliferating boogie boarders sparked a backlash from stand-up surfers, who resented the increased crowds and rained creative epithets, from "spongers" and "boogers" to "speed-bumps," on the newcomers. But the boogie board survived and thrived. The dollars may have eluded Morey, but no board designer in history provided so many converts with their first thrilling wave-riding experience.

LAPTOP SURFING

The contemporary surfer awakes in the morning and immediately checks the computer for waves. This is a big change from the days when surfers embarked for local surf sessions or long-range surfaris with a better chance of getting skunked than of scoring waves, yet willing to take the chance. Today's surfer has no need to make the daily trek to the beach to check the surf; a high-tech surf check is just a mouse click away. Internet surf reports have made it possible for big-wave riders to chase mammoth swells around the globe; they also allow inlanders to surf without fruitless runs to the coast. But surf forecasts have taken the surprise out of surfing, rewarding the lazy instead of the persistent, and increasing crowds in lineups. They have made surfing a sport of convenience instead of dedication.

The science of surf forecasting came out of World War II and the demands of amphibious warfare. In the Cold War it combined with several other military technologies—satellite remote sensing, electronic buoy networks, and the Internet.

Postwar surf forecasting at Scripps acquired importance from events that had nothing to do with rideable waves. On April 1, 1946, a hundred-foot tsunami slammed into Unimak Island in the Aleutians, obliterating a new Coast Guard lighthouse. The waves hit Hawaii five hours later with no warning whatsoever and waves several stories tall. The surge inundated some areas up to a half mile inland and killed 159 people. Waves measuring from fourteen to thirty feet also hit Washington State, California, French Polynesia, and Chile. Since the Hawaiian Islands are subject to tsunamis from seismic zones in almost every direction, early warning was crucial. In 1949 the federal government built a tsunami warning center at Ewa Beach on Oahu, which eventually became the center of a multinational Pacific warning system and, after the devastating Indian Ocean tsunami of 2004, similar systems in the Indian Ocean and South China Sea as well as the Caribbean. Surfers have been caught in the water during tsunami events in Peru and Western Samoa. In each case they managed to ride out the surge—actually catching a fast-moving tsunami on a surfboard is well-nigh impossible—but described it as a nightmare.

By the mid-1960s a variety of government agencies were interested in wave data and the U.S. Coast Guard set up a national data buoy system. The National Oceanic and Atmospheric Administration (NOAA) assumed control of wave data after its formation in 1970. The first buoys were large, ten-meter steel hulls in deep water with an array of electronic sensors measuring atmospheric pressure, temperature, wind speed and direction, and, later, wave heights. By 1979, sixteen stations were deployed in the Pacific, seven in the Atlantic, and three in the Gulf of Mexico. The Buoy Center also supported a number of near-shore buoy projects for agencies like the Army Corps of Engineers and NASA. For instance, Scripps ran the Coastal Data Information Program, well known to California surfers as CDIP, created in 1975 in collaboration with the Corps of Engineers and the state of California. CDIP runs eighteen buoys off the California coast and provides the data free to NOAA—and to surf forecasters.

Meanwhile, the U.S. government supported meteorology and then oceanography through satellite remote sensing, first for the military and then for NASA and NOAA. Previously, weather and surf forecasters had to wait several days for detailed weather charts to arrive from ground stations, or for Air Force planes or Navy ships to chart open-ocean storms. Beginning with the Tiros and Nimbus meteorological satellites of the 1960s, reams of panoramic data began beaming down from space-based sensors, first with overhead images of potential wave-spawning storms, then by the late 1970s including data from radar altimeters, microwave scatterometers, and other electronic sensors to measure open-ocean wave heights and wind fetches. Meteorologists no longer assembled weather charts from distant ground stations, and oceanographers no longer relied on data from grueling voyages that covered a single scant slice of the ocean. Satellite coverage soon expanded to cover the South Pacific, so that summer south swells from Antarctic storms acquired the same predictability as North Pacific swells. In 1988 *Time* magazine de-clared that "remote-sensing devices are revolutionizing the study of the seas."

Some surfers recognized a business opportunity. Veteran surfers Jerry Arnold of Corona del Mar and David Wilk of San Clemente started Surfline in 1985 in the first attempt to use high technology for checking the waves. The pair established "976-SURF," where surfers could get surf reports for thirty-one cents a call. Sean Collins, a surfer and self-taught meteorologist, provided Surfline's initial forecasts, using weather data from the National Weather Service buoy networks and the U.S. Navy. At its inception, the number generated nine hundred calls a day. Surfers were happy to spend the money rather than trek up and down the coast in search of rideable waves. Callers could obtain a 6:00 a.m. "dawn patrol" report for surf spots from Ventura to Orange County with details on wind direction and strength, water temperature, the day's tides, and wave height and shape. Surfline also provided afternoon up-dates and a seventy-two-hour forecast every evening. Data for individual sites was provided by reporters ranging from fifteen to twenty-two years of age; most were college students who earned from $250 to $750 a month for their daily reports. In an early major coup, Surfline predicted three straight south swells from storms off New Zealand using satellite images.

Surfline ramped up its service with the introduction of 900 numbers in 1989, charging eighty-five cents to two dollars a call. Over a million calls a year came in from surfers in California and Florida. Collins purchased Surfline in the early 1990s and added a subscription fax service that updated serious surf travelers on conditions at exotic destinations including Nias, Costa Rica, and Fiji. In 1995 Collins launched Surfline.com, the Internet version of 976-SURF. He hired a professional meteorologist to interpret electronic buoy data transmitted via satellite, along with reports from surfing correspondents around the globe. In 1996 Surfline.com streamed the first live Surfcam, the precedent for eventual worldwide camera coverage of popular surf spots. In addition to everyday surfers, surf magazines began turning to Collins before sending surf photographers to far-flung assignments, contest organizers asked for optimal heat schedules, and beer companies contacted Surfline before shooting commercials.

By the turn of the century, surfers had come to rely on the daily—or hourly—Internet surf check. One surf magazine stated that "waiting for waves is so . . . '70s. The thing now is to go to the waves—or, better yet, follow them around the world." In 1999 Collins was named one of the "25 Most Influential Surfers of the Century" by *Surfer* magazine, and in 2006, the *Los Angeles Times Magazine* placed Collins in its "Top 100" powerful and influential people in Southern California. Surfline was soon facing competition, however, from savvy surfers who realized that most of the relevant data was available for free from the U.S. government. Surfline's cams and daily reports were a value added, but the surf forecasts themselves were a government service—a legacy of the intimate relationship between surfing and war.

Not everyone was enamored with Surfline, which allowed surfers who lived away from the beach, or were too busy for surf checks, a reliable chance at good waves. Collins allowed that it likely increased crowds for good swells. Some ticked-off locals took to sabotaging surf cams to keep good waves quiet. San Francisco surfer Mark Renneker railed that forecasts "really destroy the mystery of surfing. . . . They also make surfing a commodity, something to be bought and sold. They really serve the rich and the unimaginative." On the other hand, forecasts also encouraged surfers to go off the beaten path to try spots that break only on rare swells.

In general, Internet surf forecasts have decreased surfers' connection with nature. Before, surfing rewarded those in tune with the elements, who could read wind and weather conditions—say, cloud formations that indicated a freshening offshore breeze—to score good surf. That's why fishermen, who spent many of their waking hours on the ocean, were so often the first ones to sniff out a good swell. Today, with all this data a mouse click away, surfers don't need to know how to read the elements; they just have to know how to surf the Internet.

ARTIFICIAL REEFS

"Where would you rather surf?" asked the *Los Angeles Times*. "At an artificial reef created by surfing's premier environmental group in 2000, or at a jetty protecting a nearby drainage outflow pipe built by the city of Los Angeles?" After the '82–'83 El Niño swells, Chevron Corporation built a new groin to protect an oil line leading to its El Segundo Refinery. In doing so, it caused an upcoast sand buildup that destroyed a popular wave breaking off a jetty protecting a storm drain at the end of Grand Avenue. Tom Pratte, a founder of the Surfrider Foundation, pointed out that if Chevron's new groin impacted the surf (albeit at a man-made surf spot), the company should be required to mitigate the damage by creating a new wave elsewhere.

Pratte's argument succeeded and the California Coastal Commission added damage to surf as a criterion for evaluation of environmental impact. Surfrider's monitoring confirmed that sand buildup behind the new Chevron groin destroyed the surf at the Grand Avenue jetty. The commission agreed and calculated Chevron's penalty by multiplying the number of "lost" surfing days by the cost of a daily admission to the Raging Waters theme park. The penalty amounted to about $300,000. Flush with what seemed like a nice chunk of change, Surfrider decided to create an entirely new surf spot using a reef that shaped the ocean bottom to create a breaking wave.

The shoe was now on the other foot, however: Surfrider faced the same problems as agencies in charge of shore protection. Six years and twenty-three agency signatures later, Surfrider received approval for the artificial reef. The reef had to be built in a spot that would not damage nearby surf spots by causing downcoast shore erosion. Furthermore, Surfrider was advised not to put the reef in shallow water because of the danger that someone might break his or her neck on it, leaving Surfrider liable.

Surfrider had already ventured into artificial reefs with its ill-fated collaboration with Yvon Chouinard on Patagonia Reef. Surfrider used the experience from the Patagonia-funded research to come up with a plan for El Segundo. Once again, surfers turned to military expertise. In this case, David Skelly, a surfer and coastal engineer, was tasked with installing what was being called Pratte's Reef in the fall of 2000. Skelly had spent seventeen years working for Scripps under contract with the Navy to design tactical harbors, like the temporary Mulberries used at Normandy during World War II. Skelly's reefs used specially designed sandbags that could be assembled in place, and Pratte's Reef provided a convenient test case for a sandbag reef. In 2000 a barge moored off Dockweiler State Beach, about five hundred feet south of the Hyperion sewage outfall in El Segundo, began dropping 110 geotextile bags made out of polypropylene or polyester and each filled with fourteen tons of sand.

The effect was unspectacular. The reef was in deep water for liability reasons but thus failed to produce waves. Local surfers, disappointed with the "BB in a swimming pool" reef, declared it "bogus." Surfrider decided to increase the size by adding eighty-two more bags, using a $200,000 grant from the California Coastal Conservancy. With a half million dollars of sand bags in place, Pratte's Reef still did not generate rideable waves. Skelly emphasized that the reef was experimental: "Nobody ever promised Banzai Pipeline." But surfers expected to at least be able to see a wave over the reef. The effects of Pratte's Reef were only visible if you brought along a mask and snorkel.

A decade later, after spending upwards of $850,000, Surfrider declared defeat and removed Pratte's Reef, winching the plastic remnants off the ocean floor. Chad Nelsen, Surfrider's environmental director, expressed regret and, in hindsight, noted that there "should have been more monitoring of sand bars and beach conditions before the reef was put in." To Surfrider's credit, at least it removed the bags. More often, such detritus is left in place. California's notorious "rigs to reef" program is a prominent example of powerful oil companies sawing off platforms larger than the Eiffel Tower and calling them "reefs."

The longer legacy of Pratte's Reef, however, is in establishing a precedent for surf being valued as a natural resource, requiring mitigation; when an oil company or a developer destroys a surf spot, it can be compelled to come up with a replacement. Meanwhile, surfers at El Segundo are still riding waves breaking off the jetty at the Hyperion Sewage Treatment plant, at the spot known as Shit Pipe.

Narrowneck, located on the Gold Coast of Australia, is billed as a shore protection measure first and a surf reef second. The idea was that by installing a reef offshore one can dissipate wave energy before it reaches the beach and cut back on expensive replenishment and seawalls. The reef was installed in 1999 by Amalgamate Solutions and Research (ASR), a New Zealand firm founded by oceanographers and ocean engineers at the University of Waikato in New Zealand. Narrowneck consists of twin reefs side by side forming underwater ridges perpendicular to the beach—in essence, submerged jetties. Much larger than Pratte's Reef, the reefs are made from more than four hundred sausage-shaped, geotextile sandbags. Kerry Black, a professor at Waikato and founder of ASR, was the principal designer behind Narrowneck. Narrowneck breaks cleanly on east and southeast swells but has to compete with some of the most popular breaks on Australia's Gold Coast.

ASR's success at Narrowneck was followed by New Zealand's first artificial reef at Mt. Maunganui on the northeast coast in the Bay of Plenty in 2005. Placed outside the natural sandbars, Mt. Maunganui started with three large geotex bags and immediately generated some head-high barrels. ASR continued to refine the delta-shaped reef through 2010, producing a wider variety of waves. But some locals downplayed the wave quality, and the design was far from conservative when it came to depth, as surfers occasionally reported catching a fin on a sandbag when turning to catch the wave.

Black's success led to a contract to build Britain's first artificial surf reef at Boscombe Beach at Bournemouth in Dorset, a hundred miles from London on the English Channel. Bournemouth's town council hoped to cash in on surfing as part of its redevelopment plan. ASR's Boscombe Reef was designed for surfing but also provided beach protection. Composed of fifty-five giant geotex bags, Boscombe is the size of a soccer field and cost £3.2 million, more than three times the initial cost of Mt. Maunganui. The result was less than spectacular; according to one local observer, "the reef doesn't necessarily make the waves amazing, it's just made mediocre waves a bit less mediocre." Installed in 2009, Boscombe Reef became a center of controversy when gaps were discovered in the reef, prompting the council to close it, due to concern that surfers could drown if they were sucked into the gaps. Surfers were less than supportive, calling the reef a "beached whale" when low tides exposed the upper layer of sandbags. Some complained that the wave was, in fact, *too* shallow and risky, the opposite of Pratte's Reef, and ASR and the town council are negotiating to soften the wave breaking off the reef.

Like Alexander Hume Ford a century earlier, tourist promoters viewed surfing as a lure for visitors—only the destination in this case was not a Hawaiian tropical paradise but rather the English seaside, and the waves broke over a "reef" of geotex sandbags. Boscombe's investment led to a 32 percent increase in visitor numbers, prompting a local surfer to comment that "the reef is not what it ought to have been—the waves were better before—but it's been fantastic for Bournemouth." Boscombe and even Pratte's Reef also provide a double bonus of shore protection, and might spark a trend of underwater jetties to enhance surf and at the same time save millions in shore protection costs. ASR recently built another reef off Kovalam in southern India, where coastal development for tourism caused severe beach erosion; the reef is intended to protect the beach but also to create better waves to attract surf tourists. ASR is currently working with the Army Corps of Engineers on a plan to restore waves at Oil Piers south of Santa Barbara, a surf spot destroyed when Mobil removed several derricks in 1998. Still in the planning stages, this relationship might breathe more life into the idea of large-scale artificial surfing reefs.

If breathing life doesn't work, surfers might try death. Environmentalists in the "green death" movement seek to reduce the footprint of cemeteries by having cremated remains mixed with cement and used to create artificial reefs.

SURF'S UP . . . FOREVER! WAVE POOLS

The crew of ABC's *Wide World of Sports* showed up on the North Shore of Hawaii in the winter of 1972 ready to film a serious big-wave competition. When they arrived, however, there were no waves. So they waited. And waited. Still no waves. Soon the novelty of a daiquiri on

SIXTY-EIGHTH YEAR

SCIENTIFIC AMERICAN

THE WEEKLY JOURNAL OF PRACTICAL INFORMATION

VOLUME CVII. NUMBER 4.] NEW YORK, JULY 27, 1912 [10 CENTS A COPY $3.00 A YEAR

SURF-BATHING INDOORS.—[See page 74.]

Germans enjoy the Undosa-Wellenbad, the first public wave pool, in 1912. (Scientific American, July 27, 1912)

the lanai faded, and the crew returned to New York with no footage. The impossibility of scheduling waves even with today's forecasting techniques makes surf contests very difficult to mass market. Artificial reefs might improve the waves but are still reliant on swells generated by open-ocean storms.

Every surfer knows that the sport involves long periods of downtime when there simply are no waves. Surfing's fickle nature contributed to the emergence of skateboarding, wakeboarding, and snowboarding as substitutes for surfing when the waves are flat. One potential solution was the wave pool. The idea of generating waves mechanically in a swimming pool had been around since at least 1903, when a German engineer named Hofrat Höglaner patented his system: hydraulically operated flaps pushed water back and forth, producing breaking waves in a pool. The Undosa-Wellenbad at Dresden was the first public wave pool. Surf bathing was still seen as a health benefit—visitors to Dresden's International Hygiene Exposition of 1912 touted "the massage effected by the moving water"—but many others just liked the fun, with 7,500 bathers a day lolling in the waves. At about six cents a ticket, that amounted to $450 per day, showing "that the artificial surf bath may be made a very profitable as well as a very beneficial institution." In 1934 England's Wembley Swimming Pool incorporated four electric paddles in the deep end that generated mild swells. The Summerland pool built in Japan in 1966 also utilized piston-powered paddles. This "Surf-a-Torium" was the first one utilized by surfers. Every hour the pool was cleared of swimmers and surfers could ride waist-high waves for fifteen minutes.

Wave pools reached a new level in 1969 when Big Surf opened in Tempe. The pool generated chest-high waves by dropping millions of gallons of water down a vertical forty-foot concrete chute. Big Surf was the first sign of a new swell of interest in wave pools. Once again, technology from the oil industry and naval research was finding its way into surfing. In the early 1970s Offshore Technology Corporation, which built wave tanks for oil firms to test drilling platforms, began marketing wave machines for the surf market to amusement parks. Four million dollars got you a fully operational wave pool, perhaps with rope tow to avoid tiresome paddling back to the takeoff spot, and Disney World in Orlando was already interested. The company specifically mentioned the potential for contests, since there would be no waiting for waves and an ideal arena for TV coverage.

In the 1980s wave pools allowed surfers to begin riding waves in such landlocked locales as Las Vegas, Memphis, Cleveland, Palm Springs, and Allentown. Disney World eventually built Typhoon Lagoon, its 2.5-million-gallon wave tank surreally backdropped by a decrepit fishing boat impaled on a Matterhorn-like mountain. The trend spread abroad, with a wave pool at Sun City, South Africa, an indoor pool in Edmonton, and a wave pool at Bandar Sunway in Malaysia that produced a good seven-foot wave. The apex arrived in Japan with the construction of the world's largest water park in Miyazaki. Called the Ocean Dome, the $300 million park, three hundred meters long and one hundred meters wide, was covered by the world's largest retractable roof and could accommodate over six thousand people. Part of Sheraton's Seagaia resort, the Ocean Dome was adjoined by high-end hotel rooms, restaurants, golf courses, and a zoo. Air temperature in the dome was kept at a constant 30 degrees Celsius with water temperature slightly cooler at 28 degrees. Designed by Mitsubishi and opened in July 1993, Ocean Dome's pool held 13,500 tons of water. Behind the wall twenty massive pumps lofted 1,800 tons of water and flushed it like a giant toilet, creating a downward surge across the contoured pool bottom. The result was a jacking wave up to ten feet, with groundswell strength. An Australian surfer, hired to perform at the pool, was ecstatic: "I have the best job, surfing all day in the ocean, then getting barreled every night. . . . Plus, I'm getting paid for it!" Meanwhile, a few hundred yards away was the actual ocean with rideable waves.

Not everyone shared his enthusiasm. Surf writers predicted that "purists will undoubtedly cringe, wavepools representing exactly what they seek, by surfing, to escape from: machinery, technology, computers, plastic, metal." Others recoiled from the notion of paying to surf: "Wave pools suggest elitism. They make me think of green fees and country club dues." But those fees themselves suggested the limits to wave pools, which were not based on aesthetics or ideals, but simple economics. Wave pools cost about eighty dollars per square foot to build. An eight-foot wave needed a twenty-thousand-square-foot pool, with millions of gallons of water and elaborate pumps, filters, and chlorinators, which meant a couple million dollars minimum. The only way to recoup this investment was to pack people in for swimming and wading; unlike a ski mountain, surfers don't share waves and would have to take turns. That limited the number of rides a surfer could squeeze into a day, driving the cost per wave through the roof. If wave pools were to serve the general public, not experienced surfers, avoiding lawsuits meant no big waves, no hard surfboards, and no injuries. The objective of most water park proprietors became to pack in as many people as possible. At best, surfers could enjoy short blocks of time to ride bigger waves on their hard fiberglass boards.

The economics of wave pools help explain why Seagaia, whose best waves broke in treacherously shallow water over the concrete bottom, never turned a profit. The Ocean Dome shut down for good in 2007. But surfers were just then reconsidering their attitude toward wave pools. This movement came not from recreational surfers but from pro surfers. Wave-pool backers had long viewed surf contests as a major justification for the pools. Pro surfing had always been limited by the lack of an arena (and so no paid admission), and the fickleness of Mother Nature. With a wave pool, contest organizers, surfers, spectators, and TV crews need not wait around for waves. You could build stadium seating around the pool, charge for seating, ensure excellent viewing angles for TV cameras, and broadcast live because waves arrived on demand. No more standing on the beach waiting for waves or peering through binoculars at a distant reef trying to make out contestants.

In 1985 Tom Carroll captured the first Inland World Surf Championship at the wave pool in Allentown, Pennsylvania. The surf media scorned the gutless, knee-high waves as "pathetic," "an abomination." Wave-pool contests nevertheless followed at Palm Springs in 1987, Miyazaki in 1993, and Disney World in 1997, where Kelly Slater won the inaugural Typhoon Lagoon contest. The pros complained of the monotonous waves, but third-place finisher Rob Machado, whose dreadlocked, ultra-mellow image was the epitome of the soul surfer, said, "I'd much rather surf here than Huntington. At least I know I'll get my wave count."

Slater now leads the drive for wave pools. In late 2010, shortly after running away with an unprecedented tenth world title, Slater launched the Kelly Slater Wave Company (KSWC), "devoted to making a world-class surfing experience accessible to the sport's enthusiasts across the globe." Slater is banking on new technology that can create adjustable waves to suit any surfer from beginners to pros. One possibility includes a "ring wave," a concept proposed by Offshore Technology in the early 1970s where a moving reef circled an inner island in an annular pool, generating waves that peeled around endlessly. Slater has enlisted the help of aerospace engineers at USC to help design the pool.

Slater approached the economics issue from the angle of surf travel and crowding. He acknowledged that paying customers would bear the huge cost of a scaled-up wave pool, but calculated that an average two-week surf trip to the Mentawais involved several days of exhausting and expensive travel. When you figured all the paddling and waiting for waves, that yielded less than an hour of actual time riding waves. A wave pool, Slater declared, was "cheaper than flying to Indo for five grand to stay on a boat and get your 50 minutes of surfing in 10 days." He added, "If you could go an hour from your house and get five minutes of good wave-riding any day you wanted, who wouldn't do that?" Some of Slater's zeal was rooted in his Florida upbringing: "If I'd had this when I was a kid I would have freaked out. Because the waves sucked in Florida." Even now, living in Santa Barbara, Slater lamented that he sometimes went to Rincon and ended up turning around because of the crowd: "I don't want to deal with that. I hate it. I'd rather go surf some punchy little peaky thing with two guys in the water, any day of the week." But Slater's calculations undoubtedly included the potential of wave pools for pro contests.

The technological approach to surfing won approval from a most unlikely source. In 2002 word got out that Kim Jong Il, ruthless leader of North Korea, had a wave pool. The Dear Leader liked to putter around in it on a motorized bodyboard. Meanwhile, water parks spawned another form of artificial wave in the FlowRider, a stationary wave, developed by La Jolla surfer Tom Lochtefeld and designer Carl Ekstrom, formed by a sheet of water flowing over a curved sheet of foam, like a gym mat. Lochtefeld opened his first FlowRider wave in 1991 at the Schlitterbahn Water Park Resort in New Braunfels, Texas, a mock-Bavarian resort that offered a surreal cultural mash-up of German theme park, surf culture, and Texan grandiosity. The FlowRider, called "Surfenburg," shot 100,000 gallons a minute in a sheet forty feet wide and three inches deep, creating head-high barrels. Lochtefeld's WaveLoch company began selling FlowRiders at $700,000 a pop, netting over $1 million in 2004, and by 2010 there were over a hundred FlowRiders around the world, from Singapore to Spain.

Some of these FlowRiders circled the world on Royal Caribbean Cruise Liners. Cruise ship tourists could now enjoy surfing alongside shuffleboard on the Lido Deck. Such devices, however, begged the question: was this surfing? The economics of wave pools, with surfers paying to ride waves, represented another step in the privatization of surfing. They might also represent the final step in the increasing artificiality of surfing. First surfboards went from natural wood to synthetic chemicals; surfwear went from bare skin to cotton and wool to synthetic nylon and neoprene. Finally, the waves themselves might go from natural to engineered coasts and finally to completely man-made pools. This raised a basic question for surfers: how much was nature part of surfing's attraction? If surfing was just about riding waves for fun, then go ahead with that foam-and-fiberglass board down to the chlorinated inland wave pool to get your wave count, as Slater argued. But if surfing is really about an encounter with nature, then you better grab your wooden alaia, ditch your wetsuit and go naked, and try to find an unengineered wave.

SURFERS ON THE MENU

Surfing is one of the few remaining human activities where the participant enters the food chain below its apex. Any surfer who has ever dropped over the side of a boat outside a deepwater reef or point in central or northern California will acknowledge a twinge at the thought of encountering one of nature's most efficient killing machines. The idea of a voracious predator the size of a small boat circling beneath one's feet conjures nightmares.

Popular culture has helpfully provided gruesome images to seed the surfer's subconscious. Peter Benchley's book *Jaws*, published in the summer of 1974, drew upon real events that gave his fictional tale an edge and kept it on the bestseller list for forty-four weeks. During the hot summer of 1916 five swimmers were attacked along an eighty-mile stretch of New Jersey coastline. Four died, including a twelve-year-old boy who was bathing in brackish Matawan Creek near Raritan Bay. At the time there were no records of shark attacks and the few experts at that time were surprised to see a large shark, probably a great white, feeding so close to shore. Researchers have subsequently pointed to environmental conditions that included sewage discharge from nearby cities. Steven Spielberg's subsequent 1975 movie version grossed $438 million in eleven weeks in 1975, as horrified audiences witnessed "Chrissie's last swim" and the fallout in the fictional town of Amity.

Robert Shaw's famous rant in the film about the USS *Indianapolis* is also based on a true event, the sinking of a World War II cruiser; after three and a half days in the water, 559 of the 880 men had died, many of them eaten by sharks.

Shark attacks are nevertheless very rare, although surfers may stand a higher chance due to their many hours in the ocean and resemblance, especially when clad in dark wetsuits, to seals and sea lions. Sharks rarely eat surfers; they just bite them, as a sort of taste test, though that initial bite may be fatal. As one shark researcher put it, "sharks have no hands. The only way they can learn about strange objects is to put them in their mouths." Since 2000 there have been fifty-six unprovoked attacks recorded along the coast of California and Oregon, of which 70 percent involved surfers. Of these fifty-six only four were fatal and only one of those was a surfer. In 90 percent of the cases the great white shark was identified as the suspect. Your average beachgoer has a one in 11 million chance of being attacked by a shark. Chances of getting killed are one in 263 million. Humans are "30 times more likely to be killed by lightning and three times more likely to drown at the beach than die from a shark attack."

Humans are doing all they can to make these infinitesimal odds even lower. People are far more dangerous to sharks than sharks to people. Each year sharks kill at most a dozen humans worldwide; each year humans kill up to 75 *million* sharks. Sharks are slaughtered by the boatload primarily for their fins, a delicacy in China, and meat, and sometimes just for sport. Some shark species have declined by 99 percent over the past fifty years and now face extinction.

If killing all the sharks doesn't save humans, we will also resort to technological fixes. Australia has used shark nets since the 1930s, when attacks in the Sydney area that killed six people, including one young surfer, led to the formation of a Shark Menace Advisory Committee. The state of New South Wales began netting beaches during the summer at a distance of about fifty meters from the beach, and now nets over fifty beaches. Since the netting program began in 1937, there is only one recorded fatal attack on a netted beach. One side effect of the nets is that protected species such as whales, dolphins, turtles, and manta rays can also get caught in the nets. In Queensland the Shark Control Program deploys lines of hooks baited with fresh fish in order to catch sharks outside swimming areas; such measures also result in collateral catch. Most surfers ignore the environmental questions raised by these measures: how much innocent sea life is it worth to surf waves worry-free?

Humans have tried less lethal ways of preventing shark attacks. Following the nightmare of the USS *Indianapolis* the U.S. Navy conducted research on shark repellents. Scientists discovered that sharks are repelled by the smell of dead sharks and from there deduced that copper sulfate and copper acetate seemed to drive off sharks. The result was Shark Chaser, a mixture of black dye and copper acetate that proved ineffective. In the early 1970s, Eugenie Clark, a shark expert at the University of Maryland, discovered that a flounder from the Red Sea called the Moses sole secretes a milky substance that repels sharks. Coppertone suntan lotion contacted Clark in hopes of marketing a new repellent, but Clark dissuaded them. After years of study a repellent derived from the Moses sole was abandoned because it only worked when squirted into a shark's mouth. This is not a trick most surfers or divers would bet their lives on.

In the 1990s researchers in South Africa from the Natal Sharks Board developed a Protective Ocean Device (POD) that emits an electromagnetic field jarring to the shark's sensing organs. The Shark POD was tested among great white sharks for eight years off Dyer Island near the Western Cape and deemed effective. Shark Shield, an Australian company, negotiated a licensing agreement with the Natal Sharks Board and produced a miniaturized POD for surfers and divers in 2002. The surf version mounts on the tail of a surfboard, weighs two pounds, and is advertised to keep sharks at a ten-foot distance. For $500, a surfer might ride waves in peace. But Shark Shield was called into question in 2008 when a great white ate a chunk of bait hanging from a prototype surf module, causing researchers to debate whether the device worked only when stationary. That is, it might not be effective when a surfer was paddling for a wave. Shark Shield's Rod Hartley insisted that the module was a test unit and that "our final design works 100 times out of 100." Peter Kimley, an animal behaviorist at the University of California at Davis, was unimpressed: "Anyone who says something works [with animals] 100 percent of the time is lying." Shark Shield absorbed another blow when its spokesperson Peter Clarkson was killed by two great whites while diving off Port Lincoln, west of Coffin Bay in 2011. It is not known whether Clarkson was using the Shark Shield at the time of his death.

GLOBAL WARMING

Scripps has had one more role to play in the story of surfing. After World War II, oceanographer Roger Revelle, whose relationship with the Navy helped lead to Hugh Bradner's wetsuits, built up Scripps with millions of dollars in Navy support. Revelle's own research studied the ocean's ability to absorb and dissipate radioactivity, relevant to the nuclear testing then under way in the Pacific. At the same time, however, he began collecting data on the ocean's ability to absorb carbon dioxide. Revelle was aware of the argument that increased use of fossil fuels was producing enough CO_2 to cause a greenhouse effect, altering the earth's climate and raising the sea level. Scientists assumed that the earth's vast oceans would absorb the excess carbon dioxide and prevent warming. Revelle's research showed that there were limits to the ocean's capacity as a carbon dioxide dump and that global warming would become a major environmental issue. Revelle died in 1991 but his former student, Vice President Al Gore (Revelle spent a decade teaching at Harvard), won the Nobel Prize for sounding the alarm about the inconvenient truth of fossil fuels.

In the short term, global warming would seem to be good for surfing. Warmer water, larger storms, and bigger waves—what could be better? As one conservative pundit quipped in the *National Review*, "when deserts start blooming, blizzards stop hitting, and you are enjoying surfing at your beach house in upper Newfoundland, you won't care what caused global warming, you'll just thank goodness it happened." The reality is less sanguine. In October 2012, Superstorm Sandy gave the northeastern United States a glimpse of what larger storms and bigger waves will mean. Sandy made landfall with a record low pressure of 940 millibars, and the NOAA buoy at New York Harbor registered wave heights of 32.5 feet—and that, as we know, is the significant wave height, or average of the highest third, meaning that many waves were even bigger. In such conditions surfboards became rescue devices, not playthings.

Global warming poses an additional threat to coral reefs, the largest living structures on earth, which are vulnerable to the rising temperature and increased acidity of oceans; absorbed carbon dioxide creates carbonic acid in seawater. Warm acidic water prevents corals from creating the calcareous skeletons over which many of the world's greatest waves break, including those of Waikiki. Take away these magnificent barriers and you risk losing not only the waves but also the natural shore protection they afford. Flooding, coastal erosion, and the loss of food and income from reef fisheries and tourism will devastate the economies of numerous tropical states. Surfaris to Fiji, Indonesia, Costa Rica, and other reef-lined paradises will be pointless if, by 2050, 70 percent of the world's coral disappears. Meanwhile, rising sea levels will drown islands and beachfront, even along the fortified coastline of California, and seawalls and breakwaters will become the new, unintended artificial reefs for surfers.

The environmental implications of global warming are potentially devastating for surfing's most hallowed ground. Waikiki withstood the elimination of a vast wetland and the containment of its spouting waters in the Ala Wai Canal. A forest of hotels built on fill replaced the idyllic beach. Through all of this the waves kept breaking across the remaining reefs, even after the hotels were bordered by seawalls, groins, artificial beaches, a harbor, and a man-made island. Elimination of the coral reefs by global warming will be the final desecration of surfing's cradle.

12 SURFING AT THE FRONTIERS

We are on a fortified beach at night. Just offshore gigantic waves crest and break. The moonlight barely reveals a camouflaged rider, feet strapped onto a narrow surfboard, speeding across the dark face of a sixty-foot wave. He is soon joined by two others, similarly camouflaged and outfitted with night-vision goggles and submachine guns. The surfers carve their way across the towering faces to the beach, where their surfboards slide open to reveal miniature radio antennas and other exotic gadgetry.

So begins *Die Another Day*, the 2002 installment in the James Bond film franchise. How could surfing become fodder for a high-tech spy thriller? Surfing requires no more technology than a surfboard, and from an engineering perspective surfboards could seem pretty low-tech. Surfboard makers stuck to the same materials they'd been using since the 1950s and surfboard shapes had barely evolved in the twenty-five years after the shortboard revolution and three-fin designs. Most shapers still made boards by hand and passed down the art through an apprentice system or backyard trial and error.

But surfing was becoming increasingly technological, and a new wave of innovation in the 1990s, driven by the subcommunity of big-wave surfers, dispelled the illusion of a low-tech pursuit. This small band of watermen charged waves sixty feet high and survived horrendous hold-downs and near drownings after wipeouts. And they embraced high-powered jet skis, satellite data networks and computer models for surf forecasting, and radically new surfboard designs, including hydrofoils that bore scant resemblance to any surfboard that had come before. It was no coincidence that the Bond filmmakers turned to some of these very same watermen to perform the film's stunt surfing. By the end of the century, they had helped complete surfing's transformation from a premodern pastime to a thoroughly modern, high-tech pursuit. A real-life promoter of a big-wave contest declared about the new surfing frontier, "We're looking at little miniature air tanks, GPS locators, or whatever it's going to be. We're going to be delving heavily into the James Bond gadget arena."

THE NORTH SHORE

The big-wave community first coalesced on the North Shore of Oahu in the 1950s. Before then, the Hawaii surf scene had centered on Waikiki. Although surf could get big there—the Duke reportedly rode waves as tall as a steamer's bridge—most waves on Waikiki's south-facing reefs had traveled several thousands of miles from the South Pacific, a journey that damped their energy and left mostly small surf. In the late 1930s surfers armed with the new hot curl boards had started venturing to Makaha on the west side of Oahu, which has some exposure to winter swells from the North Pacific. But while the hot curl boards could hold an edge better than contemporary boards, these heavy redwood planks still floated low in the water and didn't paddle well, keeping the biggest winter swells off-limits.

The postwar introduction of fiberglass and resin led to lighter boards and also the surfboard fin, and by the late 1940s surfers began venturing into bigger surf, first at Makaha and then in a new, almost mystical world called the North Shore. Surfers had known about the North Shore of Oahu for decades, and centuries earlier Hawaiian chiefs had apparently surfed there. But the North Shore remained a marginal spot. For starters, it was hard to reach. It lay on the far side of Oahu, a good twenty-five miles from Honolulu. As with the mainland United

States, the Cold War drove the construction of a highway system in Hawaii, to link Oahu's many military bases (and also provide access to sugarcane and pineapple plantations). The network included the Kamehameha Highway, which provided the first easy access to North Shore beaches. Surfers driving north on the highway crested a rise in the pineapple fields and saw before them, spread out like a surfing smorgasbord, a seven-mile vista encompassing a dozen world-class waves, all directly exposed to North Pacific winter swells, the surfer's equivalent of the Miracle Mile.

The few surfers traveling Kam Highway did not exactly discover the North Shore, but there is no denying their sense that they had stumbled onto surfing's Shangri-la. A small group of young men began gleefully exploring its fruits. The pioneers on this new frontier included locals George Downing and Wally Froiseth and a bunch of transplant Californians, led by Buzzy Trent, Walter "Flippy" Hoffman, and Woody Brown, joined later by Peter Cole, Ricky Grigg, and others. This crew brought surfing, and surf culture, to the North Shore in the 1950s. The young Californians had learned to stretch their few dollars through a winter season packed into Quonset huts at Makaha, foraging for pineapples and diving for fish, buying cheap beer in bulk, and pulling merciless pranks to pass time between swells.

At the North Shore's heart were three spots: Waimea Bay, Pipeline, and Sunset Beach, and on a decent winter day a surfer could stroll down the beach and sample waves at all three. They focused first on Sunset Beach, a formidable deepwater reef that can hold waves up to about thirty feet high. The slightly smaller but sharper-breaking Pipeline eluded them until 1961, and even then punished most of those who tried to surf it on longboards. By then they had conquered the biggest spot of all: Waimea Bay, a scenic bend in the coast where, on the largest days, fifty-foot waves heaved into colossal barrels and exploded off the point. The North Shore crew watched Waimea break for several years until one day in November 1957, when a nineteen-year-old Greg Noll, Mickey Muñoz, and a few others pulled their boards off their cars and paddled out.

What took them so long to surf Waimea? The usual explanation has been that they were all spooked by the place. An ancient Hawaiian temple overlooked the bay, rumored to be the site of human sacrifice of captured sailors from George Vancouver's ships in 1792, and the *heiau*'s lingering spirits haunted the local surf community. Closer at hand was the example of Dickie Cross and Woody Brown, who in 1943 found themselves caught outside at Sunset Beach when a swell jumped in size. They paddled down the coast to try get in through the channel at Waimea, but when they got there they found forty-foot waves breaking all across the bay. Caught inside by a set, Brown got pounded to within an inch of his life but finally dragged himself onto the beach. They never found Dickie Cross.

But there is another explanation for why surfers first tackled Waimea at that particular time. The name "Waimea" means "reddish water," after the runoff from the Waimea River, which empties into the bay. The red tint comes from the sediment carried into the river. This sediment, and the sand carried by long-shore currents, settled in the bottom of the bay and helped shape the waves. In 1956 the Dillingham company—the same firm that earlier engineered Waikiki—began building what would be the largest shopping mall in the United States, the Ala Moana Center in Honolulu. Dillingham continued the business model pioneered at Waikiki: the mall sat on new real estate created out of former wetlands, using crushed coral dredged from Honolulu Harbor. To make concrete for the mall, in 1957 Dillingham dredged sand from Waimea Bay, making the bay deeper in the middle. This meant that waves were less likely to close out across the bay, and instead broke farther out on the point, with a more tapered shoulder leading into the deep water. Waimea was still daunting but not a death wish. It is not likely a coincidence that Waimea was first surfed in November 1957, just after the dredging. This milestone in big-wave surfing was, in fact, enabled by environmental engineering. Since then, sand has gradually been filling in the bay, so that waves break further in, with more force on a shallower bottom and with more closeouts. Changing board designs have helped surfers compensate, to a point, but Waimea's heyday may be limited.

The Waimea session opened up what is sometimes viewed as the golden age of big-wave surfing. In addition to the original Makaha crew, the new generation, led by the flamboyant, hard-partying Noll, known as "Da Bull" for his relentless approach, and the taciturn Pat Curren,

Noll's stylistic foil, pushed the boundaries at Waimea—and paid the price. All the surf videos at the time had a wipeout segment of surfers taking horrendous beatings, going over the falls of forty-footers with pinwheeling boards and flailing limbs. Noll regularly set up his wife Beverly with a video camera on the beach, where she nervously watched through the viewfinder and waited for her husband to claw his way to the surface after yet another wipeout.

In general, though, big-wave surfing was rarely a death-defying experience. Terrifying, certainly. It took enormous cojones—not to mention physical endurance—to paddle out to a distant reef through walls of whitewater, stare up the face of a forty-foot wave, turn around, and stroke over the ledge and down the face, ignoring the thundering cauldron behind you. As big-wave pioneer Buzzy Trent put it, "Big waves are not measured in feet, but in increments of fear." On the other hand, surfers, like sportsmen everywhere, were sometimes prone to exaggerate their accomplishments. One wag joked that "big waves are not measured in feet, but in increments of bullshit." No one died at Waimea in this period, despite all the dramatic wipeouts. Not until 1995, when a young surfer named Donnie Solomon drowned in big surf, did Waimea kill anyone, although Pipeline claimed several victims. In January 1966 *Surfer* magazine ran an article titled "Big-Wave Danger—a Hoax!" One later study suggested that surfing on average was about as dangerous as fishing, and that skiing, snowboarding, and skateboarding were much more hazardous.

Death by drowning, however, is drawn out and terrifying, and surfers who had suffered long hold-downs even in relatively tame surf could appreciate the fear factor of a Waimea lip driving them thirty feet deep and thrashing them like a rag doll. If a deepwater thrashing didn't drown you, there was also the chance of being driven into the reef. The energy of a breaking wave increases as the square of its height, so a doubling of size means a quadrupling of explosive energy. North Shore waves repeatedly proved their power by snapping surfboards and surfers' limbs like twigs. Big-wave surfing acquired a mystique, with big-wave riders spoken of as a different breed or in terms of the old "waterman" ideal: the true waterman could handle anything the ocean threw at him. Some big-wave surfers, like Noll, carved out a professional niche in big waves and cultivated a ballsy image. Others stayed off the media radar by choice, and there were always a handful of carpenters and craftsmen who showed up on big Waimea days and charged.

The period from the late fifties through the sixties acquired almost mythical status as the heyday of big-wave surfing. Noll capped off this golden age in December 1969, an equally legendary winter when an El Niño kicked up bigger surf than anyone could remember. The biggest swell closed out the North Shore, washing away roads and houses, and Noll instead drove down the coast to Makaha. There he dropped into what is still viewed as the biggest wave a surfer has ever paddled into, a wave estimated at seventy feet (although no photos have survived). Noll made it to the bottom before the wave swallowed him, chewed him up, and finally released him so he could swim for his life to the beach. After this session Noll walked away from big waves for good, the gunslinger hanging up his spurs.

Noll's Makaha wave capped the early pioneering period. Big-wave surfing didn't have quite the same panache over the next two decades. The new professional tour of the 1970s focused on small waves, since contest schedulers couldn't wait around for a huge swell to arrive. As the surf media concentrated on pro contests, sponsors showered their money on the tour's small-wave wizards. Surfers began speaking of big-wave riding as "a dying art." A 1983 *Surfer* magazine article titled "Whatever Happened to Big Wave Riding?" seemed to put the nail in the coffin, when it asked, "Have surfers turned into candyasses?"

REVIVAL

Within a few years, though, around the mid-1980s, there appeared the first glimmerings of a big-wave revival. Not surprisingly, Hawaii led the way with the creation of the Quiksilver Big Wave Invitational in Memory of Eddie Aikau—more commonly known as "the Eddie." Aikau, from a prominent local family, was a famed North Shore surfer and lifeguard who won the Duke Kahanamoku Invitational in 1977. Aikau died in 1978 as part of a crew re-creating the ancient Polynesians' canoe voyage between Hawaii and Tahiti. The canoe capsized soon after leaving Oahu; Aikau tried to paddle his surfboard more than a dozen miles to save the crew, and was lost at sea. The Eddie contest began in

1984 at Sunset Point but soon moved to Waimea Bay. The twenty-eight contestants are chosen through a poll of big-wave specialists, and the contest is held only when waves at Waimea reach a minimum height of forty feet. The window for holding the Eddie extends from December through February; if the waves don't get big enough in that time, the contest doesn't happen. The Eddie has taken place only eight times since 1984 but has been the scene of dramatic big-wave heroics. It has also contributed a new phrase to the surf lexicon, a prod to any surfer afraid to take on a big wave: "Eddie would go."

Although the big-wave renaissance included the original North Shore hotbed, it also sprang from the discovery of several new spots outside Hawaii. First was Todos Santos, a small island several miles off the coast of northern Baja. In 1986 a session including reigning world champ Tom Curren put Todos on the map, with thirty-five-foot waves persuading surfers—and the surf media—to look beyond the North Shore for extreme surf. They soon found it. In the early 1960s surfers around Half Moon Bay, north of Santa Cruz, had noticed a reef outside the harbor handling huge swells. They surfed it on a smaller day and named it Maverick's, after the dog who jumped in and swam out to the lineup after his owner. But the wave was clearly not meant for longboards—or, perhaps, for anyone sane. Offshore ocean-bottom contours focused North Pacific swells onto a bedrock reef a half mile from shore, where fifty-foot waves pitched with such violence that they registered on seismic instruments at UC Berkeley thirty miles away. If the awesome spectacle of the waves themselves wasn't enough, the break was lined inside with craggy rocks, often fog-bound, and in frigid fifty-degree water and notorious white shark territory. No one tried it big except for one local, Jeff Clark, who first surfed it as a high school senior in 1975, on a short single-fin, and kept surfing there after taking up the carpenter's trade.

For fifteen years Clark surfed Maverick's solo. No photographers on the beach, no sponsors urging him out, just a desire to test himself against the hugest waves around. Finally in 1990 Clark persuaded a few Santa Cruz surfers to join him, and word spread through the local surf community and then trickled into the surf media, where early reports warned that "Maverick's holds you down and beats you as if you owed it money." Maverick's added a new image for big-wave surfing. The big-wave fraternity no longer featured tanned Hawaiian watermen, but rather guys from Westside Santa Cruz with a harder edge, a low-rent vibe of pickup trucks and street/skate attitudes, and nicknames like "Flea" and "Skindog."

Maverick's really hit general consciousness in December 1994. One day sixteen-year-old Jay Moriarity paddled for a frothing forty-foot monster, got hung up in the offshore wind, and launched over the falls. The wipeout appeared on *Surfer*'s cover and blew minds, especially when readers learned that after finally resurfacing with a splintered board, the teenager grabbed another board and paddled back out.

The next issue of the magazine had grimmer news. Later that week a few of the North Shore elite—Mark Foo, Ken Bradshaw, and Brock Little—flew over to try the new spot. The day marked something of a coming-out party for Maverick's, but the Hawaiians were disappointed to find it relatively small. They soon came to appreciate the spot's power. Little and Todos Santos regular Mike Parsons almost drowned on the same wave, both getting driven into the inside rocks and held down when their leashes snagged on the bottom. Neither one knew that Mark Foo, who had wiped out on the wave before theirs, was still underwater with them. Hours later, on their way back to the harbor, they found Foo's dead body. Foo, a noted big-wave specialist who had survived sixty-foot closeouts at Waimea, died on a wave half as big at Maverick's. The first big-wave death in fifty years—since Dickie Cross—happened not at Waimea, but in California. Foo's death changed perceptions of the big-wave possibilities: the North Shore was no longer the only arena.

One more new spot reinforced the message from Maverick's. A reef called Teahupoo, a third of a mile off of Tahiti, featured waves not as tall as the other spots, but with more volume, thicker lips, and warping barrels that detonated on the shallow reef with awesome power. Teahupoo, which translated from Tahitian as "broken skulls," began attracting surfers in the 1990s and soon acquired a reputation as the world's most dangerous wave, especially after local Briece Taerea died after a wave drove him into the reef and broke his back. Teahupoo, however, acquired legendary status for one wave, involving a particular surfer, Laird Hamilton, and a new technology: tow-in surfing.

THE TOW-IN REVOLUTION

Surfers have always paddled themselves into waves, but they have also consistently dreamed of getting into waves using some method faster and easier than paddling. Plans for motorized surfboards cropped up as early as the 1930s, and in World War II the Navy considered using them for landing craft, foreshadowing James Bond. Such ideas persisted, and a variant appeared in the 1970s in the personal watercraft, or jet ski. Amid the general postwar rise of American leisure culture was a trend that turned small-bore internal combustion engines to personal recreation. As all-terrain vehicles and snowmobiles began overrunning American landscapes, jet skis similarly started taking individuals on high-speed runs across American rivers, lakes, and oceans, and the high-pitched whine of revving two-stroke engines became a common part of the beach experience.

Surfers soon noticed these new toys, and in the 1980s Herbie Fletcher started riding waves on jet skis on the North Shore, including big Waimea. One day Fletcher used a jet ski to tow Martin Potter and Tom Carroll, two top pros, into waves at the outer reef of Pipeline, but surfers viewed the stunt as just that, a one-off novelty, and no one followed Fletcher's lead. For one thing, after jet ski accidents at Waikiki demonstrated the hazard to swimmers and surfers, the Hawaii state legislature around 1987 banned the use of jet skis in the surf zone. Only lifeguards could use them, for rescues. But the law provided a potential loophole, which Fletcher's experiment tested: the law allowed jet skis outside the surf zone, and surfers could conceivably argue that outer reefs, where waves only broke on the biggest days, might thus lie outside the restricted area.

No one followed Fletcher's precedent for several years, but in the meantime new inspiration came from yet another direction. Just as jet skis were proliferating in American waterways in the 1970s, the sport of windsurfing caught fire in Europe. It soon spread to Hawaii, and in the 1980s a number of top Hawaiian surfers took up the sport. Whereas European riders saw windsurfing as a variant of sailing, skimming across flat-water lakes and rivers, the Hawaiians focused on the "surfing" part and started sailing into, around, and over waves. A few of them—led by Laird Hamilton, Buzzy Kerbox, and Darrick Doerner, three surfers who had taken up the new sport—had a basic insight: they could zip into big waves at twenty knots on a windsurfer far more easily than paddling into waves at just a few knots. They might thus overcome a basic, built-in limitation to big-wave surfing. The speed of the water flowing on a big wave increases with size, and beyond a certain size waves move faster than a person can paddle. Nature seemed to impose a limit on how big a wave a surfer could ride—or, rather, how big a wave a surfer could *catch*. If you could get into the wave, there was no limit on how big it could be, but first you had to catch it. And speed was the solution.

Wind, though, is not generally good for surf; and windsurfing a mammoth wave with a big sail in your hands was not quite the same thing as carving unfettered across the face on a surfboard. In 1992, Hamilton, Kerbox, and Doerner decided there was yet another way to catch a wave. They fired up Kerbox's small inflatable Zodiac and ventured out on the North Shore, with one of them towed on a surfboard with a rope behind the boat, like a water-skier. As a wave approached, the Zodiac towed the surfer into it and then the rider dropped the rope to surf. The Zodiac, in other words, gave them the speed they'd previously gotten from their windsurfer sails.

They soon replaced the Zodiac with higher-speed jet skis and started towing into ever-bigger waves at outer reefs, especially a break on Maui known as Peahi or, more menacingly, Jaws. Here the new approach got a timely boost from the surf-film world. In 1993 Bruce Brown was filming *The Endless Summer II*, this time with Hollywood financial backing, and he proposed a segment on this new tow-in concept. It helped that Jaws, in addition to the dramatic name, had a perfect cliff-side vantage point for filmmakers. Brown tapped the movie budget to buy new top-of-the-line jet skis for the tow-in crew, which they could not otherwise afford. The tow-in surfers thus got faster, safer machines for exploring their new frontier. Having embraced one technology, they tried others, including another crossover from windsurfing: foot straps. The straps allowed them to hop over windchop and launch themselves into spectacular aerial flips off the backs of waves (with the downside that when they fell, the board could whipsaw their legs around in the whitewater). Hence the nickname: the "Strapped" crew.

Hamilton, in particular, emerged as the ringleader. Now known almost universally by his first name, Laird, he was the stepson of Billy Hamilton, a noted North Shore surfer of the late sixties. The good news was that Laird grew up hanging around the North Shore elite; the bad news was he was still a haole boy in Hawaiian schools, fending off attacks with a tough, chip-on-his-shoulder attitude. Laird followed in Billy's footsteps, becoming an accomplished North Shore surfer with an aggressive, powerful style. He was also photogenic and made a living early on as a model (as did Kerbox), which didn't hurt the Strapped crew when it came to media coverage. Laird made *People* magazine's "50 Most Beautiful People" list in 1996, and his physique and thrill-seeking persona attracted much media attention to the tow-in revolution.

The tow-in phenomenon demonstrated surfing's increasing interaction with other sports. We have seen how skateboarding spun off surfing and then fed new approaches, such as aerials, back into it, and tow-in surfing similarly derived from windsurfing. Another key input then came from snowboarding, yet another surfing spin-off that had reached broad popularity. Snowboarders had settled on a simple, short template for their boards, and demonstrated that such shortboards could handle high-speed turns. If snowboarders could ride mountains on small boards, why couldn't surfers ride mountains of water the same way? Big-wave surfboards had always been long, around ten feet or more—but that, the Strapped crew realized, was just for paddling speed. Once you catch the wave, you don't need the length, and Laird and his buddies had soon cut their boards down to the six-foot range.

This was a key additional step, and helped differentiate tow-in from previous big-wave surfing. That is, the tow-in revolution was not just about catching and riding these waves; it was also about what surfers were *doing* on the waves. And that meant not just the jet skis, but also the shortboards and straps. Instead of just angling across the face and racing for the safety of the shoulder, previously the main approach of big-wave riders, Laird and his buddies were carving turns across the face and arcing under (and sometimes over) the pitching lip, and in general taking small-wave surfing to a vastly greater canvas. Peter Cole, a big-wave legend from the 1950s, declared, "This tow-in surfing has made regular surfing look like a Model T."

Then came the wave at Teahupoo in 2000. Doerner towed Laird

into a monstrous mutant of a wave that reared up over the reef, warped, and then doubled over with a lip nearly as thick as the wave was high. Laird somehow steered a course through the cavern of the beast and shot through the barrel to the safety of the shoulder, where he sat down on his board and wept. Videos of the ride left surfers everywhere awestruck, and it was instantly recognized as "the Wave," the heaviest ride in surfing history. A photo of it ran on the cover of *Surfer* with a simple caption: "Oh my god . . ."

The Teahupoo wave boosted Laird's already formidable celebrity. Big-wave riders at times complained that pro surfing gave them few career opportunities, yet the most commercially successful surfer in the world came from their ranks. At least in terms of exposure, Laird dwarfed Kelly Slater, who dominated the world pro tour in the 1990s. Hamilton crossed over from surf-industry sponsors to mainstream commercial companies such as Nike and American Express, to the point where "Laird" itself became a sort of brand, with the associated image of a rugged and tanned waterman, hyper-fit and fearless. Laird's success made him not universally loved in the surf community, and the outsized ego that allowed him to challenge big waves turned off some surfers. But there was no denying that he had helped usher in a revolution in surfing.

The revolution, though, did not happen overnight, and it reached much further than many surfers realized. For one thing, surfing was no longer a solitary pursuit. Tow-in involved teams of riders, two to a ski and usually with several skis coordinated in a single session. More important, tow-in changed surfing's relationship with technology. Previously surfers had largely ignored the technologies of surfboards and wetsuits and clung to a sense that surfing was a "natural" sport, free of technological trappings. Tow-in surfing shattered that illusion.

Outer reefs became the scene of technological extravaganzas, with dozens of jet skis circling, the whine of their internal combustion engines rivaling the roar of the surf. To complete the circus, these sessions often include helicopters circling overhead and an armada of boats, all to carry the photo and film crews on hand to document the occasion. And the documentary images were far from secondary; they sustained the whole enterprise, since without industry sponsors few individuals would have the financial means to afford jet skis, trailers, sleds, fuel, and special tow-in boards. A full tow-in setup could easily run into the tens of thousands of dollars, and the travel costs of chasing big waves added to the bill. Sponsors paid for it only because the images helped move product.

Some surfers rejected tow-in surfing for just that reason. The Strapped crew had the swashbuckling air of pirates, swooping in from the sea to score rare treasures. Much of the big-wave community initially viewed them as enjoying ill-gotten gains. For one thing, they mostly stood outside the big-wave fraternity and even the surf community. The Strapped crew included several names, such as Dave Kalama, unfamiliar to the surf community but well known to windsurfers. Only Doerner, a respected North Shore lifeguard and Waimea veteran, had previous recognition among the big-wave elite. The tight-knit big-wave fraternity did not immediately appreciate having these newcomers suddenly riding seventy-foot waves at Jaws without paying their dues in the big-wave ranks.

More broadly, for many surfers tow-in smacked of cheating. If you didn't paddle into the wave yourself, it wasn't surfing; you were just waterskiing. Big-wave stalwarts such as Ken Bradshaw mocked the new approach, and resistance persisted for several years. But the Strapped crew continued pushing the boundaries, surfing fifty- and then sixty-foot waves as if they were in cartoons, while the purists sat on the beach because it was too big for paddling. Tow-in surfing gradually gained converts, and even Bradshaw came around. Laird's wave at Teahupoo in 2000 capped the revolution.

In effect, tow-in surfing required a redefinition of the waterman. Before, a true waterman pitted himself against the elements. That's why so many of the early exemplars, from Duke and Tom Blake through Peter Cole, started as competitive swimmers—because surfing often required getting yourself back to the beach in one piece, amid racing currents and relentless whitewater, without your board or anything else to bail you out. Laird and the Strapped crew changed this by adding technology to the equation. The new waterman handled a variety of equipment, from surfboards to windsurfers to jet skis (and Laird meanwhile added kitesurfing and stand-up paddling to the waterman equation). The lifeguard Doerner warned that tow-in surfers still needed to survive in the open ocean and swim through poundings in the impact zone even greater than at Waimea. But the warning was needed because the image suggested otherwise: mastering the equipment seemed to get surfers into and out of the biggest challenges. After 2000, surfers considered no waterman complete (and up to this point it was, as we shall see, always a man) unless he had towed into big waves.

As jet skis proliferated in big-wave lineups, however, resistance appeared not in the form of surfers' conservatism, but in the law. One issue concerned public safety: jet skis' high speeds endangered swimmers and other surfers, which had led to their ban at Hawaiian surf breaks. The Strapped crew apparently got a pass because North Shore lifeguards such as Terry Ahue and Brian Keaulana, themselves accomplished surfers who used jet skis as rescue craft, were the ones who defined the boundary and decided to tolerate tow-ins at outer reefs—and Doerner himself was part of this elite lifeguard community. Laird said at the outset, "If Terry or Brian ever told me to stop doing this, I would. . . . It's a family, all of these guys who know their way around big surf, and it's all based on safety. If you blow it, you hear from the family." But as tow-in teams proliferated, local governments began to regulate them, requiring ski drivers to attend classes and obtain a license, and allowing jet skis in the surf only when waves reached a certain size.

A more serious issue concerned the environment. Two-stroke jet-ski engines are extremely polluting, spewing exhaust smoke into the air and up to one-third of the fuel unburned into the water. In the late 1990s, the jet-ski industry introduced new fuel-injection systems and four-stroke engines to cut emissions, but most jet skis remained two-strokes, and their noise and pollution led federal and state governments to ban jet skis in many parks and marine sanctuaries on environmental grounds.

The environmental consequences did not appear on the radar of most surfers until tow-in teams began tackling Maverick's. The big-wave spot lay right in the middle of the Monterey Bay National Marine Sanctuary, an environmental preserve established in 1992 by the federal government to protect one of the most diverse marine ecosystems on the planet. Monterey was viewed as the crown jewel in the sanctuary system, equivalent to Yosemite in the national parks. So what were a bunch of surfers doing tooling around on two-strokes, dumping fuel and exhaust into this nature preserve? Breaking the law, that's what. That, at least, was the view of some environmentalists. The sanctuary's original designation banned jet skis except in a few existing harbors, but an ambiguous definition of "personal watercraft" in the regulations left a loophole that Maverick's tow surfers, like their Hawaiian colleagues, happily drove through.

The federal government soon moved to close it. In 2001 sanctuary managers began soliciting input on revised regulations, and twelve thousand public comments poured in. The local Surfrider Foundation chapter led the charge, urging a jet-ski ban based on environmental noise and pollution (although some of these objections also no doubt drew on the purist, "tow-in isn't real surfing" view). In response the tow-in surfers organized the Association of Professional Towriders, arguing that they used jet skis in small numbers, on few days, and in a limited area, and that jet skis in fact enhanced safety, since they could be used to rescue surfers who got in trouble in big waves. They also declared that tow-in surfers were, as Jeff Clark put it, "like astronauts"—jet skis, like rockets, got people to places no others had been, in this case not the moon but rather sixty-foot waves. A little environmental damage was just the cost of progress. Clark's speculation was not so far-fetched; rumor had it that NASA in the 1950s considered big-wave surfers as potential astronauts before settling on test pilots; if so, *Surfer* magazine observed, the first footprints on the moon might have been barefoot.

The two sides haggled for several years over possible compromises, such as allowing a limited number of jet skis at certain spots and only when surf reached a certain size. But environmentalists balked at any concessions that allowed these machines to operate at all in the sanctuary, while tow-surfers fumed that environmentalists put more value on marine life than human life, since any surfer who supported the ban would love to see a jet ski if he got stuck in the impact zone on a big day. In 2009 the government declared that jet skis could operate only from December to February, and only during high-surf warnings, but tow-surfers continued to complain that this kept them out of the water on many good days.

Restrictions on tow-in surfing were part of a wider political debate over all these personal combustion-engine devices, whether snowmobiles or ATVs or jet skis, and their effects on the environment and other people. The debate turned on the fundamental issue of government regulation of individual behavior—that is, the balance between individual liberty and public welfare. In this case it was the individual right to choose one's personal recreation versus the costs of environmental damage. The tow-in debate presented a particular dilemma for surfers, many of whom would define themselves as environmentally conscious, yet were apparently willing to compromise environmental ideals in order to ride big waves.

WHAT THE BIG-WAVE REVOLUTION MEANT

Tow-in surfing opened up still more spots around the world to big-wave surfing, including Ghost Tree, off the Pebble Beach golf course and just down the coast from Maverick's, Shipsterns Bluff in Tasmania, Dungeons in South Africa, and spots in Peru, Spain, Ireland, and Japan. Several of these were mutant waves with double-ups, warps, or wobbles in the face that made them basically impossible to paddle into but feasible with tow-in. Some tow-in spots also sparked debates over environmental effects and possible regulations, starting with Ghost Tree, which also lay in the Monterey sanctuary, but also, for example, Dungeons, which was similarly inside a South African marine preserve and where government restrictions on jet skis similarly prompted an outcry from local big-wave surfers.

All these new spots further diluted the focus on the North Shore, as big-wave surfing went increasingly global. The isolation and inconsistency of many of these waves also highlighted another role for science and technology, in surf forecasting. This same time frame saw the development of a system of satellites feeding data from space-based sensors and far-flung electronic buoys into computer weather models, which in turn fed their results onto the Internet. These data networks and online reports allowed Mark Foo to fly over to surf Maverick's on word of an imminent swell. A case in point was Cortes Bank, a seamount one hundred miles off the coast of San Diego that caught huge open-ocean swells—not a place surfers can hang around waiting for a big enough swell to arrive. In a famous session there in January 2001, Mike Parsons towed into a wave estimated at sixty-six feet high; in 2008 Parsons rode a seventy-footer.

Big waves were no longer the province of a small North Shore fraternity with a couple dozen members; now hundreds of surfers around the world were venturing into huge surf. With more surfers one would expect more deaths, and indeed more surfers have died in the last fifteen years than in the previous four decades, starting with Foo and including Donnie Solomon at Waimea, Todd Chesser at a North Shore outer reef, Taerea at Teahupoo, Peter Davi at Ghost Tree in 2007, and Sion Milosky at Maverick's in 2011 (a couple months after a Maverick's wipeout left another surfer in a coma). This trend will likely continue, and it is probably more than just a matter of numbers. Surf media lavished coverage on the latest big-wave exploits, and companies began awarding lucrative annual prizes for the largest wave, heaviest wipeout, and so on. Mike Parsons, for example, won $65,000 for his 2001 wave at Cortes Bank. That year, the surfwear firm Billabong announced a half-million-dollar prize to the first person to ride a hundred-foot wave.

This money made big-wave surfing an alternate career route for pro surfers. Noll had first pioneered this path, and Foo and Bradshaw had revived the idea of surfers getting paid for their big-wave prowess alone. The big-wave revival greatly increased the commercial prospects, especially for surfers stepping off the world tour in their thirties—such as Parsons, his friend Brad Gerlach, and Shane Dorian—and looking to sustain an income as pro surfers. Industry sponsors were crucial to paying for all this equipment—and travel, as big-wave riders routinely chased waves around the globe, stashing jet skis in backyards near the major spots and hopping red-eye flights to meet forecast swells.

Some big-wave veterans wondered whether the money and hype were pulling some surfers into waves they otherwise wouldn't, and shouldn't, ride. But most big-wave surfers were not just in it for the money. There were still guys out there doing it without sponsors, the local contractors calling in sick to surf the biggest days at Waimea or Maverick's, and most of the sponsored elite were ultimately doing it for the same reason Greg Noll and his friends had fifty years earlier: the sheer adrenaline rush that came from riding a fifty-foot wall of water.

The Strapped crew meanwhile continued to push the technological envelope. In 2003 the film *Step into Liquid* included a startling segment on them. As Laird and his friends towed into giant waves at Jaws, their

Laird Hamilton on a hydrofoil surfboard. (Source: Joel Guy)

boards suddenly rose out of the water until they were skimming two feet over the surface, with only a thin metal rod connecting them to the underwater hydrofoil that provided their main contact with the water. The hydrofoil boards not only minimized drag, further boosting tow-in speeds, but also avoided wind chop, allowing surfers to ride in any conditions.

The hydrofoil boards did not immediately catch on, perhaps because they looked utterly unlike any previous surfboard. But they highlighted the fact that the tow-in revolution had fundamental consequences for all of surfing, not just for big waves. It changed the surf community's attitude toward technology in general, introducing not only jet skis but also foot straps, short and slender big-wave boards, and finally the far-out hydrofoils, plus the Internet-based surf forecasts that themselves relied on electronic buoy networks, satellite data, and computer models. More recently, big-wave surfers have begun wearing inflatable wetsuit tops; when pushed deep underwater in a wipeout, they yank the ripcord, a carbon-dioxide canister inflates the suit, and they bob to the surface like a cork.

It is likely not coincidence that the big-wave revival coincided with an upsurge in interest in wave pools. If "surfing" could include buzzing around behind a jet ski on a hydrofoil, then it might also include riding a foam mat on a water jet in a swimming pool. Or, for that matter, towing into the wave created by a calving glacier, also known as "glacier surfing," or riding the wake created by tankers in the Galveston ship channel, which was basically wakeboarding without the rope. All of these, in this brave new world, qualified as surfing. Tow-in redefined surfing as something more than just paddling into an ocean wave on a board, and blurred the line between nature and artifice.

For that reason, some big-wave surfers sought a return to purer roots, and by 2010 enough had joined the backlash against tow-in that a paddle-in revival was clearly discernible. It did not help that tow-in surfers were making it look almost too easy, as one Aussie charger was filmed guzzling a can of beer in a massive Shipstern's barrel, while another towed in wearing a Santa suit. *Surfer* magazine proclaimed "the end of the machine" and added, "in the eyes of the big-wave vanguard, a towrope has become the equivalent of training wheels."

Surfing is more than technology. That was as true for the original North Shore pioneers as it is for the current paddle-in revivalists. Although new technology—the new foam-and-fiberglass boards with fins—helped open up the North Shore in the 1950s, cultural influences also played a role. While surfers were first dropping down big North Shore walls, rock climbers were climbing up big Yosemite walls. It is probably not just coincidence that surfers pioneered Waimea Bay and climbers ascended Yosemite's El Capitan within months of each other. The 1950s world of "the organization man" not only stimulated the development of surfing in general, but also the particular pursuit of high-risk, authentic challenges. Like Jack Kerouac and the Beats chasing their "kicks," renegade big-wave surfers and big-wall climbers became adrenaline junkies to escape fifties conformity. Real men didn't climb the corporate ladder in a gray flannel suit; rather, like the right-stuff test pilots of this same time, they hung their ass out over the edge to see if they could pull it back. Atomic-age nihilism only encouraged such behavior: why not take some risks, if the world might go up in a mushroom cloud tomorrow anyway?

A similar explanation may factor into the revival of big-wave interest in the 1990s. Again, it was not just big-wave surfing that thrived. "Extreme" sports in general had enthusiasts hucking hundred-foot cliffs on snowboards and skydiving off buildings and bridges. One theory attributes this embrace of death-defying adventure sports to the rise of the feminist movement and the coincident rise of white-collar work. For all these white males sitting in desk jobs with no physical labor, while women challenged their social roles, extreme sports helped recapture rugged male individualism.

Another development in surfing itself may support this theory. At the same time surfers returned their attention to big waves, women's surfing was bursting on the scene. Women began to challenge performance standards, pulling into barrels and boosting airs with the best male surfers, and a *Surfer* magazine cover in 1996 threw down the gauntlet to its male readers: "Lisa Andersen surfs better than you." In this post-feminist world, what could men do to keep ahead of women? Carve out a realm where they could remain dominant. The big-wave revival, in other words, could have been male surfers' way of saying, "Oh yeah? Can Lisa Andersen do *this*?" Maybe Laird Hamilton didn't have Lisa Andersen in his mind when he dropped into sixty-foot waves at Jaws. But it is striking how Laird himself emerged as the big-wave standard-bearer with an almost cartoonish image as a muscle-bound he-man. If this theory is true, what will men do now that women are beginning to encroach into big-wave surfing? Women are out surfing Maverick's and towing in at Teahupoo, where Peruvian charger Maya Gabeira won much respect for a horrendous wipeout in 2007. Keala Kennelly fearlessly threaded a monster Teahupoo barrel during what became known as the Code Red swell of 2011, after Tahitian maritime authorities issued warnings against anyone entering the ocean. Two days later Kennelly earned fifty stitches in her face after being driven headfirst into the reef. After such exploits by female big-wave chargers, how far would men go in response?

13 WOMEN AND SURFING: FROM FLAPPERS TO ROXY GIRL

In ancient Hawaii women and men participated equally in surfing. The legendary sport of kings was also the sport of queens. Queen Ka'ahumanu, favorite wife of Kamehameha, preferred what is now known as Castles, an outer reef at Waikiki that was *kapu* for all but the *ali'i*—Hawaiian royalty. Castles breaks only on huge swells that cause Waikiki's regular breaks to close out. Ka'ahumanu, who weighed over two hundred pounds, was a powerful athlete with the strength and skill to paddle an *olo* into a fifteen-foot wave at Castles. The royal couple surfed the outer reefs of Oahu together along with numerous breaks along the Kona coast. Both were adept at *lele wa'a*, or canoe leaping, where a surfer got into the wave after jumping off an outrigger canoe—an early version of tow-in surfing. For Ka'ahumanu and Kamehameha it meant catching huge waves at outside Castles and riding them through to the inside.

Early Hawaiian oral history confirms that women and men partook equally of surfing. Several miles down the coast from Waikiki, a break called Mamala honors a Hawaiian queen who was also a famous surfer. Early European accounts and engravings also emphasized the presence of women surfers, with occasional reference to children riding smaller boards closer to shore. Except on those beaches where the most dangerous swells peaked and *kapu* restrictions applied, men and women shared surfing areas equally. Compared to today's low ratio of females to males in surfing, a large percentage of wahines of early Hawaii were skillful surfers.

What happened to the wahines? Most histories claim that prude missionaries covered Hawaiian nudity with Western garb and banned their traditions, especially surfing. As we know, though, several missionaries admired surfing themselves, and many Hawaiians happily ignored the pious preachers. The real reason for the near death of surfing was the decimation of Hawaiians, women and men, by Western diseases. Surfing survived, barely, but was a sport dominated by males for most of the next century.

The return of wahines to surfing was a long, slow process. Surfing today remains a male-dominated sport with lingering sexism. When you grab a copy of *Surfer*, *Surfing*, or Australia's *Tracks*, the only marquee picture of a woman appears in advertisements featuring backside shots of topless models wearing minuscule thong bikinis. After thumbing through a few magazines, the average newcomer to the sport might conclude that women do not actually surf, but rather recline on the beach wearing negligible bathing suits. Magazines filled with stories and pictures devoted exclusively to men are not particularly attractive to female athletes. Indeed, apart from the thong bathing suits and the occasional women's wetsuit, the surfing accessories marketed in magazines are for men only. Yet women have made important inroads into surfing and their presence has changed the sport, from local lineups to industry boardrooms. How did wahines evolve from sharing waves equally with men to over half a century of near banishment from the sport? Why did it take so long for women's surfing to revive? What caused the return of the wahines?

The relative absence of women from the initial revival of surfing in the twentieth century stemmed from several factors. Culturally, the surfing revival occurred in the context of American, not Hawaiian, society. This male-dominated and prudish culture provided little encouragement for female athletes, and when women did venture into the water they were often encumbered by full-length woolens to cover their skin. Surfboard technology also posed an obstacle, as boards shifted from short alaias to massive, unwieldy planks. Women nevertheless began to make inroads. The first step came from the world of competitive swimming in the first part of the century. The second came from new surfboard technology emerging out of the Second World War. And the third and final step came through a piece of federal legislation in the early 1970s, in the context of the growing women's movement, that revolutionized all of women's sport in America and fundamentally reshaped the surfing landscape.

THE BEACHBOYS AND THE FLAPPERS

Duke Kahanamoku and his brothers, the original beachboys, introduced numerous women to the surf through surf lessons and tandem surf rides. By far the most famous woman to ride Waikiki's waves with the beachboys was Doris Duke, heir to the Duke tobacco and energy fortune, known as the "richest little girl in the world." She arrived in Hawaii while honeymooning with her first husband and thereafter often visited Waikiki for long stints. It took 250 workers five years to build Shangri La, her spectacular home above Diamond Head. The six-foot-tall heiress was an accomplished athlete who won tandem surf competitions with Sam Kahanamoku and entered paddleboard races. She fell in love with the Waikiki beach life, beachboys, and the surf, spending decades refining her magnificent home. Doris helped her lifelong friend Duke Kahanamoku and his wife purchase their home in Honolulu.

Swimming had a major role in the resurgence of surfing in the early twentieth century. Swimmers had the strength, stamina, and water knowledge to navigate the heavy boards and swim back to shore after a wipeout. Paddling to an outer reef could take half an hour or more, and losing your board in a wipeout led to another long swim back in. The pioneers among male surfers were athletes with superb swimming skills, and it is no surprise that women with similar backgrounds were among the first to join them.

Swimming was booming in popularity in the early twentieth century, and Hawaiians, born and raised in warm tropical waters, provided many of America's first swimming champions. Duke Kahanamoku, as we know, won many Olympic swimming golds starting in

1912 and spread surfing on his global swimming tours. During a visit Down Under, Duke tandem-surfed with fifteen-year-old Isabel Letham, a skilled ocean swimmer, who became the first Australian to stand up on a surfboard. Letham was hooked on surfing and helped spread the sport among women and men throughout Australia for the rest of her life. Less well known than Duke was Ruth Stacker, another Hawaiian, who held the world record for the fifty free. A publication declared in 1914, "The King and Queen of the surf both live in Hawaii," and a year later Jack London's wife Charmian watched Stacker teaching kids how to surf in the wahine zone in 1915.

Victorian values made swimming particularly difficult for women. Cultural expectations confined women to the sidelines for many sports, and when they did enter the game current fashions constrained them further. Australian beaches were segregated by sex, and American women by law wore restrictive bathing costumes. Women sea bathers in the nineteenth century wore long sleeves and loose trousers to the ankles beneath knee-length skirts, and up to the turn of the century women swimmers kept their legs and most of their arms covered. When Australian swimming champion Annette Kellerman showed up on a Boston beach in 1907 in a form-fitting one-piece exposing her calves—not even her knees—she was arrested for indecent exposure. Suits gradually climbed above the knee; in 1917 the American Association of Park Superintendents issued "bathing suit regulations" that required women's suits to expose no more than four inches above the knee, and to have "quarter-arm sleeves or close-fitting arm holes." Park officials patrolled beaches, tape measure in hand, to enforce the rules.

Even afterward, bare legs raised eyebrows. New Yorker Ethelda Bleibtrey started swimming in 1918 to recover from polio and over the next two years won every swimming championship in the country. Ethelda's career was full of firsts and not all of them involved swimming medals. In 1919, at New York's man-made Manhattan Beach, the police cited Bleibtrey for "nude swimming" when she removed her stockings before going for a swim. Her case drew attention to the absurdity of covering one's legs while swimming. Public opinion swung in her favor and stockings were no longer required.

In contrast to earlier woodcuts of naked native women surfing, images of women surfing in Hawaii from this time show them fully dressed in elaborate bathing suits that at times included stockings or lace-up boots. Today Westerners wonder at the sight of Muslim women competing in athletic burkas, forgetting that Western women in the early twentieth century similarly had to cover their skin. Even the more liberated one-piece woolen suits could soak up over ten pounds of water when immersed. Try swimming a mile or two so encumbered, with a board weighing a hundred pounds, and you can see why very few women were swimming, let alone surfing.

Pioneering female swimmers challenged the social barriers surrounding aquatic sports. While competing in Australia, Ethelda and her friend Charlotte Boyle were the first American swimmers to bob their hair. This style, favored by the "flappers" of the 1920s, was far more convenient for swimming and came to symbolize the women's liberation movement in the years after World War I, when women's suffrage and sexual liberation challenged Victorian gender roles.

Bleibtrey's visit Down Under was all business in the swimming department. She defeated the great Australian champion Fanny Durack, who had won the first-ever women's Olympic championship. Bleibtrey joined Duke Kahanamoku at the 1920 Olympic Games in Antwerp, where the competition was held in a murky tidal estuary. Ethelda told Prince Albert of Belgium that the conditions made it feel like she was swimming in mud, not water. Her three gold medals were a first for American women, and she could easily have won four if the competition had included women's backstroke, her best event. Afterward Ethelda embarked on a triumphant world tour, surfing with Duke and the Prince of Wales in Hawaii, dating oarsman Jack Kelly in Atlantic City, and triumphantly touring the Panama Canal, Australia, and New Zealand. Like the Duke's, Bleibtrey's aquatic expertise was multifold. She, too, performed a water rescue that attracted national attention and traveled the world performing as a swimmer.

Ethelda Bleibtrey's career set the stage for another swimmer who became the greatest female surfer of the early twentieth century. Like Bleibtrey, Mary Ann Hawkins overcame childhood illness through swimming, taking lessons at a YMCA. She was winning races by age ten and later swam for the Los Angeles Athletic Club in the 1930s.

Ethelda Bleibtrey and Duke Kahanamoku, July 25, 1920, just before the Antwerp Olympics. Bleibtrey's three Antwerp golds included the 100-meter freestyle, which she won by over three seconds, breaking her own world record in the bargain. Duke also won gold in the 100 meters there. (Source: Library of Congress)

Her parents moved from Pasadena to Costa Mesa, where she swam for the Corona del Mar club. Hawkins set a national junior record in the 800-yard free relay in 1933 and three years later won the AAU 500-meter freestyle and 880-yard backstroke titles, but she was already moving away from the pool toward the ocean. In 1936 she began entering long-distance paddleboard races and by 1940 won both paddleboard and surfing championships.

Hawkins had all-around aquatic ability. She was one of the best bodysurfers of her generation, man or woman; she could bodysurf faster than many surfers could ride waves on a board. She was among the first surfers to excel at Palos Verdes Cove and was a favorite of pioneering surf photographer Doc Ball. *Life* magazine included a photo of Mary Ann surfing Palos Verdes in its February 1938 edition. Two months later she appeared in the *Los Angeles Times* as the only woman to undergo the grueling test to become a Los Angeles County lifeguard, competing for the job against male swimming and water polo Olympians. She also appeared in the *Times* performing a handstand on a wave, shortly before becoming the first woman to enter the Catalina-Hermosa aquaplane race. Hawkins worked as a stunt person for Hollywood and later moved to Hawaii, where she started a swimming school and taught thousands of children how to swim.

THE POSTWAR ERA: "GIRL BOARDS," GIDGET, AND A NEW GENERATION

There is an intriguing photo of Mary Anne Hawkins smiling atop a human pyramid of her fellow Corona del Mar surf club teammates—all women. But large numbers of wahines did not join the ranks of California surfers in the sport's early years. One of the highest hurdles faced by early women surfers was the weight of surfboards. Although the Duke certainly appreciated the potential of women surfers—in 1928 he declared that "women, as a rule, make better surf-board artists than men"—one of his innovations provided a major obstacle. As we know, the initial revival had centered on alaia boards, short six-footers, but Duke soon demonstrated greater paddling and surfing stability on long ten- to twelve-footers. These long redwood planks could weigh well over one hundred pounds, and even more after soaking up water. Tom Blake's hollow paddleboards improved buoyancy but were akin to small boats and still required enormous strength to drag into the surf and then maneuver in the water. Technical advances in the years following World War II made the sport far more accessible to women. Beginning with Bob Simmons and continuing with Joe Quigg and Matt Kivlin, Southern California, and particularly Malibu, was the laboratory for production of the new boards. Quigg designed a balsawood-and-fiberglass "Girl Board" for Darrylin Zanuck, daughter of Hollywood mogul Darryl Zanuck and an avid Malibu local. At about forty pounds the "Girl Board" was lighter and more maneuverable, and subsequent models in the 1950s cut that weight in half again, so that a five-foot-tall, ninety-five-pound girl—the size of Kathy "Gidget" Kohner—could handle one. The lightweight Girl Boards performed so well that guys were soon sheepishly asking to borrow them, and shapers began shaping similar boards—minus the "girl" appellation—for male Malibu regulars. The postwar surfboard design revolution was, in part, driven by the demands of the growing crew of female surfers.

One indicator of the increasing presence of women surfers came at the Makaha International Surfing Championship, held on Oahu's west side starting in 1954. The inaugural contest had men and women competing together, and the next year a separate women's division formed. Marge Calhoun of Southern California won the Makaha contest in 1958, a particularly impressive victory considering it was her first trip to Hawaii. Calhoun learned to surf at Malibu during the early 1950s and was among the first to ride Quigg's Girl Boards. After winning at Makaha, Calhoun traveled to the North Shore and was among the first women in the modern era to surf powerful winter swells along Sunset Beach. Calhoun was a cofounder of the U.S. Surfing Association that campaigned to keep California beaches open and promoted the sport of surfing. Calhoun and her two daughters set the standard for women surfers during the 1950s and into the 1960s.

By the time *Gidget* and *Beach Blanket Bingo* arrived, women surfers had already gotten off their beach towels and were pushing performance standards. Linda Benson grew up watching her brothers surf in Encinitas, retrieving their boards when they washed up on the shore. Soon she was paddling the boards back out for a few waves herself. She started with a balsa board and was soon setting a new standard for hotdogging. Benson idolized the diminutive Dewey Weber, who jitterbugged his way up and down the deck of Dale Velzy's wide-tailed "pig" boards at Malibu Point. At five foot two, Benson was an inch shorter than Weber and equally balletic in her style. Light weight is an advantage for surfers, since it makes it easier to get up to planing speed after catching a wave. Thus Benson was among the first surfers, male or female, to master the nose ride and had a storied career in the late 1950s and 1960s.

Few athletes excel in their first competition regardless of talent.

In 1959, a fifteen-year-old Benson entered her first surfing competition, the inaugural U.S. Surfing Championships held in Huntington Beach, and won. She also won the 1959 Makaha contest and a few years later became the first woman to surf Waimea Bay. Other women quickly emerged to challenge Benson. Joyce Hoffman dominated women's surfing competitions throughout much of the 1960s, winning the Makaha competition in 1964 and five world titles between 1961 and 1971. In 1964, Margo Godfrey Oberg won the first of her numerous world titles at age fifteen. Her professional career spanned three decades, and the shift from longboards to shortboards. Hoffman and Oberg obtained limited support from sponsors and benefited from the formation of early women's professional surfing organizations, but their success was far from the rule in women's surfing in the 1960s and 1970s. Despite the advent of the women's liberation movement in wider society—or perhaps because of it—many male surfers clung to sexist views and defended their dominance in the lineup, in what another female surfing pioneer, Jericho Poppler, called the "dark age" of surfing.

THE DARK AGES

"If I catch you out here again I'll shove my board right up your cunt." This reproof greeted a woman surfer who made the mistake of cutting off one of the locals at Ala Moana during the late 1960s. It is hard enough to surf Ala Moana, a challenging spot that breaks across a shallow reef, without disgusting put-downs. Women endured insults regardless of their talent. Poppler had enough talent to be crowned U.S. surfing champion in 1970 and world champion in 1976, yet a few years earlier surfers at her local break were telling her to "come back when your tits are bigger." For women, from the 1960s into the '80s every break was potentially hostile. Another male surfer at Ala Moana punched world champion Sally Prange in the face when she inadvertently cut him off. Seventies big-wave rider Kim Hamrock paddled into practically anything the ocean could throw at her, only to hear male surfers yell, "Get out of here, bitch!"

Women faced additional insults in the nascent professional surfing scene. As contests for male surfers began attracting corporate sponsors and TV coverage from ABC's *Wide World of Sports*, women's contests languished in the background. Mary Setterholm, Jericho Poppler, and Mary Lou McGinnis formed the Women's International Surfing Association (WISA) to correct the imbalance. The first WISA contest took place at Malibu in 1975. A year later, in 1976, Fred Hemmings started International Professional Surfers (IPS) and convinced the women to join his tour, but their lower status in IPS persuaded Poppler, Rell Sunn, Lynne Boyer, Margo Oberg, and a number of other prominent women professionals to form Women's Pro Surfing (WPS) in 1979. (Setterholm, a former U.S. champion, had meanwhile fled the surf scene after a group of surfers sexually assaulted her at a party.) Even then women's surfing continued to lag behind men's in financial rewards. Total prize money for the men's tour in 1980 was $243,850. The women's tour offered $10,000.

The emergence of a pro circuit for women would eventually pave the way for a generation of professionals whose winnings could sustain the expense of competing around the world. Floridian Frieda Zamba won the first of many world titles in 1982, and the rest of the decade saw surfers such as Zamba, Kim Mearig of Santa Barbara, and Australia's Pam Burridge and Pauline Menczer open a new frontier for women's surfing. By 1990 prize money on the women's tour reached over a quarter million dollars, twenty-five times the total for 1980. But that still lagged the men by a long shot. The surf media didn't help. The masthead of most major surf magazines revealed a landscape of almost exclusively male editors, writers, and photographers. These men gave little coverage to women surfers, and the limited publicity further discouraged potential sponsors. With the surf media defining "surfer" as male, sponsors and the general public had little sense that women's surfing even existed. At the end of the 1980s, *Surfer* magazine declared that "women's surfing continues its struggle to survive. . . . Modern female surfing just isn't dynamic enough to spark any flames of public interest."

In January 1993 Matt Warshaw spotlighted surfing's chauvinism in a *Surfer* article titled "Sexism Sucks." Warshaw bluntly called out surfing as "a sexist activity in a sexist world," and declared that sexism, far from waning in the postfeminist era, was getting worse. He observed that a recent issue of *Surfer* had 226 photos, 6 of which featured women; 5 of the 6 were in ads, and none of them were surfing. For comparison, the first issue of *Surfer* in 1960 had 3 shots of women surfing, out of 93 total. Warshaw noted the frequent rhetoric of male surf journalists likening surfing to sex or, worse, rape, with frequent descriptions of male surfers ravaging the waves. He also noted that surfing's sexism reinforced its homophobia, evident in the whisperings about the sexuality of several female pros, whose "image problem," as industry insiders called it, was lesbianism.

The *Surfer* editors puckishly teased Warshaw's article with a "Bikini Issue" tag on that issue's cover. But since every issue of the magazine was the bikini issue, *Surfer* readers may have missed the joke. The article did not seem to affect *Surfer's* editorial content, which continued its almost exclusive focus on male surfers amid the bikini models in surfwear ads. Warshaw's article itself was accompanied by a handful of tiny one-by-two-inch photos of women surfing, instead of the usual full-page images. And just inside the front cover of the "Sexism" issue ran the usual Reef surfwear ad, with a full-backside shot of a thong-clad young woman.

Surfing, of course, was not alone in its chauvinism. *Sports Illustrated*'s swimsuit edition remained its most popular issue, despite the annual flood of letters from offended subscribers. Women in many professional sports perceived that they were regarded more as sex objects than as athletes, evident in the larger sponsorships garnered by attractive, swimsuit-ready sportswomen like Anna Kournikova in tennis. Several female athletes cashed in on such attitudes by posing for *Playboy*, and some female surfers contributed to the beach-bunny stereotype. In 1974 Laura Blears, the first woman to compete against men and to surf Pipeline, posed nude on her surfboard for *Playboy*. A part-time waitress who earned $3,500 surfing in 1974, Blears was paid $1,500 by *Playboy*. She later appeared on an all-woman version of TV's *Superstars*, competing with Billie Jean King, Kathy Rigby, and a host of others in a contest King later called an "unbelievable bunch of garbage." Blears told reporters, "It's a downer when people think chicks who do sports aren't chicky enough. It's a trip bein' a chick, man. A groove. Superstars? Far out, man." In 1992 four-time world champion surfer Wendy Botha removed her clothing for the short-lived Australian *Playboy*. Botha's exposure disappointed some women surfers, but it gave them some attention at a time when surf magazines ignored them. Even as Botha was stripping for the camera, however, changes were afoot for women surfers.

THE WOMEN'S SURF BOOM: ROXY GIRL, *BLUE CRUSH*, AND TITLE IX

In the early 1990s, women constituted only 5 to 8 percent of all surfers. A decade later they accounted for 15 to 20 percent of surfers and commanded a significant market share in the surf industry. Where did this increase come from? What changed?

Commentators often credit the rise of women's surfing to the first female superstar, Lisa Andersen. A combination of drive, skill, athleticism, and timeliness enabled this product of Florida's Ormond Beach to take women's surfing to a whole new level. Unlike Linda Benson, Marge Calhoun, or Wendy Botha, Andersen did not come from a surfing family or grow up on the beach. Indeed, it is amazing that she ever encountered surfing at all. Andersen grew up in Virginia and had no idea what surfing was until her family moved to Ormond Beach when she was thirteen and she taught herself to surf on borrowed boards. Lisa and her three brothers grew up in an abusive family, with an alcoholic father and a tormented mother. By the time she was sixteen Lisa was well on her way to becoming a juvenile delinquent. Her father was drunk every evening and addressed his daughter's mounting transgressions with bursts of rage, on one occasion stomping her surfboard into smithereens. Lisa's mother put up with the alcoholism and watched as her husband hit the children. In the end surfing saved Lisa. She ran away from home during her junior year of high school to Huntington Beach, where she lived on couches and with a series of boyfriends while honing her skills at local beach breaks. Ian Cairns of Bronzed Aussie fame recognized Lisa's unique talent and let her enter competitions in the fledgling National Scholastic Surfing Association (NSSA). After winning two amateur competitions and garnering limited support from sponsors, Lisa turned pro.

The women's tour had grown but remained smaller than the men's tour. Lisa did not take the women's tour by storm, although her talent was immediately apparent. Fellow Floridian Frieda Zamba still reigned as the perennial champion with Botha close on her heels. Andersen spent years training with a series of coaches and competing with top male surfers; she modeled herself after the inscrutable Tom Curren, who also cut his teeth in the NSSA during the early 1980s. She lived for three years with Dave Parmenter, an accomplished former pro, surfing along the wild coast of Central California. As her career matured, Lisa moved to Australia and picked up sponsorship from Quiksilver.

By 1990 she was the most talented woman in the water, with small-wave moves comparable to the best of the male pros, but her coaches grew frustrated with her unwillingness, at times, to apply her immense talent. Andersen reached her peak when she jettisoned the men and trained by herself, finally mastering the mental aspects of competitive surfing. She also overcame the challenge of pregnancy and motherhood after marrying Brazilian surf organizer and ASP judge Renato Hickel. She competed while pregnant in 1993; the following year, after giving birth to her daughter, she won her first world championship. She went on to win three successive championships, breaking Frieda Zamba's record. In February 1996 *Surfer* magazine taunted its male readers with the cover caption "Lisa Andersen surfs better than you."

Why was Lisa Andersen the first superstar of women's surfing? One might follow the money. Any successful surf shop owner will tell you that the money is not in boards, wetsuits, and wax. The money is in clothing. Andersen's rise took place at a time when surf companies were looking to expand their clothing lines to include women. The business model was tried and true; in the 1970s, Levi's created jeans for women, opening up a brand-new market. Quiksilver's Danny Kwock recognized the market potential and created the Roxy brand for girls. Andersen informed her sponsors at Roxy about the need for women's surf trunks. Men's surf trunks were too big for women, and for many women surfing in a bikini meant continually pulling your suit out of your nether regions, an activity particularly uncomfortable with herds of male surfers leering at you. The real problem with a bikini-style suit, female or male, is that rubbing your thighs against a wax-covered board for a day or two in sun and salt water leaves them raw. Roxy changed the cut of surf trunks to suit women's bodies and turned on the style. The result was a new industry staple with flair and color that soon influenced its male predecessor. Who better to model the new duds than the photogenic world champ—Lisa Andersen? Finally, surfing magazines

Surfer *magazine cover, February, 1996, with caption: "Lisa Andersen surfs better than you." (Source: Tom Dugan photo and* Surfer *magazine)*

had an alternative to thong ads, and serious female surfers could stop involuntarily emulating the Reef Brazil girl.

Following the money works so long as there are women out there who want to be like Lisa Andersen. Roxy provided the supply; the demand came from women whose love for waves made them willing to paddle out into a pack of idiots, put up with stink-eye and leering, and pick off some waves. Such women purchased surf gear and actually used it. That generation of the 1990s started a revolution in surfing. Where did these women come from? Why did they succeed where the women's-liberation generation of the late sixties and seventies did not? Was the rise of women's surfing due just to one talented Floridian, plus the marketing genius of Quiksilver? Or were there larger social changes in play?

To understand this new generation one must return to Hawaii and a plantation on the island of Maui where, two months after Pearl Harbor, a diminutive young Japanese American girl resolved to run for high school student-body president. Patsy Mink won that race and spent the next half century taking on the establishment in her quest to change the social fabric of America. She left Maui with the goal of becoming a medical doctor, but after graduating from university she realized that few medical schools were willing to admit women. Mink became a lawyer instead and then launched a political career that led to twelve terms as the first woman to represent Hawaii's Second Congressional District. Revered by her constituents, Mink won her last election after her death in 2002. She was the first Asian American woman elected to Congress and the first woman elected to Congress from the state of Hawaii, and in 1972 she became the first Asian American, man or woman, to seek the presidential nomination of the Democratic Party. Patsy Mink never surfed, but she had perhaps more influence on women's surfing, not to mention women's sports in general, than any other figure in the last century. And yet her name appears nowhere in the surf literature.

"No person in the United States shall, on the basis of sex, be excluded from participation in, be denied the benefits of, or be subject to discrimination under any education program or activity receiving federal financial assistance." So goes the preamble to one section of the federal Education Amendments of 1972. It may seem like an obscure and boring legal provision, but it packed a huge punch. The law Patsy Mink helped craft is now called Title IX, a term that rippled through the U.S. athletic establishment like an earthquake. Title IX specifically applied the 1964 Civil Rights Act to discrimination against women. It sent a message to school districts, colleges, and universities throughout the United States that if they wanted to continue tapping hundreds of millions of dollars in government funding, their sports programs must offer women the same opportunity as men. All of a sudden America's public educational institutions had to come up with sports for girls and women equal to those enjoyed by millions of male athletes. After Title IX, the number of women participating in varsity college athletics increased from 30,000 to 150,000 by 1980; high school sports saw an even bigger jump, from under 300,000 to over 2 million girls, a sevenfold increase. By 1978 *Time* magazine was already declaring it "a revolution that is one of the most exciting and one of the most important in the history of sport."

The revolution did not occur overnight. It took two decades for the federal government to figure out how to enforce the law and get schools to comply, against objections and legal challenges from the NCAA and individual schools. Although the statistics showed Title IX's impact in the 1970s, its effects became even more clear by the 1990s.

So, what does this law have to do with women surfing? The NCAA does not sanction surfing and it is a club sport at the few universities that field competitive teams. The answer is that the impact of Title IX runs deeper than an NCAA women's soccer or basketball tournament. Before Title IX, even elite women athletes struggled to obtain scholarships for sports. Donna de Varona won two gold medals in swimming at the 1964 Olympics in Tokyo and could not get a college scholarship. After Title IX, young girls could hone their athletic abilities at schools and colleges across the land. Elementary and secondary schools developed girls' sports teams and programs to match the boys'. Fathers and mothers coached their daughters and drove them to practices alongside their brothers. For thousands of girls, paddling out was now a trivial exercise compared to two-a-day training workouts and high-level competition. Title IX created a generation of competitive, confident, and athletic young girls with the ability and inclination to paddle out and surf. The demand from this tidal wave of women surfers drove the billion-dollar industry represented by Lisa Andersen's stardom.

Hollywood took note. In 2002 the movie *Blue Crush* showed the new generation of wahines surfing at Pipeline on the North Shore of Hawaii. Loosely based on Susan Orlean's essay about the surfer girls of Hana, Maui, in 1993, *Blue Crush* shifted the scene to Oahu and women riding surfing's ultimate showcase. Orlean was awed at the tribe of tanned, athletic, independent girls whose lives revolved around waves, surfing competition, and beach life. "To be a surfer girl in a cool place like Hawaii is perhaps the apogee of all that is cool and wild and modern and sexy and defiant," according to Orlean. "The Hana girls, therefore, exist at that highest point—the point where being brave, tan, capable and independent, and having a real reason to wear all those surf-inspired clothes that other girls wear for fashion, is what matters most." At $35 million the most expensive surf movie ever made, *Blue Crush* grossed $52 million, much of it from thousands of teenage girls transfixed by the surfing lifestyle. And many of those young women now had an athletic mindset and experience, thanks to Title IX.

The *Blue Crush* Pipeline segments suggested that women could even enter the big-wave arena. Candy Calhoun had been one of the first, women or men, to bodysurf huge summer swells at the legendary Wedge in Newport Beach during the 1950s. Women charged Makaha, Waimea, and Sunset Beach in the 1960s. More recently, competitions at Tahiti's Teahupoo, one of the most challenging waves in the world, indicate that, contrary to the posturing of male surfers, gender has little to do with riding big waves. Keala Kennelly, a supremely confident Hawaiian, showed little fear there and won the Teahupoo women's contest three times—in 2000, 2002, and 2003. She even towed in on a monster day, negotiating the tube and weaving through to the channel. Her wave opened many eyes and made the cover of *Australian Surf Life for Men*, which, laughed Kennelly, is "the most chauvinistic magazine in the world. There was never a woman on the cover before or since." Kennelly later gashed her head on the reef at Teahupoo and then missed most of the 2006 ASP season after colliding with a coral head in Fiji and suffering severe bone contusions and torn ligaments. Kennelly starred as herself in *Blue Crush* and later appeared as Kai in HBO's ill-fated surf miniseries *John from Cincinnati*.

The draw of surfing for both men and women goes beyond the exploits of surfing professionals to the "soul" side of surfing. For the vast majority, surfing is not a competitive sport but rather a bond with the ocean. Duke Kahanamoku's skill as an all-around waterman was unparalleled; more important, he was an ambassador for Hawaii's ocean culture. Rell Sunn, born in Makaha and surfing by the age of four, was, from a surfing perspective, a female equivalent of the Duke. An excellent swimmer, diver, and spear fisher who became Hawaii's first female lifeguard, Sunn helped organize the Women's Surfing Hui and the women's professional surfing tour. By 1982 she ranked first in the international ratings.

Sunn was known as the Queen of Makaha for her efforts to teach children to surf and involvement in community programs on Oahu's impoverished west side. Her Menehune Surf Meet for children was an annual event for twenty-three years. Sunn's cultural values and aloha made her bigger than surfing; she promoted Hawaiian culture and became expert at hula and the ukulele. Sunn's life and love of surfing captured the essence of a sport that for centuries emptied Hawaiian towns as the women, men, and children all paddled out when a swell hit.

Roxy Girl, *Blue Crush*, and above all Title IX helped change lineups at surf breaks around the world. From a commercial perspective, the new wave crashed through the malls of America like a twenty-footer at outside Pipeline, rewarding industry with a wave of brand-new customers. By 2006 Roxy was providing over one-fourth of Quiksilver's total sales, over $500 million a year. Top female surfers, such as Stephanie Gilmore and Carissa Moore, reportedly now make over $1 million a year from sponsors.

Meanwhile, surfing's mouthpiece, the surf journalist, stumbled along behind like a drunk frat boy. When Linda Merrill was the first woman on the front of *Surfer* in November 1964, the editor included the backhanded admission, "It took us almost five years to get around to it, but we finally gave in." Decades later, although top female surfers such as Andersen and Kennelly had appeared on the cover of *Surfer*, the editorial staffs of the main magazines, from writers to photographers, were almost exclusively male, as continued gratuitous T&A shots demonstrated. In August 2012 *Transworld Surf* ran a "women's issue," with an editorial declaring "Sexism Is Dead." The issue featured a male surfer on the cover and included the results of a reader poll asking "Who is the hottest female surfer?" The irony was apparently lost on the editors. Similarly, surf videos came almost entirely from the cameras, and viewpoints, of males. As a result, the emerging generation of women's surfers looked to new magazines such as *Surfing Girl*, *Surf Life for Women*, and *Wahine*, written by and for women surfers, and to videos produced by and for women.

RETURN OF THE WAHINES

In ancient Hawaii, the birthplace of modern surfing, women and men enjoyed the surf equally. The near decimation of the Hawaiian people from disease nearly eliminated surfing. Then, when haoles revived surfing, they did so within the context of American, not Hawaiian, culture. The days of men and women sharing waves together were all but over with the imposition of Western social mores. Because of prevailing Victorian gender values and cumbersome swimwear, women participated in surfing only in small numbers, in the "wahine surf" close to the beach. After the turn of the century pioneering sportswomen like Ethelda Bleibtrey chipped away at such social strictures, shedding stockings, bobbing their hair, and developing phenomenal physical fitness.

The post–World War II application of military technologies to surfboard design allowed another generational advance. Heavy boards limited the participation of all but the most athletic women until new lightweight materials opened the door to a new generation. Marge Calhoun honed her skills at Malibu and later Makaha, joining the first generation of women to revive women's surfing in Hawaii. Linda Benson and Joyce Hoffman surfed with grace and power at some of the most challenging breaks in the world, followed by Margo Godfrey Oberg, Jericho Poppler, Rell Sunn, and Mary Setterholm and the first professional women's surfing organizations. These pioneers and many others paved the way for the meteoric rise of Lisa Andersen, who demonstrated unequivocally that yes, indeed, she could surf better than men.

Today the wahines are back with a vengeance. Stoked young girls abound at breaks in Hawaii, California, and around the world. Although all these female surfers have increased crowding in surf lineups, they also may be helping to moderate localism and surf rage, thanks to a less confrontational attitude. Surf tourism has also accommodated the new market, setting up female-only surf camps so that women surfers need not spend weeks on small islands surrounded by beer-drinking men. The surf industry, meanwhile, has almost doubled in size to accommodate a whole new generation—and gender—of customers. Twenty-first-century women are taking the sport of surfing to entirely new levels from both an athletic and a commercial standpoint. Ironically, the wahine most responsible for this explosion never rode a wave in her life. Maui High School's softball stadium and running track are named for a woman who never participated in sports, yet who helped create a revolution in American sport. Title IX created millions of sportswomen who share in the stoke of surfing. Not too shabby for a wahine who never rode a wave.

That, then, is the difference in the Roxy Girl generation. It was not the mere presence of the original Roxy Girl, Lisa Andersen, or her industry sponsors. Surfing requires athleticism and Title IX took care of that, in spades. Patsy Mink's law created thousands upon thousands of Ethelda Bleibtreys, Mary Ann Hawkinses, and Lisa Andersens with the ability and inclination to leave the beach and catch waves. And that's why the Girl Scouts of America now offers a surfing badge.

At the 1912 Olympics in Stockholm Duke won the men's hundred-meter gold with a world record time of 1:03.4. Ninety-four years later, in 2006, ten-year old Lia Neal, an African American, swam the same hundred meters in 1:02.11 and set the U.S. national age group girls' record. Neal's swim also beat the record for ten-year-old boys. In 2008 Neal turned thirteen and dropped four seconds off her one hundred—enough time for her to be toweling off with Duke still in the water on his world record pace. Four years later she won a bronze medal in the 2012 London Olympics.

The explosion of interest in women's sports led to a revolution in women's surfing. Wahines are back riding the waves, and somewhere Rell Sunn's ancestors are smiling.

14 FROM WAIKIKI TO WALL STREET

Stroll down Waikiki's Kalakaua Avenue, the Rodeo Drive of Hawaii, and you will pass polished storefronts representing a who's who of world fashion: Gucci, Fendi, Saks, Prada. Alongside these iconic brands are equally glitzy surfwear purveyors—Quiksilver, Billabong, Rip Curl, and virtually every other major surf brand. Stepping through their gleaming doors reveals rack after rack of surf trunks and T-shirts, all carefully branded with each company's signature trademark. Off in a corner there may be a token rack of overpriced boards, but these stores have long since forsaken the basic tool of surfing. Today's surf industry is mainly the garment business, and most of Waikiki's "surf" shops are all about clothing—ironically, since the ancient Hawaiians often surfed naked.

Take a similar stroll a world away, down the Champs-Élysées in Paris. There, amid the luxury boutiques (and the American fast-food franchises), you'll find a surf shop. Well, sort of a surf shop: an outlet for the Quiksilver surfwear giant. For the global surf industry, whose $10 billion in sales mostly comes from landlocked consumers from Minnesota to Moscow, and from Paris, Texas, to Paris, France, the storefronts on Kalakaua are supposed to signal its continued commitment to the surf lifestyle. Quiksilver maintains a store in Waikiki precisely to balance its presence in Paris.

Many surfwear firms were started by young dirtbag surfers, but surfing's increasing popularity changed the business and the surfers who worked in it. Producing, marketing, and distributing billions of dollars of product around the world took more resources than a couple of sewing machines, cardboard boxes, and an old VW van. Armies of investment bankers, accountants, and lawyers brought a jarring corporate sensibility to a formerly suntanned, salt-encrusted domain. As MBAs replaced surfers and business suits replaced board shorts in the corporate offices of billion-dollar multinational surfwear firms, surfing's countercultural image came into question. Could surf companies maintain credibility while focused on IPOs and shareholder value, with corporate leaders flying off to private islands on their personal jets? How subversive could surf magazines be when they were all owned by the same giant media conglomerate? Once surfing had gone to Wall Street, could it ever go back to Waikiki?

TRUNKING IT

In the beginning, surfers made themselves the one item they needed for surfing: the surfboard. If early Hawaiians wore anything in the water, it was only a simple loincloth for men or sarong for women. The arrival of Western values brought the bathing suit to surfing, and by the turn of the century the woolen one-piece, reaching from knees to neck, had become standard swim attire on Waikiki and elsewhere. These woolen costumes, however, could soak up to ten pounds of water, dragging down swimmers and surfers. West Coast swimsuit makers early in the twentieth century set out to redefine the swimsuit, starting with Jantzen in 1909 and then Catalina and Cole. In addition to introducing new fabrics and styles, they brought modern marketing to the swimsuit business. To boost the ranks of potential customers, Jantzen backed a national campaign for swim lessons in the 1920s, sponsoring swimming pools and clubs and enlisting famous swimmers—including Duke Kahanamoku—as spokesmen. This learn-to-swim campaign, of course, also increased the number of potential surfers.

The aquatic lifestyle propagated by the Waikiki beachboys contributed to the evolution of bathing suits. The beachboys were wearing simple trunks, either belted or with a drawstring, by the late 1920s, while many mainland American beaches required men to wear the old woolen tops for another decade. Atlantic City banned topless men until 1937, wanting "no gorillas on our beaches." In 1937 Duke signed a five-year modeling contract with the Hawaiian firm Kahala, which produced drawstring trunks popular among the beachboys; the next year *Vogue* magazine's travel-issue cover featured a tandem-surfing beachboy wearing a pair of "Duke swim trunks by Kahala." Jantzen, Catalina, and other established swimsuit makers followed suit with trunks designed for the surfing lifestyle.

Hawaii's contribution to the evolution of surf trunks continued during the 1950s when M. Nii, a one-legged tailor from Waianae, together with his wife began crafting custom shorts for local and visiting surfers. Greg Noll's jailhouse-striped trunks were an M. Nii creation. The Niis' trunks were highly sought after and visiting surfers often purchased extras to sell on the mainland. Southern Californians had their own source for trunks by the early 1960s, after Nancy Katin and Birdwell Britches established iconic brands, making trunks from canvas or nylon and incorporating a drawstring fly or waist.

Around this time, in the early 1960s, Francis "Duke" Boyd and Doris Moore took surfwear into a new dimension. Boyd, a surfer and ex-marine, grew up in Hawaii and Southern California and knew the potential market. He needed money for school and approached Moore with a design for a jacket. His caricature was also wearing a pair of trunks. Moore, an experienced clothing designer and buyer out of New York, was far more interested in shorts than jackets—trunks were easy to manufacture—and pushed Boyd to come up with a prototype. She took his design and arranged for production, while Boyd began traveling the coast, knocking on doors and convincing board shops like Weber and Hobie to carry trunks. Dewey Weber agreed to buy a dozen but only all white and size 30, so if they didn't sell he could wear them himself. Boyd made inroads into the surf community using what is now a timeworn technique: handing out free gear to standout surfers at places like Huntington Beach, Newport, and Laguna.

The shorts sold, but "Doris Moore Productions" was not a catchy brand. Moore asked Boyd, "What would be the equivalent of a 'Hole in One' in surfing?" Boyd responded with the "hang ten"—the sensation of hanging all ten toes off the front of a longboard while trimming down the line on a glassy face. Duke captured the stoke of a surfer perched on the nose with the name Hang Ten, and his two golden feet soon graced shorts, shirts, and jackets in what became surfing's first great branding triumph. The golden footprints conjured up images of sinking your toes into a sandy beach, while the graffiti-style "Hang Ten" lettering was reminiscent of the scrawling on the wall at Malibu. Moore trademarked "Hang Ten" in 1964 and immediately purchased a yearlong advertising run in the fledgling quarterly *Surfer* magazine.

Meanwhile Moore began selling the trunks at department stores. She knew the big money was at stores catering to the back-to-school crowd; moms were far more likely to shop at department stores than at a local surf shop, if the town even had one. Moore used her contacts to take the brand into the big time, and in less than a year Hang Ten became the surf industry's first major success. By June of 1965, the *Los Angeles Times*' Father's Day fashion column was calling Hang Ten's lace-up striped surf trunk and nylon jacket combination the "sun uniform for 1965." Hang Ten stitched up the cachet of surfing and sold it in department stores to customers who had never seen a surfboard.

Duke Boyd and Doris Moore held on to the Hang Ten brand until 1971, when they sold it for $3 million to Ratner, a national garment firm best known for developing the leisure suit. That might have cost Hang Ten some credibility in the surf world, but it didn't hurt its bottom line. At the time of the sale Hang Ten was collecting annual royalties on a wholesale volume of over $30 million, with licenses in the United States, New Zealand, Japan, and South Africa. A decade later, Ratner collected royalties on over $250 million of wholesale revenue in thirty-five countries, with Hang Ten products ranging from men's, women's, and children's sportswear to roller skates, skateboards, tote bags, umbrellas, and doll clothes.

Duke Boyd was not the only surfer to ride the surfwear craze of the 1960s. Dave Rochlen, another ex-marine, was a veteran surfer of postwar Malibu, where he dated a young Marilyn Monroe. In 1963 Rochlen left his job as an analyst for the Rand Corporation for Oahu, where he opened a surf shop. Soon after, Rochlen saw a photo in *Life* of Russian beachgoers wearing rolled-up pajamas as they waded on the Black Sea shoreline. Keanuenue Rochlen, Dave's Hawaiian wife (and an accomplished surfer, swimmer, and paddler herself), produced a pair of knee-length, Hawaiian-print, drawstring trunks in 1963, modeled on the Russian pajamas, and called them "Jams" for short. The baggy trunks were an immediate hit with surfers. Within a couple years Rochlen's Surfline Hawaii Company was producing millions of pairs a year for mainland department stores, and "Jams" came full circle by appearing in *Life* magazine in 1965, now as a surfwear trend.

Australia came late to the surfwear industry but made up for lost time. Alan Green, a surfer and high school dropout from Melbourne, cut his teeth in the business world as a personal gofer for Sir Reginald Ansett, founder of Ansett Airlines, and then as a bookkeeper for Lieutenant Commander Maurice "Bats" Batterham's Australian Divers in North Melbourne. Batterham had served in the war with a Royal Australian Navy team that disarmed Japanese mines for amphibious assaults, earning an Order of the British Empire for his efforts. After World War II Batterham started Australia's first scuba school and founded Australian Divers, with Jacques Cousteau as an investor, to supply the booming diving industry. Green approached Batterham about making wetsuits for surfers, and his boss told him to do it himself and sold him the materials at cost to get him started.

Green took Batterham's advice, borrowed $1,500 from his dad, and joined forces with Doug Warbrick, principal of a failing surfboard company called Rip Curl. Green and Warbrick turned Rip Curl into Australia's leading domestic wetsuit brand before Green moved into the greener pastures of surf trunks. He used technologies from his experience with Australian Divers to provide an alternative to heavy canvas board shorts, replacing bulky buttons and lace-up flies with flat snaps and Velcro, and in 1970 created a new boardshort that he branded "Quicksilver"—soon dropping the *c* to avoid copyright issues with a rock band. Quiksilver got a boost from a fabric wholesaler with contacts in East Germany, who provided surplus cloth from behind the Iron Curtain and dyed it to Green's specifications.

Soon Quiksilver was thriving in Australia and making inroads in the United States. In 1976 Jeff Hakman—"Mr. Sunset," just starting a downward spiral into heroin addiction—came to Australia to compete in the venerable Bells contest near Melbourne, sponsored by Rip Curl and Quiksilver. Hakman had seen Quiksilver trunks and liked them, and approached Green about the American license. He won the Bells contest stoned to the gills and went out with Green to celebrate. At the tail end of a drunken dinner, Green challenged Hakman to eat a paper doily as a sign of his commitment to Quiksilver. Hakman duly downed the doily, and the impressed Green granted the license. In forming Quiksilver USA Hakman was joined by Bob McKnight, a twenty-two-year-old business major from USC making surf films, whom Hakman had met and befriended on a surf trip to Indonesia.

It is worth noting how many surf companies involved women at the start-up. Surf literature invariably celebrates the men of these firms as surfwear visionaries: M. Nii, Duke Boyd, Dave Rochlen. The women who played crucial roles in several of these episodes—Mrs. Nii, Doris Moore, Keanuenue Rochlen—are often forgotten. (Boyd, to his credit, is quick to acknowledge Moore's role in Hang Ten.) Another prime example involved Billabong, founded in the early 1970s by a young couple on Australia's Gold Coast, Gordon and Rena Merchant. Gordon had grown up surfing and his mother was a seamstress, and to supplement his board-shaping business he and Rena began making surf trunks on their kitchen table and selling them out of their station wagon. The business benefited from a catchy brand name: "Billabong," the Aboriginal name for a waterhole, conveyed Australian cachet just as Australian surfers were taking over the competitive surf world. After Billabong went public in 2000, Gordon Merchant's net worth was estimated at close to $100 million. A couple years earlier Rena, after a drawn-out divorce from Gordon, had sold her stake for $26 million.

Quiksilver and Billabong developed exceptional staying power. Many a surf brand turned out to be a flash in the pan. Hang Ten's heyday in the 1960s gave way to Golden Breed and Lightning Bolt in the '70s (other brands developed by impresario Duke Boyd), followed by Ocean Pacific in the '80s, where Boyd again lent his magic marketing touch to sell hundreds of millions of dollars of surfwear to the American mainstream. Another prime example from the 1980s was Gotcha, founded in 1978 by South African Michael Tomson (Shaun's cousin). Gotcha cultivated a self-consciously rebellious image and a corporate culture of rock-star-style partying (and drug use). One ad campaign featured photos of dorky nonsurfers, with the slogan "If you don't surf, don't start." Other ads featuring middle-aged guys in suits were captioned "We have an aversion to all the new surfwear companies being run by people who don't surf." Gotcha designs similarly embraced a bad-boy sensibility, highlighting retina-burning neon colors and New Wave graphics. Gotcha also introduced an ironic line of Bermuda shorts to see if kids would embrace clothes associated with the fuddy-duddy fifties of their fathers' generation. The kids did, and Gotcha was soon grossing hundreds of millions of dollars in sales through such hard-core surf outlets as Nordstrom, Robinson's, and Bullock's. After selling a 40 percent stake to Merrill Lynch in 1989, Tomson went out and bought houses in Laguna Beach and on the North Shore. But Gotcha grew too big, too fast, and the company's meteoric rise flamed out in the 1990s. Pushing product into department stores, Gotcha lost touch with its roots—at one point, Tomson discovered the Gotcha line no longer included surf trunks, the brand's original reason for existence. Tomson summed it up: "Size is the enemy of cool."

Surf trunks were relatively generic from their Waikiki beginnings through the next four decades. Probably the biggest change was in price. Joining mainstream fashion came at a cost, especially at glitzy surf boutiques where one could easily spend over a hundred dollars on a pair of trunks. The most significant style development came in the 1990s when surfing sensation Lisa Andersen ("She can surf better than you") decided it was time women had surf trunks of their own. Andersen's trunks became the mainstay of the Roxy brand, which provided a quarter of Quiksilver's sales by 2006—a half billion dollars. Other brands followed as the surf industry mined the new and lucrative frontier of women's surf fashion.

SELLING SURF

Surfwear firms entered a profitable symbiosis with the surf media. The postwar surf boom had spawned several magazines in the 1960s, including *Surfer* and *Surfing* in the United States and several Australian counterparts. Although both *Surfer* and *Surfing* went through a countercultural phase in the late 1960s, they were otherwise generally conservative, presenting a clean, healthy sport as a way to popularize surfing—and increase potential readership. Their basic business model depended on advertising revenue, not subscriptions. And that landed them in bed with the surf industry. Surfwear firms bought ad pages, and the magazines covered surfers sponsored by the surfwear firms. Such ties did not exactly encourage investigative reporting. The incestuous relationship extended to journalists themselves, who regularly used the revolving door between the magazines and surf companies. A few prime examples: Duke Boyd edited *Surfing* while still with Hang Ten; Drew Kampion quit as *Surfing*'s editor in 1978 to head O'Neill's advertising department; Gotcha later hired both *Surfing* editor Dave Gilovich and *Surfer* editor Paul Holmes to its marketing team.

The surf magazines were not the only ones in bed with sponsors. So were the surf contests. Surfwear firms evolved alongside the new professional tour. In the early years of the tour several of the lead judges were surfwear executives—in part because the tour couldn't afford to pay travel costs for judges, and industry managers were the only ones who had an interest in following the tour and could afford it. In the early 1980s pro surfers accused them of a conflict of interest at least, and bias at worst. How could Jack Shipley of Lightning Bolt or Doug Warbrick of Rip Curl judge a heat featuring Bolt or Rip Curl riders? The tour eventually barred judges with industry ties, but that did not entirely solve the problem. As surfwear firms increasingly sponsored pro contests, rumors persisted that judges favored, say, a Quiksilver rider in a Quiksilver-sponsored contest.

In the 1980s the surfwear industry took off, aided by several factors. A major defense buildup revived Southern California's aerospace economy and encouraged more middle-class California kids to surf. Also similar to the 1950s, a conservative national mood, captured by President Reagan's sunny California optimism, repeated Gidget's embrace of surfing as a wholesome outdoor sport. Pro surfing in particular burnished the clean-cut image. *Surfing* magazine noted "a kind of tacit agreement among pro surfers, no matter how demented or wild or offbeat they may be in the comfort of their own homes, and that is: we want a clean act."

In the early 1980s California's Ocean Pacific, another surfwear firm created in the 1970s, stepped in as a major backer of the world tour, with its annual OP Pro contest at Huntington Beach the centerpiece. The OP Pro presented the surf contest as beach party, with bleachers, crowds, skate ramps, and bikini contests. The recovery of California competitive surfing produced a prodigy named Tom Curren, a young surfer with a fluid, graceful style honed on Santa Barbara's point breaks. Curren blazed up the amateur ranks while in high school and turned pro in late 1982, at the age of seventeen. He soon won the OP Pro, and then in 1985 the first of three world titles, while sponsored by Ocean Pacific and Rip Curl.

Part of Curren's appeal was that while dominating the world tour, he maintained a soulful image. Some surf industry insiders grumbled that Curren, as the first American world champ, was not doing enough to promote the sport in the United States. Curren's reticence was genuine, not calculated; he was by nature aloof and introspective, and not given to self-promotion. But it was also the best thing for surfing's commercial prospects. The more Curren shunned publicity, the more popular he got. He helped surfing keep its soul at a time of rampant commercialism.

Most important, surfing once again became hip for nonsurfers. GQ ran a series of photo layouts featuring surfers as fashion models. Indeed, a number of top surfers in this period found modeling a more lucrative career niche than pro surfing. In 1985 *Rolling Stone* ran a photo spread titled "The Boys of Summer," featuring Madonna cavorting with "six hunky surfers." Two years later *Rolling Stone* profiled Curren, with photography by fashion icon Herb Ritts. *Interview* magazine similarly ran photo features on top Hawaiian surfers, alongside ads from Quiksilver and other surfwear companies; its competitor Gotcha ran ads in New York's *Village Voice*. Surfing seemed to be taking over New York City, including a new surf-themed nightclub, the Big Kahuna. *Time* magazine and the *Wall Street Journal* ran articles on the new "surfing chic," and ESPN and *Sports Illustrated* similarly flocked to the surf craze. *Time* estimated that Americans would spend $1 billion on surfwear in

Amid the 1980s surf revival, The Economist *portrayed Gorbachev surfing the waves of geopolitics. (Source:* Economist, *September 16, 1989)*

1986. Former world champion Mark Richards, meanwhile, was selling beer, Ford cars, and Kentucky Fried Chicken on Australian TV. The surf industry was mainstream on two continents.

Hollywood completed the sense of revival, with *The New Gidget*, featuring a grown-up and married Gidget and Moondoggie, and *Back to the Beach*, with Frankie and Annette rediscovering the California surf lifestyle. There was also the movie *North Shore*, featuring an aspiring Arizona teenager who wins a wave pool contest and goes to Hawaii. Real-life wave pools at the time were bringing surfing to such landlocked locales as Allentown, Memphis, Las Vegas, Cleveland, Edmonton, Palm Springs, and Orlando. Even towns without wave pools got into the act; in 1986 Williamsburg, Iowa, trucked in 3 million pounds of sand for a beach party.

The trend encouraged the surf industry's expansion to landlocked markets. Quiksilver brought in John Warner, formerly a senior manager of Macy's, to oversee the expansion; he was hired not for his surf knowledge but for his marketing expertise. The strategy worked; Quik's annual sales went from $19 million in 1986 to $30 million in 1987, $48 million in 1988, and $70 million in 1989. That is, sales more than doubled in two years, and tripled in three years. OP, meanwhile, was topping out at $370 million in revenues in 1989. Quiksilver, OP, Gotcha, and other labels turned Orange County into "Velcro Valley," the center of the national, and increasingly global, surf industry.

To finance its expansion into mainstream markets, Quiksilver went public in 1986. Selling stock was a sign of the increasing maturity of the surf industry. In 1983 new Quiksilver USA directors, to McKnight's chagrin, booted Hakman, who had spiraled deeper into drug abuse. But embracing Wall Street also meant an invasion of surfwear firms by troops of accountants and lawyers. Quiksilver veterans wondered whether it was losing touch with its roots, and its market credibility, as "the suits" took over from "the surfers." Selling stock also introduced an increasingly short-term focus on dividends and stock price, as shareholders zeroed in on quarterly goals.

PROS AND CLOTHES

Pro surfing had little effect on surfing itself, or on surfers. Rather, pro surfing changed nonsurfers' image of surfing. Pro surfers entered into a tacit agreement: in exchange for money, they would clean up their act and present a wholesome, clean-cut image as elite athletes. As *Surfing* magazine observed, "Thanks to this pro surfing thing, Johnny Public is actually beginning to believe surfers are nice, clean, OK human beings—and that may be the biggest change of all."

Had the surfers themselves changed? They had in one respect: the top pro surfers looked different than previous generations. Lightweight shortboards and urethane leashes meant no wrestling heavy boards through surf or long swims to the beach. Contests often held in small waves also meant that smaller, gymnastic types replaced the longer, stronger surfers of earlier periods. Unlike big and burly he-men like Greg Noll of previous generations, the pro tour in the eighties and nineties was dominated by lithe, gymnastic surfers under five foot ten. At the same time, a few pro surfers actually began to train out of the water, with exercise and nutrition regimes. Older surfers were bemused by the trend, believing surfers should be watermen, not gym rats: surfers previously didn't need to train because wrestling with heavy boards and swimming thousands of yards each session was training itself. But in some respects pro surfers hadn't changed much. They were still mostly young men, barely out of their teens, who were paid to ride waves. Most of them still spent flat spells—or even nights before contests—drinking beer, smoking pot, and chasing girls.

By summer 1986 surfing appeared poised, as *Surfing* magazine put it, to take off like a rocket. The OP Pro contest that summer at Huntington Beach had everything going for it; thirty thousand spectators in stadium-style bleachers enjoying Labor Day weekend, sunny skies, and the best south swell of the summer. By the last day the contest looked like a triumph of the three-ring-circus beach festival. But as the finals hit the water, a crowd behind the contest grandstands turned ugly and a full-fledged riot broke out. Drunken revelers overturned and burned several police and lifeguard vehicles, and threw the wreckage through the windows of the lifeguard headquarters. The mob overran overmatched police officers and drove off a police helicopter with a barrage of beer bottles; a lifeguard captain fired warning shots to keep the rioters from storming the headquarters itself. This did not exactly fit the public image of laid-back surfers, and the riot attracted sensational news coverage, with video of fiery columns of smoke from burning police cars instead of surfers cruising on sun-spangled waves. Amid much soul-searching, some pro surfers feared that surfing had lost touch with its roots. Ian Cairns quit in disgust as head of the ASP, predicting that the riot might "put a lid on professional surfing for five to ten years."

With the OP Pro riot surfing paid the price for its association with sex, and sexism. The riot was initiated not by surfers, but by drunken revelers leering at scantily clad young women. A bikini contest had been a central part of the OP Pro beach party since its inception. There had been warning signs the preceding years, when contest organizers, not to mention the young women themselves, grew nervous as crowds of drunken young men tried to break down the fence around the stage in order to reach the contestants. But OP had continued to hold the bikini contest, no doubt because they recognized, as a *Surfing* magazine survey of male beachgoers found, that most of the male spectators came specifically to see the bikini contest, not the surfing. The riot did not change anything. The OP Pro was back the next year—and so was the bikini contest.

The beach-festival philosophy, meanwhile, hurt pro surfing by removing the surf itself. The best waves often land on remote, inaccessible beaches, presenting promoters with a choice between great waves and no spectators or lame waves and a good crowd. Contest promoters went with the crowds, which meant accessible beaches and convenient heat times. The frequent result was contests held in crappy waves. In 1984, dead-flat surf at the Wave Wizards Challenge in Florida caused tour officials to waive the minimum eighteen-inch wave height, and to hire a large powerboat to motor up and down the coast in hopes contestants could at least surf the boat wake. Four-time world champ Mark Richards wandered onto the beach, took one look at the flat ocean, and said, "Take me to the airport."

The zenith, or nadir, came the following year in a contest held in a wave pool in that noted surf town, Allentown, Pennsylvania. World champion Tom Curren caught one wave in his first heat, rode the weak ankle-slapper to the "beach," stepped off his board, and walked out in disgust. Pro surfer Matt George won more money than most of his colleagues by entering a Hot Buns contest the night before the final. The enterprising George, the lone male contestant, stripped to a Speedo, stuffed a newspaper down the front, and walked away with a thousand dollars, more than the fifth-place surfers earned in the actual surf contest. Celebrating his win later that night, George blew out his ankle in a breakdancing move and spent the next month on crutches.

Meanwhile, surfing's burgeoning image as a lifestyle also underscored that surfing was not, in fact, a profession. Pro surfing was not exactly fulfilling the vision of the Free Ride generation. There were indeed hundreds of surfers competing in contests, surfing in exotic locales and getting paid for it. But the economic reality belied the glamorous image of tanned young men riding perfect waves and bedding beach bunnies. By the end of the 1980s the world tour consisted of twenty events spread across eight months, nine countries, and five continents. The travel grind made the tour a young man's game; most pros started straight out of high school, or even earlier, since it usually took a few years to work up the ranks. Travel costs meant most pros were actually losing money. Only the top thirty on the tour were breaking even, and the top fifteen making as much as an average schoolteacher or fireman; a mere handful of surfers at the top were making six figures. Women fared even worse, with the female champion in 1987 making less than the number 16 male finisher.

For even the most successful surfers, the "profession" only lasted for five or ten years. The travel grind wore them down, and the media and contest judges latched on to hot newcomers, leaving older surfers in the dust. By their late twenties, most pros found themselves off the tour, with no income, a high school education at best, and no other job experience. A savvy few transitioned to jobs in surf media, the surfwear industry, or surfboard shaping; most tried desperately to catch on with the industry, often as low-level sales reps hawking product to surf shops.

Some pros didn't even make it that far. In the mid-1980s, David Eggers, Nicky Wood, and Jason Buttonshaw were all seen as can't-miss kids. All of them, with the possible exception of Wood, missed. Eggers, for example, a hot teenage surfer out of La Jolla, turned pro in 1985 at age fifteen, with $30,000 from sponsors Body Glove and Gotcha in his pocket. The huge hype soon flamed out in partying and drug addiction. Eggers recalled, in the midst of his comeback attempt at age nineteen (!): "I had the money, I had the fame, I had the attitude. . . . Girls, parties, drinking, drugs . . . shit, I was 16, man, and could pretty much do whatever I wanted." Similarly, Matt Archbold signed with Gotcha at age sixteen for $70,000 a year and began a long slide into drug addiction ending in a prison sentence.

By the late 1980s a sense of disillusionment set in for pro surfers. They realized that making surfing into a profession meant that surfers were now working *for* somebody: namely, the sponsors. And that meant no longer just surfing whenever and wherever they wanted. Sometimes The Man asked surfers to do something they didn't want to do, like surfing crummy waves, or showing up for a press conference or marketing meeting, in return for a paycheck. And surfers, like workers everywhere, complained about it. Top pros began muttering of "revolt," but the ASP tour manager quickly squashed such talk in a letter to the top thirty pros: "The events are not there because of you. . . . If all the Top 30 were killed in a plane crash tomorrow, the following day the event would be advertising a new Top 30."

And that was in the good times. The recession of the early nineties hit Southern California especially hard. The end of the Cold War decimated the defense industry and with it Southern California's middle class, but consumers across the country felt the pinch and stopped buying boardshorts and surfing tees at the local mall. Meanwhile, early nineties trendsetters looked away from the beach toward the inner city and the Northwest, as hip-hop and grunge replaced surf trunks with baggy jeans and flannels. The economic downturn cleaned out several major surfwear labels—Ocean Pacific filed for bankruptcy in 1991—which in turn left pro surfers and contests without sponsors.

Surfing once again proved resilient. One can't-miss kid avoided the pitfalls of teenage stardom and merged his freakish surfing talent with media savvy. In 1990 a young Kelly Slater signed an exclusive deal with Quiksilver for six figures annually for three years. By 1996 Slater was making a million a year from Quiksilver, after winning three of his eventual, unprecedented eleven world titles. That year Slater appeared in a come-hither pose on *Interview* magazine's cover with the tagline "Half Fish, Total Dish." Million-dollar contracts revived the old question: was surfing a sport, an art, or a lifestyle? Calling it a lifestyle implied that surfing was about more than fat contracts; it was an idealistic, even spiritual pursuit. How, then, did the best surfer in the world end up as an actor on *Baywatch*?

Hollywood had continued to look to surfing as a pop-culture touchstone since the Beach Party/Gidget days, with surfers often cast as one of two types: the surf bum or the mysto guru. The apotheosis of the first was Sean Penn's brilliant turn as surfer-stoner Jeff Spicoli—"all I need are some tasty waves and a cool buzz and I'm fine"—in

Fast Times at Ridgemont High (1982), which launched Penn's career. For the second, there was 1991's *Point Break*, featuring Patrick Swayze as a surfer whose name, Bodhi, unsubtly suggested his mystical soulfulness. Spiritual claptrap reached a peak with *In God's Hands* in 1998. Written by the breakdancing Matt George and starring several pro surfers, it was quite possibly the worst surf movie ever. Unlike the Beach Party movies, it took itself all too seriously, and lasted only a week in general release. *Box Office* magazine called it an "abysmally turgid and pretentious mess of quasi-documentary, tepid adventure, ponderous philosophizing, unromantic romance, forced symbolism, bogus mysticism and vapid travelogue."

Most surfers viewed such spiritual excursions as unintentional comedies. But Hollywood movies from *Big Wednesday* to *Blue Crush* defined the surfer for the general public. Millions of moviegoing Americans imbibed the public image of the surfer either as a drug-addled burner like Spicoli or a mysto guru like Bodhi. HBO recently framed an entire series around surfers on literally a higher plane of consciousness, in *John from Cincinnati*. This makes Kelly Slater's star turn on *Baywatch* noteworthy. Slater represented the return of the clean-cut heartthrob, the wholesome middle-class jock—in other words, the renewed triumph of Moondoggie over Kahuna. *Baywatch* had first aired in 1989 and soon became the world's most popular TV show, conveying Southern California's beach lifestyle to landlocked masses on several continents. Slater joined the cast in 1992 as Jimmy Slade, a surfer from Malibu High, and appeared in ten episodes. Slater's acting gig was roundly ridiculed in the surf community—in one regrettable scene, he wrestled an octopus in a cave. His agent, Bryan Taylor, however, defended the attempt to expand Slater's horizons, and his income: "What I don't want is for Kelly to surf until he's 30, and then end up as a rep for a clothing company." The mere fact that Slater, even as a teenager, had an agent from Hollywood's William Morris Agency suggested surfing's increasing commercialization. Taylor, however, noted that of all the sports businesses he had worked in, "the surf industry is by far the most unsophisticated."

Slater's foray into Hollywood followed in the hallowed footsteps of the Duke himself, who had turned to acting sixty years earlier as a way to make a living off of surfing. Duke had also signed clothing deals, and the most lucrative approach remained the surfwear industry. Most pro surfers on the contest tour made more money from surfwear sponsors than from contest winnings. Tom Curren summed it up in 1993: "All pro surfing is—all it means to be a pro surfer—is to sell trunks."

Some pro surfers took this a step further and ignored contests altogether, in the career niche of "photo pro," whose contracts depended on getting exposure for their sponsors in magazines and videos. This approach was not new; Miki Dora had pursued it in the 1950s and 1960s and Pipe master Gerry Lopez in the 1970s. Like Dora, the new photo pros seemed to reject pro surfing, and indeed based their image on a noncommercial stance. For this reason some preferred the sobriquet of "soul surfer" or "free surfer," which implied that they shunned the world of contests and ratings for the pure joy of surfing—although their lifestyle was underwritten by a billion-dollar multinational corporation. These soul surfers couldn't have sat around in Irish pubs reading poetry in between surf sessions if their sponsors weren't supporting them generously. They were every bit as professional as contest surfers, but without the contest jerseys, judging standards, and priority buoys. Instead, they knew how to burnish a carefully scripted brand image on photo trips and were as conversant with lighting angles and logo placements as any fashion model.

The cost of these increasingly scripted and targeted marketing campaigns eventually showed up in surfwear prices. Industry veterans debated whether these sponsored pros were worth the investment: did that surfer on a $500,000 contract really help bring in that much profit each year? Did tens of thousands of teenagers buy T-shirts and shorts because that surfer wore them? Surfwear corporate managers decided they did, and continued to ratchet up contract amounts for top surfers. They were no doubt encouraged in this strategy because however much pro surfers were making, the surfwear titans were making many times more.

Above all, sponsoring pro surfers maintained brand credibility even as surfwear firms became billion-dollar behemoths. By 2005, Quiksilver was grossing $2 billion. The big American and Australian companies—Quiksilver, Billabong, Rip Curl, Volcom—were joined by new players from abroad, such as Reef Brazil, founded by two

Argentinian brothers in 1985. In 2002 they sold a controlling interest to investment bankers, and in 2005 the VF Corporation, the giant clothing conglomerate, bought Reef for $188 million in cash. Reef was no longer a surf company; it was a subdivision of a global clothing distributor, which promptly laid off all 120 staff at Reef's San Diego distribution center.

Reef's fate suggested that surfwear firms transcended single countries, since they were billion-dollar multinational corporations. Half of Quiksilver's sales, for example, came from the international market. Thus Roxy, for example, signed Sofia Mulanovich of Peru when she was fifteen and underwrote her surf travels. She won the women's world title in 2004 and became a national hero; her victory was front-page news in the Peru press, a crowd of twenty thousand greeted her plane in Lima, and she was voted Peru's most popular person. Roxy sales in some parts of Latin America jumped 50 percent, and Mulanovich became one of Roxy's highest-paid surfers. This example was multiplied in ensuing years, as surf firms sought young stars in new markets and cultivated their careers. By 2011, *Surfer* magazine's "Hot 100" list of up-and-coming youngsters included surfers from the usual suspects—Hawaii, California, Australia, South Africa—but also France, Italy, Mexico, Costa Rica, Peru, the French West Indies, Réunion Island, Tahiti, New Zealand, plus a slew of Brazilians and a New Yorker (Balaram Stack). This international spread had the salutary effect of finally expanding surfing's ethnic horizons. Surfwear firms discovered the easiest way to expand their market was to tap into large minority populations and attract more minorities to surfing.

Like many other international businesses, the surf industry began eyeing the two largest markets: India and China, with 2 billion potential consumers—about a third of the world's population—between them. Those two countries were noticeably absent from the surf community, despite thousands of miles of surfable coastlines. Several barriers thwarted surfing's emergence in India and China, including lack of swim lessons, environmental pollution, widespread poverty, and lack of lesiure time. But the surf industry had long realized it didn't need people to surf in order to sell them stuff. In 2005 skateboarder Danny Way jumped the Great Wall of China in a celebrated stunt. Quiksilver spent a half million dollars building the huge skate ramp that launched Way over the Wall.

The ramp was liberally festooned with Quiksilver logos, and anyone who thought Quiksilver chose China for this spectacle by accident failed Business 101.

•

CROSSOVER

What was Quiksilver, a surf company, doing sponsoring a skateboarder? In the eyes of industry, surfing was just one of an entire class of sports. In the 1990s "extreme" sports took off: snowboarding, skateboarding, windsurfing, kiteboarding. In 1995 ESPN tapped the trend with the first X Games. They were also sometimes called "alternative" sports, which suggested a reaction against traditional, mainstream sports like football or baseball. But with these sports defined and propagated by multinational corporations like ESPN and Quiksilver, could one credibly maintain that they were "alternative"? After snowboarding joined the Olympics in 1998, was it still outside the mainstream? Some academic theorists preferred to view them as "postmodern" sports, typifying the fragmented, image-conscious, aesthetic, and performative trends of postmodernism—words that probably won't cross the mind of an X Games analyst.

So, was surfing an "extreme" sport? Many of these sports involved the act of riding, whether it was a surfboard, skateboard, snowboard, or windsurfer. The French lumped many of them together as *sports de glisse* (*glisser* means to slide or glide). Surfing also shared the element of risk and danger, and a countercultural, nonconformist image. In fact, surfers spawned several of these sports, especially skateboarding and snowboarding, to mimic the sensation of riding waves, so it was no coincidence there was crossover. Skateboarding wasn't called "sidewalk surfing" for nothing. Extreme skiers Mike Douglas, Cody Townsend, and Chuck Patterson recently took crossover to a new level by riding big waves on Maui, towing in on water skis.

Industry encouraged the crossover trend, with surf companies like Quiksilver sponsoring skiers, skaters, and snowboarders and making gear for them. The business philosophy saw these extreme outdoor sports as one large market. Thus, in 2005 Quiksilver bought French ski maker Rossignol. The deal, however, may have revealed the uniqueness of surfing. Skiing seemed to offer many, yes, parallels to surfing. Skiers exulted over carving turns on bluebird powder days as enthusiastically as surfers cherished glassy overhead barrels. And, like surfing, skiing's romantic attraction centered on the individual's encounter with natural wilderness. There were many more similarities. Like surfing, skiing was practiced for centuries in isolation before emerging in the twentieth century as popular recreation. It was identified with a particular place (the Alps), and enthusiasts embraced that region's culture and made regular pilgrimages to the sport's ancestral home. Skiing shed natural wood for new high-tech materials after World War II and became a baby-boom leisure lifestyle, in the process combining a dirtbag, outlaw counterculture with the middle-class mainstream (and remaining overwhelmingly white as well). And it underwent commercialization and professionalization to become a multibillion-dollar international industry, even as the pure fun of the sport continued to attract legions of new enthusiasts. In short, skiing, like surfing, went from an isolated premodern pursuit to an industrialized leisure commodity.

Ultimately, however, surfing was different. Its roots were literally a world away from skiing's. Alpine and Polynesian geography are about as different as you can get, and their cultures reflect this—unless you count lederhosen as a sort of surf trunk, and yodeling as a sort of vocal slack-key. Cold, forbidding Alpine peaks meant hardship. Warm Waikiki waters meant pleasure. Certainly huge Hawaiian waves could deal out unforgiving punishment; but the image, from ancient Hawaiians through the beachboys to Gidget to today, was fun. Skiing reflected its setting in its emphasis on discipline. Early skiing was utilitarian, initially for hunting and then taken up by European militaries, whose influence on the sport persisted well into the twentieth century. Skiing's element of discipline is still exercised by the ever-present ski patrol, and by the systematic regime of technical ski instruction. Surfing suggests the opposite: casting aside discipline in pursuit of fun. Surfing might have been useful for getting from an offshore boat to a beach, but ancient Hawaiian chants reveal that it was mostly just for fun all along.

That helps explain why Quiksilver's Rossignol deal turned into a business disaster that left Quiksilver looking for an exit strategy. But skiing was easier to justify than other crossovers attempted by the surf industry. As part of the Rossignol deal, Quiksilver found itself owning Cleveland Golf, a golf club manufacturer. Yes, golf—that new "alternative," "extreme" sport. In late 2007 Quiksilver sold off this business, thereby disappointing all its young riders enjoying their pro deals on new golf clubs. The fact that young surfers had made golf a hip trend on the world tour suggested how much surf culture had changed: from counterculture rebels to country-club duffers.

DEMOGRAPHICS

Crossover sports suggested demographic trends in surf culture. The X Games had two connotations: extreme sports, and Generation X. It was a stroke of marketing genius by ESPN to combine them into one term.

But before there was Generation X, there was the baby boom generation. By the 1990s, the boomers were starting to enter their fifties, with disposable income. They helped fuel a longboard revival and also drove a thriving memorabilia market, with replicas of 1950s boards selling for thousands of dollars and originals for far more. The surfwear industry targeted these aging surfers as a lucrative niche market; Quiksilver, for example, re-signed several graying legends from the 1970s to promote its "Quik*silver* Edition." Here surfing's appeal as a lifestyle had a literal sense, captured in the popular documentary *Surfing for Life*, which spotlighted several waveriders in their seventies, eighties, and nineties. The message: once a surfer, always a surfer. Thus Madison Avenue made TV ads for insurance and brokerage firms featuring old guys out longboarding.

At the other end of the demographic spectrum were the grommets. The surf industry, in its eternal quest for youth, extended "pro surfing" to children, and young surfers not yet in their teens began earning six-figure salaries for their surfing ability. Again, such early investments wete motivated by the occasional success story, such as that of Hawaiian John-John Florence, born in October 1992, who competed in pro contests on the North Shore at age thirteen. The trend encouraged preteen boys and girls to prepare promo videos of themselves surfing, which they shopped to potential sponsors.

Like the can't-miss kids of the 1980s who ended up drug addicts, the latest crop of starry-eyed aspiring pros raised troubling questions. A documentary called *Chasing the Dream* presented a surfing version of

Hoop Dreams: it followed a number of Huntington Beach high schoolers pursuing competitive surfing and showed what happened down the line. Youngsters might make money from the surf industry in the short run, while the surfwear companies used them for marketing, but most were soon cast aside for the next crop of hot youngsters. The opposite danger was that these kids would succeed as pro surfers but still hurt surfing in the long run by becoming clones. When Kolohe Andino, a sixteen-year-old hotshot, signed sponsorship deals with Target, Nike, and Red Bull, his friends mocked him with the nickname "Corporate." Graham Stapelberg, Billabong's marketing head, said, "If all we're creating is a bunch of little competitive robots then we've all failed. Surfing has always thrived on characters, but true characters are getting harder and harder to find." The trend threatened to further undermine surfing's countercultural, nonconformist image—the very source of its mass-market appeal. How could young surfers rebel against authority with corporate minders overseeing their careers?

By turning children into pro surfers, surfing joined the general commodification of childhood. Clothing companies sought to establish brand identities before children grew old enough to question it; marketers began paying popular kids to wear particular brands to school. Popular culture was more and more defined by youth—not a new trend, as surfers were well aware, but one that was accelerating, and pushing "youth" back beyond the early teens. If you think eight-year-old kids these days aren't familiar with Quiksilver and Billabong, then you don't have an eight-year-old kid.

BLOWING FOAM

Surfboard manufacturers also faced a new era. They were another major part of the surf industry, with their own international markets and business cycles. Early in the twenty-first century the surfboard market was whipsawed by the forces of global manufacturing, and by the whims of one man.

The whims were those of Gordon "Grubby" Clark, whose Clark Foam dominated the production of surfboard blanks. (A blank is the block of foam that shapers carve into a surfboard, which is then coated with fiberglass and resin.) Clark had entered the business with Hobie

Alter in the late 1950s, just after the introduction of polyurethane foam. He had a bachelor's degree in engineering from Pomona College, where he also studied math, physics, and chemistry. He picked up the nickname "Grubby" because he often surfed after his job in the Huntington Beach oil fields. In 1961 he started Clark Foam up in Laguna Canyon. The process was tetchy; workers mixed up the ingredients and poured them into massive steel-and-concrete molds to expand and cool; variations in the recipe, temperature, or humidity left air bubbles and other weak spots in the foam. Over the years Clark perfected his formula, scaled up his operation, and squeezed out competitors. By 2000 Clark had an iron grip on at least 95 percent of the $200 million U.S. market and 70 percent of the world market for polyurethane blanks. The secretive Clark did not divulge his production figures, but rumor had it he shipped a thousand foam blanks a day, several times more than his closest competitor. Three years earlier, *Surfer* magazine dubbed Clark the second most powerful man in surfing (after Bob McKnight of Quiksilver). The article included a photo of Grubby with both middle fingers raised in a double-barreled salute to the surfing community.

Clark won market share by keeping prices low. He undercut competitors in part because of a ruthless business philosophy—if Clark learned a shaper was also buying a competitor's blanks, he would punish him with slow deliveries. But Clark also had the ideals of surf culture at heart. Clark believed in the romantic, individualistic approach to surfboard design and nobly supported small-scale backyard shapers, pointedly refusing to give large-scale producers a price break. He could do so because of the quality of his products and the scale of his operation. He bought raw chemicals by the ton, built massive, multiton concrete molds and reactor vessels, and invested in high-tech ventilation and environmental control systems. His process used large volumes of toluene diisocyanate, a highly hazardous material, combined with a polyester polyol blend. In short, the proliferation of small-scale backyard shapers starting in the late 1960s depended on the supply of cheap foam blanks from Clark, which in turn rested on the cheap raw chemicals supplied by Bayer and other major firms in the global chemical industry. Like the idyllic tropical reefs surfers loved, the do-it-yourself ideal in surfboard making was supported by a vast, unmentioned infrastructure. Surfers, however, certainly noticed this submerged structure when they wiped out and hit a coral reef, and shapers eventually recognized their own industrial infrastructure on the day when Grubby Clark wiped them out.

Over the years Clark regaled his customers with annual letters describing the state of the industry. On a Monday in December 2005, surfboard shapers received a rambling fax declaring that Clark Foam was closing immediately. To make it irreversible, Clark dismantled his plant and ordered his workers to destroy his concrete blank molds. The shattered molds up in Laguna Canyon, source of world-championship boards, became a pilgrimage site for surfers. Dubbed "Blank Monday," Clark's abrupt demise shocked the surfing world. Why did he quit? His fax claimed that government regulators and health-related lawsuits by employees threatened to ruin his company: "I may be looking at very large fines, civil lawsuits, and even time in prison." He had had visits from state and federal environmental agencies and the local fire marshal; though none had taken action, he had also been served with several workers' compensation claims, one of which included a wrongful death lawsuit focusing on isocyanate exposure.

Blank Monday produced apocalyptic pronouncements; a prominent article by William Finnegan in the *New Yorker* was subtitled "Could Grubby Clark Destroy Surfing?" The global supply of blanks disappeared in a day, and shapers desperately scrambled to find foam. Because Clark so abruptly quit the business, he screwed those same backyard shapers his business philosophy had supported. Many of them now found themselves with no blanks to shape and going underwater financially. When new blank makers slowly filled the vacuum, their blanks proved of spotty quality, and shapers took the blame for the boards' poor performance.

Some in the surfboard industry viewed Blank Monday as a blessing in disguise. Without the sheer inertia of Clark Foam, perhaps the industry could finally break the stranglehold of the polyurethane foam and polyester resin model. In particular, perhaps surfboard shapers could finally address the serious health and environmental hazards of existing boards, with more low-tech, environmentally friendly materials: balsawood or sugarcane foam instead of isocyanate-laced polyurethane, linseed resin instead of polyester, and hemp, silk, or bamboo instead of fiberglass. (Wetsuit and boardshort makers similarly experimented with limestone-based "geoprene" instead of petroleum-based neoprene for wetsuits, and recycled plastic or organic cotton instead of synthetic nylon or polyester boardshorts.)

The strength-to-weight ratios of the new "green" board materials, however, did not approach those of polyurethane and polyester. The old paradigm remained entrenched. Sixty years after Bob Simmons introduced new materials from synthetic chemistry after World War II, well over 90 percent of new boards used polyurethane foam and polyester resin. As shaper Rich Price put it, the foam-and-resin model was "the heart and soul of the industry." Another shaper, Jesse Fernandez, downplayed the new "green" materials: "You can do a killer bamboo board with a sugar-cane based core and some corn oil resin, but when you pick the 10-lb thing up, it's like, '*Whoa*.' And not in a good way." Fletcher Chouinard, shaper for Patagonia, invoked the source of the prevailing paradigm: "All the veggie-based epoxies I've tried are pretty much garbage. They've come a long way, but like any major breakthrough, you need the military or someone with really deep pockets to develop something that really works." *Surfing*'s board design forum for 2009 summed it up: "So much for the revolution."

There was another path open after Blank Monday. Instead of going low-tech and organic, surfboard shaping could go even more high-tech. Most manufacturers chose this route. This included both the materials involved, such as less toxic polystyrene formulas or hollow carbon-fiber shells, and the production process. Windsurfing provided key experience here, in the mass production of foam cores in molds instead of hand-shaped foam blanks. (Since the boards were popped out of the molds during production, they were often called "pop-outs.") The extensive windsurfing market, especially in Europe, embraced these mass-produced boards in the 1980s, and companies cut their teeth on these boards before turning to surfboards.

Most pop-out surfboards came from a single factory in Thailand run by Cobra International, which specialized in mass production of composite materials. The company was created in 1985 by Vorapant Chotkipanich, a Thai professional windsurfer, and began making surfboards in 1991. Just before Blank Monday, with spectacularly good timing, Cobra opened a new factory in an industrial park in Chonburi, outside Bangkok, where Sony, Mitsubishi, and Toyota had plants. The Cobra factory cost $20 million to build and employed 2,800 workers. It was soon cranking out 200,000 epoxy and 70,000 polyurethane boards each year, generating $30 million in sales. The Cobra factory was a model of high-tech mass production: it made foam cores by injection molding, followed by vacuum-press molding of the fiberglass-resin laminate. The Cobra factory helped make Surftech, a pop-out line sold in many surf shops, the bestselling surfboard label in the world by 2005. A number of old-school shapers found that licensing their designs to Surftech not only made them more money; it even increased sales of their custom, hand-shaped boards: new surfers tried their shapes as pop-outs, then moved on to custom boards. Channel Islands' Al Merrick, for instance, a preeminent shaper, had an "Anacapa" line of pop-outs from the Cobra factory.

The dominance of the Cobra factory suggested that the surfboard industry had just swapped one monopoly for another, Clark for Cobra. A labor lockout at Cobra in 2008 shut down production for five days and left the market scrambling, in shades of Black Monday. Chinese factories, however, were catching up in molded composite manufacturing and eagerly entering the pop-out surfboard market. The burgeoning competition in Asia suggested another possible cause for Blank Monday—namely, that Grubby Clark quit not because of environmental regulations and lawsuits, but because he feared competing against Asian manufacturers. Clark himself had suggested as much. In 2004, the year before Blank Monday, his annual missive had warned that surfboard production, like many other American manufacturing industries, would soon be offshored to Asian factories with cheap labor. Clark may have seen the handwriting on the wall and jumped out of the business before Asian competitors could push him out.

The proliferation of Asian-made pop-outs, at less than half the price of a board down at the local surf shop, caused much hand-wringing about the end of the backyard-craftsman model of surfboard shaping. The double whammy of Blank Monday, with Clark no longer supporting small-scale shapers, and cheaper Asian competition threatened finally to drive the local backyard shaper out of business. A surfboard would be just another widget cranked out by the thousands at a faceless Asian assembly line, not a work of art painstakingly created to your detailed specifications by the local guy standing in surf trunks and sandals in his backyard covered in foam dust, who was as hard-core about surfing as you were. And another piece of surfing's soul would vanish.

The hue and cry over Asian factories, however, obscured the fact that many local shapers were far from a handcrafted, garage operation in the twenty-first century. Many were now "shaping" boards at their computers, using CAD software driving CNC (computerized numerical control) routers. A shaper sat down at the computer, pulled up the shaping software to tweak the dimensions of a particular model, and hit "enter," and the router carved the programmed shape out of the foam blank. The "shaper" just had to sand out any rough patches left by the machine. Instead of a handsaw and a planer, shapers used a computer keyboard and mouse. These machine-shaped boards undermined the hand-crafted ideal, which included an assumption about custom surfboards. Ever since the shortboard revolution, surfers had viewed surfboard shaping as immune to standardization. A surfboard shape needed to reflect an individual surfer's height and weight, surfing ability, performance style (for instance, cruising in trim, or aggressively carved turns?), and size and type of waves (small mushy point break, quickly barreling beachbreak, or macking outer reef?). *Surfing* magazine in 1983 declared that "standardization is virtually impossible" because of these many variables.

Standardized computer models undermined the old custom ideal. Surfing followed the arc, common to modern sports, from idiosyncrasy to standardization of equipment—and standardization of fun. Most surfboard labels began offering a dozen or so basic models, each available in several sizes. That range of options was enough to satisfy most surfers. By 2011, *Surfer* magazine estimated 90 percent of surfboards sold in surf shops were shaped by machine, and most of the top one hundred pros—the surfers most sensitive to subtle gradations—rode machine-shaped boards. Even small-volume shapers produced boards on computers, wangling or renting machine time from higher-volume producers. This was not exactly the backyard-craftsman model, in particular since these shaping machines were very expensive. (That's one reason they took so long to catch on; they had been around since at least the 1980s.) A single shaping machine cost over $50,000—complete top-end setups could run in the million-dollar range—and some surfboard labels, like their surfwear counterparts, began looking to outside investors to come up with the cash. With those kinds of costs, labels had to do a huge volume to recoup investment. Channel Islands, for example, had a gleaming factory, paid for by an infusion of cash from its new corporate owner, Burton. The factory, a stone's throw from the world-class testing grounds of Rincon south of Santa Barbara, didn't match the scale of the Cobra factory, but neither was it anything like a backyard operation.

Most surfers accepted this level of technological modernization but drew the line at Asian pop-outs. Few dedicated surfers would be caught riding a pop-out, although that stigma may be starting to erode. This resistance, a desperate clinging to the romantic notion of the handcrafted surfboard, maintained surfing's self-image as a soulful sport. Of course, that surfboard was made out of polyurethane and other synthetic chemicals, not wiliwili wood. And the neighborhood shaper was increasingly likely to type a few numbers into a shaping machine rather than get his hands dirty with a planer.

In the end, the one thing keeping surfboard production from going even more high-tech and mass-produced was probably not so much the values of surf culture, but rather the relative smallness of the market: 20 million surfers was not chump change, but neither was it a market like, say, T-shirts. Unlike the surfwear brands, surfboard makers couldn't sell their products in Midwestern malls. That helps explain why the threat of Asian mass production soon proved overblown. When the first container of cheap boards arrived at the average surf shop, they sold quickly; the second container arrived soon after and sold slower; then the third container arrived, and retailers were practically giving surfboards away because the fourth container was en route. Most surfers only bought a new board every year or two, and there just weren't that many new surfers joining the sport. Asian factories had tooled up to meet a nonexistent demand.

SURFING THE MAINSTREAM

Hollywood, Madison Avenue, Asian factories, Wall Street—there seemed to be no part of the modern business realm untouched by surfing's liquid cultural diffusion. All of these markets, from Hollywood and high fashion to middlebrow Midwestern malls, rested on surfing's romantic appeal as a natural, individualistic pursuit outside the mainstream. But, as companies like Gotcha and OP learned the hard way, it was all too easy to lose your cool in pursuit of mainstream markets. The surf industry had to achieve a delicate balancing act, maintaining surfing's countercultural image even as it increasingly entered the mainstream.

This balancing act could have tragic consequences. In November 2010 Andy Irons, a three-time world champion and an icon in the surfing world, died alone in a Dallas airport hotel room en route from Puerto Rico to Hawaii after a contest. Initial reports tiptoed around the cause of his death, at first attributing it to dengue fever. Only later did journalists connect the tragedy to Irons's well-known but little-mentioned partying streak, including drug abuse, which exacerbated an undetected heart condition. Others noted that Irons was not an isolated example, since drugs pervaded pro surfing, and they called on the surf media and industry to confront the issue rather than continue to sweep it under the rug. Pro surfing was again caught between its desire to be a mainstream competitive sport and the countercultural lifestyle. The world tour had no drug-testing program, probably because, as one former ASP official put it, too many pro surfers would fail any test for recreational drugs. As with Michael Peterson and Jeff Hakman in the 1970s, surfing distinguished itself in a bad way for its association with drugs. What other sport stood by while its best athletes spiraled into addiction? Finally, the ASP announced that it would begin drug testing of tour surfers in 2012, apparently at the urging of the Surf Industry Manufacturers Association, the industry trade group. Longtime Hawaiian contest director Randy Rarick declared, "It's been a long time coming."

Surfing's countercultural inclinations may have kept it from becoming even bigger. As a sport, it still occupied a fairly small niche, closer in size to bowling than to football or baseball, and not even close to tennis or golf, let alone NASCAR. You can't turn on the TV on a weekend afternoon and catch a surf contest. One possible reason: only so many people live near coastlines and know firsthand about surfing. On the other hand, many major sports are not participatory; people watch the Super Bowl even if they don't play tackle football. Major money comes into these sports through *spectator* interest, especially from TV deals. Surfing could have gone this route. In 1997 surfers and surfwear firms shot down a major TV deal with London-based Communications Services International, one of the largest distributors of TV sports programming, with connections to Rupert Murdoch's broadcast empire. CSI offered to televise all twelve world-tour events in more than one hundred countries and spend up to $7 million promoting pro surfing over the next four years. Surfers on the ASP board rejected the deal. One writer at the time asked, "Did pro surfing blow its shot at the truly big time, or has cool triumphed over greed?" But another way to view this issue is that surfing, by not getting even bigger, helped keep its countercultural credibility. Surfing in general, and the surf industry in particular, walks a fine line between staying cool and selling out, between Waikiki and Wall Street. Going even more big-time may cost surfing its cool and kill the goose that lays golden eggs.

It has been a decade and a half since the CSI offer, and surfing still doesn't have a major TV deal, relying on webcasts to publicize pro surf contests. One problem was that surfing on TV demanded good surf—and preferably accessible surf, with multiple vantage points, not some distant offshore reef. As contest promoters learned in the 1970s, network executives would hang out in Hawaii drinking mai tais for about a week, waiting for a swell to arrive, before they started asking, "When are you going to run this freakin' contest?" The answer, of course: wave pools! Even better, wave pools could better accommodate live spectators as well, providing the sense of spectacle that large crowds conveyed for pro football or baseball games. Kelly Slater and others began working anew to develop wave pools for just this reason. Wave pools would let pro surfing reach the lazy landlocked masses, as spectators for surf contests in person and on TV. For the more adventurous, wave pools offered inlanders the opportunity to try surfing themselves. You could live in Nebraska and be a surfer. Wave pools would complete surfing's trajectory from Waikiki to Wall Street . . . and finally to Main Street.

15 THE WORLD IN THE CURL

Duke Kahanamoku, the world's fastest swimmer for almost sixteen years and the greatest surfer of all time, ruled the waves for much of the twentieth century. His lifetime spanned the transition to modern surfing. Duke was born when surfing was dead. He learned to swim and surf as a young *keiki* on Waikiki Beach in the 1890s, when a handful of surfers plied the waves. Seven decades later, he stood on a California beach at the 1963 West Coast Surfing Championships in front of thirty thousand cheering teenage surfers, every one of whom knew his name. By that time, surfing was well on its way to becoming a cultural and commercial juggernaut, incorporating both high-tech advances from the military-industrial complex and Hollywood hokum. Also by that time, Duke could look over a Waikiki utterly transformed from the beach of his youth, its streams diverted by concrete canals and its beach lined with imported sand and high-rise hotels built on dredged fill. Like Waikiki Beach itself, Duke at times struggled with these changing circumstances. But he emerged with his spirit of aloha intact and continued to epitomize the pure stoke of wave riding.

By the start of the twenty-first century, surfing had gone from an exotic tropical pastime to a mainstream lifestyle practiced by millions of people around the world and envied by millions more. Surfing's image of casual mastery has carried its influence far beyond the surf community itself to Hollywood, music, fashion, and business (not for nothing do we call it "surfing" the Internet). Today, surf culture is woven into the fabric of societies whose members will never catch a wave. That's why you can walk through a mall in Midwestern America, or Munich or Moscow, and pick up a pair of surf trunks.

LOOKING BACK

Much of surfing's cultural and commercial appeal came from its image of an individualistic pursuit, where a person could escape modern society and find solitary communion with nature. This book has sought to paint a more interesting picture. Surfing is not an isolated pursuit on the margins of society. It has been a major cultural phenomenon across centuries and around the globe. Along the way it has been deeply entwined with social forces: colonialism, capitalism, race and gender relations, the military-industrial complex, multinational corporations, environmental change, and globalization.

Surfing's story is that of the modern world: it shows how these broad social forces reach into seemingly simple and pure pursuits. And, like much of what we see as modern, surfing poses difficult questions. Is surfing sexist? Is it racist? Why don't more minorities surf? Who is a "native"? What defines a local? Can a wave be private property? Is surfing popular only because marketing campaigns made it cool?

Surfing reflects the modern world in another key respect. Surfing is increasingly artificial. Surfboards went from hand-carved natural wood to a blend of mass-produced synthetic chemicals. Surfwear evolved from mulberry-bark loincloths (or just plain naked skin) to synthetic nylon and neoprene. Most surfers would not have it otherwise. How many want to wrestle a hundred-pound redwood plank through walls of whitewater? How many want to spin out on every other wave and make constant long swims to the beach to retrieve the board? Who wants to do all this in fifty-four-degree water, shivering and sinking in sopping-wet wool? Not us. We *like* our lightweight foam contrivances, which let us ride all over and even inside of waves, and we *like* the 4-mil neoprene that lets us surf for hours year-round in toasty comfort. But we recognize these come with a cost.

Then there are the waves themselves, from environmentally engineered and polluted coastlines to artificial reefs and landlocked wave pools. Because surfers sit at the very interface between civilization and wilderness—between human communities and the oceanic frontier—they are ideally placed to reveal the increasing encroachments of modern industrial society on the natural world. Surfers have a front-row seat for the ongoing assault on earth's last wilderness—the ocean. The conquest of nature is a messy business, and surfers are swimming in it.

Surfers increasingly face a basic question: how much is nature part of surfing's attraction? If surfing is just about riding waves for fun, then grab your foam-and-fiberglass board and head down to the chlorinated, inland wave pool to get your wave count, as Kelly Slater argues. But if surfing is really about an encounter with nature, you're going have to go pretty far afield with your hand-carved alaia to find an untouched wave. And gas is expensive, so chances are you'll be checking your laptop for a surf forecast regardless of what kind of board is under your arm.

LOOKING FORWARD

Surfing is more popular than ever. An estimated 20 million people surf worldwide. The U.S. surf industry has sales of over $5 billion a year, the global industry $10 billion. Starting in 2008 the economic crisis put a dent in the industry. Quiksilver's stock price cratered, from over $15 to under $1 a share, and as the company skirted bankruptcy it laid off hundreds of workers. At the same time, however, pro surfing boasted record prize purses from surfwear sponsors, with some contest winners walking away with six-figure checks. Pro surfer Taj Burrow said at the end of 2009, "You know how they say that the only things that do well during a recession are the beer companies and bars? Well, maybe pro surfing is like that too." On the other hand, those six-figure checks were a pittance compared to the money in other sports—and to the executive compensation in the surf industry.

Where will surfing go from here? Surfing in the past has undergone waves of popularity, followed by lulls: for example, California's surf boom of the late 1950s and early 1960s, followed by the 1970s doldrums. But the overall trend has been inexorably upward: increasing numbers of surfers, increasing dollars in the surf industry, and increasing crowds in surf lineups. Surfing's future prospects, like its past, depend on trends in technology, economics, demographics, the environment, and culture. Will new surfboard materials again boost surfing's accessibility and spark another revolution, or will scarce materials lead to stagnation? Can surf culture thrive without a real countercultural edge? Will economic decline stifle surfing along with the middle class? Will global population growth and development render the oceans unsurfable with sewage? Have surfers finally found their political voice on environmental issues? How will surfing cope with global warming? Will surfing continue to spread into new regions, and how will these cultural encounters shape surf culture? Will India and China, with their thousands of miles of surfable coastline, embrace surfing? If surfers think it's crowded now, what happens when the 2 billion people in these two countries hit the waves?

Most fundamentally, can surfing maintain its split personality? Much of its appeal has come from its rebellious, countercultural spirit—like rock 'n' roll, but even better because it involves nature. But surfing is tangled up with such dominant social forces as tourism, warfare, environmental engineering, and global commerce. Surfing is business, whether it's selling surfboards, surfwear, tourism, magazines, forecasting websites, or pro contests. As Wall Street and Madison Avenue co-opted surfing, it became more accessible but also lost some of its original appeal. The more people got turned on to the stoke, the less fun there was in surfing. How subversive is surfing, when it is a billion-dollar business run by multinational conglomerates? When twelve-year-old kids from Manhattan, New York, to Manhattan, Kansas, spend their parents' money on surf trunks that will never get wet? And when most surf lineups are bastions of middle-class white males? Can surfing go mainstream and still be a counterculture? Or does surfing's popularity carry the seeds of its own demise?

Surfers recognize the dangers and have sought to defend their sport's iconoclastic roots, from the Santa Cruz locals tipping contest scaffolds off the cliff at Steamer Lane in 1969 to every surfer who refuses to buy a mass-produced Asian pop-out today. Amid surfing's increasing high-tech commodification, a veritable ashram of authors has emerged to celebrate surfing's spiritual purity, with mysto titles like "Surfing into Spirituality," *The Surf Guru*, *Saltwater Buddha*, *The Zen of Oceans and Surfing*, *West of Jesus*, and *Walking on Water*. A similar sensibility sparked the backlash against tow-in surfing among some of the big-wave brethren, and has also spurred a recent revival of interest in ancient alaia boards. For every Laird Hamilton consulting the latest in industrial carbon-fiber molding techniques, and for every Kelly Slater seeking to perfect wave-pool technology, there are scores of surfers jumping in the ocean with nothing but a simple wooden alaia plank, seeking an unmediated encounter with a wave. Many surfers believe they should at one point in their surfing life shape their own board. This impulse is something few other sports exhibit—picture golfers making their own clubs or baseball players carving bats.

A few intrepid surfers recently took up a challenge thrown down decades ago by Miki Dora, who said that the test of a true surfer would be to ride as long a wave as possible, on a self-made wooden board, with no industrial-age technology. That meant no synthetic-chemical surfboard, no neoprene wetsuit or nylon trunks, no urethane surf leash. Three old-school surfers—Robert "Wingnut" Weaver, the longboarding star of *The Endless Summer II*, Marc Andreini, a longtime underground shaping guru, and Mickey Muñoz, a headline hotdogger from the late 1950s—surfed Jeffrey's Bay in South Africa on one of the biggest days of the year, on hand-shaped wood boards, wearing only wool trunks and vests in the fifty-degree water. They found the same stoke that ancient Hawaiians experienced surfing giant south swells at Waikiki, riding wooden boards and wearing nothing at all.

BACK TO WAIKIKI

Lots of sports are fun. Sportswriters wax rhapsodic about a well-struck three-iron or topspin forehand, or a well-climbed 5.13 pitch, or a waist-deep powder run in skiing. What's special about surfing? Surfing's basic appeal has always derived, even if subconsciously, from its association with the tropical paradise of Hawaii. Early European explorers perceived Polynesia as the antithesis of modern society, and today's kids still perceive surfing that way. They do so despite—or perhaps because of—surfing's increasing entanglements with the modern industrial world. The more modern society enfolds surfing in technology and commerce, the more important that Polynesian heritage. This self-conscious appeal to a premodern Polynesian past, and to the ideal, if not the reality, of escaping modern society, further sets surfing apart from other pursuits. What other sport cultivates its roots so assiduously, to the point where many enthusiasts today reject current equipment in favor of centuries-old technology? How many skiers, or golfers, or tennis players, happily set aside the latest carbon-composite contraptions for hand-carved wooden gear?

That's why it is important that modern surfing emerged in Hawaii. Hawaii is a world apart, a uniquely positioned geological gem populated by a people of unparalleled aquatic prowess. To surf you must swim. In ancient Hawaii swimming was a key to survival; Hawaiians were the world's greatest water people and surfing was a byproduct of their oceanic lifestyle. And Hawaiians had time for fun because of their ability to grow large quantities of protein-rich foods. In short, Hawaiians taught the world that the ocean might be feared, but it was also full of fun.

Surfing expresses the tension between the romantic and the modern, the natural and the artificial, the communal and the commercial—ultimately, between the heart and the mind. The mind knows surfing's litany of sexism, racism, marketing, environmental apathy, and the rest of it. And yet. You step onto Waikiki Beach on a tropical summer evening, and you turn your back on the skyscraping hotels, on the engineered landscape, on the whole sordid history of political and economic exploitation, chauvinism and bigotry, pollution, and localism. You look out to sea, heft your board under your arm, and jump into the warm salt water. Paddling out, you sense the purple mass of Diamond Head aglow with the setting sun and hear slack-key guitar warbling out from a beach bar. You scan the horizon for that telltale bump. A wave approaches and you turn toward shore. You feel the speed gathering under your board, and you are once again upright, propelled as if by magic carpet, arcing through the twilight. And everything else drops away.

ACKNOWLEDGMENTS

This book started as a course at the University of California, Santa Barbara, and we first thank our colleague Mike Osborne, the UCSB History and Environmental Studies departments, and the UCSB Coastal Fund for getting the course off the ground. Fellow historians Nicolas Rasmussen, Patrick McCray, Dan Kevles, John Heilbron, Ruth Cowan, Lawrence Badash, Rod Nash, Carroll Pursell, Greg Graves, John Talbott, Bill Deverell, and Dan Lewis provided welcome encouragement and advice, as have several writer friends, especially Wade Graham, Stephen Murdoch, and Matthew Stewart; Charles Donelan read and critiqued the whole manuscript. Alison Rose Jefferson, Patrick Moser, Stuart Sweeney, and Isaiah Walker collegially shared perspectives on surf history. We presented some of this material at conferences at the Huntington Library (organized by Volker Janssen), Oregon State (Anita Guerrini and Helen Rozwadowski), and Princeton (Michael Gordin, D. Graham Burnett, and David Kaiser), where participants provided useful feedback.

Many very knowledgeable members of the surf community shared their insights, in casual conversations or formal interviews: Bernie Baker, Rick Blocker, Duke Boyd, Joe Burke, Spencer Conway, Bill Delaney, Fred Hemmings, Greg Huglin, Danny Kwock, Tom Morey, Kevin

Naughton, Andy Neumann, Steve Pezman, Randy Rarick, Shawn Stussy, Steve Tepper, and Shaun Tomson. We also greatly benefited from conversations with several scientists and engineers: Hugh Bradner, John Crowell, Adam Fincham, Michael Neushul Jr., and Walter Munk.

We naturally must thank a number of archives and archivists: DeSoto Brown and Tia Reber at the Bishop Museum in Honolulu; Dick Metz, Barry Haun, Steve Wilkings, and Linda Michael at the Surfing Heritage Foundation; Charles Johnson at the Museum of Ventura County; Deborah Day and Caroline Rainey at Scripps; Shelley Irwin at Caltech; Simon Elliot at UCLA; and the Huntington Library. For help with photos: Rick Hilts; Scott Bass, Ty Ponder, Ralph Kellogg, and Gregg Samp; Jeff Divine; and Bob Barbour. Several friends surfed and talked surfing with us: John Rapp, Brian McWilliams, John Murphy, Mike Kelley, Mike Randolph, Kelly Smith, Harry Rabin, and Jim Smart; also our brothers, Stephen Neushul and John Westwick. Special thanks to Stephen and Suzanne Neushul for sharing their home and aloha on Oahu. Stephen also shared his insights on hydrodynamics and engineering. Our student Craig Nelson contributed back issues of surf magazines gathered during research on his senior thesis at UCSB on surfing and environmentalism.

We thank our agent Andrew Stuart, who immediately understood what we were trying to do. Our editor, Vanessa Mobley of Crown Books, similarly got it, and brought her sharp editorial eye to the project. The irony of writing this book is that we often had to skip surfing itself in order to finish it. Too often, especially in the epic winter of 2010, we opted for surfboards instead of keyboards. Fortunately for Vanessa, California had a lousy winter for surf the next year so we could finish off the manuscript. Vanessa's assistants Miriam Chotiner-Gardner and Claire Potter shepherded the book to publication.

We must finally thank our wives, Cathy Neushul and Medeighnia Westwick, and kids, Kiley, Jamie, and Ryann Neushul and Dane and Caden Westwick, for sharing the stoke.

NOTES

For books cited below with only author and title, see the bibliography for full publication information. For works not listed in the bibliography, the notes give publication details.

CHAPTER 1. THE CRADLE OF SURFING

7 *"rode the entire distance"*: Charles Kenn, "Hawaiian Sports and Games," box 17.6, Kenn papers, Bishop Museum, Honolulu.

7 *fishing villagers rode waves*: Felipe Pomar, "Surfing in 1,000 BC," *Surfer*, April 1988.

7 *in West Africa*: Sam George, "Pre-contact: The Surfing Tradition of Sao Tome," *Surfer's Journal* 16, no. 3 (2007): 40–49.

8 *Hawaii's extreme geographic isolation*: Walter A. McDougall, *Let the Sea Make a Noise: A History of the North Pacific from Magellan to MacArthur.*

8 *"Give me the waves"*: "Naihe" chant, in *Pacific Passages: An Anthology of Surf Writing*, ed. Patrick Moser, 41.

8 *"Arise! Arise"*: Ben R. Finney and James D. Houston, *Surfing: The Sport of Hawaiian Kings*, 52–55.

8 *One legend told of Kelea*: Most of these legends from Finney and Houston, *Surfing*. Quote from Kelea legend in Moser, *Pacific Passages*, 20. See also

Dave Zurick, "Surfing Among the Ancient Hawaiians," *Surfer*, August 1987, 60.

9 *Surfing was a form of courtship*: John R. K. Clark, *Hawaiian Surfing: Traditions from the Past*, 46–47.

9 *Another popular saying*: Finney and Houston, *Surfing*, 42–44; Charles Kenn, "Notes on Surfing," box 18.9, Kenn papers; Moser, *Pacific Passages*, 48.

10 *Anthropologists have concluded*: Patrick Vinton Kirch, *Feathered Gods and Fishhooks: An Introduction to Hawaiian Archaeology and Prehistory*.

11 *The evolution of Hawaiians*: Kenn, "Hawaiian Sports and Games"; George S. Kanahele, *Waikiki, 100 BC to 1900 AD: An Untold Story*; Don Hibbard and David Franzen, *The View from Diamond Head: Royal Residence to Urban Resort*.

12 *sophisticated system of aquaculture*: Kirch, *Feathered Gods and Fishhooks*, 199–214; Elspeth Sterling and Catherine C. Summers, eds., *Sites of Oahu*, 47–49; Diane Lee Rhodes, "Overview of Hawaiian History," in *A Cultural History of Three Traditional Hawaiian Sites on the West Coast of Hawai'i Island* by Linda Wedel Greene.

13 *In other words*: David E. Stannard, *Before the Horror: The Population of Hawai'i on the Eve of Western Contact*, 68.

13 *Surfing has always been*: Kenn, "Notes on Surfing"; Lorrin Andrews, *A Dictionary of the Hawaiian Language* (Honolulu: Henry M. Whitney, 1865), see "nalu"; Mary Kawena Pukui and Samuel H. Elbert, *Hawaiian Dictionary* (Honolulu: University of Hawaii Press, 1986), see "kanalu" and "nalu." See also Abraham Fornander, *An Account of the Polynesian Race: Its Origin and Migrations*, Vol. 3, 244.

14 *Several of his crew wondered*: James King and Charles Clerke, *The Journals of Captain James Cook on His Voyages of Discovery*, quoted in Moser, *Pacific Passages*, 74, 67; William Ellis, *An Authentic Narrative of a Voyage Performed by Captain Cook and Captain Clerke*, quoted in Moser, *Pacific Passages*, 69.

14 *David Samwell, surgeon's mate*: David Samwell, *The Voyages of Captain James Cook on His Voyages of Discovery*, quoted in Moser, *Pacific Passages*, 71.

14 *In 1837 a Hawaiian scholar, David Malo*: Quoted in Gavan Daws, *Shoal of Time: A History of the Hawaiian Islands*, 106.

15 *Kamehameha, a tall, strong*: Daws, *Shoal of Time*, 29.

15 *The sandalwood trade*: Rhodes, "Overview of Hawaiian History."

16 *Hundreds of whaling ships*: Eric Jay Dolin, *Leviathan: The History of Whaling in America*, 12, 245–7.

16 *Sailors, after months on*: Sarah Vowell, *Unfamiliar Fishes*, 110–11.

16 *Honolulu became a*: C. S. Stewart, *A Visit to the South Seas*, 114, 217.

16 *Whaling accelerated Hawaii's*: Rhodes, "Overview of Hawaiian History."

16 *That meant another displacement*: Daws, *Shoal of Time*, 128.

18 *"After some hesitation"*: William Ellis, *Narrative of a Tour Through Hawaii, or Owhyhee*, 6.

18 *In 1827, irate sailors on*: Jennifer Fish Kashay, "Competing Imperialisms and Hawaiian Authority: The Cannonading of Lahaina in 1827," *Pacific Historical Review* 77, no. 3 (2008): 369–90.

18 *The mission scored a*: Daws, *Shoal of Time*, 75; McDougall, *Let the Sea Make a Noise*, 175.

19 *"Formerly, old and young"*: James Jackson Jarves, *History of the Hawaiian or Sandwich Islands*, 121–22.

19 *"There are those living"*: In Finney and Houston, *Surfing*, 64.

19 *A visitor in 1838*: W. R. S. Ruschenberger, *Narrative of a Voyage Round the World* (1838), quoted in Finney and Houston, *Surfing*, 60.

19 *Bingham and other missionaries*: Joint letter of the missionaries (H. Bingham et al.) to C. B. W. Finch, commander of USS *Vincennes*, November 14, 1829, in Stewart, *A Visit to the South Seas*, 259–60.

19 *Bingham complained about*: Hiram Bingham, *A Residence of Twenty-One Years in the Sandwich Islands*, 3rd ed., 137, 215.

20 *By 1870 only a quarter of*: Daws, *Shoal of Time*, 98, 160. An earthquake and tsunami in 1837, seen as signs of God's displeasure, provoked a brief revival movement, but the revival itself suggested decline had already set in.

20 *One missionary complained*: Thomas Hopu, quoted in Moser, *Pacific Passages*, 3.

21 *A missionary wife in 1834*: Sarah Lyman, quoted in Clark, *Hawaiian Surfing*, 49; Charles Wilkes, *Narrative of the United States Exploring Expedition*, Vol. 4, 46–47.

21 *In the 1850s a visitor*: S. S. Hill, *Travels in the Sandwich and Society Islands*, 197–203.

21 *"a large company of naked natives"*: Mark Twain, *Roughing It* , 525.

22 *"expert surfers going upland"*: Both quotes from Daniel Duane, *Caught Inside: A Surfer's Year on the California Coast*, 85.

22 *Historians have even suggested*: Andy Martin, "Surfing the Revolution: The Fatal Impact of the Pacific on Europe," *Eighteenth-Century Studies* 41, no. 2 (2008): 141–47.

23 *"To see fifty or a hundred persons"*: Ellis, *Narrative of a Tour*, 278–80.

23 *"The sport is so attractive"*: Rev. Henry Cheever, *Life in the Sandwich Islands* (1851), quoted in Moser, *Pacific Passages*, 104–105.

23 *Such views resonated*: Alain Corbin, *The Lure of the Sea: The Discovery of the Seaside in the Western World, 1750–1840*, 78. See also Roderick Nash, *Wilderness and the American Mind*, 4th ed..

23 *Seaside resorts sprang up in*: John Towner, *An Historical Geography of Recreation and Tourism in the Western World, 1540–1940*, 170–1; Lena Lenček and Gideon Bosker, *The Beach: The History of Paradise on Earth*, 71–72.

23 *Michelet himself saw the sea*: Jules Michelet, *The Sea*, 398–399.

24 *Sea bathing became a way*: Corbin, *The Lure of the Sea: The Discovery of the Seaside in the Western World, 1750–1840*; Charles Sprawson, *Haunts of the Black Masseur: The Swimmer as Hero*; Lenček and Bosker, *Beach*, 54–55, 95–106; Nick Ford and David Brown, *Surfing and Social Theory: Experience, Embodiment and Narrative of the Dream Glide*, chap. 2.

25 *There was no winter cold*: O. A. Bushnell, *The Gifts of Civilization: Germs and Genocide in Hawai'i*; David E. Stannard, *Before the Horror: The Population of Hawai'i on the Eve of Western Contact*.

26 *Venereal disease arrived*: Stannard, *Before the Horror*, 70.

26 *His sailors, seeing healthy*: Bushnell, *Gifts of Civilization*. See also David Igler, "Diseased Goods: Global Exchanges in the Eastern Pacific Basin, 1770–1850," *American Historical Review* 109 (June 2004): 693–719.

27 *Sailors the world over*: Bushnell, *Gifts of Civilization*, 181–83.

27 *An estimated 142,000*: Anderson, *Hawaiian Islands*, 271.

27 *From 800,000 to 40,000*: Stannard, *Before the Horror*, 45. Other scholars continue to argue for lower numbers but have reached no consensus. See Patrick V. Kirch, " 'Like Shoals of Fish': Archaeology and Population in Pre-contact Hawaii" and Ross Cordy, "Reconstructing Hawaiian Population at European Contact," in *The Growth and Collapse of Pacific*

Island Societies: Archaeological and Demographic Perspectives, ed. Patrick V. Kirch and Jean-Louis Rallu, 52–69, 108–28.

27 "all the causes": Rufus Anderson, *The Hawaiian Islands: Their Progress and Condition Under Missionary Labors* (Boston, 1864), 275–76. Italics in original.

29 *The Navy became a*: Noel J. Kent, *Hawaii: Islands Under the Influence*, 66–67.

29 *In August 1898*: Daws, *Shoal of Time*, 252–88; McDougall, *Let the Sea Make a Noise*, 389–98.

CHAPTER 2. THE DUKE, DILLINGHAM, AND THE WAIKIKI DREAM

32 *He was soon the*: Joel T. Smith, "Reinventing the Sport, Part III: George Freeth," *Surfer's Journal* 12, no. 3 (2003): 90–94; Arthur C. Verge, "George Freeth: King of the Surfers and California's Forgotten Hero," *California History*, 53(Summer/Fall 2001): 82–105.

33 "*There's something spiritual*": Quoted in Ian Whitcomb, "The Father of Surfing," *American Heritage*, July/August 2000.

33 "*When he left*": Charmian Kittredge London, *Our Hawaii*, 53.

33 "*Charmian tried the gentle*": London, *Our Hawaii*, 74.

33 "*the big, bearded man surf*": Jack London, "The Kanaka Surf," in *Island Tales*, 211.

33 *London quickly wrote up*: Jack London, "Riding the South Seas Surf," *Woman's Home Companion* (October 1907); Jack London, *The Cruise of the Snark* (New York, 1911); Alexander Hume Ford, "Riding the Surf in Hawaii," *Collier's*, August 14, 1909. London's tales made an impression on Alexander Solzhenitsyn, evident in *The Oak and the Calf* (1980): "Two novels of mine appearing simultaneously in the West? A double? I felt like the Hawaiian surf riders described by Jack London, standing upright on a smooth board . . . on the crest of the ninth wave." Quoted in *Los Angeles Times*, August 4, 2008.

34 *Charmian London's account*: London, *Our Hawaii*, 75.

34 "*no one has done more*": *Pacific Commercial Advertiser*, July 7, 1907, quoted in Smith, "Reinventing the Sport," 91.

34 *Tourism took the*: James Buzard, *The Beaten Track: European Tourism, Literature, and the Ways to 'Culture', 1800–1918*, 2.

35 *During the first several*: Don J. Hibbard, *Designing Paradise: The Allure of the Hawaiian Resort*, 5.

35 *The government pitched*: Thomas Kemper Hitch, *Islands in Transition: The Past, Present, and Future of Hawaii's Economy*, 117–18.

35 *Several factors encouraged*: Jane C. Desmond, *Staging Tourism: Bodies on Display from Waikiki to Sea World*, 37.

35 *The Hawaiian display*: Desmond, *Staging Tourism*, 277–78; Hibbard, *Designing Paradise*; Norman Bolotin and Christine Laing, *The World's Columbian Exposition: The Chicago World's Fair of 1893* (Champaign: University of Illinois Press, 2002), 125.

35 *These efforts generated*: Hitch, *Islands in Transition*, 117.

36 *In 1901 the*: Desmond, *Staging Tourism*, 35.

36 *Surfing provided just*: Buzard, *Beaten Track*, 2, 5.

37 *A 1905 article*: Elinor Langton, "Give the Tourists More Variety," *Paradise of the Pacific*, March 1905, quoted in Cristina Bacchilega, *Legendary Hawai'i and the Politics of Place: Tradition, Translation, and Tourism*, 102; see also "Hawaiian Aquatic Sports," *Los Angeles Times*, October 11, 1908.

37 *"The water is a place"*: Desmond, *Staging Tourism*, 125; Bacchilega, *Legendary Hawai'i*, 96.

37 *The Moana quickly*: Grady Timmons, *Waikiki Beachboy*, 26–27.

37 *One such tourist was the British*: G. Hevesy, "Francis William Aston," *Obituary Notices of Fellows of the Royal Society* 5, no. 16 (1948): 635–50.

37 *Hawaii's tourism marketing*: Lynn Ann Davis, "Photographically Illustrated Books About Hawai'i, 1854–1945," *History of Photography* 25, no. 3 (Fall 2001), 288–305.

38 *By 1911 there*: Ben R. Finney and James D. Houston, *Surfing: The Sport of Hawaiian Kings*, 71.

38 *In 1899 Benjamin Dillingham built*: Hitch, *Islands in Transition*, 117.

39 *The drainage and sanitation*: Kai White and Jim Kraus, *Images of America: Waikiki*, 19.

40 *Pinkham's appointment as*: White and Kraus, *Waikiki*, 69.

40 *Thus well connected*: Paul T. Yardley, *Millstones and Milestones: The Career of B. F. Dillingham*.

40 *Starting a dredging*: Benjamin to Walter Dillingham, November 4, 1910, box 1, Walter Francis Dillingham Papers, Huntington Library, San Marino,

California; Walter to Benjamin Dillingham, October 14, 2010, box 8, Dillingham papers; "B. F. Dillingham Passes Fifty Years in Hawaii," January 28, 1916, box 12, Dillingham papers; "Early Railroad," *Honolulu Advertiser*, April 17, 1938.

42 *Soon every plot*: Jerald K. Crane, *History of the Marine Structures on Waikiki Beach and Their Effects Upon the Beach* (Honolulu: Department of Ocean Engineering, University of Hawaii, 1972); Robert L. Wiegel, *Waikiki, Oahu, Hawaii, an Urban Beach: Its History from a Coastal Engineering Perspective* (Berkeley, CA: Hydraulic Engineering Laboratory, University of California, 2002).

43 *On the plus side*: Crane, *History of the Marine Structures*; Wiegel, *Waikiki, Oahu, Hawaii*.

43 *Once the streams*: Timmons, *Waikiki Beachboy*, 45; Fred Hemmings, *The Soul of Surfing*, 1.

43 *On occasion the*: Crane, *History of the Marine Structures*; Wiegel, *Waikiki, Oahu, Hawaii*.

43 *Some of this sand*: Sarah Park, "Argument Raised on Surfing; New Beach Project Started," *Honolulu Star-Bulletin*, May 5, 1953.

45 *Duke then beat*: Sandra Kimberley Hall, *Duke: A Great Hawaiian*, 35.

46 "*he would have starved*": Timmons, *Waikiki Beachboy*, 73.

47 *By the late*: Elizabeth Buck, *Paradise Remade: The Politics of Culture and History in Hawai'i*.

47 *Soon afterward Pacific*: Craig Stecyk, "Pacific System: Birth of the Surfboard Factory," *Surfer's Journal* 6, no. 4 (1997): 32–39.

47 "*barely getting along*": *Honolulu Star-Bulletin*, August 6, 1961, reproduced in Hall, *Duke*, 84.

48 *Newport's police chief*: "Five Are Drowned When Waves Capsize Yacht," *Los Angeles Times*, June 15, 1925.

48 "*it took Tarzan*": Duke quoted in Stuart Holmes Coleman, *Eddie Would Go*, 62; Weissmuller quoted in Hall, *Duke*, 57.

49 *Dozens of cities built*: J. E. Van Hoosear, "Pacific Service Supplies the World's Largest Baths," *PG&E Magazine*, September 1912; Charles Sprawson, *Haunts of the Black Masseur: The Swimmer as Hero*, 268.

50 *Private pools, at*: C. Howard Hopkins, *History of the Y.M.C.A. in North America* (New York: Association Press, 1951), 154–55; David I. Macleod, *Building Character in the American Boy: The Boy Scouts, YMCA, and*

Their Forerunners, 1870–1920 (Madison: University of Wisconsin Press, 1983).

50 *By early in the*: Jeff Wiltse, *Contested Waters: A Social History of Swimming Pools in America*.

50 *Toward the end*: Joseph L. Brennan, *Duke: The Life Story of Hawai'i's Duke Kahanamoku*, 254.

CHAPTER 3. THE DARK SIDE OF PARADISE: RACE AND SEX IN HAWAII

51 *"the most sensational purple"*: *Honolulu Advertiser*, March 25, 1922.

52 *"The waitress said"*: Sandra Kimberly Hall, *Duke: A Great Hawaiian*, 53.

52 *Jack London glowingly*: Jack London, "Riding the South Seas Surf," *Woman's Home Companion*, October, 1907; Charmian London, *Our Hawaii*, 74.

52 *Ford himself made*: Alexander Hume Ford, "Riding the Surf in Hawaii," *Collier's*, August 14, 1909.

52 *"none but natives"*: Mark Twain, *Roughing It*, 288.

53 *He set dues at*: Grady Timmons, *Waikiki Beachboy*, 25.

53 *An immediate rivalry*: Isaiah Helekunihi Walker, "Hui Nalu, Beachboys, and the Surfing Boarder-Lands of Hawaii," *Contemporary Pacific* 20, no. 1 (2008): 89–113; Isaiah Helekunihi Walker, *Waves of Resistance: Surfing and History in Twentieth-Century Hawaii*, 62. In 1897 Hawaiian canoe surfers had organized a concession on Waikiki and called themselves the Hui Pakaka Nalu. They charged tourists one dollar an hour for canoe surfing—see John R. K. Clark, *Hawaiian Surfing: Traditions from the Past*, 69–70. Today Hui Nalu is primarily a paddling club. See http://info.huinalucanoeclub.com/page/3/ for a brief history of the club.

54 *Hui Nalu and Outrigger*: Other local swim teams included the Waikiki Swimming Club, the Healanis, and the Myrtles. Freeth swam for the Healanis as a youth but later joined Hui Nalu. Duke's rival, George Cunha, swam for the Healanis. Duke initially applied for membership in the Healanis but was rejected; he later jumped from Hui Nalu to Outrigger.

54 *one famous photo*: The Hui Nalu photo appears in Matt Warshaw's *The History of Surfing* and Leonard Lueras, *Surfing: The Ultimate Pleasure*.

55 *Many of these*: Daws, *Shoal of Time*, 305, 318.

56 *The LAAC hired*: Betty Lou Young, *Our First Century: The Los Angeles Athletic Club, 1880–1980*, 83.

57 *Savvy beachboys knew*: Jane C. Desmond, *Staging Tourism: Bodies on Display from Waikiki to Sea World*, 125–26.

57 *James Michener, in*: Quoted in Robert C. Allen, *Creating Hawai'i Tourism*, 17.

58 *A Vogue magazine cover*: *Vogue*, December 15, 1938.

58 *One young female*: Timmons, *Waikiki Beachboy*, 138–40. There is reason to question how much really went on with the beachboys. Tales of sexual exploits may have compensated for the fact that the job itself was often menial and demeaning, handing out towels and umbrellas as essentially a beach servant for white tourists. And, as longtime beachboy Harry Robello pointed out, while expressing skepticism about sex tales, the hotels that employed them did not tolerate affairs with clients. If the beachboys were plying tourists with sex as well as surfing lessons, they were not unique. Similar stories abound from ski instructors, climbing guides, and rafting guides; Ernest Hemingway's story from that period, "The Short Happy Life of Francis Macomber," featured a hunting guide who assumed sex with female clients was part of the deal.

58 *A 1932 mainland magazine*: Donald Barr Chidsey, "A Paradise Gone Mad: Facing the Facts in Hawaii," *Liberty*, March 26, 1932. Sarge Kahanamoku commented about one of his brother's boards, "Bruddah Duke like dis one best because it floated better and he take out many 'Haole' girls surfing. But he no surf; he keep on paddling way outwards and 'get' dem one good Hawaiian fucking." Inscription attached to Duke Kahanomoku hollow board at the Surfing Heritage Foundation in San Clemente, CA.

59 *Dillingham's company would*: H. Brett Melendy, *Walter Francis Dillingham, 1875–1963: Hawaiian Entrepreneur and Statesman*.

60 *By the late 1920s*: Thomas Kemper Hitch, *Islands in Transition: The Past, Present, and Future of Hawaii's Economy*, 122–25; Brian McAllister Linn, *Guardians of Empire: The U.S. Army and the Pacific, 1902–1940*; Erwin N. Thompson, *Pacific Ocean Engineers: History of the U.S. Army Corps of Engineers in the Pacific, 1905–1980* (Honolulu: Army Corps of Engineers, 1981).

60 *In particular, many military*: David Stannard, "The Massie Case: Injustice and Courage," *Honolulu Advertiser*, October 14, 2001.

60 *The five went*: David Stannard, *Honor Killing: How the Infamous 'Massie Affair' Transformed Hawai'i*. See also Daws, *Shoal of Time*.

61 *The* New York Times: Stannard, *Honor Killing*, 3–5.

62 *The U.S. Department*: William Atherton Du Puy, *Hawaii and Its Race Problem* (Washington, 1932), 129–31.

62 *In fact, there*: Stannard, *Honor Killing*, 4, 53.

62 *Another commentator cautioned*: Donald Barr Chidsey, "A Paradise Gone Mad: Facing the Facts in Hawaii," *Liberty*, March 26, 1932.

62 *Hollywood actress*: Timmons, *Waikiki Beachboy*, 33.

63 *Native Hawaiians and Asian*: Stannard, *Honor Killing*, 2.

63 *Younger generations*: Ibid., 80.

63 *He was the first*: Malcolm Gault-Williams and Gary Lynch, "The Last Chapter: Stories of Gene 'Tarzan' Smith," *Surfer's Journal* 7, no. 4 (1998): 44–51.

CHAPTER 4. INVENTING SURFURBIA: SURFING TO CALIFORNIA

64 *Waikiki had already sent*: Rex Dalton, "Manhattan: Isle's Sandman," *Daily Breeze*, October 13, 1973.

64 *"complete water-dogs"*: Richard Henry Dana, *Two Years Before the Mast,* 94.

65 *The permanent California*: Joel T. Smith, "Reinventing the Sport, Part III: George Freeth," *Surfer's Journal* 12, no. 3 (2003): 90–94. See also Ian Whitcomb, "The Beach Boy," *American Heritage*, July/August 2000.

65 *A local paper*: *The Daily Outlook*, July 22, 1907, quoted in Arthur C. Verge, "George Freeth: King of the Surfers and California's Forgotten Hero," *California History* 53,(Summer/Fall 2001): 86.

65 *At the time many*: John Grissim, "California Roots," *Surfing*, November 1981.

65 *Newspaper ads promised*: Classified ads in the *Los Angeles Times*, April 5, 1907 and May 5, 1908.

66 *beach towns later dubbed*: "Surfurbia" was coined by Reyner Banham in *Los Angeles: The Architecture of Four Ecologies*. See also Ronald A. Davidson, "Before 'Surfurbia': The Development of the South Bay Beach Cities Through the 1930s," *Yearbook of the Association of Pacific Coast Geographers* 66 (2004): 80–94; Lawrence Culver, "America's Playground:

Recreation and Race," in *A Companion to Los Angeles*, ed. William Deverell and Greg Hise, 421–37.

66 "*Take surf-boarding*": Quoted in Ben R. Finney and James D. Houston, *Surfing: The Sport of Hawaiian Kings*, 66.

67 *English beach resorts*: Laura Chase, "Public Beaches and Private Beach Huts: A Case Study of Inter-war Clacton and Frinton, Essex," in *Histories of Tourism: Representation, Identity, and Conflict*, ed. John K. Walton, 211–27.

67 *Unlike the old*: Verge, "George Freeth."

67 *The* Los Angeles Times *described*: "Snatch Eleven Men from Death's Jaws," *Los Angeles Times*, December 17, 1908.

68 *An ocean lifeguard*: Verge, "George Freeth."

69 *One of Duke Kahanamoku's*: Finney and Houston, *Surfing*, 71, 74.

69 *Balsa was also*: George Orbelian, *Essential Surfing*, 171–73.

70 *Blake was born*: Gary Lynch and Malcolm Gault-Williams, *Tom Blake: The Uncommon Journey of a Pioneer Waterman*.

71 *One of Blake's*: "Vultee Shows His Heels," *Los Angeles Times*, Mar 8, 1920; "Manning Cup Goes to Gerard Vultee," *Los Angeles Times*, March 15, 1920; "Swimmers to Compete at Redondo," *Los Angeles Times*, August 11, 1926.

71 *LAAC swim meets*: Betty Lou Young, *Our First Century: The Los Angeles Athletic Club, 1880–1980*, 59–60, 82–83, 105, 111.

71 *Vultee also surfed with Duke:*: "Five Are Drowned When Waves Capsize Yacht," *Los Angeles Times*, June 15, 1925.

71 *Vultee studied aeronautical*: S. Thomas Long, *To Undreamed-of Marks: A Tribute to Jerry Vultee* (Falls Church, VA: General Dynamics, 1991).

72 *Probably because the*: Craig Stecyk, "Pacific System: Birth of the Surfboard Factory," *Surfer's Journal* 6, no. 4 (1997): 32–39.

72 *An article in*: Paul W. Gartner, "Hawaiian Water Sled Is Easy to Build," *Modern Mechanix*, June 1933; "Paddle Surf Canoe," *Popular Mechanics*, November 1937, 769; Tom Blake, "Improved Hollow Surfboard for All Around Sport," *Popular Science*, June 1939; "Lifeguards Use Surfboards," *Modern Mechanix*, December 1937.

72 *In addition to hollow boards*: Stecyk, "Pacific System."

73 "*the emergence of a pleasure-seeking*": Kevin Starr, *The Dream Endures: California Enters the 1940s*, 3–27, quote on 4, surfing discussed on 10–11.

75 *Rindge fell in love*: See Frederick Hastings Rindge, *Happy Days in Southern California* (Cambridge, MA, 1898).

75 *Her opponents included*: Frank Norris, *The Octopus: A Story of California* (New York: Doubleday, 1901); William Deverell, *Railroad Crossing: Californians and the Railroad, 1850–1910*.

75 *Rindge knew that*: For a history of the Rindge railroad see http://www.ci.malibu.ca.us/index.cfm/fuseaction/detail/navid/9/cid/428/.

76 *When state construction*: Rumor had it Rindge's men shot at at early surveying crews plotting routes for the highway. Carlos Izan, "Malibu: Curse of the Chumash," *Surfer*, June/July 1976.

76 *In the 1920s*: "Beach Frontage Soaring: Ferguson Corporation Announces Malibu Beach to Be Listed at $500 per Front Foot," *Los Angeles Times*, October 14, 1928.

76 *a friend of Duke Kahanamoku*: Thomas W. Doyle et al., *The Story of Malibu* (Malibu, CA: Malibu Lagoon Museum, 1995) available at www.malibucity.org.

76 *May Rindge declared*: "Rancho Malibu Acreage Sold: Deal Announced Involving More Than $6,000,000," *Los Angeles Times*, November 20, 1928.

77 *Littoral flow rates*: Gary Griggs, Kiki Patsch, and Lauret Savoy, *Living with the Changing California Coast*, 51.

77 *Created by jetties*: Sean Reily, "Big Corona," *Surfer*, February 1984.

77 *The breakwater did*: Tami Abdollah, "Sea Wall Stops, Yet Makes, Waves," *Los Angeles Times*, July 24, 2007; Deborah Scoch, "A Possible Sea Change," *Los Angeles Times*, June 30, 2008.

78 "*foul and septic*": Blake Gumprecht, *The Los Angeles River: Its Life, Death, and Possible Rebirth*, 124.

78 *Finally, in 1950*: On the history of sewage treatment systems, see Joel A. Tarr et al., "Water and Wastes: A Retrospective Assessment of Wastewater Technology in the United States, 1800–1932," *Technology and Culture* 25 (1984), 226–263; Jamie Benidickson, *The Culture of Flushing: A Social and Legal History of Sewage*.

78 *Southern California sat*: Paul Sabin, *Crude Politics: The California Oil Market, 1900–1940*.

78 *A beachside oil boom*: Fred W. Viehe, "The Social-Spatial Distribution in the Black Gold Suburbs of Los Angeles, 1900–1930," *Southern California*

Quarterly 73, no. 1 (1991), 33–54. See also Nancy Quam-Wickham, " 'Cities Sacrificed on the Altar of Oil': Popular Opposition to Oil Development in 1920s Los Angeles," *Environmental History* 3 (April 1998): 189–209.

79 *So before they*: Fred W. Viehe, "Social-spatial Distribution," 33–54.

79 *"cavort and gambol"*: "State Victor in Beach Fight," *Los Angeles Times*, July 3, 1928.

80 *The decision drove oil drilling*: Robert Sollen, *An Ocean of Oil: A Century of Political Struggle over Petroleum off the California Coast*, 18–19.

CHAPTER 5. WAR AND SURFING

83 *That led to an FBI*: Naomi Oreskes and Ronald Rainger, "Science and Security Before the Atomic Bomb: The Loyalty Case of Harald U. Sverdrup," *Studies in History and Philosophy of Modern Physics* 31 (2000): 309–69.

83 *The shallow-draft*: Walter Munk, interview by authors, April 23, 2009; John Crowell, interview by authors, May 12, 2009; John C. Crowell, "Sea, Swell, and Surf Forecasting Methods Employed for the Allied Invasion of Normandy, June 1944," (master's thesis in meteorology, UCLA, 15 February 1946); Charles C. Bates, "Sea, Swell, and Surf Forecasting for D-Day and Beyond: The Anglo-American Effort," 2010, available at scilib .ucsd.edu/sio/hist/bates__sea-swell-surf.pdf; Charles C. Bates and John E. Fuller, *America's Weather Warriors*.

85 *In September 1942*: Bates, "Sea, Swell, and Surf Forecasting."

86 *He then relaxed*: Crowell interview.

86 *For each landing*: Ibid.

88 *Two weeks later*: Charles C. Bates, "Utilization of Wave Forecasting in the Invasions of Normandy, Burma, and Japan," *Annals of the New York Academy of Sciences* 51, no. 3 (May 1949), 569–72.

88 *Berkeley had turned*: For the Berkeley program, see Robert L. Wiegel, "Coastal Engineering: Research, Consulting, and Teaching, 1946–1997," oral history interviews by Eleanor Swent, 1997, Bancroft Library, UC Berkeley.

88 *In one of the*: Willard Bascom, *The Crest of the Wave: Adventures in Oceanography*.

90 *Among other daring raids*: J. Valerio Borghese, *Sea Devils: Italian Naval*

Commandos in World War II; Jack Greene and Alessandro Massignani, *The Black Prince And The Sea Devils: The Story of Valerio Borghese and the Elite Units of the Decima Mas*, Churchill quoted on p. 91.

91 *Some sported necklaces*: Valerie Monson, "Pioneering Frogmen Return to Maui Training Site," http://www.northofseveycorners.com/udt14/udt14-2.htm.

92 *At the Navy's*: Francis D. Fane, *The Naked Warriors*.

92 *Revelle was very*: Roger Revelle to J. S. Coleman (National Research Council), September 3, 1952, box 1, General Correspondence, Diving, 1946–1960, Hugh Bradner papers, Scripps Institution of Oceanography archives, University of California, San Diego. The National Academy panel, overseen by the National Research Council, had different names at different times. See Panel on Underwater Swimmers, 1954, CF: DNRC: PS: Com on Undersea Warfare, 1954, National Academy of Sciences Archives, Washington, DC; G. P. Harnwell to Lt. Robert Agness, May 18, 1953, G. P. Harnwell to F. D. Fane, March 26, 1953, and Committee on Undersea Warfare, annual report, FY 1952–3, CF: DNRC: PS: Com on Undersea Warfare, 1953, National Academy of Sciences Archives.

92 *After graduation*: Hugh Bradner, telephone interview by Peter Neushul, July 21, 2004. Bradner's career is also described in Carolyn Rainey, "Wet Suit Pursuit: Hugh Bradner's Development of the First Wet Suit," copy in Archives, Scripps Institution of Oceanography, University of California, San Diego, CA, 1998.

93 *Many scoffed at*: Bradner, interview by Neushul.

94 *A 1952 Navy*: H. A. Gerdes to F. B. Allen, November 24, 1952, and Hugh Bradner to R. Revelle, January 8, 1952, February 11, 1952, and April 4, 1952, Hugh Bradner papers.

95 *In fact, gasoline*: Peter Neushul, "Science, Technology and the Arsenal of Democracy: Production Research and Development During World War II" (PhD thesis, Department of History, UC Santa Barbara, 1993).

95 *Wallace Carothers*: Matthew E. Hermes, *Enough for One Lifetime: Wallace Carothers, Inventor of Nylon* (Philadelphia: Chemical Heritage Foundation, 1996).

96 *Body Glove founder*: Sam George, "Baby, It's Cold: Surfing in the Age of Neoprene," *Surfer's Journal* 17, no. 5 (2008): 26–40.

97 *The presence of*: Peter Neushul and Peter J. Westwick, "Aerospace and

Surfing: Connecting Two California Keynotes," in *Where Minds and Matters Meet: Technology in California and the West*, ed. Volker Janssen, 231–52.

97 *Although some materials*: Games Slayter, "Fiberglass: A New Basic Raw Material," *Industrial and Engineering Chemistry* 32, no. 12 (December 1940), 1568–71. See also John A. Morgan and Leon E. McDuff, "Fiber Glass in the Space Age," *Glass Industry* (June 1960).

98 *Simmons took up*: John Elwell, "The Enigma of Simmons," *Surfer's Journal* 3, no. 1 (1994): 30–49; Richard Kenvin, "Remember the Future," *Surfer's Journal* 17, no. 6 (2008–9): 32–41.

98 *Contrary to existing*: Elwell, "Enigma of Simmons." Matt Warshaw, *Encyclopedia of Surfing*, follows Elwell.

98 *In fall 1946*: Course record of Robert Wilson Simmons, 1939–1947, Caltech Registrar.

98 *Caltech was one*: Judith R. Goodstein, *Millikan's School: A History of the California Institute of Technology* (New York: Norton, 1991), 156–64; Clayton R. Koppes, *JPL and the American Space Program* (New Haven: Yale University Press, 1982), 1–17; Richard P. Hallion, "The Impact of the California Institute of Technology on American Air Transport and Aeronautical Development, 1926–41," appendix 1 in *Legacy of Flight: The Guggenheim Contribution to American Aviation* (Seattle: University of Washington Press, 1977).

98 *Traditionally, Caltech hydrodynamics*: Caltech course catalogs for 1942–1945, Caltech Archives.

99 *American torpedo bombers*: Maurice A. Biot, "The Mechanism of Water Entry of Projectiles," Morris Dam report no. 88, September 1, 1943, box 13.3, Bruce Rule Papers, Caltech Archives, Pasadena, California; M. A. Biot to Robert T. Knapp, December 15, 1941, box 13.6, Bruce Rule Papers.

99 *The torpedo research*: "Explosive Water Tops Array of Odd Subjects at Caltech," *Los Angeles Times*, 6 Mar 1949; James W. Daily, "History of the Pump Lab, part 1," available at www.me.caltech.edu/centennial/history; "Mechanical Engineering Celebrates Its Centennial," *Caltech Engineering & Science* 72, no. 2 (2007), 5–6; George Housner oral history, July 1984, Caltech Archives. On Morris Dam, see project reports *Aircraft Torpedo Development and Water Entry Ballistics*, OSRD report 2550 (Caltech, Pasadena, 1946) and *Water Entry and Underwater Ballistics of Projectiles*,

OSRD report 2551 (Caltech, Pasadena, 1946), both in the Joseph Foladare papers, box 3.7, Caltech Archives. In summer 1945 the lab also built a ten-thousand-square-foot wave tank in nearby Azusa to test designs of a new harbor in Guam for the U.S. Navy. Robert T. Knapp, summary of wartime work, April 10, 1947, Section Y: War Activities, Y1.1, Caltech Archives; "Outline of General Headings Only," September 15, 1948, Robert Knapp papers, box 2.3, Caltech Archives; "Typhoon Laboratory," *Life*, August 23, 1948; Craig Quintana, "Curious 'Eyesore,' Once Site of Wave Lab, Will Be Razed," *Los Angeles Times*, June 18, 1989.

99 *It is not clear*: Student researchers were not mentioned in project reports. Another engineering student, Eb Rechtin, worked on the torpedo project but is not mentioned: see Rechtin interview, Institute of Electronic and Electrical Engineers online archive at http://www.ieeeghn.org/wiki/index.php/Oral-History:Eberhardt__Rechtin. Robert Simmons is listed in the Caltech staff directory for 1941–1942.

99 *Edward "Dewey" Simmons*: Knapp's teaching of the hydraulics course to ME students is in the Caltech course catalogs. "Dewey" Simmons, Bob's older brother, an eccentric engineer with a master's degree from Caltech, inspired his brother, similarly eccentric and technically gifted, to follow his path to Caltech. Dewey invented the strain gage, an instrument that proved central to aerospace and many other engineering fields, and then entered a long litigious struggle with Caltech for the rights to it. Peter K. Stein, "The Invention of the Bonded Resistance Wire Strain Gage," *Experimental Techniques* (September/October 2004); Jane S. Dietrich, "Simmons and the Strain Gage," *Caltech Engineering and Science* (September 1986), 19–23.

99 *Simmons's hybrid boards*: The plywoods used in both Blake's hollow board and Simmons's postwar veneers also had military origins, including aviation: first, in World War I for marine plywood, then in interwar aviation, and finally with new high-strength, aircraft-grade plywoods in World War II with stronger adhesives and a stronger wood combination. Several World War II aircraft, including the British-built Mosquito bomber (the "wooden wonder"), capitalized on new plywoods.

101 *Lord's test surfaces*: Lindsay Lord, *Naval Architecture of Planing Hulls* (New York: Cornell Maritime Press, Inc., 1946).

101 *Simmons thereafter*: Lord, *Naval Architecture*; Richard Kenvin, "Remember the Future," *Surfer's Journal* 17, no. 6 (2008–9): 32–41.

101 *"Simmons was the one"*: Quotes in Elwell, "Enigma of Simmons."

CHAPTER 6. THE SURF BOOM

104 *By 1934 Fortune*: Jeff Wiltse, *Contested Waters: A Social History of Swimming Pools in America*.

105 *"I'm just crazy about swimming"*: Frederick Kohner, *Gidget*, 9. On the Santa Barbara high school swim program, see "Novel Departure: Santa Barbara Students Will Be Allowed Credit Marks for Proficiency in Swimming," *Los Angeles Times*, September 27, 1912. On El Segundo, see Jim and Lynne Norris, *Urho Saari: Olympian* (Los Olivos, CA, 1988).

105 *Malibu by the late*: Ben Marcus, "Sweet Sixteen," *Surfer's Journal* 17, no. 4 (2008): 90–97. See photos of Malibu in the late 1940s in the John Larronde photo collection, Museum of Ventura County.

105 *"aerospace capital of the world"*: Ann Markusen et al. *Rise of the Gunbelt: The Military Remapping of Industrial America* [quote], chap. 5; Roger Lotchin, *Fortress California, 1910–1961: From Warfare to Welfare*; Gerald D. Nash, *The American West Transformed: The Impact of the Second World War*; Allen J. Scott, *Technopolis: High-Technology Industry and Regional Development in Southern California*; Peter J. Westwick, ed., *Blue Sky Metropolis: The Aerospace Century in Southern California*.

105 *They not only had*: Kirse Granat May, *Golden State, Golden Youth: The California Image in Popular Culture, 1955–1966*.

105 *"surfing's East Coast boom"*: *Sports Illustrated*, July 18, 1966.

105 *White-collar engineers*: Kevin Welsh, "The Space Coast," *Surfer*, October 2008, 202–10.

106 *Wallace Stegner famously declared*: Kevin Starr, *Endangered Dreams: The Great Depression in California*, vii.

106 *By 1960 there were*: *Historical Statistics of the United States: Colonial Times to 1970*, Part 1. (Washington, DC, 1970).

106 *100,000-strong "army"*: "Southern California Beaches Prove Mecca for Army of 100,000 Surfers," *Los Angeles Times*, June 28, 1963; Jeff Prough, " 'Surf's Up'—Thousands Hop Boards, Ride Waves," *Los Angeles Times*, June 28, 1963.

106 *Urethane foams were*: "Urethane Plastics—Polymers of Tomorrow," *Industrial and Engineering Chemistry* 48 (September 1956): 1383–91.

107 *Nuclear subs like the*: Benjamin S. Collins, "Foamed Plastic Replaces 50-Year-Old Method of Filling Submarine Voids," *Marine Engineering* 63 (1958): 82–83.

107 *Nopco built plants*: "Nopco to Build Plastics Plants," *New York Times*, June 30, 1955; "Expansion Planned by Nopco Chemical," *New York Times*, August 25, 1955.

107 *In the early 1960s*: "Nopco to Build in Jersey," *New York Times*, February 14, 1961.

107 *In 1954, after a friend*: Mark Fragale, "Dave Sweet: First in Foam," *Longboard Magazine*, September/October 2000.

108 *Starting in the late 1950s*: Drew Kampion, *Stoked!: A History of Surf Culture*, 103. See also "Greg Noll's Scrapbook," *Surfer's Journal* 6, no. 2 (1997): 45–46.

108 *Greg Noll knocked out*: Nat Young, *The History of Surfing*, rev. ed, 84; Greg Noll and Andrea Gabbard, *Da Bull: Life over the Edge*.

108 *For a time in*: Gordon Clark, "History of Surfboard and Sailboard Construction," in George Orbelian, *Essential Surfing*, 174.

108 *Hawaiian surfers tried*: Malcolm Gault-Williams, "Woody Brown: Pilot, Surfer, Sailor," *Surfer's Journal* 5, no. 3 (1996): 94–107; "Rabbit Kekai, Talking Story," *Surfer's Journal* 3, no. 4 (1994): 62–77; Malcolm Gault-Williams, "Surf Drunk: The Wally Froiseth Story," *Surfer's Journal* 6, no. 4 (1997): 94–109.

109 *available in sporting goods stores*: See, for example, the Robertson-Sweet ad in the first issue of *Surfer* magazine, 1960.

109 *One surf journalist*: Paul Gross, quoted in Peter Lunenfeld, "Gidget on the Couch: Freud, Dora (No, Not That Dora), and Surfing's Secret Austro-Hungarian Roots," *The Believer* (June 2008).

110 *Among those endorsing*: Lena Lenček and Gideon Bosker, *The Beach: The History of Paradise on Earth*, 188–89.

110 *Among those Jantzen*: Matt Warshaw, "Green on Blue," *Surfer's Journal* 5, no. 3 (1996): 22–35.

110 *publisher of then-new*: Kampion, *Stoked!*, 88.

110 *Madison Avenue meanwhile*: Beer and surfers certainly went together, and even occasionally while riding waves, but in this particular case the

teenaged Miller was not of legal drinking age. The photographer made a thousand bucks for the Hamm's photo and gave Miller 15 percent, $150, but Miller's parents complained he'd been exploited. *Surfer's Journal* 5, no. 1 (1996): 69.

111 *Malibu surf scene*: Lunenfeld, "Gidget on the Couch"; Charles Champlin, "The Novel Origins of Gidget," *Los Angeles Times*, September 13, 1986; Deanne Stillman, "America's Mermaid," *Truthdig*, May 24, 2011, http://www.truthdig.com/report/item/americas__mermaid__20110524/.

111 *One of them replied* : "Gidget Makes the Grade," *Life*, October 28, 1957.

112 *Despite the innuendo*: Gary Morris, "Beyond the Beach," *Journal of Popular Film and Television* 21, no. 1 (1993), 2–11; R. L. Rutsky, "Surfing the Other: Ideology on the Beach," *Film Quarterly* 52 , no. 4 (1999), 12–23.

113 *California's beaches in a sense*: Gary Morris, "Beyond the Beach," *Journal of Popular Film and Television* 21, no. 1 (1993).

114 *The swift onset*: John Whitehead, "Alaska and Hawaii: The Cold War States," in *The Cold War American West, 1945–1989*, ed. Kevin J. Fernlund, 189–210.

114 *"If there is a single aura"*: Joan Didion, "Letter from Paradise, 21°19′N., 157°52′W" in *Slouching Towards Bethlehem*, 190, 196.

114 *Surfing was not part*: On mountaineering, see Maurice Isserman and Stewart Weaver, *Fallen Giants: A History of Himalayan Mountaineering from the Age of Empire to the Age of Extremes*.

114 *For starters, many*: Michael Scott Moore, *Sweetness and Blood: How Surfing Spread from Hawaii and California to the Rest of the World, with Some Unexpected Results*, 75.

115 *bubbling through middle-class culture:* Orvar Löfgren, *On Holiday: A History of Vacationing*, 216–19.

115 *coming by ship*: Thomas Kemper Hitch, *Islands in Transition: The Past, Present, and Future of Hawaii's Economy*, 121–22.

115 *500,000 in 1965*: Cristina Bacchilega, *Legendary Hawai'i and the Politics of Place: Tradition, Translation, and Tourism*, 103–8.

115 *By the 1970s*: Hitch, *Islands in Transition*.

115 *High-rise hotels*: Noel J. Kent, *Hawaii: Islands Under the Influence*.

116 *After the war*: Mark S. Foster, *Henry J. Kaiser: Builder in the Modern American West* (Austin: University of Texas Press, 1989).

116 *The new stretch of*: Mainlanders—many of whom couldn't even pronounce

"Hawaii"—could spell and pronounce "Kahanamoku." *Honolulu Star-Bulletin*, August 4, 1956, clipping from Hawaii Scrapbook, Henry J. Kaiser Papers, Bancroft Library, University of California, Berkeley.

116 *Kaiser's gigantic hotel*: "Pasha of the Pacific," *Parade Magazine*, February 9, 1958, Kaiser Papers.

117 *A local Honolulu*: Supervisor Clarence A. Crozier, quoted in *Honolulu Star-Bulletin*, January 19, 1955, Kaiser Papers.

118 *Hawaii's new Kamehameha*: Mike Gordon, "Henry Kaiser," *Honolulu Advertiser*, July 2, 2006.

119 *Dillingham called Kaiser*: Clipping from *Honolulu Star-Bulletin*, May 13, 1959, Kaiser Papers.

119 *He created an*: Kaiser shipped the dredge *Judah* from the mainland. *Honolulu Star-Bulletin*, June 27, 1959, Kaiser Papers.

119 *The Kaiser juggernaut*: Mike Gordon, "Henry Kaiser."

120 *The highbrow* New Yorker: Susan Lardner, "The Current Cinema: Surfers and Beasts," *New Yorker*, July 9, 1966, 78; Matt Warshaw, *The Encyclopedia of Surfing*, see "Endless Summer."

122 *Noll recalled the*: Noll, quoted in the film *Riding Giants*.

122 *"We took special pride"*: Yvon Chouinard, *Let My People Go Surfing: The Education of a Reluctant Businessman*, 18.

122 *The same impulse*: Rutsky, "Surfing the Other."

123 *It was no coincidence*: Sheila Weller, "Malibu's Lost Boys," *Vanity Fair*, August 2006.

123 *One of his empoloyees summarized*: Tak Kawahara quoted in Noll, *Da Bull*, 114.

124 *"Affluence makes it possible"*: Alvin Toffler, *Future Shock*, 364, 288.

124 *In 1963 one writer*: Remi Nadeau, *California: The New Society*, 140.

124 *The next year*: "Cleanup at County Line," *Surf Guide*, October 1964. John Severson, *Surfer* editor, complained that "the surfer has become the UGLY SURFER, and while a surfboard sticking out of your car once labeled you as something unique—a real sportsman—or possibly just 'one of those crazy guys that rides waves,' now it seems to carry the label of 'bum'! The real surfers are disgusted and have reached the end of their patience." Severson editorial, *Surfer*, Summer 1961, 1.

124 *A few years earlier*: Ray Kovitz, "Surfers: Good Kids or Gangs of Rowdies?," *Los Angeles Times*, April 23, 1961.

124 *"200,000 half-naked"*: "The Surfing Supermen," *Saga*, September 1964, quoted in Matt Warshaw, "Paperweight," *Surfer's Journal* 6, no. 3 (1997): 70–79, on 74.

124 *Descriptions of surfers*: Quote from Don Smith, "Surfers Out to Improve Their Image," *Los Angeles Times*, March 17, 1966; see also Sylvie Reice, "Pray for Surf . . . and Surfers," *Los Angeles Times*, June 23, 1966.

124 Time *magazine noted:* "Surfing: Shooting the Tube," *Time*, January 10, 1964.

124 *Wolfe recounted an*: Tom Wolfe, *The Pump House Gang* (New York: Farrar, Straus and Giroux, 1968).

125 *After his piece appeared*: Steve Barilotti, "Pump House Redux," *Surfer*, January 1995.

126 *He finally returned*: David Rensin, *All for a Few Perfect Waves: The Audacious Life and Legend of Rebel Surfer Miki Dora.*

126 *And Dora's rants*: Dora in *Surfer*, January 1968.

CHAPTER 7. CHARLIE DON'T SURF: SURFING AND COUNTERCULTURE

128 *He did not think*: Mike Hynson, *Transcendental Memories of a Surf Rebel*, 29–30.

129 *Hakman was probably*: Phil Jarratt, Mr. *Sunset: The Jeff Hakman Story*; Sean Doherty, *MP: The Life of Michael Peterson.*

129 *Sutherland meanwhile*: Allan Weisbecker, "Jock's Night Trip," in *Zero Break: An Illustrated Collection of Surf Writing, 1777–2004*, ed. Matt Warshaw.

129 *Bunker Spreckels, Clark Gable's*: C. R. Stecyk III and Art Brewer, *Bunker Spreckels: Surfing's Divine Prince of Decadence.*

130 *"The town was insane"*: Wayne Rabbit Bartholomew, *Bustin' Down the Door*, 140–41.

130 *"You could buy 40 bucks'* ": Chris Mauro, "The *Surfer* Interview: Allan Weisbecker," (http://surfermag.com/magazine/archivedissues/allan/index.html); see also Allan Weisbecker, *In Search of Captain Zero.*

130 *At one point Jeff Hakman*: Jarratt, *Mr. Sunset*, 69–73.

130 *A group of Laguna Beach*: Nicholas Schou, *Orange Sunshine: The Brotherhood of Eternal Love and Its Quest to Spread Peace, Love, and Acid to the World.*

131 *The U.S. government belatedly: Hashish Smuggling and Passport Fraud: "The Brotherhood of Eternal Love,"* hearing, U.S. Senate, Committee on the Judiciary, Ninety-third Congress, First Session, October 3, 1973.

131 *"The Evolutionary Surfer"*: Steve Pezman, "The Evolutionary Surfer: Dr. Timothy Leary Interview," *Surfer*, January 1978.

131 *Despite the mystical beliefs*: Stewart Tendler and David May, *The Brotherhood of Eternal Love: From Flower Power to Hippie Mafia*, 67.

133 *Hynson was smuggling drugs*: Hynson, *Transcendental Memories*, 177, 235. Hynson claims to have invented the hollow board technique, but other sources suggest the Brotherhood was already using it.

133 *"all surfboards coming in from Hawaii"*: Joe Eszterhas, "The Strange Case of the Hippie Mafia," *Rolling Stone*, December 7, 1972.

133 *Gale gave no resistance*: Neil Purcell, telephone interview with authors, January 28, 2009; Nicholas Schou, *Orange Sunshine*, 277–78; Gary Jarlson, "Drug Figure John Gale Dies in Auto Crash," *Los Angeles Times*, June 23, 1982.

133 *One was Mike Boyum*: Michael Oblowitz, "Sea of Darkness" video, August, 2009.

133 *In 1997 the feds*: "Two Men Indicted in Federal Drug Case," *Honolulu Star-Bulletin*, May 22, 1997; Gregory Foley, "Ketchum mulls uses for drug money," *Idaho Mountain Express*, October 8, 2004; Jarratt, *Mr. Sunset*, 148; Randy Rarick, interview by authors, June 8, 2009.

134 *In the winter of*: Matt Warshaw, "Goodbye Sunshine Superman," *Surfer's Journal* 3, no. 4 (1994): 7–25.

134 *Out of 2.5 million*: Charles Wollenberg, "California and the Vietnam War: Microcosm and Magnification," in *What's Going On? California and the Vietnam Era*, ed. Marcia Eymann and Charles Wollenberg, 15; Sizemore quote from Scott Bass, Ty Ponder, and Troy Page, *Between the Lines: The True Story of Surfers During the Vietnam War*, 27; see also Pat Farley, *Surfing to Saigon*.

135 *Soldier-surfers learned*: "A Little Slice of Surfing Paradise," *Surfer*, July 1967; John Robinson, "Larry Martin: Founding Member of the China Beach Surf Club," *Surfer*, September 1989, 74–79; Bass, Ponder, and Page, *Between the Lines*.

136 *"That's Charlie's point"*: John Milius, *Apocalyse Now* screenplay, is quoted

in Warshaw, *Zero Break*, 70–86. The quotes in our text are from the movie itself.

136 "*California surfer as existential cowboy*": Bruce Newman, "Her Dog Can Surf, All Right, but What About Her Students?" *New York Times*, March 11, 1998.

136 *According to* Apocalypse Now: John Milius, interview with Scott Bass, at www.betweenthelinesfilm.com.

136 *War correspondent Michael Herr*: Michael Herr, *Dispatches*, 43.

136 *Some American servicemen*: Herr, *Dispatches*, 176.

137 "*there was nothing in the world*": Daniel Ellsberg, *Secrets: A Memoir of Vietnam and the Pentagon Papers* (New York: Viking, 2002), 302–3.

138 *Coca-Cola used Greenough's*: Coke ad ("It's the real thing") at http://www.tunnelism.com/tag/george-greenough/. On Greenough see, for example, Paul Gross, "George Greenough: The Ageless Artist," *Surfer's Journal* 3, no. 1 (1994): 102–123.

138 "*the greatest surfer in the world*": Duke Boyd, *Legends of Surfing*, 50.

138 *Bob McTavish, meanwhile*: Greenough, "Moving Forward," *Surfer's Journal* 7, no. 4 (1998): 68–121; Bob McTavish, "So How Come No One Asked Sooner?" *Surfer's Journal* 4, no. 3 (1995): 44–54. See also McTavish response to Pezman in *Surfer's Journal* 8, no. 2 (1998): 125.

138 "*As far as I'm concerned*": Drew Kampion, "Profile: The Life and Work of Richard Brewer," *Surfer's Journal* 8, no. 1 (1998): 88.

139 *John Witzig set the tone*: Witzig, "We're Tops Now," *Surfer*, May 1967.

139 "*We were a little surprised*": McTavish, "So How Come No One Asked Sooner," *Surfer's Journal* 4, no. 3 (1995): 44–54.

140 "*A little chemical stimulation*: Gerry Lopez, "Prodigy," *Surfer's Journal* 6, no. 1 (1996), 22.

140 "*There are large parts of '69*": Mauro, "*Surfer* Interview."

141 "*greatest conceptual shift*": Quoted in David Rensin, *All for a Few Perfect Waves: The Audacious Life and Legend of Rebel Surfer Miki Dora*, 183.

141 *Counterculture rebellion*: Andrew Kirk, *Counterculture Green: The* Whole Earth Catalog *and American Environmentalism* (Lawrence: University Press of Kansas, 2007); E. F. Schumacher, *Small Is Beautiful: Economics As If People Mattered* (New York: Harper and Row, 1973); Carroll Pursell,

"The Rise and Fall of the Appropriate Technology Movement in the United States, 1965–1985," *Technology and Culture* 34 (1993): 629–37.

141 *In this age of backyard*: When the Pasadena Art Museum held annual "California Design" exhibitions in the 1960s and 1970s, its curator, Eudorah Moore, "went round the garages looking for surfers and climbers, the real innovators." Paola Antonelli, "Economy of Thought, Economy of Design," *Arbitare* no 329 (May 1994), 242–49. On Chouinard, see his book *Let My People Go Surfing*. The trend at the time to name particular boards—Greenough had "Baby" and then "Velo"; McTavish had "Sam" and "Betsy"—highlighted the turn to individuality, away from mass production.

141 *as* Surfer *magazine intoned*: Steve Pezman, "The Art Form," *Surfer*, August/September 1974.

143 *"We're on top"*: Witzig, "We're Tops Now."

143 *They instead followed*: Charles Kaiser, *1968 in America: Music, Politics, Chaos, Counterculture, and the Shaping of a Generation* (New York: Weidenfeld & Nicolson, 1988). Clad in white pajamas, Leary made his famous proposal in 1966 at a twenty-thousand-strong Gathering of the Tribes in San Francisco's Golden Gate Park: "Turn on to the scene. Tune into what is happening and drop out—of high school, college and grad school, junior executive, senior executive—and follow me, the hard way."

144 *African Americans bore a*: The proportion declined after 1966 as the military responded to charges of racism. Statistics from David Coffey, "African American Personnel in U.S. Forces in Vietnam," in *The Encyclopedia of the Vietnam War*, ed. Spencer Tucker (Oxford: Oxford University Press, 1998), 3–4. Eighty percent of Vietnam soldiers had a working-class background: Christian G. Appy, *Working-Class War: American Combat Soldiers and Vietnam* (Chapel Hill: University of North Carolina Press, 1993).

144 *"attended the Watts riots"*: Wolfe, *Pump House Gang*, quoted in Leonard Lueras, *Surfing: The Ultimate Pleasure*, 144.

144 *"the people who stand to lose"*: "Oiling the Economic Wheels," *Surfing*, November 1970, 38, 76.

145 *"Surfers are among the most"*: Craig Lockwood, "California Close Out," *Petersen's Surfing*, December 1968.

CHAPTER 8. SURFING TURNS PRO

147 *The development of lifeguarding*: Douglas Booth, *Australian Beach Cultures: The History of Sun, Sand and Surf*, 86–87; Colleen McGloin, "Surfing Nation(s)—Surfing Country(s)" (PhD thesis, University of Wollongong, 2005), 91.

148 *Lifeguards trying to*: Booth, *Australian Beach Cultures*, 110.

148 *Lifesaving clubs provided*: For example, Sean Doherty, *MP: The Life of Michael Peterson*, 19.

148 *The SLSA aimed*: Douglas Booth, "Ambiguities in Pleasure and Discipline: The Development of Competitive Surfing," *Journal of Sport History* 22, no. 3 (1995): 194.

148 *Australians had long*: Robert Hughes, *The Fatal Shore: The Epic of Australia's Founding*.

149 *So the "new nationalism"*: Richard White, *Inventing Australia: Images and Identity, 1688–1980*, 154–57, 161–63, 169; Colleen McGloin, "Surfing Nation(s)."

149 *Most notable in this*: Wayne Rabbit Bartholomew, *Bustin' Down the Door*; also Matt Warshaw, "Odyssey: Wayne Bartholomew Profile," *Surfer's Journal* 2, no. 4 (1993): 98–123.

150 *Cairns and PT took*: It also represented, implicitly at least, an extension of lifeguard culture. While Americans assumed that "Bronzed Aussie" meant one tanned by the sun, the term had a particular meaning in Australia, derived from lifeguard culture. A Bronze Medallion was the basic lifeguarding test, required of all lifeguard applicants, so a "Bronzed" Aussie meant someone qualified as a lifeguard. We thank Nicolas Rasmussen—historian of science, surfer, and qualified lifeguard—for this insight.

151 *Delaney financed it*: Bill Delaney, interview by authors, February 4, 2009.

151 *"Our surfing has improved"*: Quoted in Matt Warshaw, "Stayin' Alive: 1976 and the Birth of the World Professional Surfing Circuit," *Surfer's Journal* 4, no. 1 (1995): 62–81.

151 *"The fact is that when"*: Wayne Bartholomew, "Bustin' Down the Door," *Surfer*, January 1977.

153 *His conservative style*: Fred Hemmings, *The Soul of Surfing*; see also Warshaw, "Stayin' Alive."

153 *In 1977 Shaun Tomson*: Randy Rarick, interview by authors, June 8, 2009; Nat Young, *History of Surfing*, 143.

153 *MR was perhaps*: Phil Jarratt, " 'Mr. Humble' Finishes First," *Surfer*, May 1980, 28; Matt Warshaw, "Green on Blue," *Surfer's Journal* 5, no. 3 (1996): 22–35.

154 *As Rarick put it*: Matt George, "The 80s," *Surfer*, January 1990, 71.

155 "*Ian Cairns is an asshole*": Hemmings quote in Matt George, "The '80s," *Surfer*, January 1990; "Conversations: Randy Rarick," *Surfing*, June 1982; "New Beginnings for Pro Surfing," *Surfing*, May 1983. Cairns and Townend won the financial backing of surfwear company Ocean Pacific, and pro surfers followed the money. Rarick recalled how Cairns won pro surfers to his side. "It was really funny, because he came walking in with a check, a $25,000 check. We were having a meeting at the Turtle Bay, and he walked in and he said, 'I have $25,000'—which was a lot of money in those days—'Who's with me?' Well, everybody looked at me and said, 'Well, what have you got, Randy?' And I said, 'I've got a case of beer.' And they just went, 'pfft,' and in one swoop he bought the tour off" (interview by authors).

155 "*the days of hippies*": "Conversations: Ian Cairns," *Surfing*, November 1983.

155 "*ridiculous meetings*": Rarick, interview by authors; Paul Holmes, "Pro Surfing: Breaking Through or Falling Apart?" *Surfer*, December 1982.

155 *Cairns and the ASP*: Leonard Brady, "Hawaii Triple Crown Not ASP Rated," *Surfer*, March 1984, 24.

156 "*The kids started paddling out*": Kimo Hollinger, quoted in Booth, "Ambiguities in Pleasure and Discipline: The Development of Competitive Surfing," *Journal of Sport History* 22, no. 3 (1995): 196.

156 *At the inaugural*: Drew Kampion, "North Shore '70–'71," *Surfer*, March 1971; Booth, "Ambiguities," 198.

157 *In 1975* Surfing: "Where Are the Hot Californians," *Surfing*, 1975; John Witzig, "The Tropic of Cancer? Part One," *Surfer*, January 1981.

157 *Thanks to the earlier*: Roy Crump, "Nothing New, Just a Little Better," *Surfer*, December/January 1974, 76.

158 Time *concluded*: David De Voss, "Whatever Happened to California?" *Time*, July 18, 1977.

158 *It reduced youth*: Wayne Lynch interview by Steve Pezman, *Surfer's Journal* 2, no. 2 (1993): 120–21.

158 *By the mid-eighties*: Brian Gillogly, "Is Style Dead?" *Surfer*, September 1985.

158 *"If aloha is really out"*: Reno Abellira, "Whatever Happened to Hawaiian Style?" *Surfer*, September 1989, 124–33.

159 *"drug addict dole bludgers"*: Richards and Tomson, quoted in Nick Carroll, ed., *The Next Wave: The World of Surfing*, 105–6.

160 *Established sports like baseball*: John L. Crompton, "Sponsorship of Sport by Tobacco and Alcohol Companies," *Journal of Sport and Social Issues* 17, no. 2 (1993): 148–67; Robert C. Post, *High Performance: The Culture and Technology of Drag Racing, 1950–2000*, 237, 256.

160 *"The most popular sports activities"*: H. E. Christopher, trip report to T. E. Sandefur, Jr., September 5, 1975, UCSF Tobacco Legacy Project, available at http://legacy.library.ucsf.edu/tid/tgv85a00.

160 *"the renowned sport of Hawaiian"*: H. E. Christopher to Walter Iaea, Jr., September 10, 1975, UCSF Tobacco Legacy Project, http://legacy.library.ucsf.edu/tid/uua59d00.

160 *That particular deal*: Fifteen years later the Triple Crown was still pursuing RJR as a potential sponsor: Greg Littell to Fred Williamson, July 10, 1990, UCSF Tobacco Legacy Project, http: //legacy.library.ucsf.edu/tid/mwf27a00.

161 *"Oh my God, can we"*: Rarick, interview by authors.

161 *Smirnoff supported the most*: On Smirnoff and Rabbit: Phil Jarratt, "Rabbit," *Surfer*, November 1981. On Lucky Lager: Jarratt, *Mr. Sunset*.

162 *So* Wide World: Jim McKay, *The Real McKay: My Wide World of Sports* (New York: Dutton, 1998); Roone Arledge, *Roone: A Memoir* (New York: Harper, 2003); Arledge interview, ABC Sports, espn.go.com/abcsports/wwos/rarledge.html.

163 *Hawaiian pro Rory Russell*: Neil Stebbins, "North Shore Winter 75–76," *Surfer*, April/May 1976, 46–48.

165 *Starting in the 1960s*: Douglas Booth, "Hitting Apartheid for Six? The Politics of the South African Sports Boycott," *Journal of Contemporary History* 38, no. 3 (2003): 477–93.

165 *Local authorities had to issue*: Shaun Tomson, *Surfer's Code: 12 Simple Lessons for Riding Through Life*, 12.

165 *The pro tour itself*: Phil Jarratt, "The ASP Returns to South Africa," *Surfer*, November 1986; Nick Carroll, "Surfing Sun City," *Surfing*, June 1986. The boycott may have grown in part because international concern over apartheid undermined exchange rates and, hence, the prize money at stake.

165 *Other nations retaliated*: Tomson, *Surfer's Code*; Paul Holmes, "Barbados Political Pepper Sauce," *Surfer*, July 1989, 56–61.

165 *The ASP tour*: Matt George, "Encore," Shaun Tomson profile, *Surfer*, August 1988, 144.

165 *The pro tour continued to hold*: By the mid-1980s even rugby, the other holdout, had turned its back on South Africa. Booth, "Hitting Apartheid for Six?" 480.

167 *In 1971 Bob Cooper*: Bob Cooper ad reproduced in Mike Perry, "Bob Cooper: Further Down the Line," *Surfer's Journal*, 8, no. 4 (1999): 64. On recent participation, see McGloin, "Surfing Nation(s)."

167 *The rise of the One Nation party*: One scholarly compilation of 1972 passed pessimistic judgment on racism in Australia and declared, "Australian native policy can only be descried as a complete and abject failure. . . . The past history of Aboriginal affairs clearly shows that it is based on racist assumptions. There is no indication that the situation in 1971 has changed." F. S. Stevens, "Introduction," in *Racism: The Australian Experience*. Vol. 2, *Black Versus White* (New York: Taplinger, 1972), 4–5. See also Jon Stratton, *Race Daze: Australia in Identity Crisis* (Annandale, Australia: Pluto Press, 1998): "In Australia there has been a persistent myth since the ending of the White Australia policy in the early 1970s . . . that race has not only been expelled from the political vocabulary, but that it no longer plays a part in everyday Australian life. . . . Neither of these things is the case (p. 9)." John Chesterman and Brian Galligan, in *Citizens Without Rights: Aborigines and Australian Citizenship* (Cambridge: Cambridge University Press, 1997), note that the 1960s legislation was mostly symbolic and that the granting of Aboriginal rights was a drawn-out process. A more optimistic appraisal is A. T. Yarwood and M. J. Knowling, *Race Relations in Australia* (North Ryde, Australia: Methuen, 1982).

168 *African Americans wound up*: Douglas Flamming, *Bound for Freedom: Black Los Angeles in Jim Crow America*; Lawrence Culver, *The Frontier of Leisure: Southern California and the Shaping of Modern America*, 68–74; Josh Sides, *L.A. City Limits: African American Los Angeles from the Great Depression to the Present*, 21; Cecilia Rasmussen, "Resort Was an Oasis for Blacks Until Racism Drove Them Out," *Los Angeles Times*, July 21, 2002.

168 *After subsequent confrontations*: Alison Rose Jefferson, "African American

Leisure Space in Santa Monica: The Beach Sometimes Known as the 'Inkwell,' 1900s-1960s," *Southern California Quarterly* 91 (2009): 155–89; Adrienne Crew, "Revisiting Santa Monica's Ink Well Beach," *LA Observed*, March 10, 2008.

168 *"minute number of Negroes"*: "Surfing: Young Californian Is Expert at New Sport," *Ebony*, May 1965, 109–13.

168 *In the 1990s, Cab Spates*: Amy Van Sant, "Cab Spates," *Surfer*, February 1993.

168 *In 1979 one surfing magazine*: Warshaw, *The Encyclopedia of Surfing*, see "racism and surfing." For the general history of black surfers, see the documentary *White Wash* (2011), directed by Ted Woods.

168 *A few years later*: "Montgomery 'Buttons' Kaluhiokalani Is Mr. Honolulu," *Surfer*, November 1984. The only charitable explanation is that the photo may have referred to a joke three years earlier, when Buttons showed up at an IPS meeting wearing a gorilla mask. Even if it was an inside joke, most readers probably missed the reference, and in any case it showed an appalling lack of judgment.

169 *the surfers involved*: For this view, see C. R. Stecyk, "Surf Nazis and Other Objectionable Material," *Surfer's Journal* 1, no. 4 (1992): 36–43; see also "Fads: The Surfer's Cross," *Time*, April 22, 1966, and the comments by Greg Noll and Steve Pezman in the 1950s segment of the film *Riding Giants*.

169 *In later letters Dora ranted*: David Rensin, *All for a Few Perfect Waves: The Audacious Life and Legend of Rebel Surfer Miki Dora*, 117, 175–76, 275, 317, 359.

169 *Nat Young has lent*: Drew Kampion, "Animal tracks: Nat Young at 50," *Surfer's Journal* 7, no. 2 (1998): 102.

169 *A major demographic trend*: For one thoughtful perspective, see Jack Lopez, *Cholos and Surfers: A Latino Family Album*.

170 *The increasing presence*: See also Nick Ford and David Brown, *Surfing and Social Theory: Experience, Embodiment and Narrative of the Dream Glide*, 178n3.

170 *In 2008 USA Swimming*: David Crary, "New Study: 58 Percent of Black Children Can't Swim," AP newswire, May 1, 2008, abcnews.go.com/US/wireStory?id=4766578; Kevin Baxter, "Programs Seek to Ensure Everyone's into the Pool," *Los Angeles Times*, August 19, 2008.

171 *The many public pools*: Jeff Wiltse, *Contested Waters: A Social History of Swimming Pools in America.*

CHAPTER 9 ENGINEERING THE COAST

172 *"that terrific book"*: Frederick Kohner, *Gidget* (New York, 1957; 2001 reprint), 9.

173 *These measures have trapped*: John McPhee, "Los Angeles Against the Mountains," in *Land of Sunshine: An Environmental History of Metropolitan Los Angeles*, ed. William Deverell and Greg Hise, 179–200.

174 *The channelized L.A. River*: Blake Gumprecht, *The Los Angeles River: Its Life, Death, and Possible Rebirth*; Jared Orsi, *Hazardous Metropolis: Flooding and Urban Ecology in Los Angeles.*

174 *The quest for shore protection*: William J. Herron, telephone interview by Peter Neushul, Los Angeles, August 13, 1998. On littoral sand flows, see Douglas L. Inman and T. K. Chamberlain, "Littoral Sand Budget Along the Southern California Coast," *Report of the 21st International Geological Congress* (Copenhagen, Denmark: 1960), 245–46; Douglas L. Inman, "Beach and Nearshore Processes Along the Southern California Coast," *Geology of Southern California* 170 (1954): 29–34; "Littoral Processes" (1964), unpublished manuscript in Shore Protection file, LA District, Army Corps of Engineers. See also Gary Griggs, Kiki Patsch, and Lauret Savoy, *Living with the Changing California Coast.*

175 *"by throwing more and more technology"*: Wallace Kaufman and Orrin H. Pilkey, Jr., *The Beaches Are Moving: The Drowning of America's Shoreline*, 9.

175 *Scientists estimated*: Sharon Begley et al., "The Vanishing Coasts," *Newsweek*, September 24, 1984, 14–15.

175 *But the problem is particularly*: Charles Perry, "On the Beach," *Los Angeles Times Magazine*, June 24, 1990, 8.

175 *Yet California spends*: Perry, "On the Beach."

175 *The government agency*: For a historical review of Los Angeles District shore protection activities see Anthony Turhollow, *A History of the Los Angeles District, U.S. Army Corps of Engineers 1898–1965*, 116–43; William J. Herron, "The Influence of Man upon the Shoreline of Southern California," *Shore and Beach* 51 (July 1983): 17–27; Martha J. Shaw, *Artificial Sediment Transport and Structures in Coastal Southern*

California (La Jolla, CA: Scripps Institution for Oceanography, 1980); Susan Pritchard O'Hara and Gregory Graves, *Saving California's Coast: Army Engineers at Oceanside and Humboldt Bay* (Spokane, WA: Arthur H. Clark Company, 1991); and William Herron, *An Oral History of Coastal Engineering Activities in Southern California 1930–1981* (U.S. Army Corps of Engineers, Los Angeles District, 1986). For a more recent assessment see Alan Abrahamson, "Sand Slowly Disappearing from L.A.-Area Shoreline," *Los Angeles Times*, July 4, 1998.

177 *The city fathers*: Leeds and Barnard Consulting Engineers, *Report on Possible Yacht Harbor for Santa Barbara*, 1923, unpublished manuscript available at U.C. Riverside library, OCLC No. 48924911; William J. Herron, "The Influence of Man"; Erin Graffy de Garcia, "Safe Haven: The Santa Barbara Yacht Club and the Harbor," *Noticias: Journal of the Santa Barbara Historical Museum* 53, no. 3 (2010): 77–124.

177 *The continuous, costly*: Herron, *Oral History of Coastal Engineering*, 4–13.

178 *The Wedge attracts*: Photos of Kwock boardsurfing the Wedge appeared in the February 1980 issue of *Surfer*, and he was interviewed by David Keyes. Keyes, "It's Cold; and the Surfing Is Hot," *Los Angeles Times* January 13, 1980; Travis Hunter, " 'Surfing's Mosh Pit'; The Mutant Break of the Wedge Off Newport Beach Is the Grand Slam for High-Impact Bodysurfers," *Los Angeles Times*, August 3, 2004. In later years board riding became more common at the Wedge, causing bodysurfers to push back. See Phuong Le, "Surfers Rally Against Board Ban at the Wedge Protest," May 9, 1993.

179 *The public disagreed*: Donald Spencer, telephone interview by Peter Neushul, April 29, 1999.

179 *After that beach*: Herron interview. Technically, groins and jetties are different coastal engineering technologies. Groins trap sand on the beach while jetties are located adjacent to inlets and used to enhance navigation. Both trap sand. Surfers almost always refer to groins as "jetties." Hereafter the terms will be used interchangeably in the text.

179 *After severe storms*: *Santa Ana Register*, February 15, 1970.

179 *To anchor the jetties*: *Daily Pilot* (Newport Beach, CA), November 23, 1972.

179 *They were considerably longer*: Spencer interview.

179 *Saving Newport's beach*: U.S. Army Corps of Engineers, *Water Resources Development in California* (Army Corps of Engineers, Los Angeles District, 1995) 66; U.S. Army Corps of Engineers, *Explore 12, The California Coastline: Point Fermin to Newport Beach* (Army Corps of Engineers, Los Angeles District, 1980), 10.

180 *The waves were so good*: Richard Henry Dana, *Two Years Before the Mast*, 144.

180 *"Killer Dana" remains*: John Kendall, "$22 Million Harbor at Dana Point Will Berth 2,100 Boats," *Los Angeles Times*, April 24, 1967; Gordon Grant, "At 15 Dana Point Is a Booming Harbor," *Los Angeles Times*, June 16, 1986.

181 *"we are choosing not to move"*: Lila Fujimoto, "Expansion plan off for Maalaea harbor," *The Maui News* (Maui, HI), May 4, 2012.

181 *So could the list of waves*: Richard Apple, "Stanley's Isn't There Anymore," *Surfer*, February 1984.

181 *Consider Petacalco*: Craig Peterson, "Centroamerica: On the Way Home," *Surfer*, December/January 1973.

181 *By August 1975*: Gerald Saunders, "Memories of Peta," *Surfer's Journal* 8, no. 4 (1999): 10–21.

182 *But many Corps engineers*: Spencer interview.

183 *All this offal*: Ronald Fayer, Jitender P. Dubey, and David S. Lindsay, "Zoonotic Protozoa: From Land to Sea," *Trends in Parasitology* 20, no. 11 (2004): 531–36.

183 *A head-dip maneuver*: David Gilovich, "Santa Cruz: Reflections on a Northern Sky," *Surfer*, December/January 1974. The Pleasure Point outfall has since closed, and the sewage there is piped to the treatment plant that feeds the outfall off Steamer Lane.

183 *Malibu has no sewage*: Martha Groves, "In Malibu, Surf, Sewage Form a Combustible Mix," *Los Angeles Times*, January 7, 2009.

184 *In the ecological*: See the Hyperion history on its website: http://www.lasewers.org/treatment__plants/hyperion/index.htm. See also Bill Sharpsteen, *Dirty Water: One Man's Fight to Clean Up One of the World's Most Polluted Bays*.

185 *The pollution prompted*: Michael Fitzpatrick, "Trashing the Shore," *Surfer*, November 1987; Allston James, "The Dirty Dozen," *Surfer*, November 1988; "Our Filthy Seas," *Time*, August 1, 1988.

185 *Until the 1970s*: Richard Borreca, "How Hawaii Politics Cleaned Up Our Sewers," *Honolulu Star-Advertiser*, July 2, 2010.

185 *County planners identified*: City and County of Honolulu Planning Department, *North Shore Development Plan*, Public Review Draft, December 1998, and *North Shore Sustainable Communities Plan*, July 2000. Tourist statistics from Haleiwa Town Plan, July 26, 1991, Waialua Public Library. On sewage at Sunset: "Surfers Report Seeing Raw Sewage at Popular North Shore Spot," KHON-2 report, May 10, 2011.

185 *A surfer who fell*: Rod Antone, "Tracing Oliver Johnson's Final Hours," *Honolulu Star-Bulletin*, April 30, 2006.

186 *The so-called BEACH Act*: And BEACH Act monitoring tests depended on precarious funding: Tony Barboza, "U.S. to Cut Beach Water Test Funding," *Los Angeles Times*, February 16, 2012.

186 *They are often*: Steve Barilotti, "Sick Spray," *Surfer*, November 1998.

186 *"Primary" treatment*: On biological sewage treatment, see Daniel Schneider, *Hybrid Nature: Sewage Treatment and the Contradictions of the Industrial Ecosystem*.

186 *Many sewage districts*: Donna Oakley, "Upwellings of Discontent," *Surfer*, May 1985.

187 *The news images*: Robert Easton, *Black Tide: The Santa Barbara Oil Spill and Its Consequences*.

188 *Since shore protection*: Herron interview.

189 *"a passive minority"*: Craig Lockwood, "California Close Out," *Petersen's Surfing*, December 1968, quoted in Craig Nelson, "The Evolution of Environmentalism in the California Surfing Community" (senior honors thesis in history, University of California, Santa Barbara, 2009).

189 *"disheartened with the attitude"*: James "Bud" Bottoms interview, *Surfer*, 1969, quoted in Nelson, "The Evolution of Environmentalism."

189 *The surf media*: Robert Caughlan, "Making Waves," *Surfer*, December 1972; Steve Pezman, "Our Mother Ocean," *Surfer*, November 1970.

189 *A* Surfer *writer*: Richard Casperson in *Surfer*, June 1974, quoted in Nelson, "The Evolution of Environmentalism."

190 *Finally, in 1984*: Tom Pratte, "Malibu Lagoon Revisited," *Surfer*, March 1985.

190 Surfer *magazine declared*: Editor's note, *Surfer*, March 1990; Allston James, "Surfrider Foundation's Scott Jenkins," *Surfer*, October 1990.

190 *For an industry*: Allston James, "Cross-currents," *Surfer*, December 1991.

190 *The group wasted much energy*: Ken McAlpine, "Patagonia Reef," *Surfer*, June 1989; "Essential Man: An Interview with Yvon Chouinard," *Surfer*, March 1990; letters to the editor and editor's note, *Surfer*, August 1989; James, "Surfrider Foundation's Scott Jenkins." Surfrider and Patagonia leaders seemed stunned by the incredulous reaction from the surf community, many of whom wrote lambasting letters to surf magazines. The critics pointed out that these erstwhile environmentalists wanted to put giant plastic bags on the ocean floor just to please surfers. They also noted that the proposed reef was a convenient five minutes from Patagonia's headquarters.

191 "*major environmental player*": "Revolt on the Beach: Surfers Established as Major Environmental Player," *Los Angeles Times*, September 12, 1991.

191 *Surfrider board member*: Steve Hawk and Allston James, "Lawyers, Surf, and Money," *Surfer*, April 1993; Steve Hawk, "Looking Forward," *Surfer*, May 1993; Steve Barilotti, "Tribal Warfare," *Surfer*, February 1994. Surfrider's environmental director declared, "It's been like a religious war. It was like the Protestants and the Catholics: both sides believe in God, but somehow they've ended up hating each other."

192 *A small fraction*: Gary Roberts, "Our Rapidly Diminishing Coastlines," *Surfer*, April 1982.

193 *Five sheriff's deputies*: "Free to Sit on the Sand," *Los Angeles Times*, August 26, 2003.

193 "*aquatic nature religion*": Bron Taylor, "Surfing into Spirituality: A New, Aquatic Nature Religion," *Journal of the American Academy of Religion* 75, no. 4 (2007): 923–51.

CHAPTER 10. BEATING THE CROWDS, LITERALLY AND OTHERWISE

196 *Scholars and the Hawaiian public*: George S. Kanahele, "The Hawaiian Renaissance," May 1979, accessed at Polynesian Voyaging Society Archives, kapalama.ksbe.edu/archives/pvsa/primary 2/79 kanahele/kanahele.htm.

196 *In this view*: Isaiah Helekunihi Walker, "Terrorism or Native Protest? The Hui 'O He'e Nalu and Hawaiian Resistance to Colonialism," *Pacific Historical Review* 74, no. 4 (2005): 575–601. Isaiah Walker, *Waves of Resistance: Surfing and History in Twentieth-Century Hawai'i*.

196 *the apparent basis for Da Hui*: North Shore lifeguard Mark Cunningham recalled, "I was at one of the first meetings, and it took all the balls I had to say, 'I want to be a part of this, but I'm not beating anybody up.' All the guys were like, 'What the hell are you talking about? We're going to kick some ass here.' " Bruce Jenkins, "Kaku: Mark Cunningham Profile," *Surfer's Journal* 3, no. 3 (1994): 117.

196 *Rothman was acquitted*: Walter Wright, "Man Undaunted by Charges in Attack," *Honolulu Advertiser*, December 1, 1999; Ken Kobayashi, "Charges Dropped in North Shore Assault," *Honolulu Advertiser*, March 8, 2000.

196 *For decades*: Ken Kobayashi, "Reign of Terror on North Shore Told," *Honolulu Advertiser*, July 21, 1987; Ken Kobayashi, "Rothman Was Feared, Witness Says," *Honolulu Advertiser*, July 28, 1987; John O'Neill, "Surfers Wax Fearful over Drug Gang," *Sydney Morning Herald*, June 10, 1988; see also Hawaii Crime Commission, *Organized Crime in Hawaii*, 1978 report; Jim Dooley, "Shadow Links: A Yen for Golf," series on Japanese yakuza, *Honololu Advertiser*, August 21–25, 1988.

197 *The number of annual*: Don J. Hibbard, *Designing Paradise: The Allure of the Hawaiian Resort*, 55.

197 *With economic growth*: Bureau of the Census, *Statistical Abstract of the United States* (Washington, DC: Government Printing Office), 1971 and 2008 editions. Hawaiian population growth: 500,000 (1950); 633,000 (1960); 769,000 (1970); 965,000 (1980); 1.1 million (1990).

197 *In 1970, an anonymous*: "Haole Go Home!," *Surfer*, January 1970.

197 *But still, every day*: Randy Rarick, interview by authors, June 8, 2009.

198 *"We don't condone it"*: Guy Trebay, "A Line in the Sand—and in the Stores," *New York Times*, May 15, 2008.

199 *In the settlement*: "Turf War Between Surfers in Lunada Bay Is Settled," *Los Angeles Times*, December 4, 1996; Ben Marcus, "Pay Boys," *Surfer*, June 1997.

199 *The documentary film*: John Orlando, "P.O.P.," *Surfer*, December/January 1974, 45–48.

199 *As visiting surfers*: Ben Marcus, "The Face of Localism," *Surfer*, August 1996. In 1997 local Daniel Ortega attacked an older surfer, a schoolteacher from Santa Monica, giving him a headbutt and breaking his ribs. Ortega pled guilty to battery and was sentenced to three years of probation, with a twist: he was banned from surfing his home break. Two days later, local

police caught Ortega on the beach, and he got six months in jail. Violent locals often adopted an environmental defense. Ortega complained, "I am spending six months in jail for trying to protect a beach." The Bay Boys of Palos Verdes similarly claimed they were protecting Lunada Bay "for future generations." Their environmental stewardship included building a concrete cabana on the beach, before authorities forced them to remove it. Daniel Nazer, "The Tragicomedy of the Surfers' Commons," *Deakin Law Review* 9, no. 2 (2004): 697.

200 *Two separate convictions*: John Grissim, "Brain Waves," *Surfing*, July 1982. As a San Diego district attorney put it in 1995, after a local surfer pled guilty to felony assault for a surfing-inspired brawl, "we want to send the message that it won't be tolerated." "Payback Time: Surfer in Del Mar Attack Pleads Guilty to Felony Assault," *Surfer*, November 1995.

200 *"America is far less aggressive"*: Nat Young, quoted in Tim Ryan, "All the Rage," *Honolulu Star-Bulletin*, January 26, 2001.

200 *"I did what any other Australian"*: "My Punch-up at San Diego," *Sunday Telegraph*, October 23, 1966, appears in Nat Young, *Nat's Nat and That's That: A Surfing Legend*.

200 *In addition to redefining*: Derek Hynd, "The Carpark and the Code," *Surfer*, September 1988, 85.

201 *First they had*: Angela Kamper and Charles Miranda, *My Brother's Keeper: The True Story of a Vicious Killing and a Powerful Surf Brotherhood*, 4.

201 *A few years later*: "Abberton Faces More Charges," *Southern Courier* (Sydney), March 22, 2005.

201 *Jai Abberton was*: "Hines Killing Justified," *Southern Courier*, May 10, 2005; Lisa Davies, "Hines a 'Rapist and a Maggot,' " *Southern Courier*, June 15, 2004.

201 *"Ours" lay just*: Robert Hughes, *The Fatal Shore: The Epic of Australia's Founding*, 51–55; Sean Doherty, "All Yours," *Surfer*, August 2011.

202 *Surfers bumping into*: One might think the major increase in women surfers would have a calming effect, but men do not have a monopoly on bad behavior. A few years ago two women pro surfers in Australia mixed it up over a wave in a contest; Trudy Todd grabbed young Sam Cornish in a headlock and drove her face into the sand.

202 *Some surfers are happy*: Nazer, "Tragicomedy of the Surfers' Commons," 687.

202 *Surfing's informal code*: Consider Maroubra. In reality Maroubra is a pleasant little town with two surf lifesaver clubs on a magnificent beach. A homeowner's association cultivates a positive local image to boost property values. A small segment of the town consists of public housing, but this is not a seaside St. Louis or Newark. Maroubra's police, for example, defended their gentrifying town's image as a "safe seaside suburb," and they began prosecuting the Bra Boys for such transgressions as offensive language in public (see Wendy Fitzgibbon, "Suburb Still Safe, Says Local Police Chief," *Southern Courier* [Sydney], Sept 2, 2003, and Justin Cote, "Bra Boys Say They Are Being Harassed by Police," *Transworld Surf*, October 30, 2008). The makers of the Bra Boys documentary film would have you believe that "tribes of surfers" are waiting on the beach to beat you senseless. This image, like the effluent from nearby Malabar Sewage Treatment plant, is utter crap.

202 *In 1999 San Diego's*: Nazer, "Tragicomedy of the Surfers' Commons," 710–12.

202 *The Bra Boys*: Simon Canning, "Bra Boy Rides a Giant Wave of Sponsorship Opportunity," *Australian* (Mar 8, 2007); Guy Trebay, "Line in the Sand."

203 *"Oxnard surfers are not travelers"*: John Witzig, "Hotel California," *Surfer*, February 1981.

203 *A pair of young*: Kevin Naughton, Craig Peterson, and Greg Carpenter, "Centroamerica," *Surfer*, August/September 1973; Naughton and Peterson, "Beneath the African Sun," *Surfer*, June/July 1975; see also Randy Rarick, "Angola," *Surfer*, August/September 1974.

203 *The early exploration*: In the 1930s, the Dutch colonial government, in league with Dutch shipping lines, propagated an image of Bali as an enchanted tropical paradise—perhaps the last unspoiled Eden, since other tropical oases (such as Hawaii, the campaign politely did not say) had been spoiled by tourism. The wartime Japanese occupation and then postwar conflict stopped tourism, but Suharto's overthrow of Sukarno in the late 1960s led to a gradual consolidation of control and economic development, including tourism. David Shavit, *Bali and the Tourist Industry* (Jefferson, NC: McFarland, 2003); Leo Howe, *The Changing World of Bali* (New York: Routledge, 2005).

204 *Actor Bill Murray*: Bill Boyum, "A Place of Challenge," *Surfer's Journal* 2, no. 1 (1993): 108–23. For Bill Murray's visit, see Rory Russell comment in *Sea of Darkness* documentary.

204 *The Indonesian national*: Gavan Daws and Marty Fujita, *Archipelago: The Islands of Indonesia* (Berkeley: University of California Press, 1999).

204 *Literally: he poured*: Mark Cherry, "Nothing Really Organized," *Surfer's Journal*, 19, no. 4 (2010): 94.

205 *By the 1980s*: "Jungle Cats," *Surfer*, July 1991, 72; Gerald Saunders, "Jungle Nights . . . and Other G-Land Stories," *Surfer's Journal* 7, no. 3 (1998): 10–19. It could have been worse: in 1990 rumors swirled about an eight-hundred-room luxury hotel at G-Land, but nothing came of it.

205 *By the mid-1990s*: Erik Aeder, "Nias: Right Stuff in a Land of Lefts," *Surfer*, March 1989, 120–29; D.C. Green, "The Nias Myth," *Surfer*, March 1990, 76–89; Saunders, "Jungle Nights"; Matt Warshaw, "Snakes in the Garden," *Surfer*, January 1994, 62–71; Craig Jarvis, "Imported Surf Rage," in Nat Young, ed., *Surf Rage*, 158–59.

206 *Infrastructure did not*: Andrew Marshall, "Holidays in Hell: Bali's Ongoing Woes," *Time*, April 9, 2011; Kirk Owers, "The Crush," *Surfer*, December 2011, 52–61.

206 *Malaria in particular*: Kevin J. Lovett, "Custodians of the Point," *Surfer's Journal* 7, no. 1 (1998): 84–119.

206 *Rasmussen was later*: See the documentary *Sea of Darkness*, and Michael Daly, "The Cadet and the Surfer," *New York* (November 1, 1982), 44–52.

207 *Daly freely admitted*: Tim Baker, "The Sinking Islands," *Surfer*, September 1998; Ben Marcus, "A Man and His Motor Vessel," *Surfer*, March 1997.

207 *And since the average boat trip*: This could pose a problem for surf industry marketers, who wanted to retain the old romantic image of feral surf travel. In the mid-1990s Quiksilver launched a "Surfers of Fortune" campaign, promoting the idea that surfers were hard-core mercenary travelers. Quiksilver chartered the *Indies Trader* but then had to hire a beat-up fishing junk for the posed photos. As one of the surfing mercenaries observed, "our boat was a little too plush for real soldiers of fortune." Keoni Watson, "Wasteland," *Surfer's Journal* 5, no. 3 (1996): 10, 21.

207 *The old distinction*: James Buzard, *The Beaten Track: European Tourism, Literature, and the Ways to 'Culture,' 1800–1918*, 2–5. Randy Rarick recalled the dirtbag style of 1970s surf travel: "I can say that was very

romantic and it was really neat, but I've been to 150 or 160 countries now and surfed in half that many—and it was real romantic, but it was gritty, it was time-consuming, and it took forever. Now guys can just fly in, surf, get the best swell of the year, take pictures, and fly back out. The guy who comes clunking along with the camper on the back of his old pickup and sets up in a camp for a month, he's obsolete" (interview by authors).

208 *By 2008 the local*: "Elite Indo Playground," *Surfer's Journal* 5, no. 3 (1996): 123; Baker, "Sinking Islands"; Mentawais Marine Tourist Association, "Unlicensed Charter Boats to Be Controlled," http://mentawai.groupsite.com/beta/discussion/topics/59119/messages.

208 *At that point*: Baker, "Sinking Islands."

209 *Villagers seemed happy*: Chief Druku, asked whether villagers should take over Tavarua from nonnatives, replied: "Why would we want to take it from them? . . . They've done so much for the villages and this country. They build houses, send villagers to hospitals in America, give scholarships. . . . We're family, bro." Mark Borden, "Who Owns This Wave?" *Sports Illustrated*, April 18, 2005; William Finnegan, "Liberated?" *Surfer*, March 2011, 70–76.

210 *In short, localism*: Craig Jarvis, "Imported Surf Rage," in Young, ed., *Surf Rage*, 172.

210 *In 1996 the Fijian*: Borden, "Who Owns This Wave?"

210 *Fiji's tourism minister*: Zach Weisberg, "Fiji Opens Its Waves to the World," *Surfer*, October 2010, 39–40; Nick Carroll, "Tavarua Resort Doomed?" July 2, 2010, available at http://blogs.surfingmagazine.com/news/tavarua-resort-doomed/; Jed Smith, "Storm Gathers Around Cloudbreak," available at http://www.stabmag.com/jed/cloud-of-uncertainty-shrowds-tavarua/.

211 *Tavarua was not*: On the Maldives: Derek Rielly, "Mainlining," in Young, *Surf Rage*, 49.

211 *Such "dedicated access privileges"*: Gregg Easterbrook, "Privatize the Seas," *Atlantic*, July/August 2009, 58.

211 *Some economists indeed*: Bart Frazier, "Better Surfing Comes with Property Rights," *Freedom Daily*, July 2006. The economic approach is also analyzed in Stuart H. Sweeney, "The Spatial Behavior of Surfers," unpublished manuscript, University of California, Santa Barbara. See also Tom Selwyn, "Privatising the Mediterranean Coastline," in *Contesting the Foreshore:*

Tourism, Society, and Politics on the Coast, ed. Jeremy Boissevain and Tom Selwyn (Amsterdam, 2004), 35–60.

212 *Some enterprising surfers*: Andy Neumann, interview by Peter Westwick, June 2, 2009.

212 *The new ranch manager*: Dick LaRue, "The Ranch Reality," *Surfer*, July 1972.

212 *LaRue added*: Quoted in Nazer, "Tragicomedy of the Surfers' Commons."

213 *Santa Barbara County*: Allston James, "Love and Rockets," *Surfer*, October 1992.

213 *Such intransigence spurred*: Nazer, "Tragicomedy of the Surfers' Commons," 703.

213 *Santa Barbara surfers*: C. R. Stecyk, "Ghost Dance," *Surfer's Journal* 1, no. 2 (1992): 82.

213 *Ranch owners wrote*: "Moving Forward: A George Greenough Scrapbook 1960–1970," *Surfer's Journal* 7, no. 4 (1998): 68–121, and response in *Surfer's Journal* 8, no. 2 (1999): 125.

214 *Even Ranch owners*: Glenn Hening, "Stain on the Soul of Surfing," in Young, *Surf Rage*, 131–45.

214 *The Hollister Ranch*: Joan Didion, *Where I Was From* (New York: Knopf, 2003), 52–63.

214 "*It could have been 20,000 people*": Jan Hansen-Gates, "The Place Called Hollister Ranch," *Santa Barbara Magazine*, Spring 1977, quoted in Josi Ward, "Cattle on the Coast: Hollister Ranch and Californian Landscape Preservation" (master's thesis, University of Virginia, School of Architecture, 2008).

215 *Places like Tavarua*: Kevin Naughton, "Surf Resorts: Pay to Play," *Surfer*, May 1985, 48–55.

215 *Surfers viewed their sport*: Steve Hawk, "Intro," *Surfer*, February 1997.

215 "*All things in life*": Kevin Naughton, "Dispatch from Cloudbreak," *Surfline*, posted January 7, 2011, www.surfline.com/surf-news/kevin-naughton-on-the-fiji-surfing-decree__51294/. See also William Finnegan, "Liberated?" *Surfer*, March 2011, 70–76.

215 *In this way surfing infiltrated*: On Antarctica: http://www.surfline.com/travel/tripwire/tripwire.cfm?id=1321.

215 *Popular Moroccan*: Yassine Ouhilal, "Castles Made of Sand," [on Morocco], *Surfer*, July 2011; Helene Cooper, "On Liberia's Shore, Catching a New

Wave," *New York Times*, January 24, 2010; statistics on Japan from Matt Warshaw, *The Encyclopedia of Surfing*; statistics on Britain from Michael Scott Moore, *Sweetness and Blood: How Surfing Spread from Hawaii and California to the Rest of the World, with Some Unexpected Results*, 140.

216 *In Bulgaria, dozens*: Ithaka, "Surf Mythos," *Surfer's Journal* 19, no. 5 (2010): 12–13; Audrey Sykes, "Building Bridges in the Balkans," *Transworld Surf*, June 2012, 76–78.

216 *Surfing still represents*: Lewis Samuels, "Borrowed Boards: The Aftermath," *Surfer*, January 2012, 36–38.

216 *On Vancouver Island*: Joel Patterson, "The Ice Age," *Surfer*, May 2011, 56.

216 *The Munich surf*: Moore, *Sweetness and Blood*, 68–71.

216 *For example, by 2002 British*: Joanna Walters, "Cornwall's Artificial Reef to Cash in on Surf Boom," *Observer* (November 3, 2002).

217 *This may be in part*: Nick Ford and David Brown, *Surfing and Social Theory: Experience, Embodiment and Narrative of the Dream Glide*, 50; Moore, *Sweetness and Blood*, 303–4. On the *Ama* women divers, and Japanese swimming generally, see Charles Sprawson, *Haunts of the Black Masseur: The Swimmer as Hero*, chap. 8.

217 *But even Japan*: Steve Tepper, interview by authors, October 14, 2010.

217 *Garden-variety surf localism*: Rielly, "Mainlining," 46; (on Vancouver) Kevin Brooker, "Surf? What Surf," *Surfer*, July 1994, 74; Dave Parmenter, "Alaska: The Land Duke Forgot," *Surfer*, January 1993; "Bali Black Shorts?" *Surfer*, January 1993.

217 *Stories circulated*: Rielly, "Mainlining," 34.

CHAPTER 11. SURF TECH

218 *Hemmings christened*: "The Big Surf," *Life*, Mar 6, 1970.

219 *Surfboards themselves*: Steve Barilotti, "Search for the Green Board" (in 2 parts), *Surfer*, July and August 1994.

220 *The W.A.V.E. boards*: Ads for W.A.V.E. in *Surfer*, June/July 1973 and September 1976.

220 *The U.S. Coast Guard*: "Power Trip," *Surfing*, May 1983.

220 *A particular leap*: Sam George, "Baby, It's Cold: Surfing in the Age of Neoprene," *Surfer's Journal* 17, no. 5 (2008): 26–40.

221 *The neoprene-and-nylon*: Adam Kaye, "Neoprene Dreams," *Surfer*, November 1992.

222 *for lost boards*: Corky Carroll, "How Bob Neely Turned His Passion into a Business," *Orange County Register*, September 10, 2010. Neely's aquatic lifestyle includes surfing Cottons Point on a regular basis and winning the 2012 World Water Polo Masters Championship in Riccione, Italy.

222 *All this is why*: Sam George, "Fit to Be Tied," *Surfing*, December 1983.

222 *But the changes wrought*: Drew Kampion, "As Years Roll By," *Surfing*, February 1980.

222 *This experience led*: Tom Morey, telephone interview with authors, April 14, 2009.

223 *After several years*: George Orbelian, *Essential Surfing*, 171–73.

223 *For twenty-five dollars Morey*: Paul Gross, "Inventions," *Surfer's Journal* 8, no. 3 (1999): 80–89.

223 *That level of production*: Charles Duhigg, "Stoking the Masses," *Los Angeles Times*, August 3, 2004.

225 *In each case*: Ricky Grigg, *Big Surf, Deep Dives, and the Islands*, 89.

225 On NOAA see Eileen Shea, *A History of NOAA* (Washington: National Oceanic and Atmospheric Administration, 1987).

226 *Satellite coverage soon*: "Prior Knowledge," *Surfing*, February/March 1976.

226 *In 1988* Time: Eugene Linden, "Windows on a Vast Frontier," *Time*, September 12, 1988, 68; see also George Alexander, "High Technology Aids Study of World's Oceans," *Los Angeles Times*, March 31, 1984.

226 *Veteran surfers Jerry Arnold*: "Reach Out and Check the Surf," *Surfing*, June 1985.

226 *Sean Collins*: "So the Surf's Up—but When?" *Surfing*, January 1986. Surfline soon hired a professional meteorologist, Chris Borg; another of Surfline's managers, Craig Masuoka, noted that Collins was a "hobbyist." Collins left to form his own 976 service. Paul Holmes, "Surf Reporting in the Eighties," *Surfer*, August 1987.

226 *In an early major*: "Daily Reports Aid Search for Perfect Wave: 'Surfin' Safari' Now Being Conducted by Phone," *Los Angeles Times*, April 28, 1985.

227 "*waiting for waves is so*": Sam George, "Chasing the Blob," *Surfer*, August 2008.

227 "*really destroy the mystery*": "So the Surf's Up"; Steve Barilotti, "1–900-Crystal-Ball," *Surfer*, August 1993.

228 *"Where would you rather surf"*: Joe Mozingo, "New Artificial Reef Barely Makes a Ripple for Surfers," *Los Angeles Times*, November 26, 2000.

228 *Tom Pratte, a founder*: Bob Pool, "Wave Goodbye to Reef Experiment That Failed," *Los Angeles Times*, October 9, 2008.

228 *The penalty amounted*: Pool, "Wave Goodbye."

228 *Furthermore, Surfrider*: "Pratte's Reef Pulled Down," *Your Local Surf*, September 10, 2008, http://your-local-surf.blogspot.com/2008/10/prattes-reef-pulled-down.html.

229 *The effects of*: Joe Mozingo, "New Artificial Reef Barely Makes a Ripple for Surfers," *Los Angeles Times*, November 26, 2000.

229 *Chad Nelsen, Surfrider's*: Pool, "Wave Goodbye"; See also Paul Holmes, "Artificial Surf Reefs: Boon or Bust?" *Surfer's Journal* 20, no. 3 (2011): 88–91.

230 *But some locals*: Holmes, "Artificial Surf Reefs."

230 *The result was*: Jasmin Bradley, "Everybody's Goin' Surfing?" . . . Erm, No, Apparently," 20 April 2010, http://jasminb1989.wordpress.com/tag/surf-reef-review/.

231 *Installed in 2009*: "Wave Goodbye: Britain's £3.2million Artificial Surf Reef Closed After Only 2 Years as It's Unsafe," *Daily Mail*, April 4, 2011.

231 *ASR recently built*: "India's First Artificial Reef to Protect Kovalam," *Times of India*, May 20, 2010.

231 *Soon the novelty*: Randy Rarick, interview by authors, June 8, 2009.

232 *The idea of generating*: Thomas A. P. van Leeuwen, *The Springboard in the Pond: An Intimate History of the Swimming Pool*, 48–49.

233 *At about six cents*: Daniel C. Schlenoff, "July 1912," *Scientific American*, July 27, 2012.

233 *The company specifically*: "Interview with Victor Grinius," *Surfer*, August/September 1973; "The Four Million Dollar Wave," *Surfing*, May 1981.

233 *Disney World eventually*: Bill Sharp, "Way to Go Ohio," *Surfing*, January 1985; Bill Sharp, "Palm Springs Weekend," *Surfing*, July 1987; "1986 Surf Yearbook," *Surfing*, March 1987; Evan Slater, "Freshwater Future," *Surfer*, June 1997.

234 *"purists will undoubtedly cringe"*: Matt Warshaw, "Ahhh . . . I Love the Smell of Chlorine in the Morning," *Surfer*, September 1985.

234 *"Wave pools suggest elitism"*: Steve Hawk, "Intro," *Surfer*, February 1997.

235 *The Ocean Dome*: "Death of the World's Best Wave Pool," *Transworld Surf*, January 9, 2008.

235 *The surf media*: Matt Warshaw, "Notes from the Deep End," *Surfer*, November 1985; Matt George, "The 80s," *Surfer*, January 1990.

235 "*I'd much rather surf here*": Evan Slater, "Freshwater Future," *Surfer*, June 1997.

235 *Slater has enlisted*: Jake Howard, "Slater Makes Waves . . . Literally," *ESPN Action Sports*, November 30, 2011, http://espn.go.com/action/surfing/blog/__/post/5868192/slater-makes-waves-literally.

236 "*cheaper than flying to Indo*": Stuart Cornuelle, "A Conversation with Kelly Slater: Part 3," *Surfing Magazine*, October 16, 2010, online edition, http://www.surfingmagazine.com/news/a-conversation-with-kelly-slater-part-3/.

236 *The Dear Leader*: Donald Macintyre, "The Supremo in His Labyrinth," *Time*, February 18, 2002.

236 *Lochtefeld's WaveLoch company*: Jon Cohen, "Making Waves," *Wired*, August 1999, 2; Ben Marcus, "Texas Tubin'" *Surfer*, December 1991; Steve Barilotti, "The Lone Star Project," *Surfer*, August 1994; Christopher Steiner, "The Making of Hay Makers," *Forbes*, November 14, 2005; "The Best Surf Parks, Surf Pools, and Artificial Waves," *Surfer Today*, web post, Mar 29, 2011, available at http://www.surfertoday.com/surfing/5283-the-best-surf-parks-surf-pools-and-artificial-waves.

238 *Robert Shaw's famous*: Richard G. Fernicola, *Twelve Days of Terror: A Definitive Investigation of the 1916 New Jersey Shark Attacks* (Guilford, CT: Lyons, 2001); Doug Stanton, *In Harm's Way: The Sinking of the USS* Indianapolis *and the Extraordinary Story of Its Survivors*, (New York: Henry Holt, 2001).

238 "*sharks have no hands*": David Ainley, quoted in Howard Davidson, "Sharks," *Surfer*, March 1992.

238 *Humans are*: Michael Reilly, "Shark Attacks: What Are the Odds?," *Discovery News*, August 2, 2010. See also Tony Barboza, "U.S. Shark Attacks Continue to Drop," *Los Angeles Times*, February 9, 2012.

239 *In the early 1970s*: Eugenie Clark, "Shark Repellent Effect of the Red Sea Moses Sole, *Pardachirus marmoratus*," *National Geographic Society Research Report* 13 (1981): 177–86.

239 *After years of study*: Walter Clark, "Natural Shark Repellent Is Alluring to Scientists," *New York Times*, January 20, 1981.

239 *"Anyone who says something works"*: Lisa Katayama, "Mixed Signals," *Popular Science*, July 2008.

240 *It is not known*: Doug Robertson, "Lost Diver Peter Clarkson Aware of Shark Risk," *Courier-Mail* (Brisbane), February 19, 2011; Liza Kappelle, "Diver 'Would Oppose Cull'," *Courier-Mail*, February 19, 2011.

240 *Revelle's research showed*: Spencer Weart, *The Discovery of Global Warming*.

240 *As one conservative*: James S. Robbins, "Hooray for Global Warming," *National Review Online*, August 8, 2006, http://www.nationalreview.com/articles/218408/hooray-global-warming/james-s-robbins.

CHAPTER 12. SURFING AT THE FRONTIERS

243 *"We're looking at little"*: Bill Sharp, quoted in Susan Casey, *The Wave: In Pursuit of the Rogues, Freaks, and Giants of the Ocean*, 242.

245 *Dillingham continued the*: H. Brett Melendy, *Walter Francis Dillingham, 1875–1963*, 267.

245 *To make concrete*: Bernie Baker and Matt Warshaw, "The Crunch: A Disturbing State of Affairs at Waimea," *Surfer*, July 1988, 102–11; Peter Cole, "Evolution: Is the Window of Opportunity Closing?" *Surfer*, September 1990, 76–77. See also Gerry Lopez, *Surf Is Where You Find It*, 208, and Ricky Grigg, "Twenty Years of Big Wave Riding," in John Long, ed., *The Big Drop: Classic Big Wave Surfing Stories*, 227.

246 *"Big waves are not measured"*: "The 25 Greatest Moments in Big-Wave Riding," *Surfer*, December 1992.

246 *One wag joked*: Nick Carroll in *Surfing*, October 1984, 13.

247 *After this session*: Bruce Jenkins, "Mr. Clean: The Extraordinary Surfing Life of Randy Rarick," *Surfer's Journal* 7, no. 3 (1998): 60.

247 *Surfers began speaking*: Ricky Grigg, "25 Years of Big Wave Riding," *Surfer*, January 1985.

247 *"Whatever Happened to Big Wave"*: Leonard Brady, "Whatever Happened to Big Wave Riding?" *Surfer*, May 1983.

248 *It has also contributed*: On Aikau, see Stuart Holmes Coleman, *Eddie Would Go*. On the Eddie contest see Burl Burlingame, "Eddie Riding on the Crest of the Myth," *Honolulu Star-Bulletin*, March 6, 1998, and Jesse McKinley, "Bruising Surf at a Rare Big-Wave Event in Hawaii," *New York Times*, December 8, 2009, and the contest website at http://quiksilverlive.com/eddieaikau/2012/profiles%2c269%2cHonorary.en.html.

248 *In 1986 a session*: Dave Parmenter, "Big Time," *Surfing*, July 1987.

248 *Offshore ocean-bottom*: Dan Weikel and Sachi Cunningham, "On the Face of Giants," *Los Angeles Times*, November 14, 2010.

248 *No one tried it*: Sam George, "Maverick Man," *Surfer*, November 1993.

248 *Finally in 1990*: Ben Marcus, "Cold Sweat," *Surfer*, June 1992.

250 *As all-terrain vehicles*: Paul R. Josephson, *Motorized Obsessions: Life, Liberty, and the Small-Bore Engine*.

250 *Surfers soon noticed*: Brian Surrat was using a Jet Ski for water patrol at Pipeline by 1977. See Extra, *Surfer*, July 1977.

250 *For one thing*: Greg Ambrose, "Out of Gas: Jet-Skiers Given the Boot in Waikiki," *Surfer*, March 1988, 20. Brothers Randy and Wes Laine had earlier towed into waves with jet skis: Chris Carter, "There's Life in the Fastest Lane," *Surfing*, April 1984. In the early 1960s Don Davis, the inventor of a motorized "sea sled," claimed to have "launched surfers into waves"; see *Surfer* 3, no. 1 (spring 1962): 14.

250 *But the law provided*: Bruce Jenkins, "The Next Realm?" *Surfer*, December 1993, 48–55, 88.

251 *The Zodiac*: Ibid.

251 *The tow-in surfers*: Lopez, "Quantum Leap—JATO," *Surfer's Journal* 4, no. 1 (1994): 82–103.

251 *Hence the nickname*: Ben Marcus, "Power Surfing: The Next Realm, Take II," *Surfer*, September 1994.

252 *Peter Cole, a big-wave legend*: "Condition Black," *Surfer*, June 1998.

253 *Laird's success made him*: Bruce Jenkins, "Laird Hamilton," in John Long, ed., *The Big Drop: Classic Big Wave Surfing Stories*, 203.

255 "*If Terry or Brian*": Jenkins, "Next Realm?"

256 *A little environmental*: Ashley Powers, "Proposal Could Leave Surfers Cooling Their Jets," *Los Angeles Times*, November 25, 2006.

256 *Clark's speculation was*: *Surfer*, February 1996, 62. The movie *The Right Stuff* popularized the surfer-as-astronaut rumor.

257 *In a famous session*: Chris Dixon, *Ghost Wave: The Discovery of Cortes Bank and the Biggest Wave on Earth*.

258 *That year, the surfwear*: Casey, *The Wave*, 11–13.

258 *There were still guys*: Taylor Paul, "Keep the Change," *Surfer's Journal* 20, no. 5 (2011): 22–37.

260 *More recently*: Casey Koteen, "Guns over Skis," *Transworld Surf*, April 2012.

260 *For that reason*: Kimball Taylor, "Arm Strength," *Surfer*, July 2012; Koteen, "Guns over Skis"; Chris Dixon, "Big-wave Paddle Battle," *Outside*, March 19, 2012.

260 Surfer *magazine proclaimed*: Jeff Mull, "The End of the Machine," *Surfer*, January 2013.

261 *For all these white males*: Kyle Kusz, "Extreme America: The Cultural Politics of Extreme Sports in 1990s America," in Belinda Wheaton, ed., *Understanding Lifestyle Sports: Consumption, Identity and Difference*, 197–213.

CHAPTER 13. WOMEN AND SURFING: FROM FLAPPERS TO ROXY GIRL

264 *The relative absence of women*: Books devoted to women's surfing include Andrea Gabbard, *Girl in the Curl: A Century of Women in Surfing*; Linda Chase, *Surfing: Women of the Waves*.

265 *Doris helped her*: Stephanie Mansfield, *The Richest Girl in the World: The Extravagant Life and Fast Times of Doris Duke* (New York: G. P. Putnam's Sons, 1992).

266 *A publication declared in 1914*: W. D. Boyce, *United States Colonies and Dependencies, Illustrated* (Chicago, 1914), 169–70; Charmian Kittredge London, *Our Hawaii*.

266 *When Australian swimming*: Christine Schmidt, "Second Skin: Annette Kellerman, the Modern Swimsuit, and an Australian Contribution to Global Fashion" (PhD thesis, Queensland University of Technology, 2008); "Annette Kellerman Sullivan, 87, 'Million Dollar Mermaid,' Dead," *New York Times*, November 6, 1975. She was later acquitted on the condition that she wear a concealing cloak before and after swimming. Kellerman, born in Sydney in 1888, is considered the originator of the one-piece bathing suit. Kellerman was portrayed by Esther Williams in the MGM movie *Million Dollar Mermaid* in 1952.

266 *Park officials patrolled*: Lena Lenček and Gideon Bosker, *The Beach: The History of Paradise on Earth*, 189–94.

266 *Public opinion swung*: "New Record Is Set by Miss Bleibtrey," *New*

York Times, August 27, 1920; "Ethelda Bleibtrey, 76, Won 3 Medals For Swimming in 1920 Olympic Games," *New York Times*, May 9, 1978.

267 *She, too, performed*: "Australian Yields to American Girl: Miss Bleibtrey Defeats Miss Durack in Record Time in Quarter-Mile Title Swim," *New York Times*, August 17, 1919; "Woman Swimmer Saves Mother and Children: Miss Bleibtrey, Olympic Champion in 1920, Swims to Rescue in Narragansett Bay," *New York Times*, August, 18, 1925.

268 *Hawkins set a*: Jack Singer, "Many Stars Entered in A.A.U. Swim Tomorrow," *Los Angeles Times*, August, 3, 1933; Jack Singer, "Four Swim Marks Fall," *Los Angeles Times*, August 5, 1933; "Mary Hawkins Annexes Swim," *Los Angeles Times*, July 15, 1935; "Miss Hawkins Race Favorite," *Los Angeles Times*, June 22, 1937.

269 *Hawkins worked as a*: Cal Whorton, "Rodecker Wins Channel Race: Hermosa Lifeguard Speeds to Victory in Aquaplane Classic," *Los Angeles Times*, August 8, 1938.

269 *There is an intriguing photo*: "Frolicking on the Sands at Santa Monica with the Aquatic Stars of Del Mar," *Los Angeles Times*, August 21, 1935.

270 *Calhoun and her two*: Chase, *Surfing: Women of the Waves*.

270 *Thus Benson was*: Gabbard, *Girl in the Curl*.

271 *This reproof greeted*: Chase, *Surfing: Women of the Waves*, 20.

271 *Poppler had enough talent*: Douglas Booth, "Surfing: From One (Cultural) Extreme to the Other," in Belinda Wheaton, ed., *Understanding Lifestyle Sports: Consumption, Identity and Difference*, 100.

271 *Seventies big-wave*: Chase, *Surfing: Women of the Waves*, 145.

272 *Setterholm, a former*: Gabbard, *Girl in the Curl*, 54; Steve Lopez, "A Wave of Forgiveness," *Los Angeles Times*, July 19, 2009. On women's surfing in the seventies, see also Patti Paniccia, "Seventies Pro Genesis," *Surfer's Journal* 12, no. 2 (2003): 42–53.

272 *But that still*: Brian Gillogly, "Post Modern Surf Femme," *Surfer*, June 1989, 92–99.

272 "*women's surfing continues its struggle*": Matt George, "The 80s," *Surfer*, January 1990.

272 *In January 1993 Matt Warshaw*: Matt Warshaw, "Sexism Sucks," *Surfer*, February 1993; on homosexuality, see also Gillogly, "Post Modern Surf Femme."

273 *A part-time waitress*: "Laura in the Sea Near Diamond Head Hangs 10 on Her Way to Fame," *People*, February 10, 1975.

273 *She later appeared*: Curly Kirkpatrick, "There Is Nothing Like a Dame," *Sports Illustrated*, January 6, 1975, 24.

273 *Blears told reporters*: Kirkpatrick, "There Is Nothing Like a Dame," 24.

273 *In 1992 four-time world*: "World's Number One Surfer Wendy Botha: Sensational Nude Pictorial," *Australian Playboy*, September 1992, cover.

273 *Botha's exposure disappointed*: "Wendy Botha—Biography," *World Champions of Surfing* website, http://www.worldchampionsofsurfing.com.

274 *After winning two amateur*: Martha Sherrill, "Gidget Kicks Ass," *Outside*, May 2, 2004; Nick Carroll, *Fearlessness: The Story of Lisa Andersen*.

275 *In February 1996*: "Lisa Andersen Surfs Better Than You," *Surfer*, February 1996, cover.

277 *And yet her name*: Elissa Gootman, "Patsy Mink, Veteran Hawaii Congresswoman, Dies at 74," *New York Times*, September 30, 2002; Mechelle Voepel, "Remembering the Mother of Title IX," ESPN.com, December 27, 2002, http://a.espncdn.com/ncw/columns/voepel/1479394.html; Dan Nakaso, "Mink Remembered for Her Resolve, Integrity," *Honolulu Advertiser*, September 29, 2002.

278 *By 1978* Time: "Comes the Revolution," *Time*, June 26, 1978; Allen Guttman, *A Whole New Ball Game: An Interpretation of American Sports*, 151.

279 "*The Hana girls*": Susan Orlean, "Life's Swell," *Women's Outside* (Fall 1998).

279 *Her wave opened*: Keala Kennelly interview at http://www.filmbug.com.

279 *Kennelly starred as herself*: Jeff Mull, "Keala Kennelly Interview: The Kauaian Charger on the State of Women's Surfing and Her Fateful Tahiti Session," *Surfer*, September 29, 2011; Jon Coen, "Keala Talks Waves, Big and Small," http://espn.go.com, June 12, 2012.

280 *By 1982 she ranked*: Bruce Jenkins, "Rell Sunn: With Her Death, There Is Life," *San Francisco Chronicle*, January 10, 1998; Gabbard, *Girl in the Curl*.

CHAPTER 14. FROM WAIKIKI TO WALL STREET

284 *West Coast swimsuit makers*: Lena Lenček and Gideon Bosker, *The Beach: The History of Paradise on Earth*, 187–89.

285 *Jantzen, Catalina, and*: Lenček and Bosker, *Beach*, 213.

286 *By June of 1965*: Roger Dee, "Father and Fashion," *Los Angeles Times*, June 14, 1965.

286 *Hang Ten stitched up*: Duke Boyd, interview by authors, June 5, 2009.

286 *Hang Ten products*: Anthony Ramirez, "Having the Right Name Keeps Others Following in Hang Ten's Footsteps," *Los Angeles Times*, April 26, 1983.

287 *Within a couple years*: Phil Jarratt, *Salts and Suits*, 74.

287 *Green approached Batterham*: Jarratt, *Salts and Suits*, 106.

288 *In forming Quiksilver*: On Quiksilver formation, see Phil Jarratt, *Salts and Suits* and *The Mountain and the Wave: The Quiksilver Story*.

288 *The women who played*: Duke Boyd interview.

289 *Tomson summed it up*: Kevin O'Sullivan, *Goin' Big: Gotcha and the Evolution of Modern Surf Style*, 202.

290 *As surfwear firms*: Paul Holmes, "Power Without Glory," *Surfer*, April 1982; Nick Carroll, "Hawaii: A Working Holiday," *Surfing*, May 1982; Graham Cassidy, "How to Score," *Surfing*, March 1986.

290 "*a kind of tacit agreement*": Nick Carroll, "Ten Years," *Surfing*, March 1986.

291 *Curren blazed up*: "Tom Curren Joins Pro Ranks," *Surfer*, January 1983.

291 *The more Curren*: Steve Hawk, "Tom Curren Knows What Time It Is," *Surfer*, May 1991.

291 *Two years later*: "The Boys of Summer," *Rolling Stone*, May 9, 1985; Kem Nunn, "Chairman of the Board: Tom Curren," *Rolling Stone*, July 16, 1987.

291 Time *estimated that*: Kathleen A. Hughes, "Riding the Wave: Variety of Businesses Seek to Cash in on Surge in Surfing Chic," *Wall Street Journal*, May 11, 1987; Kathleen Brady, "If Everybody Had an Ocean," *Time*, August 18, 1986.

292 *Former world champion*: Chris Carter, "Shaun, MR, Rabbit," *Surfing*, November 1987.

293 *Quiksilver, OP, Gotcha*: Jarratt, *Salts and Suits*, 173.

293 *Selling stock also*: Ibid.

293 "*Thanks to this pro surfing*": Carroll, "Ten Years."

294 *Ian Cairns quit*: Bill Sharp, "Smoke on the Water," *Surfing*, January 1987; Matt Warshaw, "Winners and Losers," *Surfer*, January 1987; "Ian Cairns Calls It Quits," *Surfer*, January 1987; "Ian Cairns Quits as ASP Head," *Surfing*, January 1987.

295 *Four-time world champ*: Tony Arruza, "Wave Wizards Challenge," *Surfing*, June 1984; Mike Daniels, "A Shot in the Dark," *Surfer*, June 1984.

296 *Women fared even worse*: Steve Barilotti, "Money or Nothin': The Realities of Pro Surfing," *Surfer*, September 1991; see also statistics in *Surfer*, December 1987.

296 *Eggers recalled, in the*: Matt Warshaw, "What Happened to David Eggers," *Surfer*, February 1990; Bill Sharp, "Small Wonders," *Surfing*, May 1984; "The Boys," *Surfer*, December 1989; Dean La Tourrette, "A Reckoning," *Surfer's Journal* 16, no. 5 (2007): 76–85.

296 *Similarly, Matt Archbold*: Chris Mauro, "Mortification," *Surfer*, June 2008, 102–14.

297 *Top pros began muttering*: Matt Warshaw, "Message to the ASP: Give It Back to the Surfers," *Surfer*, December 1988; Graham Cassidy and Al Hunt, letters to *Surfer*, February 1989.

297 *The economic downturn*: Chris Woodyard, "Surf Wear in Danger of Being Swept Aside by Slouchy, Streetwise Look," *Los Angeles Times*, June 21, 1992.

297 *That year Slater*: *Interview*, May 1996.

298 Box Office *magazine*: Dale Winogura, review, *Box Office* magazine, quoted in Ben Marcus, "Wet Dream," *Surfer*, September 1998.

298 *Slater's acting gig*: See Kelly Slater, *Kelly Slater: For the Love*.

298 *His agent, Bryan Taylor*: Ben Marcus, "Bottom Line," *Surfer*, December 1992.

299 *Tom Curren summed it*: Drew Kampion, "Tom Curren: Still Waters Run Deep," *Surfer's Journal* 2, no. 3 (1993): 113.

299 *Did tens of thousands*: Matt Warshaw, "Green on Blue: Kelly Slater's Million-Dollar Deal, and Other Thoughts on Surfing-For-Hire," Surfer's Journal 5, no. 3 (1996): 22–35.

300 *Reef was no longer*: Dean LaTourrette, "El Otro Che," *Surfer's Journal* 17, no. 5 (2008): 62–71.

300 *Roxy sales in some*: Pete Thomas, "Peru's Villaran Is Trying to Make His Own Breaks," *Los Angeles Times*, July 20, 2007.

300 *By 2011,* Surfer *magazine's*: "Hot 100," *Surfer*, May 2011.

301 *Some academic theorists*: Belinda Wheaton, "Introduction: Mapping the Lifestyle Sport-Scape," in Belinda Wheaton, ed., *Understanding Lifestyle*

Sports: Consumption, Identity and Difference, 1–28. Scholars have applied postmodern French philosophers such as Bourdieu and Foucault to "the surfing gaze" and "surf imaginaries." See, for example, *Surfing and Social Theory*.

302 *In short, skiing*: E. John B. Allen, *The Culture and Sport of Skiing*; John Fry, *The Story of Modern Skiing*.

303 *It was a stroke of marketing*: Kyle Kusz, "Extreme America: The Cultural Politics of Extreme Sports in 1990s America," in Belinda Wheaton, ed., *Understanding Lifestyle Sports: Consumption, Identity and Difference*, 197–213.

304 *When Kolohe Andino*: Chas Smith, "Corpo Andino," *Surfing*, June 2010, 84–93.

304 *Surfing has always*: Jake Howard and Chris Mauro, "Of Age and Innocence," *Surfer*, March 2008, 125.

304 *By turning children*: Daniel Thomas Cook, *The Commodification of Childhood: The Children's Clothing Industry and the Rise of the Child Consumer*.

305 *The secretive Clark*: William Finnegan, "Blank Monday: Could Grubby Clark Destroy Surfing?" *New Yorker*, August 21, 2006; Steve Tepper, interview by authors, October 14, 2010, Goleta, CA (Tepper poured blanks for Walker Foam during the 1970s); market statistics from Jason Smith, "Blank Check," *Surfer*, November 1998. Finnegan says Clark controlled 90 percent of the U.S. market, 60 percent of the world market.

305 *The article included*: Finnegan, "Blank Monday."

306 *He had had visits*: Ibid.

306 *Many of them now*: Leslie Earnest, "Dead in the Water," *Los Angeles Times*, May 30, 2008.

307 "*the heart and soul*": "Surfboards 2009: Back to Earth," *Surfing*, January 2009, 112–25; see also Mike Anton, "For Eco-Friendly Surfboard Shapers, More Kelp in the Lineup," *Los Angeles Times*, April 16, 2010; Joni Martin, "Material Benefits: Toward Greener Surfboards," *Surfer's Journal* 16, no. 6 (2007/2008): 88–97.

307 *Most pop-out surfboards came*: Amanda Jacob, "Cobra Strikes Out into Industrial Markets," *Reinforced Plastics*, May 2004, 24–29; Mark Borden, "Wave Maker," *Fortune*, September 1, 2005, available at http://money.cnn

.com/magazines/fsb/fsb__archive/2005/09/01/8277774/index.htm. See also Tim Baker, "Made in Thailand," *Surfing*, January 2003.

308 *Clark may have*: Finnegan, "Blank Monday"; Randy Rarick, interview by authors, June 8, 2009.

309 *Instead of a handsaw*: Kyle Denuccio, "How New Technology Is Shaping the Designer," *Surfer*, June 2012, 10.

309 Surfing *magazine in 1983*: Nick Carroll, "By Design," *Surfing*, October 1983.

309 *Surfing followed the arc*: Allen Guttmann, *From Ritual to Record: The Nature of Modern Sports*.

309 *By 2011,* Surfer *magazine*: Joel Patterson, "Power Tools," *Surfer*, July 2011.

309 *That's one reason they*: Darrell Jones, "Star Wars Shaping Machine," *Surfer*, December 1984.

311 *Hollywood, Madison Avenue, Asian factories*: Surf companies like Quiksilver and Volcom created entertainment divisions and began sponsoring rock bands and producing movies and TV shows, all to help promote the surf brands. That's why you can run out now and buy your special Metallica trunks from Billabong. Marc Graser, "It Surfs H'wood Right," *Variety*, June 26, 2002. Meanwhile, a Quiksilver outlet opened at Disneyland, and luxury L.A. hotels began offering Quiksilver boardshorts in poolside vending machines. Booth Moore, "Hotel Gift Shops Go Glam," *Los Angeles Times*, July 18, 2010.

311 *All of these markets*: For high-fashion influence, see Tetsuhiko Endo, "Sand on the Runway," *Surfer*, August 2010, 86. Quiksilver and other brands sold surfwear at Barney's and other New York high-fashion hotspots; their sales reps no doubt neglected to tell the Barney's buyers that in surfing a "barney" is the ultimate kook.

311 *Only later did*: Brad Melekian, "Last Drop," *Outside*, November 22, 2010, and "Crashing Down," *Outside*, August 1, 2011; Jake Howard, "Andy Irons Died of Heart, Drug Issues," ESPN.com, June 9, 2011.

311 *Others noted that Irons*: Steve Shearer, "Derek Hynd and the Philosophy of Free Friction," *Surfer*, October 2011; see also Zander Morton, "Death of a Disco Dancer," *Transworld Surf*, April 2012.

311 *The world tour*: Melekian, "Crashing Down."

311 *"It's been a long time coming"*: Fred Pawle, "ASP to Introduce Drug Testing

from 2012," *Australian*, November 10, 2011; Jake Howard, "Pro Surfing Gets Drug Testing," ESPN.com, November 10, 2011.

312 "*Did pro surfing blow its shot*": Fred Pawle, "Branding the Leper," *Surfer's Journal* 6, no. 4 (1997): 5–9. See also Steve Hawk, "Tour de Force," *Surfer*, December 1995.

312 *As contest promoters learned*: Rarick, interview by authors.

CHAPTER 15. THE WORLD IN THE CURL

315 *Because surfers sit at the*: On nature and civilization, see the essays in William Cronon, ed., *Uncommon Ground: Rethinking the Human Place in Nature.*

315 *Quiksilver's stock price*: Hang Nguyen, "Quiksilver Announces More Layoffs," *OC Register*, April 4, 2008; Jessica Lee, "Quiksilver Outlook Dims," *Orange County Business Journal*, December 1, 2008. Our estimate of 20 million surfers seeks middle ground among various numbers, from 5 million (Surf Industry Manufacturers Association) to 35 million (International Surfing Association). See Matt Warshaw, *The Encyclopedia of Surfing*, 605, and www.isasurf.org/isa-info/presidents-message/.

315 *Pro surfer Taj Burrow*: Brendon Thomas, "Too Big to Fail," *Surfer*, December 2009.

316 *Much of its appeal*: Tom Curren, interview by Matt George, "The Second Time Around," *Surfer*, August 1987, 56.

317 *a veritable ashram of authors*: Bron Taylor, "Surfing into Spirituality: A New, Aquatic Nature Religion," *Journal of the American Academy of Religion* 75, no. 4 (2007): 923–51; Peter Heller, *Kook: What Surfing Taught Me About Love, Life, and Catching the Perfect Wave* (New York: Free Press, 2010); Doug Dorst, *The Surf Guru* (New York: Penguin, 2010); Jaimal Yogis, *Saltwater Buddha: A Surfer's Quest to Find Zen on the Sea* (Somerville, MA: Wisdom Publications, 2009); Steven Kotler, *West of Jesus: Surfing, Science, and the Origins of Belief* (New York: Bloomsbury, 2006); Katherine Wroth, ed., *The Zen of Oceans and Surfing: Wit, Wisdom, and Inspiration* (Seattle: Skipstone, 2009); Jeremy V. Jones, *Walking on Water: The Spirituality of the World's Top Surfers* (Ventura, CA: Regal, 2006).

317 *A few intrepid surfers*: See the film *Chasing Dora*.

SELECTED BIBLIOGRAPHY

In addition to the works below that influenced our thinking, our references include many more primary and secondary sources, in particular back issues of *Surfer* and *Surfing* magazines and *Surfer's Journal*. We also profited from the general histories by Finney and Houston, Lueras, Young, Kampion, and Warshaw, all listed below; for readers seeking more details on the history of surfing, we happily refer them to Warshaw's engaging and exhaustive history.

Allen, E. John B. *The Culture and Sport of Skiing: From Antiquity to World War II*. Amherst, MA: University of Massachusetts Press, 2007.

Allen, Robert C. *Creating Hawai'i Tourism*. Honolulu: Bess Press: 2004.

Anderson, Rufus. *The Hawaiian Islands: Their Progress and Condition under Missionary Labors*. Boston: Gould and Lincoln, 1864.

Bacchilega, Cristina. *Legendary Hawai'i and the Politics of Place: Tradition, Translation, and Tourism*. Philadelphia: University of Pennsylvania Press, 2006.

Banham, Reyner. *Los Angeles: The Architecture of Four Ecologies*. Berkeley: University of California Press, 1971.

Bartholomew, Wayne Rabbit. *Bustin' Down the Door*. Sydney: HarperSports, 1996.

Bascom, Willard. *The Crest of the Wave: Adventures in Oceanography*. New York: HarperCollins, 1988.

Bass, Scott, Ty Ponder, and Troy Page. *Between the Lines: The True Story of Surfers During the Vietnam War*. Cardiff-by-the-Sea, CA: Headline Graphics, 2008.

Bates, Charles C. "Sea, Swell, and Surf Forecasting for D-Day and Beyond: The Anglo-American Effort," 2010, available at scilib.ucsd.edu/sio/hist/bates__sea-swell-surf.pdf.

———, and John F. Fuller. *America's Weather Warriors, 1814–1985*. College Station: Texas A&M University Press, 1986.

Benidickson, Jamie. *The Culture of Flushing: A Social and Legal History of Sewage*. Vancouver, British Columbia: University of British Columbia Press, 2007.

Bingham, Hiram. *A Residence of Twenty-One Years in the Sandwich Islands*. 3rd ed. Canandaigua, NY: H. D. Goodwin, 1855.

Boissevain, Jeremy, and Tom Selwyn, eds. *Contesting the Foreshore: Tourism, Society, and Politics on the Coast*. Amsterdam: Amsterdam University Press, 2004.

Booth, Douglas. "Ambiguities in Pleasure and Discipline: The Development of Competitive Surfing." *Journal of Sport History* 22, no. 3 (1995): 189–206.

———. "Surfing: The Cultural and Technological Determinants of a Dance." *Sport in Society* 2, no. 1 (1999): 36–55.

———. *Australian Beach Cultures: The History of Sun, Sand, and Surf*. London: Frank Cass, 2001.

———. "Hitting Apartheid for Six? The Politics of the South African Sports Boycott." *Journal of Contemporary History* 38, no. 3 (2003): 477–93.

Borghese, J. Valerio. *Sea Devils: Italian Naval Commandos in World War II*. Annapolis, MD: Naval Institute Press, 1995.

Boyd, Duke. *Legends of Surfing*. Minneapolis, MN: MVP Books, 2009.

Brawley, Sean. " 'Surf Lifesaving Owes No Person a Living': A Third Sector Case Study." *Labour History* 81 (November 2001): 75–91.

Brennan, Joseph L. *Duke: The Life Story of Hawai'i's Duke Kahanamoku*. Honolulu: Ku Pa'a Publishing, 1994.

Brown, DeSoto. *Surfing: Historic Images from the Bishop Museum Archives*. Honolulu: Bishop Museum Press, 2006.

Buck, Elizabeth. *Paradise Remade: The Politics of Culture and History in Hawai'i*. Philadelphia: Temple University Press, 1993.

Bushnell, O. A. *The Gifts of Civilization: Germs and Genocide in Hawai'i*. Honolulu: University of Hawai'i Press, 1993.

Buzard, James. *The Beaten Track: European Tourism, Literature, and the Ways to 'Culture', 1800–1918*. Oxford: Oxford University Press, 1993.

Cahn, Susan. *Coming on Strong: Gender and Sexuality in Twentieth-Century Women's Sport*. New York: Free Press, 1994.

Carroll, Nick, ed. *The Next Wave: The World of Surfing*. New York: Abbeville Press, 1991.

———. *Fearlessness: The Story of Lisa Andersen*. San Francisco: Chronicle Books, 2007.

Casey, Susan. *The Wave: In Pursuit of the Rogues, Freaks, and Giants of the Ocean*. New York: Doubleday, 2010.

Chase, Laura. "Public Beaches and Private Beach Huts: A Case Study of Inter-war Clacton and Frinton, Essex." In *Histories of Tourism: Representation, Identity, and Conflict*, edited by John K. Walton, 211–27. Buffalo, NY: Channel View, 2005.

Chase, Linda. *Surfing: Women of the Waves*. Salt Lake City, UT: Gibbs Smith, 2008.

Chouinard, Yvon. *Let My People Go Surfing: The Education of a Reluctant Businessman*. New York: Penguin, 2005.

Clark, John R. K. *Hawaiian Surfing: Traditions from the Past*. Honolulu: University of Hawai'i Press, 2011.

Coleman, Stuart Holmes. *Eddie Would Go: The Story of Eddie Aikau, Hawaiian Hero and Pioneer of Big Wave Surfing*. New York: St. Martin's Griffin, 2004.

———. *Fierce Heart: The Story of Makaha and the Soul of Hawaiian Surfing*. New York: St. Martin's Press, 2009.

Cook, Daniel Thomas. *The Commodification of Childhood: The Children's Clothing Industry and the Rise of the Child Consumer*. Durham, NC: Duke University Press, 2004.

Corbin, Alain. *The Lure of the Sea: The Discovery of the Seaside in the Western World, 1750–1840*. Berkeley: University of California Press, 1994.

Crompton, John L. "Sponsorship of Sport by Tobacco and Alcohol Companies." *Journal of Sport and Social Issues* 17, no. 2 (1993): 148–67.

Cronon, William, ed. *Uncommon Ground: Rethinking the Human Place in Nature*. New York: W. W. Norton, 1996.

Crowell, John C. "Sea, Swell, and Surf Forecasting Methods Employed for the Allied invasion of Normandy, June 1944." Master's thesis in meteorology, UCLA, 1946.

Culver, Lawrence. "America's Playground: Recreation and Race." In *A Companion to Los Angeles*, edited by William Deverell and Greg Hise, 421–37. Malden, MA: Wiley-Blackwell, 2010.

———. *The Frontier of Leisure: Southern California and the Shaping of Modern America*. New York: Oxford University Press, 2010.

Dana, Richard Henry. *Two Years Before the Mast: A Personal Narrative*. New York: Harper, 1868.

Davidson, Ronald A. "Before 'Surfurbia': The Development of the South Bay Beach Cities Through the 1930s." *Yearbook of the Association of Pacific Coast Geographers* 66 (2004): 80–94.

Davis, Lynn Ann. "Photographically Illustrated Books About Hawai'i, 1854–1945." *History of Photography* 25, no. 3 (Fall 2001): 288–305.

Daws, Gavan. *Shoal of Time: A History of the Hawaiian Islands*. Honolulu: University of Hawai'i Press, 1968.

Desmond, Jane C. *Staging Tourism: Bodies on Display from Waikiki to Sea World*. Chicago: University of Chicago Press, 1999.

Deverell, William. *Railroad Crossing: Californians and the Railroad, 1850–1910*. Berkeley: University of California Press, 1996.

Didion, Joan. "Letter from Paradise, 21°19′N, 157°52′W." In *Slouching Towards Bethlehem*, New York: Farrar, Straus & Giroux, 1968.

Dixon, Chris. *Ghost Wave: The Discovery of Cortes Bank and the Biggest Wave on Earth*. San Francisco: Chronicle Books, 2011.

Dixon, Peter. *Men Who Ride Mountains: Incredible True Tales of Legendary Surfers*. Guilford, CT: Lyons Press, 2001.

Doherty, Sean. *MP: The Life of Michael Peterson*. Sydney: HarperSports, 2004.

Dolin, Eric Jay. *Leviathan: The History of Whaling in America*. New York: W. W. Norton, 2007.

Duane, Daniel. *Caught Inside: A Surfer's Year on the California Coast*. New York: North Point Press, 1997.

Du Puy, William Atherton. *Hawaii and Its Race Problem*. Washington, DC: U.S. Government Printing Office, 1932.

Easterbrook, Gregg. "Privatize the Seas." *Atlantic*, July/August 2009.

Easton, Robert. *Black Tide: The Santa Barbara Oil Spill and its Consequences*. New York: Delacorte Press, 1972.

Ellis, William. *Narrative of a Tour Through Hawaii, or Owhyhee*. London, 1827. Reprint, Honolulu: Hawaiian Gazette, 1917.

Elwell, John. "The Enigma of Simmons." *Surfer's Journal* 3, no. 1 (1994): 30–49.

Eszterhas, Joe. "The Strange Case of the Hippie Mafia." *Rolling Stone*, December 7, 1972.

Fane, Francis D., and Don Moore. *Naked Warriors: The Story of the U.S. Navy's Frogmen*. New York: St. Martin's Press, 1996.

Farley, Pat. *Surfing to Saigon*. Santa Cruz, CA: Ranger Publications, 1994.

Fayer, Ronald, Jitender P. Dubey, and David S. Lindsay. "Zoonotic Protozoa: From Land to Sea." *Trends in Parasitology* 20, no. 11 (2004): 531–36.

Ferincola, Richard G. *Twelve Days of Terror: A Definitive Investigation of the 1916 New Jersey Shark Attacks*. Guilford, CT: Lyons Press, 2001.

Finnegan, William. "Playing Doc's Games." *New Yorker*, August 24, 1992.

———. "Blank Monday: Could Grubby Clark Destroy Surfing?" *New Yorker*, August 21, 2006.

Finney, Ben R., and James D. Houston. *Surfing: The Sport of Hawaiian Kings*. Rutland, VT: Tuttle, 1966.

Flamming, Douglas. *Bound for Freedom: Black Los Angeles in Jim Crow America*. Berkeley: University of California Press, 2005.

Ford, Alexander Hume. "Riding the Surf in Hawaii." *Collier's*, August 14, 1909.

Ford, Nick, and David Brown. *Surfing and Social Theory: Experience, Embodiment and Narrative of the Dream Glide*. New York: Routledge, 2006.

Fornander, Abraham. *An Account of the Polynesian Race: Its Origin and Migrations*. London: Trubner and Company, 1880.

Fragale, Mark. "Dave Sweet: First in Foam." *Longboard*, September/October 2000.

Frank, Thomas. *The Conquest of Cool: Business Culture, Counterculture, and the Rise of Hip Consumerism*. Chicago: University of Chicago Press, 1997.

Fry, John. *The Story of Modern Skiing*. Lebanon, NH: University Press of New England, 2006.

Gabbard, Andrea. *Girl in the Curl: A Century of Women in Surfing*. Seattle, WA: Seal Press, 2000.

Gault-Williams, Malcolm, and Gary Lynch. "The Last Chapter: Stories of Gene 'Tarzan' Smith." *Surfer's Journal* 7, no. 4 (1998): 44–51.

George, Sam. "Baby, It's Cold: Surfing in the Age of Neoprene." *Surfer's Journal* 17, no. 5 (2008), 26–40.

———, ed. *The Perfect Day: 40 Years of Surfer Magazine*. San Francisco: Chronicle Books, 2001.

———. "Pre-contact: The Surfing Tradition of Sao Tome." *Surfer's Journal* 16, no. 3 (2007): 40–49.

Goodstein, Judith R. *Millikan's School: A History of the California Institute of Technology*. New York: W. W. Norton, 1991.

Graves, Gregory, and Susan Pritchard O'Hara. *Saving California's Coast: Army Engineers at Oceanside and Humboldt Bay*. Spokane, WA: A. H. Clark, 1991.

Greene, Jack, and Alessandro Massignani. *The Black Prince and the Sea Devils: The Story of Valerio Borghese and the Elite Units of the Decima Mas*. Cambridge, MA: Da Capo Press, 2004.

Griffin, Donald F., Charles W. Eliot, and Simon Eisner. *Coastline Plans and Action for the Development of the Los Angeles Metropolitan Coastline*. Los Angeles: Haynes Foundation, 1944.

Grigg, Ricky. *Big Surf, Deep Dives, and the Islands*. Honolulu: Editions Limited, 1998.

Griggs, Gary, Kiki Patsch, and Lauret Savoy. *Living with the Changing California Coast*. Berkeley: University of California Press, 2005.

Gumprecht, Blake. *The Los Angeles River: Its Life, Death, and Possible Rebirth*. Baltimore: Johns Hopkins University Press, 1999.

Guttmann, Allen. *A Whole New Ball Game: An Interpretation of American Sports*. Chapel Hill: University of North Carolina Press, 1988.

———. *From Ritual to Record: The Nature of Modern Sports*. Rev. ed. New York: Columbia University Press, 2004.

Hall, Sandra Kimberley. *Duke: A Great Hawaiian*. Honolulu: Bess Press, 2004.

Hemmings, Fred. *The Soul of Surfing*. New York: Thunder's Mouth, 1999.

Hening, Glenn. "The Stain on the Soul of Surfing." In *Surf Rage*, edited by Nat Young, 131–45. Angourie, NSW: Nymboida, 2000.

Herr, Michael. *Dispatches*. New York: Knopf, 1977.

Herron, William J. "The Influence of Man upon the Shoreline of Southern California." *Shore and Beach* 51 (July 1983): 17–27.

Hibbard, Don, and David Franzen. *The View from Diamond Head: Royal Residence to Urban Resort*. Honolulu: Editions Limited, 1986.

———, David Franzen, and Augie Salbosa. *Designing Paradise: The Allure of the Hawaiian Resort*. New York: Princeton Architectural Press, 2006.

Hill, S. S. *Travels in the Sandwich and Society Islands*. London: Chapman & Hall, 1856.

Hitch, Thomas Kemper, and Robert M. Kamins. *Islands in Transition: The Past, Present, and Future of Hawaii's Economy*. Honolulu: University of Hawai'i Press, 1992.

Hughes, Robert. *The Fatal Shore: The Epic of Australia's Founding*. New York: Knopf, 1986.

Hynson, Mike. *Transcendental Memories of a Surf Rebel*. Dana Point, CA: Endless Dreams Publishing, 2009.

Igler, David. "Diseased Goods: Global Exchanges in the Eastern Pacific Basin, 1770–1850." *American Historical Review* 109 (June 2004): 693–719.

Isserman, Maurice, and Stewart Weaver. *Fallen Giants: A History of Himalayan Mountaineering from the Age of Empire to the Age of Extremes*. New Haven, CT: Yale University Press, 2008.

Jarratt, Phil. *The Mountain and the Wave: The Quiksilver Story*. Huntington Beach, CA: Quiksilver Entertainment, 2006.

———. *Mr. Sunset: The Jeff Hakman Story*. London: Gen X, 1997.

———. *Salts and Suits*. Melbourne: Hardie Grant, 2010.

Jarves, James Jackson. *History of the Hawaiian or Sandwich Islands*. Boston: Tappan and Dennet, 1843.

Jenkins, Bruce. *North Shore Chronicles: Big Wave Surfing in Hawaii*. Berkeley: Frog, 1999.

Josephson, Paul R. *Motorized Obsessions: Life, Liberty, and the Small-Bore Engine*. Baltimore: Johns Hopkins University Press, 2007.

Kamper, Angela, and Charles Miranda. *My Brother's Keeper: The True Story of a Vicious Killing and a Powerful Surf Brotherhood*. Crows Nest, NSW: Allen & Unwin, 2006.

Kampion, Drew. *Stoked!: A History of Surf Culture*. Salt Lake City, UT: Gibbs Smith, 2003.

Kanahele, George S. *Waikiki, 100 BC to 1900 AD: An Untold Story*. Honolulu: University of Hawai'i Press, 1995.

Kashay, Jennifer Fish. "Competing Imperialisms and Hawaiian Authority: The Cannonading of Lahaina in 1827." *Pacific Historical Review* 77, no. 3 (2008): 369–90.

Kaufman, Wallace, and Orrin H. Pilkey, Jr. *The Beaches Are Moving: The Drowning of America's Shoreline*. Garden City, NY: Anchor Press, 1979.

Keauokalani, Kepelino. *Kepelino's Traditions of Hawai'i*. Edited and translated by Martha Warren Beckwith. Honolulu: Bernice P. Bishop Museum, 1932. Reprinted 2007.

Kent, Noel J. *Hawaii: Islands Under the Influence*. New York: Monthly Review Press, 1983.

Kenvin, Richard. "Remember the Future." *Surfer's Journal* 17, no. 6 (2008/2009): 32–41.

Kirch, Patrick Vinton. *Feathered Gods and Fishhooks: An Introduction to Hawaiian Archaeology and Prehistory*. Honolulu: University of Hawai'i Press, 1985.

Kirch, Patrick V., and Jean-Louis Rallu, eds. *The Growth and Collapse of Pacific Island Societies: Archaeological and Demographic Perspectives*. Honolulu: University of Hawai'i Press, 2007.

Kohner, Frederick. *Gidget*. New York: Putnam, 1957.

Kusz, Kyle. "Extreme America: The Cultural Politics of Extreme Sports in 1990s America." In *Understanding Lifestyle Sports: Consumption, Identity and Difference*, edited by Belinda Wheaton, 197–213. London: Routledge, 2004.

Leeuwen, Thomas A. P. van. *The Springboard in the Pond: An Intimate History of the Swimming Pool*. Cambridge, MA: MIT Press, 1998.

Lenček, Lena, and Gideon Bosker. *The Beach: The History of Paradise on Earth*. New York: Viking, 1998.

Linn, Brian McAllister. *Guardians of Empire: The U.S. Army and the Pacific, 1902–1940*. Chapel Hill: University of North Carolina Press, 1997.

Löfgren, Orvar. *On Holiday: A History of Vacationing*. Berkeley: University of California Press, 1999.

London, Charmian Kittredge. *Our Hawaii*. New York: Macmillan, 1917.

London, Jack. *The Cruise of the Snark*. New York: Macmillan, 1911.

———. *Island Tales*. London: Mills, 1920.

———. "Riding the South Seas Surf." *Woman's Home Companion*, October 1907.

Long, John, ed. *The Big Drop: Classic Big Wave Surfing Stories*. Helena, MT: Falcon, 1999.

Long, S. Thomas. *To Undreamed-of Marks: A Tribute to Jerry Vultee*. San Diego, CA: General Dynamics Corporation, 1991.

Lopez, Gerry. *Surf Is Where You Find It*. Ventura, CA: Patagonia Books, 2008.

Lopez, Jack. *Cholos and Surfers: A Latino Family Album*. Santa Barbara, CA: Capra Press, 1998.

Lord, Lindsay. *Naval Architecture of Planing Hulls*. 4th ed. Cambridge, MD: Cornell Maritime Press, 1963.

Lotchin, Roger. *Fortress California, 1910–1961: From Warfare to Welfare*. New York: Oxford University Press, 1992.

Lueras, Leonard. *Surfing: The Ultimate Pleasure*. New York: Workman, 1987.

Lunenfeld, Peter. "Gidget on the Couch: Freud, Dora (No, Not That Dora), and Surfing's Secret Austro-Hungarian Roots." *The Believer*, June 2008.

Lynch, Gary, Malcolm Gault-Williams, and William K. Hoopes. *Tom Blake: The Uncommon Journey of a Pioneer Waterman*. Corona del Mar, CA: Croul Family Foundation, 2001.

Mansfield, Stephanie. *The Richest Girl in the World: The Extravagant Life and Fast Times of Doris Duke.* New York: G. P. Putnam's Sons, 1992.

Marcus, Ben. "Sweet Sixteen." *Surfer's Journal* 17, no. 4 (2008): 90–97.

Markusen, Ann, Peter Hall, Scott Campbell, and Sabina Deitrick. *Rise of the Gunbelt: The Military Remapping of Industrial America.* New York: Oxford University Press, 1991.

Martin, Andy. "Surfing the Revolution: The Fatal Impact of the Pacific on Europe." *Eighteenth-Century Studies* 41, no. 2 (2008): 141–47.

Mauro, Chris, and Steve Hawk, eds. *The Best of Surfer Magazine.* San Francisco: Chronicle Books, 2007.

May, Kirse Granat. *Golden State, Golden Youth: The California Image in Popular Culture, 1955–1966.* Chapel Hill: University of North Carolina Press, 2001.

McDougall, Walter A. *Let the Sea Make a Noise: A History of the North Pacific from Magellan to MacArthur.* New York: Basic Books, 1993.

McGloin, Colleen. "Aboriginal Surfing: Reinstating Culture and Country." *International Journal of the Humanities* 4, no. 1 (2006): 93–100.

———. "Surfing Nation(s)—Surfing Country(s)." PhD thesis, University of Wollongong, 2005.

McPhee, John. "Los Angeles Against the Mountains." In *Land of Sunshine: An Environmental History of Metropolitan Los Angeles,* edited by William Deverell and Greg Hise, 179–200. Pittsburgh: University of Pittsburgh Press, 2005.

McTavish, Bob. "So How Come No One Asked Sooner?" *Surfer's Journal* 4, no. 3 (1995): 44–54.

Melendy, H. Brett. *Walter Francis Dillingham, 1875–1963: Hawaiian Entrepreneur and Statesman.* Lewiston, NY: Edwin Mellen Press, 1996.

Michelet, Jules. *The Sea.* English translation. New York: Rudd & Carleton, 1861.

Moore, Michael Scott. *Sweetness and Blood: How Surfing Spread from Hawaii and California to the Rest of the World, with Some Unexpected Results.* New York: Rodale, 2010.

Morris, Gary. "Beyond the Beach." *Journal of Popular Film and Television* 2, no. 1 (1993): 2–11.

Moser, Patrick, ed. *Pacific Passages: An Anthology of Surf Writing*. Honolulu: University of Hawai'i Press, 2008.

Nadeau, Remi. *California: The New Society*. New York: David McKay, 1963.

Nash, Gerald D. *The American West Transformed: The Impact of the Second World War*. Bloomington: Indiana University Press, 1985.

Nash, Roderick F. *Wilderness and the American Mind*. 4th ed. New Haven, CT: Yale University Press, 2001.

Nazer, Daniel. "The Tragicomedy of the Surfers' Commons." *Deakin Law Review* 9, no. 2 (2004): 655–713.

Neushul, Peter, and Peter Westwick. "Aerospace and Surfing: Connecting Two California Keynotes." In *Where Minds and Matters Meet: Technology in California and the West*, edited by Volker Janssen, 231–48. Berkeley and San Marino, CA: University of California Press and the Huntington Library, 2012.

Nicholson, Joy. *The Tribes of Palos Verdes*. New York: St. Martin's Press, 1997.

Noll, Greg, and Andrea Gabbard. *Da Bull: Life over the Edge*. Berkeley: North Atlantic Books, 1989.

O'Dell, James Douglas. *The Water Is Never Cold*. Washington, DC: Brassey's, 2000.

Orbelian, George. *Essential Surfing*. 3rd ed. San Francisco: Orbelian Arts, 1987.

Oreskes, Naomi, and Ronald Rainger. "Science and Security Before the Atomic Bomb: The Loyalty Case of Harald U. Sverdrup." *Studies in History and Philosophy of Modern Physics* 31 (2000): 309–69.

Orsi, Jared. *Hazardous Metropolis: Flooding and Urban Ecology in Los Angeles*. Berkeley: University of California Press, 2004.

O'Sullivan, Kevin. *Goin' Big: Gotcha and the Evolution of Modern Surf Style*. Irvine, CA: Full Force, 2008.

Post, Robert C. *High Performance: The Culture and Technology of Drag Racing, 1950–2000*. Baltimore: Johns Hopkins University Press, 1994.

Pursell, Carroll. "The Rise and Fall of the Appropriate Technology Movement in the United States, 1965–1985." *Technology and Culture* 34 (1993): 629–37.

Quam-Wickham, Nancy. " 'Cities Sacrificed on the Altar of Oil': Popular Opposition to Oil Development in 1920s Los Angeles." *Environmental History* 3 (April 1998): 189–209.

Rensin, David. *All for a Few Perfect Waves: The Audacious Life and Legend of Rebel Surfer Miki Dora*. New York: Harper Entertainment, 2008.

Rhodes, Diane Lee. "Overview of Hawaiian History." In *A Cultural History of Three Traditional Hawaiian Sites on the West Coast of Hawai'i Island*, by Linda Wedel Greene. Denver, CO: National Park Service, 1993.

Rielly, Derek. "Mainlining." In *Surf Rage*, edited by Nat Young, 33–53. Angourie, NSW: Nymboida, 2000.

Rutsky, R. L. "Surfing the Other: Ideology on the Beach." *Film Quarterly* 52, no. 4 (1999): 12–23.

Sabin, Paul. *Crude Politics: The California Oil Market, 1900–1940*. Berkeley: University of California Press, 2004.

Schmidt, Christine. "Second Skin: Annette Kellerman, the Modern Swimsuit, and an Australian Contribution to Global Fashion." PhD thesis, Queensland University of Technology, 2008.

Schneider, Daniel. *Hybrid Nature: Sewage Treatment and the Contradictions of the Industrial Ecosystem*. Cambridge, MA: MIT Press, 2011.

Schou, Nicholas. *Orange Sunshine: The Brotherhood of Eternal Love and Its Quest to Spread Peace, Love, and Acid to the World*. New York: St. Martin's Press, 2010.

Scott, Allen J. *Technopolis: High-Technology Industry and Regional Development in Southern California*. Berkeley: University of California Press, 1993.

Severson, John. *Modern Surfing Around the World*. Garden City, NY: Doubleday, 1964.

Sharpsteen, Bill. *Dirty Water: One Man's Fight to Clean Up One of the World's Most Polluted Bays*. Berkeley: University of California Press, 2010.

Sides, Josh. *L.A. City Limits: African American Los Angeles from the Great Depression to the Present*. Berkeley: University of California Press, 2004.

Silva, Noenoe. *Aloha Betrayed: Native Hawaiian Resistance to American Colonialism*. Durham, NC: Duke University Press, 2004.

Slater, Kelly. *Kelly Slater: For the Love*. San Francisco: Chronicle Books, 2008.

———, with Jason Borte. *Pipe Dreams: A Surfer's Journey*. New York: ReganBooks, 2003.

Sollen, Robert. *An Ocean of Oil: A Century of Political Struggle over Petroleum off the California Coast*. Juneau, AL: Denali Press, 1998.

Smith, Joel T. "Reinventing the Sport, Part III: George Freeth." *Surfer's Journal* 12, no. 3 (2003): 90–94.

Sprawson, Charles. *Haunts of the Black Masseur: The Swimmer as Hero*. New York: Pantheon Books, 1992.

Spurrier, Jeff. "A Generation of Gidgets." *Atlantic Monthly*, April 2002.

Stannard, David E. *Before the Horror: The Population of Hawai'i on the Eve of Western Contact*. Honolulu: University of Hawai'i Press, 1989.

———. *Honor Killing: How the Infamous 'Massie Affair' Transformed Hawai'i*. New York: Viking, 2005.

———. "The Massie Case: Injustice and Courage." *Honolulu Advertiser*, October 14, 2001.

Starr, Kevin. *The Dream Endures: California Enters the 1940s*. New York: Oxford University Press, 1997.

———. *Embattled Dreams: California in War and Peace, 1940–1950*. New York: Oxford University Press, 2002.

———. *Endangered Dreams: The Great Depression in California*. New York: Oxford University Press, 1996.

———. *Material Dreams: Southern California Through the 1920s*. New York: Oxford University Press, 1990.

Stecyk, Craig R., III. "Pacific System: Birth of the Surfboard Factory." *Surfer's Journal* 6, no. 4 (1997): 32–39.

———. "Surf Nazis and Other Objectionable Material." *Surfer's Journal* 1, no. 4 (1992): 36–43.

———, and Art Brewer. *Bunker Spreckels: Surfing's Divine Prince of Decadence*. Los Angeles: Taschen, 2007.

———, and Drew Kampion. *Dora Lives: The Authorized Story of Miki Dora*. Santa Barbara, CA: T. Adler Books, 2005.

Stedman, Leanne. "From Gidget to Gonad Man: Surfers, Feminists and Postmodernisation." *Journal of Sociology* 33, no. 1 (1997): 75–90.

Steinberg, Philip E. *The Social Construction of the Ocean*. Cambridge, UK: Cambridge University Press, 2001.

Sterling, Elspeth, and Catherine C. Summers, eds. *Sites of Oahu*. Honolulu: Bishop Museum, 1978.

Stewart, Charles S. *A Visit to the South Seas*. New York: J. P. Haven, 1831.

Stratton, Jon. "On the Importance of Subcultural Origins." In *The Subcultures Reader*, edited by Ken Gelder and Sarah Thornton, 181–90. New York: Routledge, 2001.

Tarr, Joel A., with J. McCurley, F. C. McMichael, and T. F. Yosie. "Water and Wastes: A Retrospective Assessment of Wastewater Technology in the United States, 1800–1932." *Technology and Culture* 25 (1984): 226–263.

Taylor, Bron. "Surfing into Spirituality: A New, Aquatic Nature Religion." *Journal of the American Academy of Religion* 75, no. 4 (2007): 923–951.

Tendler, Stewart, and David May. *The Brotherhood of Eternal Love: From Flower Power to Hippie Mafia; The Story of the LSD Counterculture*. London: Cyan, 2006.

Timmons, Grady. *Waikiki Beachboy*. Honolulu: Editions Limited, 1989.

Toffler, Alvin. *Future Shock*. New York: Random House, 1970.

Tomson, Shaun. *Bustin' Down the Door: The Surf Revolution of '75*. New York: Abrams, 2008.

———. *Surfer's Code: 12 Simple Lessons for Riding Through Life*. Salt Lake City, UT: Gibbs Smith, 2006.

Towner, John. *An Historical Geography of Recreation and Tourism in the Western World, 1540–1940*. New York: John Wiley, 1993.

Trask, Haunani-Kay. *From a Native Daughter: Colonialism and Sovereignty in Hawaii*. Honolulu: University of Hawai'i Press, 1993.

Turhollow, Anthony. *A History of the Los Angeles District, U.S. Army Corps of Engineers, 1898–1965*. Los Angeles, CA: U.S. Army Engineer District, Los Angeles, 1975.

Twain, Mark. *Roughing It*. London: Routledge, 1870.

Verge, Arthur C. "George Freeth: King of the Surfers and California's Forgotten Hero." *California History* 80, no. 2/3 (Summer/Fall 2001): 82–105.

Viehe, Fred W. "The Social-Spatial Distribution in the Black Gold Suburbs of Los Angeles, 1900–1930." *Southern California Quarterly* 73, no. 1 (1991): 33–54.

Vowell, Sarah. *Unfamiliar Fishes*. New York: Riverhead Books, 2011.

Walker, Isaiah Helekunihi. "Hui Nalu, Beachboys, and the Surfing Boarder-Lands of Hawai'i." *Contemporary Pacific* 20, no. 1 (2008).

———. "Terrorism or Native Protest? The Hui 'O He'e Nalu and Hawaiian Resistance to Colonialism." *Pacific Historical Review* 74, no. 4 (November 2005).

———. *Waves of Resistance: Surfing and History in Twentieth-Century Hawai'i*. Honolulu: University of Hawai'i Press, 2011.

Ward, Josi. "Cattle on the Coast: Hollister Ranch and Californian Landscape Preservation." Master's thesis, School of Architecture, University of Virginia, 2008.

Warshaw, Matt. *The Encyclopedia of Surfing*. Orlando, FL: Harcourt, 2003.

———. "Goodbye Sunshine Superman." *Surfer's Journal* 3, no. 4 (1994): 7–25.

———. "Green on Blue: Kelly Slater's Million-Dollar Deal, and Other Thoughts on Surfing-for-Hire." *Surfer's Journal* 5, no. 3 (1996): 22–35.

———. *The History of Surfing*. San Francisco: Chronicle Books, 2010.

———. *Surf Movie Tonite!* San Francisco: Chronicle Books, 2005.

———, ed. *Zero Break: An Illustrated Collection of Surf Writing, 1777–2004*. Orlando, FL: Harcourt, 2004.

Weisbecker, Allan. *In Search of Captain Zero: A Surfer's Road Trip Beyond the End of the Road*. New York: Jeremy P. Tarcher/Putnam, 2001.

Weller, Sheila. "Malibu's Lost Boys." *Vanity Fair*, August 2006.

Westwick, Peter J., ed. *Blue Sky Metropolis: The Aerospace Century in Southern California*. Berkeley and San Marino, CA: University of California Press and Huntington Library, 2012.

Wheaton, Belinda, ed. *Understanding Lifestyle Sports: Consumption, Identity and Difference*. London: Routledge, 2004.

Whitcomb, Ian. "The Beach Boy." *American Heritage*, July/August 2000.

White, Kai, and Jim Kraus. *Images of America: Waikiki*. Charleston, SC: Arcadia, 2007.

White, Richard. *Inventing Australia: Images and Identity, 1688–1980*. Sydney: Allen & Unwin, 1981.

Whitehead, John. "Alaska and Hawaii: The Cold War States." In *The Cold War American West, 1945–1989*, edited by Kevin J. Fernlund, 189–210. Albuquerque: University of New Mexico Press, 1998.

Wigo, Bruce. *The Golden Age of Swimming: A Picture History of the Sport & Pools that Changed America*. Fort Lauderdale, FL: Bruce Wigo, 2009.

Wilkes, Charles. *Narrative of the United States Exploring Expedition*, Vol. 4. Philadelphia: Lea and Blanchard, 1844.

Wiltse, Jeff. *Contested Waters: A Social History of Swimming Pools in America.* Chapel Hill: University of North Carolina Press, 2007.

Witzig, John. "Interesting Times." *Surfer's Journal* 4, no. 3 (1995): 60–66.

Wolfe, Tom. *The Pump House Gang.* New York: Farrar, Straus & Giroux, 1968.

Wollenberg, Charles. "California and the Vietnam War: Microcosm and Magnification." In *What's Going On? California and the Vietnam Era,* edited by Marcia Eymann and Charles Wollenberg. Berkeley: University of California Press, 2004.

Wright, Ralph R. "A Historical Study of the Development of the Competitive Swimming of Hawai'i up to 1916." Master's thesis, University of Hawai'i, November 1947.

Yardley, Paul T. *Millstones and Milestones: The Career of B. F. Dillingham, 1844–1918.* Honolulu: University of Hawai'i Press, 1981.

Young, Betty Lou. *Our First Century: The Los Angeles Athletic Club, 1880–1980.* Los Angeles: LAAC Press, 1979.

Young, Nat. *The History of Surfing.* Rev. ed. Angourie, NSW: Palm Beach Press, 1994.

———. *Nat's Nat and That's That.* Frenchs Forest, NSW: Nymboida Press, 1998.

———. "The New Era." *Surfer's Journal* 4, no. 3 (1995): 56–69.

———, ed. *Surf Rage.* Angourie, Australia: Nymboida Press, 2000.

INDEX

Note: Page numbers in *italics* indicate illustrations.

ABOUT THE AUTHORS

PETER WESTWICK is an assistant research professor in history at USC and director of the Aerospace History Project at the Huntington–USC Institute on California and the West. He received his BA in physics and PhD in history from Berkeley and has held fellowships at Caltech and Yale. He is the author of *Into the Black: JPL and the American Space Program, 1976–2004* and *The National Labs: Science in an American System, 1947–1974*, and editor of *Blue Sky Metropolis: The Aerospace Century in Southern California*, which was selected for the Best Nonfiction of 2012 list by the Los Angeles Public Library. He lives and surfs in Santa Barbara.

PETER NEUSHUL is a visiting senior associate researcher in the department of history at the University of California at Santa Barbara. He received a BA and PhD in United States history from UCSB. His postdoctoral appointments include fellowships at Caltech and UCSB. He has written extensively on defense industries, the history of oceanography, and on environmental history. He lives and surfs in Goleta.